THEORY AND TREATMENT OF ANOREXIA NERVOSA AND BULIMIA

Biomedical,

Sociocultural, and

Psychological Perspectives

THEORY AND TREATMENT OF ANOREXIA NERVOSA AND BULIMIA

Biomedical, Sociocultural, and Psychological Perspectives

Edited by

Rev. Steven Wiley Emmett, Ph.D.

NEW YORK AND LONDON

First published 1985 by Routledge

Published 2009 by Routledge
711 Third Avenue, New York, NY 10017
2 Park Square, Milton Park, Abingdon, Oxfordshire OX14 4RN

First issued in paperback 2014

Routledge is an imprint of the Taylor and Francis Group, an informa business

Library of Congress Cataloging in Publication Data
Main entry under title:

Theory and treatment of anorexia nervosa and bulimia.

Includes bibliographies and index.
1. Anorexia nervosa. 2. Bulimarexia. I. Emmett, Steven W., 1948-   . [DNLM: 1. Anorexia Nervosa. 2. Appetite Disorders. WM 175 T396]
RC552.A5T48   1985   616.85'2   84-29267
ISBN 0-87630-384-X

Copyright © 1985 by Steven Wiley Emmett

All rights reserved. No part of this book may be reproduced by any process whatsoever without the written permission of the copyright owner.

ISBN 13: 978-0-87630-384-9 (hbk)
ISBN 13: 978-1-138-00443-6 (pbk)

For all those striving to help anorexics
and bulimics on their journey to recovery

Foreword

The incidence of eating disorders is reaching epidemic proportions. Estimates for the occurrence of anorexic or bulimic behavior patterns in the female population are alarmingly high. Just as startling is the apparent spread of eating disorders across most ethnic and socioeconomic groups. The consequences are tragic. In the absence of a reliable means for recovery, the cost of treatment is extraordinarily expensive. Although mortality rates appear to be constant, the absolute number of deaths is probably rising. Always, the presence of an eating disorder creates family disruption and personal anguish. The epidemic nature of the problem is dramatically illustrated when the recent nationwide media coverage of anorexia and bulimia is compared to the relative obscurity in which Hilde Bruch first published her classic treatise. In one, or perhaps two decades, anorexia and bulimia have undergone a remarkable metamorphosis — from psychiatric curiosities to publically recognized mental health emergencies.

Indeed, eating disorders can be described as the emotional disturbances that most characterize and captivate the present time. Perhaps, then, they are also a profound reflection of the psychological strains that are embedded in contemporary life. Underlying anorexia and bulimia are pervasive anxiety and a deep sense of personal ineffectiveness. Eating-disordered symptoms express an unwillingness or an inability to desire, to grow, and to accept or risk change. They represent an effort to ensure psychological safety and certainty. As a result, they create a kind of self-protection that becomes entrapping self-stagnation. Regardless of the specific etiology, those who develop anorexia or bulimia are conveying the deeply held conviction that they are not yet prepared to continue living. The question, at least, seems clear. What has happened in the past 20 years — at all levels of psychological influence and experience — to cause an exploding number of adolescents and young adults to turn away from growth and towards eating disorders? Even more to the point, why is it women in particular who are suffering so much from anorexia and bulimia?

Some of the rising incidence and the cross-cultural spread of eating disorders may be a function of increasing variation in etiology. Broadly speaking, there may be two different kinds of people who are developing anorexia and bulimia. There are those who become eating disordered because their psychological circumstances specifically predispose them to food- and weight-related symptomatology. Theirs can be regarded as a psychologically active symptom choice, grounded in and propelled by particular conflicts. These anorexics and bulimics have been well described in the literature, and themselves reveal a wide range of etiologies.

However, it may be nowadays that a great many people are becoming eating disordered via simple contagion—because anorexia and bulimia are the emotional disturbances of the present time. In this situation the symptom choice is passive. It will "happen" that someone develops an eating disorder whenever any problem in living becomes troubling enough to require a symptomatic expression that will command notice and appropriate attention. Given that this is so, the consequence will be a snowball effect. Anorexia and bulimia will occur in an ever expanding etiological context.

The proliferation of eating disorders is a challenge to the mental health professionals who are striving to better understand and treat anorexia and bulimia. Clinicians, as well as researchers, must have an opportunity to remain informed about new and recent developments in the field. In this regard, *Theory and Treatment of Anorexia Nervosa and Bulimia* makes an impressive and invaluable contribution to the literature. Dr. Emmett has compiled an extremely comprehensive work that truly represents the state of the art. The book's division into biomedical, sociocultural, and psychological perspectives is an excellent structure because it helps to emphasize the complex and multifaceted nature of eating disorders. Furthermore, through inclusion of such diverse viewpoints between two covers, this volume makes a significant statement about the absolute importance of collaboration. Professionals who are working with anorexics and bulimics must make a concerted effort to share with each other and to learn from each other. Without mutual support and respect, there is a danger of lapsing into the central dilemma of eating disorders—sterile self-protectiveness at the expense of innovative and beneficial change.

William N. Davis, Ph.D.
Executive Director
Center for the Study of
Anorexia and Bulimia
New York City

Contents

Foreword by William N. Davis, Ph.D. vii
Acknowledgments xi
Contributors xiii
Introduction xvii

PART I. BIOMEDICAL PERSPECTIVE

1. Medical Complications of Anorexia Nervosa
   and Bulimia 5
   Norman P. Spack
2. Nutritional Aspects of Anorexia Nervosa and Bulimia ... 20
   Johanna Dwyer
3. Neuroendocrine Aspects of Eating Disorders 51
   Paul M. Copeland
4. Biological Treatments of Eating Disorders 73
   Harrison Pope and James Hudson

PART II. SOCIOCULTURAL PERSPECTIVE

5. Anorexia Nervosa and Bulimia:
   The Sociocultural Context 95
   *Donald M. Schwartz, Michael G. Thompson, and
   Craig L. Johnson*
6. Bulimarexia: A Sociocultural Perspective 113
   Marlene Boskind-White

7. Visibility/Invisibility: Social Considerations
   in Anorexia Nervosa—A Feminist Perspective 127
   Susie Orbach

PART III. PSYCHOLOGICAL PERSPECTIVE

8. Long-Term Dynamic Group Therapy with Bulimic Patients:
   A Clinical Discussion 141
   W. Nicholson Browning
9. Psychotherapeutic Partnering: An Approach to the
   Treatment of Anorexia Nervosa and Bulimia 154
   April Benson and Linda Futterman
10. Eating Disorders and the Family: A Model
    for Intervention 174
    Barry Dym
11. Eating and Monsters: A Psychodynamic View
    of Bulimarexia 194
    Ana-Maria Rizzuto
12. An Inpatient Model for the Treatment of
    Anorexia Nervosa 211
    Philip G. Levendusky and Catherine P. Dooley
13. Structuring a Nurturant/Authoritative Psychotherapeutic
    Relationship with the Anorexic Patient 234
    Steven Levenkron
14. Bulimarexia: Intervention Strategies and
    Outcome Considerations 246
    William C. White, Jr.
15. Therapeutic Dilemmas in the Treatment of
    Anorexia Nervosa: A Self-Psychological
    Perspective 268
    Richard A. Geist

PART IV. CONCLUSION

16. Do Anorexics and Bulimics Get Well? 291
    Michael G. Thompson and Margery T. Gans
17. Future Trends 304
    Steven Wiley Emmett

Index 321

Acknowledgments

This book is the result of a challenging two-year period, during which the merits of writings encompassing a varied array of material on anorexia and bulimia were assessed. Many people participated in the project as it developed; to all who generously shared in the endeavor go my thanks.

I wish to acknowledge the invaluable assistance of Paul Copeland, M.D., and Harrison Pope, M.D., and the hearty support and friendship of my colleagues at The Renfrew Center, Allen Davis and Samuel Menaged, Esq. Sincerest gratitude is extended to my clients, who are a continual source of inspiration. I am especially indebted to Ann Alhadeff, managing editor of Brunner/Mazel, Publishers, for her wise and gentle counsel. Finally, the great encouragement and humor of my wife, Deborah, are deeply appreciated.

Steven Wiley Emmett

Contributors

APRIL BENSON, Ph.D., is Director of Training at the Center for the Study of Anorexia and Bulimia, New York, and practices privately in New York City. Currently, she is involved in the creation of a specialty training program for therapists who want to learn to treat patients with eating disorders and is writing a paper on the merger experience in psychotherapy.

MARLENE BOSKIND-WHITE, Ph.D., is Co-author with her husband, William, of *Bulimarexia: The Binge/Purge Cycle*. She has written and lectured extensively on the treatment of bulimarexia.

W. NICHOLSON BROWNING, M.D., is a Psychiatrist in private practice in Lexington, MA. He was formerly Clinical Assistant in Psychiatry and Supervisor in Child Psychiatry at Massachusetts General Hospital.

PAUL M. COPELAND, M.D., is a Clinical Instructor in Medicine at Harvard Medical School, and Staff Endocrinologist at Salem Hospital, Salem, MA. He specializes in neuroendocrine functioning at Massachusetts General Hospital in Boston.

CATHERINE P. DOOLEY, M.S., is a Supervisor at McLean Hospital Weight Management Clinic, and is Co-Director of the Eating Disorder Program, McLean Hospital, Belmont, MA. She is Principal Investigator of "A Study of the Effectiveness of the Treatment of Eating Disorders" at McLean Hospital.

JOHANNA DWYER, R.N., D.Sc., is Associate Professor in the Departments of Medicine and Community Health, Tufts Medical School, and an Adjunct Associate Professor at the School of Nutrition at Tufts University. She is director of the Frances Stern Nutrition Center at New England Medical Center Hospital in Boston and is the author of over 200 publications.

BARRY DYM, Ph.D., is a Psychologist and a Founder and Director of the Family Institute of Cambridge, Cambridge, MA. He has worked with numerous anorexic and bulimic families.

STEVEN WILEY EMMETT, M.Div., Ph.D., editor, is a Unitarian-Universalist Minister and Psychotherapist specializing in the treatment of eating disorders. He is Director of the Anorexia Nervosa Aid Society of Rhode Island and Clinical Consultant of the Renfrew Center, Philadelphia, PA, the nation's first freestanding institution devoted solely to the treatment of anorexics and bulimics.

LINDA FUTTERMAN, Ph.D., is a Psychoanalyst practicing in New York City and Larchmont, N.Y. Her special interest in the field of eating disorders is the interaction of parent-child psychopathology in the genesis and perpetuation of these disorders.

MARGERY T. GANS, M.Ed., is a Doctoral Student in counseling at the Harvard Graduate School of Education. She is a Clinical Associate with the Eating Disorders Unit at the Massachusetts General Hospital and is on the Eating Disorders Team at North Shore Children's Hospital.

RICHARD A. GEIST, Ed.D., is Clinical Associate, Department of Psychiatry, Massachusetts General Hospital in Boston, and Clinical Instructor in Psychology, Department of Psychiatry, Harvard Medical School.

JAMES HUDSON, M.D., is an Assistant Psychiatrist at Mclean Hospital, Belmont, MA, and Instructor in Psychiatry at Harvard Medical School. He is author of more than 20 articles, the majority of which relate to eating disorders.

CRAIG L. JOHNSON, Ph.D., is a long-term Researcher of eating disorders and past Editor of *The International Journal of Eating Disorders*. He is the Director of the Anorexia Nervosa Project, Michael Reese Hospital, Chicago.

Contributors

PHILIP G. LEVENDUSKY, Ph.D., is Director and Psychologist-in-Charge of the Behavior Therapy Unit at Mclean Hospital, in Belmont, MA. He is also Instructor, Department of Psychiatry, Harvard Medical School.

STEVEN LEVENKRON, M.A., is a Psychotherapist at Montefiore Hospital and Medical Center, Department of Pediatrics, Division of Adolescent Medicine, and Clinical Consultant at the Center for the Study of Anorexia and Bulimia in New York City. He is author of the best-selling novel, *The Best Little Girl in the World*, and *Treating and Overcoming Anorexia*.

SUSIE ORBACH is a Founder of The Women's Therapy Centre in London, England, and Co-founder of The Women's Therapy Center Institute in New York City, an institution providing postgraduate training related to eating problems and women's psychology. She is author of the best-selling books *Fat is a Feminist Issue* and *Fat is a Feminist Issue II*, co-author of *What Do Women Want?* and *Understanding Women: A Psychoanalytic and Feminist Approach*. Her latest book is *Hunger Strike: Anorexia as a Metaphor for Our Time* (in press).

HARRISON POPE, M.D., is Assistant Psychiatrist at Mclean Hospital in Belmont, MA, and Assistant Clinical Professor of Psychiatry at Harvard Medical School. He has written 40 articles and three books in the field of psychiatry and related topics, and is co-author with James Hudson of *New Hope for Binge-Eaters: Advances in the Understanding and Treatment of Bulimia*.

ANA-MARIA RIZZUTO, M.D., is a Practicing Psychoanalyst who teaches at the Psychoanalytic Institute of New England in Boston. She is Clinical Professor of Psychiatry at Tufts University School of Medicine and is author of *The Birth of the Living God, A Psychoanalytic Study*.

DONALD M. SCHWARTZ, Ph.D., is a Psychotherapist in private practice in Evanston, IL.

NORMAN P. SPACK, M.D., is a Clinical Instructor in Pediatrics, Harvard Medical School, and Associate in Medicine, Children's Hospital, Boston.

MICHAEL G. THOMPSON, Ph.D., founded the Anorexia Nervosa Research Project at Michael Reese Hospital, Chicago. He has written on the subject of sociocultural influences on the eating disorders. At present, he teaches and supervises at the Massachusetts Mental Health Center and is in private practice in Cambridge, MA.

WILLIAM C. WHITE, Jr., Ph.D., is Director of Psychological Health Services at Cornell University and, with his wife Marlene, facilitator of nationally-known workshops for bulimarexics.

Introduction

There is a growing awareness among clinicians and researchers alike (despite a paucity of solid, supporting epidemiological data) that the eating disorders, anorexia nervosa and bulimia, are appearing in certain segments of the population* at an increasingly alarming rate (Lucas, Bearn, Kranz, & Kurland, 1983). While a variety of theories and treatment strategies have emerged during the past two decades, one area of agreement between specialists in the field is clearly discernible: anorexia and bulimia are continually viewed as complex heterogenous disorders, both in their etiology and symptomatology (Boskind-White, 1983; Bruch, 1973; Garfinkel & Garner, 1982; Lacey, 1983). The collection of writings making up this book encompasses a broad spectrum of ideas which, hopefully, do justice to the multifaceted nature of a phenomenon constituting the paradigmatic psychosomatic disorder of our age. Thus, this volume, intended for research academicians and helping professionals, approaches the enigmatic eating disorders under consideration from the three perspectives—biomedical, sociocultural, and psychological—around which all thorough investigations addressing anorexia and bulimia revolve.

The link between our bodies and emotions has been gaining heightened attention as the worlds of psychology and medicine continue to merge (Benson, 1979). Interdisciplinary studies issuing in a movement of great breadth have provided a holistic perspective from which to view and understand physical and mental illness that is unprecedented in medical history. More-

---

*The pronoun "she" will be used throughout the book when referring to anorexic/bulimic patients due to the preponderance of females struggling with eating disorders.

over, one can trace, since Freud, psychology's (and society's) fascination with a particular illness or constellation of diseases, which, in some distinct manner, seem to reflect the distinguishing malaise of the time. From the conversion hysteria of the Victorian epoch to the narcissism of the 1970s, psychoanalysis has functioned to somehow capture the psychic spirit of the era, transforming it into a force less intimidating, more manageable.

Given this, it is not surprising to discover anorexia and bulimia, so intriguing as both symptomatic and symbolic states of anguish, attracting more notice as they filter through the strata of society. The mind/body interface reflected in phrases pervading our everyday speech—"fed up," "can't stomach it," "leaves a bad taste in my mouth," "consumed by rage," "hungering for love," "all choked up," "starving for attention," "makes me sick to my stomach," "hard to swallow"—simply underscores the fact that " . . . eating, from birth on, is always closely intermingled with interpersonal and emotional experiences, and its physiological and psychological aspects cannot be strictly differentiated" (Bruch, 1973, p. 3).

Along with provision of shelter, there is no greater fundamental act of love than the offering of food. No other human behavior is more essential to the establishment of trust, bonding, and security than the consistent feeding of an infant by its parents. It is little wonder that food and its consumption are so readily enlisted in the service of irrational belief systems imbued with special significance, destructively utilized to mask damaged or unresolved feelings arising out of family-centered pain and conflict. Indeed, it would not be too outlandish to suggest that food represents the earliest and most widespread substance abused by humankind. From the Roman vomitorium to the "buling" of today's collegians, history seems to support such a speculation. (For a detailed historical perspective, see Chapters 2 and 12 in Hilde Bruch's classic study, *Eating Disorders*, 1973.)

The past decade has witnessed a burgeoning awareness of the prevalence of anorexia and bulimia as the media, academic conferences, literature, clinics and self-help organizations have begun to vigorously explore the myriad aspects of both disorders. The writings assembled here continue this process by offering the first comprehensive consideration of both illnesses vis-à-vis theoretical and treatment perspectives. Part I examines pertinent biomedical elements: the clinical presentation and physiological complications; an analysis of the nutritional issues, coupled with a nutrition treatment program; the critical pituitary and neuroendocrine factors; and consideration of a psychopharmacological therapeutic approach. Part II offers an overview of the insidious sociocultural influences so often instrumental in swaying the hearts and minds of impressionable anorexics and bulimics: an integrative psychosocial model examining the interplay between sociocultural forces and psycho-

Introduction

pathology; an historical sociocultural analysis of bulimia; and a feminist understanding of anorexia.

In Part III, treatment and theoretical models are advanced: a psychodynamic approach to group therapy with bulimics; an innovative, collaborative, multidimensional psychotherapeutic model involving two therapists working in tandem with the patient and her family; an integrative family systems theory model; a theoretical psychodynamic interpretation of bulimia; a multimodal inpatient treatment program; a reparenting nurturant/authoritative approach to the treatment of anorexia; short-term intervention strategies with bulimics; and a unified psychoanalytic understanding of anorexia employing a self-psychological perspective. Part IV is devoted to the most recent outcome studies and future considerations.

It is the consensus of both clinicians and theorists that, owing to the multiplicity of factors noted above, any creatively productive treatment plan must reflect the diversity of the eating disorder's complex causation. Hence, an all-inclusive approach to theory and therapy appears to offer the most promise. Familiarity with the biomedical, sociocultural, and psychological features linked to the etiology and evolution of the illness is imperative if the person is to be sufficiently understood and adequately helped. As no single therapeutic strategy can yet lay claim to an undisputed superiority of success, it is our contention that exposure to a broad, rich spectrum of theories and treatment philosophies can best serve researchers and therapists as they struggle to stem the tide of what may prove to be a problem of epidemic proportions. This book is guided by the hope that such an endeavor will result in a better understanding of one of the most critical mental health problems of our time.

Steven Wiley Emmett
The Renfrew Center
475 Spring Lane
Philadelphia, PA 19128

REFERENCES

Benson, H. (1979). *The mind/body effect*. New York: Berkley Books.
Boskind-White, M., & White, W. (1983). *Bulimarexia*. New York: W. W. Norton.
Bruch, H. (1973). *Eating disorders*. New York: Basic Books.
Garfinkel, P., & Garner, D. (1982). *Anorexia Nervosa: A multidimensional perspective*. New York: Brunner/Mazel.
Lacey, J. (1983). An outpatient treatment program for bulimia nervosa. *International Journal of Eating Disorders, 2*(4), 209-214.
Lucas, A., Bearn, C., Kranz, J., & Kurland, L. (1983). Epidemiology of anorexia nervosa and bulimia. *International Journal of Eating Disorders, 2*(4), 85-90.

THEORY AND TREATMENT OF ANOREXIA NERVOSA AND BULIMIA

Biomedical,

Sociocultural, and

Psychological Perspectives

Part I

Biomedical Perspective

Chapter 1

Medical Complications of Anorexia Nervosa and Bulimia

Norman P. Spack

The physical appearance of bulimic and anorexic patients reflects their qualitative and quantitative nutritional intake. Whereas anorexic behavior and weight loss usually draw attention to the patient's "problem," even if the actual diagnosis remains elusive, most bulimics have been purging themselves for months or years before discovery. In one recent study of college freshmen, 4.5% of the women and 0.4% of the men admitted bulimic behavior (Pyle, Mitchell, Eckert, Halvorson, Neuman, & Goff, 1983). These bulimics maintain themselves at, or even above, ideal body weight and consider purging to be absolutely necessary to achieve any semblance of desirable body weight.

Their apparent external physical normality, however, may belie subtle physical changes, such as dental erosion from gastric acid or parotid swelling. Serious electrolyte losses from the individual or combined effects of laxatives, diuretics, or vomiting (or a superimposed gastroenteritis) render these patients potassium-depleted, with little margin to prevent hypokalemia. At some point of lowered serum potassium, myocardial contractility is affected and a fatal arrhythmia or total asystole may ensue (Keys, Brozek, Henschel, Mickelson, & Taylor, 1950). This catastrophic event probably represents the most common cause of death in bulimics and in anorexics who vomit. It tends to occur in outpatients not subject to the nutritional protocols and biochemical scrutiny of the hospital inpatient unit. Since weight is often the criterion for hospitalization, these outpatients succumb at a weight above that at which they had previously been or would be hospitalized (Bruch, 1971).

Whereas bulimics may be above or below or even at ideal body weight, the physical similarities between anorexia nervosa patients is striking. The symptoms and physical signs are well outlined in Warren and VandeWiele's (1973) series of 42 patients (see Table 1).

ENDOCRINE MANFIESTATIONS

Virtually every endocrine system is altered by anorexia nervosa, as it is by starvation. Hormonal concentrations are increased or decreased in predictable fashion, usually proportional to the degree of weight loss. These alterations reflect perturbations in rate of hormonal secretion, degree of binding to serum proteins and receptors, and altered rate of metabolic clearance.

Amenorrhea is a sine qua non for anorexia nervosa with 80% of patients developing it, even before significant weight loss (Warren & VandeWiele, 1973). This finding has been responsible for anorexia nervosa being considered a primary hypothalamic disorder, even though stress alone may account for this phenomenon. Ultimately, when weight loss has been sufficient to reduce total body fat content to less than 20% of total body weight, menses will usually cease for any woman (Eisenberg, 1981; Frisch & McArthur, 1974).

The amenorrhea is the result of reduced estrogen levels secondary to re-

Table 1*

Symptoms	% of Patients Affected	Reported in Starvation?
Amenorrhea	100	Yes
Constipation	62	Yes
Preoccupation with food	45	Yes
Abdominal pain	19	Yes
Intolerance to cold	19	Yes
Vomiting	5	No

Physical Signs	% Affected	Reported in Starvation?
Hypotension	86	Yes
Hypothermia	64	Yes
Dry skin	62	Yes
Lanugo type hair	52	Yes
Bradycardia	26	Yes
Edema	26	Yes
Systolic murmur	14	No
Petechiae	9	Yes

*Reprinted with permission from Warren, M. P., & VandeWiele, R. L., 1973.

duced hypothalamic production of the gonadotrophins, LH and FSH. Twenty-four-hour monitoring of LH levels in anorexics reveals secretory patterns similar to prepubertal children, and patients 25%-50% below ideal body weight have markedly impaired LH responses to gonadotrophin-releasing hormone (GnRH) (Boyar et al., 1974; Sherman, Halmi, & Zamudio, 1975). Even when the amplitude of the reponse to GnRH is normal, it is delayed; similar findings have also been reported in male anorexics (Crisp, Hsu, Chen, & Wheeler, 1982; Vigersky, 1977). Weight-related decreased testosterone levels occur in both sexes accompanied by a diminution in libido (Andersen, Wirth, & Strahiman, 1982; Wesselius & Anderson, 1982). When weight is regained, many patients fail to menstruate at a weight higher than that at which they had lost their menses. Falk and Halmi described this latter group as "more anorexic in their attitudes and behaviors" (p. 799) than patients who menstruated at the attainment of the critical weight (Falk & Halmi, 1982). Although hyperprolactinemia has been associated with amenorrhea, prolactin concentrations are normal in anorexia and play no role in the hypogonadotrophic hypogonadism (Vigersky, 1977).

Thyroid function tests often appear grossly abnormal. Serum T_4 levels may be low due to decreased levels of thyroid-binding globulin, but *Free* (unbound) T_4 levels are normal (Williams, 1981). Under no circumstances should an anorexia nervosa patient be given thyroid hormone on the sole basis of a low serum T_4, as the resultant increased metabolic rate will exacerbate weight loss. The most metabolically active thyroid hormone is triiodothyronine (T_3) which is generated not by thyroidal secretion but by peripheral conversion from T_4. Low T_3 levels are the hallmark of starvation and serve to reduce the metabolic rate, thus conserving calories. The TSH response to thyroid-releasing hormone (TRH) is delayed in patients who lose weight (Vigersky, Andersen, Thompson, & Loriaux 1977), and bulimics at normal weight also exhibit a delayed response, one of the few endocrine changes observed in such patients (Gwirtsman, Roy-Byrne, Yager, & Gerner, 1983). The significance of this is unclear.

Growth hormone and cortisol levels are the only hormones typically in the higher than normal range in anorexia nervosa—a finding that is shared with patients starved from other causes. The growth hormone secretory response to arginine and insulin in anorexia is normal, although the response to hypoglycemia may be diminished (Mecklenburg, Loriaux, Thompson, Andersen, & Lipsett, 1974). Increased evening cortisol levels may be secondary to an increased cortisol half-life, a consequence of reduced metabolic clearance of the hormone (Boyer et al., 1977). Decreased affinity of cortisol for its binding globulin also contributes to an elevated free cortisol (Casper, Chatterton, & Davis, 1979).

Growth arrest typically accompanies a reduction in calories significant enough to produce weight loss, and this may be most evident during adolescence when a growth spurt is expected. Peak height velocity antedates menarche by approximately 18 months in normal females, and mean menarchal age in the United States is 12.6 years (Marshall & Tanner, 1969). Despite the wide standard deviation around mean menarchal age, girls who develop anorexia prior to menarche will not only fail to develop estrogen-induced secondary sexual characteristics, but their skeletal age will arrest (despite their elevated growth hormone levels) (Lacey, Hart, Crisp, & Kirkwood, 1979). Crisp (1969) has reported narrower pelvic measurement in fully grown anorexics and has hypothesized that the cause is years of reduced estrogen effect on the pelvic growth centers. No data exist concerning the propensity for such women to require Caesarean sections due to their pelvic narrowing.

The relationship between estrogen deficiency and osteoporosis has been well-established in postmenopausal women and has been associated with an increased risk of long bone fractures (Lindsay, Aitkin, Anderson, Hart, Macdonald, & Clarke, 1976). An increased incidence of fractures and decreased bone density (osteopenia) has also been observed in premenopausal women with surgically-produced estrogen deficiency (Johansson, Kaij, Kullander, Lenner, Svonberg, & Astedt, 1975). Recently, hypoestrogenic anorexia nervosa patients showed similar loss of bone mass (Ayers, Gidwani, Schmidt, & Gross, 1984).

Additional studies will be required to ascertain whether fractures can be anticipated in those anorexics who exercise vigorously. The question of estrogen replacement for anorexics to prevent osteopenia cannot be answered until additional data are known about the natural course of this condition.

Catch-up growth is a frequent concomitant of recovery from illness or starvation in children and adolescents. Height velocities four times normal and bone age velocity three times normal have been reported (Prader, Tanner, & von Harnack, 1963). Whether or not catch-up growth will enable the patient to regain her position on her pre-morbid growth chart depends on the duration of slowed growth and the presence of hormones, particularly gonadal or adrenal-derived sex steroids, which affect the maturational potential of the epiphyseal growth centers in the long bones. Neither the mechanism for catch-up growth nor the signals triggering return to a normal growth rate are sufficiently understood.

Gross and colleagues (1979), in a study of catecholamine metabolism, measured plasma norepinephrine levels, 24-hour urinary 3-MHPG and homovanillic acid measurements in anorexics. Decreased levels were present in all patients who were 20-25% below ideal body weight. All patients were bradycardic and hypotensive, and catecholamine measurements returned to normal with subsequent weight gain. A norepinephrine deficit in the central nervous system may be responsible for the failure of dexamethasone administered at night to suppress cortisol levels at 4:00 P.M. the following day. This is a finding that anorexics and depressed bulimics share with endogenously depressed patients (Carroll, Curtis, & Mendels, 1976; Gerner & Gwirtsman, 1981). Since norepinephrine normally inhibits hypothalamic cortisol-releasing factor (CRF), decreased circulating levels of norepinephrine may allow more CRF to be released, resulting in more cortisol production by the adrenal.

FLUID AND ELECTROLYTE COMPLICATIONS

In a manner observed in severely obese individuals, abnormalities in water balance mediated via a defect in pituitary antidiuretic hormone secretion (ADH) has recently been reported in anorexics by Gold, Kaye, Robertson, & Ebert (1983). Intravenous saline, a potent stimulus for ADH secretion, was infused into anorexics. The ADH response of the patients was subnormal as compared to controls and follow-up studies showed very slow correction with weight gain. This explains the observation of inappropriately low urine specific gravity when anorexics are fluid-restricted. Failure to adequately concentrate their urine renders them even more prone to dehydration at times of heat exposure or incidental gastroenteritis.

In obese volunteers, a defect in renal concentrating ability can be produced after a four-day fast (Macaron, Schneider, & Ertel, 1975). Furthermore, anorexics and starved volunteers fail to adequately excrete a water load, i.e., they cannot adequately dilute their urine, in response to decreased plasma osmolality even when overhydrated (Russell & Bruce, 1966). Thus, anorexics are also prone to edema due to reductions in glomerular filtration rate, renal plasma flow (secondary to decreased cardiac output), and reduced renal-concentrating ability (Berkman, Weir, & Kepler, 1947). These abnormalities have also been reported in malnourished children (Klahr & Alleyne, 1973), but unlike protein-calorie malnutrition, anorexics have a reduced filtration fraction (Aperia, Broberger, & Fohlin, 1978). The qualitative nutritional difference between anorexics and malnourished children may account for the physiologic difference, since protein deficiency is not a typical feature of anorexia.

Some of the fluid abnormalities can be linked to the effect of chronic potassium depletion on the kidney tubule where vacuolation has been associated with decreased urine-concentrating ability (Wigley, 1960; Wolff et al., 1961). Potassium depletion reflects reduced intake of this cation, coupled with enhanced excretion in the urine and stool in the case of diuretic and laxative abuse. Vomiting does not shed potassium through the GI tract as much as it augments urinary loss. Vomiting chloride (hydrochloric acid) produces potassium loss via reduced renal tubular reabsorption of sodium with chloride (as less is available for absorption) and an increased reabsorption of sodium ion in exchange for potassium and hydrogen (Kassirer & Schwartz, 1966). Thus, a hypochloremic, hypokalemic metabolic alkalosis is the renal effect of chronic vomiting. Serum bicarbonate levels higher than 55 mEq/1 and occasionally exceeding the serum chloride have been observed (Wallace, Richards, Chesser, & Wrong, 1968). As previously noted, hypokalemia poses a potential threat of reduced muscle contractility. Skeletal, smooth, and cardiac muscle are affected, with muscular weakness, gastric atony and cardiac arrhythmias or asystole being the potential consequences of a profoundly reduced serum potassium concentration. Treating hypokalemia demands slow intravenous administration of potassium chloride, keeping in mind that only a tiny fraction of the total body potassium is extracellular. While a low serum potassium indicates marked depletion of the body's cation, normal serum levels are no guarantee of repletion.

Sodium values, however, may be low, normal, or high. Overhydration can be conscious on the part of patients who water load themselves to reach a goal weight, or it may be iatrogenic from the overzealous administration of intravenous fluids in patients who fail to excrete water loads adequately. In either case, the hyponatremia may be profound enough to provoke cerebral edema and seizures (Jose, Barton, & Perez-Cruet, 1979).

OTHER BIOCHEMICAL EFFECTS

Other biochemical changes also reflect the idiosyncratic diets and purgatives of anorexics and bulimics. Massive laxative abuse has produced hypophosphatemia (Sheriden & Collins, 1983). Hypercarotenemia is frequently noted in anorexics and in some bulimics and has been linked to amenorrhea even in normal weight individuals for reasons that are unknown (Kemmann, Pasquale, & Skaf, 1983). Patients who vomit are less likely to exhibit such elevated serum carotenes (Bhanji & Mattingly, 1981).

Zinc deficiency has been reported by Casper and by Thomsen who reversed a case of acrodermatitis enteropathica complicating anorexia nervosa with zinc supplements (Casper, Kirschner, Sandstead, Jacob, & Davis, 1980; Thomsen, 1978). Although Casper found hypogeusia in his study of anorexics, the serum levels failed to correlate with the dysfunction in taste sensation. Two separate recent case reports have suggested that oral zinc supplementation has improved taste sensation and appetite in two severely malnourished anorexics (Bryce-Smith & Simpson, 1984; Safai-Kutti & Kutti, 1984). Controlled studies of the effect of zinc supplements in anorexics must obviously be performed before any additional conclusion can be drawn.

Lipid values in anorexia have been the source of controversy. Crisp and Klinefelter and Mordasini all reported increased cholesterol values (Crisp, Blendis, & Pawan, 1968; Klinefelter, 1965; Mordasini, Klose, & Greten, 1978).

Mordasini et al. found only the LDH fraction increased; triglycerides were normal and cholesterol values failed to correlate with the amount of weight lost. Refeeding returned serum cholesterols to normal. Blendis and Crisp (1968) hypothesized that the intermittent bulimia may have accounted for the abnormal lipid values. Three of Nestel's (1974) four patients had increased serum cholesterol concentrations in spite of decreased cholesterol synthesis. Decreased bile acid excretion, also seen in starvation, may have accounted for the increased serum values. In contrast, Halmi and Fry (1974) were unable to find a statistically significant elevation in cholesterol in their series of anorexics, even when they sub-sampled patients with and without bulimia, both in the phase of anorexia and after recovery.

GASTROINTESTINAL COMPLICATIONS

Liver enzymes are often mild to moderately elevated in anorexia for reasons that are unclear. Fatty liver from malnutrition may compress the parenchyma sufficiently to release hepatic enzymes into the circulation (Halmi & Falk, 1981). Pancreatic enzyme release in the form of an increased serum amylase is a concomitant of suddenly impaired nutrition, termed "refeeding pancreatitis" (Gryboski et al., 1980; Schoettle, 1979). One hypothesis links pancreatic obstruction to back pressure on the duodenum in a manner similar to the development of the superior mesenteric artery syndrome (Rampling, 1982). In this syndrome, marked loss of fat allows the artery to compress the duodenum, producing small bowel obstruction (Burrington & Wayne, 1974; Froese, Szmuilowicz, & Bailey, 1978).

Acute gastric dilatation and rupture have been reported in anorexia and bulimia (Evans, 1968; Jennings & Klidjian, 1974). Saul and colleagues (1981) described one unfortunate bulimic whose stomach contained eight liters of undigested food and fluid at the time of surgery. The patient ultimately succumbed to gastric infarction and perforation.

Delayed gastric emptying is measurable in anorexics who commonly report early satiety, belching, and postprandial pain (Dubois, Gross, Ebert, & Castell, 1979; Saleh & Lebwohl, 1980). Metoclopramide, a properistaltic agent, has been effective in facilitating gastric emptying via pyloric relaxation (Saleh & Lebwohl, 1980). Constipation is the result of delayed gastric emptying, altered composition of food, dehydration, decreased metabolic rate, and, possibly, hypokalemia.

Painless parotid swelling seen in both anorexics who binge and bulimics is another curious manifestation of refeeding (Levin, Falko, Dixon, Gallup, & Saunders, 1980). It has also been noted two to six days after a binging episode in refed prisoners of war (Watt, 1977).

Glucose metabolism is indirectly affected by malnutrition and by anorexia nervosa. Hypoglycemia may be a manifestation of diminished hepatic gluconeogenesis or an increased insulin receptor sensitivity (Elias & Gwinup, 1982; Soman & Felig, 1980; Wachslicht-Rodbard, Gross, Rodbard, Ebert, & Roth, 1979). This author has confirmed the observations of Hillard, Powers, and Roland and their colleagues on the occurrence of bulimia and/or anorexia in patients with diabetes mellitus (Hillard, Lobo, & Keeling, 1983; Powers, Malone, & Duncan, 1983; Roland & Bhanji, 1982). Clearly, patients intent on losing calories will utilize whatever mechanism is at hand, including reduction or withdrawal of insulin to produce ketosis, glycosuria, and weight loss. This was best expressed by one 17-year-old with recurrent ketoacidosis who stated, "Ketones are my friends because they let me know I am burning my fat. Insulin is my enemy because it makes me gain weight."

CARDIOVASCULAR COMPLICATIONS

Bradycardia, hypotension, and decreased maximal heart rate with exercise are the expected physical signs of anorexia (Fohlin, 1967). The reduced maximal physical performance is probably secondary to decreased skeletal muscle mass. Peripheral circulation is diminished by an increased peripheral vascular tone, hence the cold extremities. Cardiac arrhythmias reported include supraventricular premature beats, sinus arrests, sinus tachycardia, nodal escape beats, and even ventricular ectopy, particularly with exercise (Gottdiener, Gross, Henry, Borer, & Ebert, 1978; Mitchell & Gillum, 1980; Simonson, Henschel, & Keys, 1948; Thurston & Marks, 1974). Many of these same findings were reported by Tur (1944), who studied patients starving during the siege of Leningrad. These findings were also reported in the classic treatises by the Jewish physicians of the Warsaw ghetto and in the Minnesota study of 32 volunteers during World War II (Apfelbaum-Kowalski, Pakszwer, Zarchi, Heller, & Askanas, 1979; Simonson et al., 1948). Both groups reported a marked reduction in cardiac output in addition to the above noted heart rate and EKG changes. The Warsaw physicians, themselves the victims of malnutrition, noted that "even at rest cardiac muscle is lacking in oxygen and functionally damaged . . . and the adaptive cardiac regulation becomes 'fixed'" (p. 151). This reduction in cardiac reserve may well be the consequence of myocardial damage, as has been seen post mortem in a previous obese patient who succumbed while on a starvation diet (Garnett et al., 1961). Although cardiac function ultimately returns to normal with nutritional reconstitution of the starved patient, the stress of rapid refeeding or an excessive exercise challenge may threaten the still compromised cardiac reserve. The result may be sudden cardiac decompensation and death, even in patients who have regained substantial weight.

Using technology of the 1980s for anorexia nervosa patients, echocardiograms reveal a decrease in the size of the left ventricle, left atrium and aorta (Gottdiener et al., 1978). Myocardial contractility, assessed by the "systolic time interval" was impaired, according to Kalager, Brubakk, and Bassoe (1978), who also noted an increased pre-injection period.

Actual alterations in intracardiac anatomy may occur secondary to profound weight loss. The new ventricular dimensions can produce a secondary mitral prolapse including a "new" mitral click, which is physiologically benign (Levine, Isner, & Salem, 1982). Lastly, cardiorespiratory function may decompensate suddenly secondary to the accumulation of subcutaneous emphysema, pneumomediastinum, and pneumoretroperitoneum from forceful vomiting of any cause (Al-Mufty & Bevan, 1977).

HEMATOLOGIC AND IMMUNOLOGIC COMPLICATIONS

Anemias, leukopenia (neutropenia and lymphopenia) and, less frequently, thrombocytopenia have all been reported in anorexia nervosa (Lampert & Lau, 1976; Mant & Faragher, 1972). Erythrocyte sedimentation rates and plasma fibrinogen levels are low, which distinguishes anorexia from many mimickers of the condition, such as inflammatory bowel disease (Anyan, 1974). Hematocrits poorly reflect the circulating red cell mass in anorexics, due to the presence of dehydration. Red blood cell morphology varies from the normochromic normocytic anemias similar to those seen in concentration camp victims, to macrocytosis and acanthocytosis (despite normal Beta lipoprotein concentrations) (Amrein, Friedman, Kosinski, & Ellman, 1979; Mollison, 1946). Bone marrow examinations are markedly hypocellular with decreased erythroblasts, megakaryocytes, and myeloid precursors, despite normal peripheral counts. All investigators have noted decreased bone marrow fat and an increased amorphous ground substance consistent with gelatinous acid mucopolysaccharide (Lampert & Lau, 1976; Mant & Faragher, 1972; Pearson, 1967).

Gotch and Palmblad and their colleagues found that neutrophils of anorexics had diminished chemotaxis and are deficient in their ability to kill staph aureus and E. coli in vitro (Gotch, Spry, Mowat, Beeson, & MacLennan, 1975; Palmblad, Fohlin, & Lunstrom, 1977). Yet, despite the previously noted neutropenia, the clinical significance of the above finding is unclear. Anorexics, in contrast to patients with protein-calorie malnutrition, are remarkably free from recurrent or infectious diseases (Bowers & Eckert, 1978; Golla, Larson, Anderson, Lucas, Wilson, & Tomasi, 1981; Palmblad et al., 1977). Kim and Michael (1975) reported one 18-year-old anorexic with recurrent staph infections whose decreased complement levels normalized with increased caloric intake. Antibody response to flu vaccine in 15 anorexic patients was similar to that of the age-matched controls (Armstrong-Esther, Crisp, Lacey, & Bryant, 1978).

Delayed hypersensitivity, in the form of Candida, streptokinase-streptodornase, and mumps skin tests, showed anergy in 27% of the patients of Pertschuk and co-workers (1982), despite normal total proteins, albumins, and transferrins. Anergy correlated best with anthroprometric indices of malnutrition. Also, in contrast to protein-calorie malnutrition, anorexics have normal T lymphocyte populations with unimpaired proliferative responses to stimuli such as PHA and concanavalin A (Golla et al., 1981). Perhaps the key to the difference between anorexics and other starved individuals again stems from the relative maintainence of protein intake as opposed to carbohydrate and fat in the former group.

PSYCHOLOGIC, NEUROLOGIC, AND OPHTHALMOLOGIC COMPLICATIONS

The psychological consequences of severe starvation are so profound as to preclude effective treatment until nutritional reconstitution has been begun. Even normal volunteers, aware that their period of food deprivation is finite, exhibited behavior quite similar to anorexics during their 24 weeks of semi-starvation (1660 calories/day) in Keys et al.'s landmark World War II study (1950). Decreased mental concentration, indecisiveness, obsessional behavior, preoccupation with food, mood lability, and sleep disturbances were all observed.

The recent availability of CAT scans has documented generalized reversible cerebral and cerebellar atrophy in anorexics (Enzemann & Lane, 1977; Sein, Searson, Nicol, & Hall, 1981). Heinz also reported dilated lateral and third ventricles (Heinz, Martinez, & Haenggeli, 1977). EEG background abnormalities appeared in 59% of anorexics as opposed to 22% of controls in Crisp's series of 32 patients (Crisp, Fenton, & Scotton, 1968). The abnormalities correlated with length of illness and degree of sodium, potassium, and chloride depletion. Transient theta bitemporal discharges were the reversible findings in Sein's patient, a 14-year-old with a normal neurological exam (Sein et al., 1981). Frank seizures are to be anticipated in patients who are profoundly hyponatremic.

Peripheral neuropathies have also been seen in patients who lose weight abruptly whatever the cause, secondary to the external compression of these less padded nerves. Foot drop was seen in one anorexic and transient bilateral peroneal nerve palsies are a frequent complication in emaciated prisoners of war who squatted or sat through most of their captivity (Schott, 1979).

Cataracta cachectica, reported by Archer (1981) in three anorexics, had previously been seen in starvation, in severe chronic anemia, and in patients with chronic diarrhea. These metabolic cataracts can be produced in experimental animals by hypokalemia and hypomagnesemia. Affected patients, however, have no metabolic or endocrine changes to distinguish them from other anorexics.

DENTAL COMPLICATIONS

Chronic vomiting can wreak havoc on the teeth of anorexics and bulimics. Chronic exposure to gastric acid may produce extensive decay and a nonreversible perimylolysis seen initially on the lingual surfaces of the incisors, the teeth most bathed by the vomitus. Contributory factors include the tendency of anorexics to ingest citrus fruits and juices and for bulimics to consume highly sugared foods during binge eating. Decreased saliva production in dehydrated anorexics also contributes to enamel erosion (Schleimer, 1980). Surprisingly little periodontal disease has been observed, unless the tooth decay is extensive (Hurst, Lacey, & Crisp, 1977; Stege, Visco-Dangler, & Rye, 1982).

CONCLUSION

The medical complications of anorexia and bulimia are a challenge for any physician, particularly when the patient is not allied with the therapeutic team. At times the patient will deliberately sabotage efforts to assess her true clinical status.

As has been shown, not all serious medical complications are related to absolute weight loss, and patients warrant periodic biochemical (particularly serum electrolyte) evaluation regardless of their weight. Obviously, normal serum electrolytes, especially in a bulimic with profound binge-purge cycles, may fail to predict the patient's status two days later, and no single test can provide a full measure of confidence in any patient's well-being.

REFERENCES

Al-Mufty, N. S., & Bevan, D. H. (1977). A case of subcutaneous emphysema, pneumomediastinum and pneumoretroperitoneum associated with functional anorexia. *British Journal of Clinical Practice, 31*, 160.

Amrein, P. C., Friedman, R., Kosinski, K., & Ellman, L. (1979). Hematologic changes in anorexia nervosa. *Journal of the American Medical Association, 241*, 2190-91.

Andersen, A. E., Wirth, J. B., & Strahiman, E. R. (1982). Reversible weight-related increase in plasma testosterone during treatment of male and female patients with anorexia nervosa. *International Journal of Eating Disorders, 1*, 74-85.

Anyan, W. R., Jr. (1974). Changes in erythrocyte sedimentation rate and fibrinogen during anorexia nervosa. *Journal of Pediatrics, 85*, 525-527.

Aperia, A., Broberger, O., & Fohlin, L. (1978). Renal function in anorexia nervosa. *Acta Paediatrica Scandinavica, 67*, 219-224.

Apfelbaum-Kowalski, E., Pakszwer, R., Zarchi, S., Heller, A., Askanas, Z. (1979). Pathophysiology of the circulatory system in hunger disease. In *Hunger Disease* (Winick M., Ed.). New York: John Wiley.

Archer, A. G. (1981). Cataract formation in anorexia nervosa. *British Medical Journal, 282*, 274.

Armstrong-Esther, C. A., Crisp, A. H., Lacey, J. H., & Bryant, T. N. (1978). An investigation of the immune response of patients suffering from anorexia nervosa. *Postgraduate Medical Journal, 54*, 395-399.

Ayers, J. W. T., Gidwani, G. P., Schmidt, I. M. V., & Gross, M. (1984). Osteopenia in hypoestrogenic young women with anorexia nervosa. *Fertility and Sterility, 41*, 224.

Berkman, J. M., Weir, J. F., & Kepler, E. J. (1947). Clinical observations in starvation edema, serum protein and the effect of forced feeding in anorexia nervosa. *Gastroenterology, 9*, 357-390.

Bhanji, S., & Mattingly, D. (1981). Anorexia nervosa: Some observations in "dieters" and "vomiters." *British Journal of Psychiatry, 139*, 238-241.

Blendis, L. M., & Crisp, A. H. (1968). Serum cholesterol levels in anorexia nervosa. *Postgraduate Medical Journal, 44*, 327-330.

Bowers, T. K., & Eckert, E. (1978). Leukopenia in anorexia nervosa. *Archives of Internal Medicine, 138*, 1520-23.

Boyar, R. M., Hellman, L. D., Roffwarg, H., Katz, J., Zumoff, B., O'Connor, J., Bradlow, H. L., & Fukushima, D. K. (1977). Cortisol secretion and metabolism in anorexia nervosa. *New England Journal of Medicine, 296*, 190-193.

Boyar, R. M., Katz, J., Finkelstein, J. W., Kapen, S., Weiner, H., Weitzman, E. D., & Hellman, L. (1974). Anorexia nervosa: Immaturity of the 24-hour luteinizing hormone secretory pattern. *New England Journal of Medicine, 291*, 861-865.

Bruch, H. (1971). Death in anorexia nervosa. *Psychosomatic Medicine, 33*, 135-144.

Bryce-Smith, D., & Simpson, R. I. D. (1984). Case of anorexia nervosa responding to zinc sulphate. *Lancet, II*, 350.

Burrington, J. D., & Wayne, E. R. (1974). Obstruction of the duodenum by the superior mesenteric artery: does it exist in children? *Journal of Pediatric Surgery, 9*, 733-741.

Carroll, B. J., Curtis, G. C., & Mendels, J. (1976). Neuroendocrine regulation in depression. I. Limbic system-adrenocortical dysfunction. *Archives of General Psychiatry, 33*, 1039-1044.

Casper, R. C., Chatterton, R. T., & Davis, J. M. (1979). Alterations in serum cortisol and its binding characteristics in anorexia nervosa. *Journal of Clinical Endocrinology and Metabolism, 49*, 406-411.

Casper, R. C., Kirschner, B., Sandstead, H. H., Jacob, R. A., & Davis, J. M. (1980). An evaluation of trace metals, vitamins, and taste function in anorexia nervosa. *American Journal of Clinical Nutrition, 33*, 1801-1808.

Crisp, A. H. (1969). Some skeletal measurements in patients with primary anorexia nervosa. *Journal of Psychosomatic Research, 13*, 125-142.

Crisp, A. H., Blendis, L. M., & Pawan, G. L. S. (1968). Aspects of fat metabolism in anorexia nervosa. *Metabolism, 17*, 1109-1118.

Crisp, A. H., Fenton, G. W., & Scotton, L. (1968). A controlled study of the EEG in anorexia nervosa. *British Journal of Psychiatry, 114*, 1149-1160.

Crisp, A. H., Hsu, L. K. G., Chen, C. N., & Wheeler, M. (1982). Reproductive hormone profiles in male anorexia nervosa before, during and after restoration of body weight to normal. *International Journal of Eating Disorders, 1*, 3-9.

Dubois, A., Gross, H. A., Ebert, M. H., & Castell, D. O. (1979). Altered gastric emptying and secretion in primary anorexia nervosa. *Gastroenterology, 77*, 319-323.

Eisenberg, E. (1981). Toward an understanding of reproductive function in anorexia nervosa *Fertility and Sterility, 36*, 543-550.

Elias, A. N., & Gwinup, G. (1982). Glucose resistant hypoglycemia in inanition. *Archives of Internal Medicine, 142*, 743-746.

Enzemann, D. R., & Lane, B. (1977). Cranial computed tomography findings in anorexia nervosa. *Journal of Computer Assisted Tomography, 1*, 410-413.

Evans, D. S. (1968). Acute dilatation and spontaneous rupture of the stomach. *British Journal of Surgery, 55*, 940-942.

Falk, J. R., & Halmi, K. A. (1982). Amenorrhea in anorexia nervosa: Examination of critical body weight hypothesis. *Biological Psychiatry, 17*, 799-806.

Fohlin, L. (1967). Body composition, cardiovascular and renal function in adolescent patients with anorexia nervosa. *Acta Paediatrica Scandinavica* (suppl), 268.

Frisch, R. E., & McArthur, J. W. (1974). Menstrual cycles: Fatness as a determinant of minimum weight for height necessary for their maintenance or onset. *Science, 185*, 949-951.

Froese, A. P., Szmuilowicz, J., & Bailey, J. D. (1978). The superior-mesenteric artery syndrome. Cause or complication of anorexia nervosa? *Canadian Psychiatric Association Journal, 23*, 325-327.

Garnett, E. S., Barnard, D. L., Ford, J., et al. (1961). Gross fragmentation of cardiac myofibrils after therapeutic starvation for obesity. *Lancet, 1*, 916-941.

Gerner, R. H., & Gwirtsman, H. E. (1981). Abnormalities of dexamethasone suppression test and urinary MHPG in anorexia nervosa. *American Journal of Psychiatry, 138*, 650-653.

Gold, P. W., Kaye, W., Robertson, G. L., & Ebert, M. H. (1983). Abnormalities in plasma and CSF arginine vasopression in patients with anorexia nervosa. *New England Journal of Medicine, 308*, 1117-1123.

Golla, J. A., Larson, L. A., Anderson, C. F., Lucas, A. R., Wilson, W. R., Tomasi, T. B. Jr. (1981). An immunological assessment of patient with anorexia nervosa. *American Journal of Clinical Nutrition, 34*, 2756-2762.

Gotch, F. M., Spry, C. J. F., Mowat, A. G., Beeson, P. B., & MacLennan, I. C. M. (1975). Reversible granulocyte killing defect in anorexia nervosa. *Clin Exp Immunol, 21*, 244-249.

Gottdiener, J. S., Gross, H. A., Henry, W. L., Borer, J. S., Ebert, M. H. (1978). Effects of self-induced starvation in cardiac size and function in anorexia nervosa. *Circulation, 58*, 425-433.

Gross, H. A., Lake, C. R., Ebert, M. H., Ziegler, M. G., & Kopin, I. J. (1979). Catecholamine metabolism in primary anorexia nervosa. *Journal of Clinical Endocrinology and Metabolism, 49*, 805.

Gryboski, J., Hillemeier, C., Kocoshis, S., et al. (1980). Refeeding pancreatitis in malnourished children. *Journal of Pediatrics, 97*, 441-443.

Gwirtsman, H. E., Roy-Byrne, P., Yager, J., & Gerner, R. H. (1983). Neuroendocrine abnormalities in bulimia. *American Journal of Psychiatry, 140*, 559-563.

Halmi, K. A., Falk, J. R. (1981). Common physiologic changes in anorexia nervosa. *International Journal of Eating Disorders, 1*, 16-27.

Halmi, K. A., & Fry, M. (1974). Serum lipids in anorexia nervosa. *Biological Psychiatry, 8*, 159-167.

Heinz, E. R., Martinez, J., Haenggeli. (1977). Reversibility of cerebral atrophy in anorexia nervosa and Cushing's syndrome. *Journal of Computer Assisted Tomography, 1*, 415-418.

Hillard, J. R., Lobo, M. C., & Keeling, R. P. (1983). Bulimia and diabetes: A potentially life-threatening combination. *Psychosomatics, 24*, 292-295.

Hurst, P. S., Lacey, J. H., & Crisp, A. H. (1977). Teeth, vomiting and diet: A study of the dental characteristics of 17 anorexia nervosa patients. *Postgraduate Medical Journal, 53*, 298-305.

Jennings, K. P., Klidjian, A. M. (1974). Acute gastric dilatation in anorexia nervosa. *British Medical Journal, 2*, 477-478.

Johansson, B. W., Kaij, L., Kullander, S., Lenner, S. C., Svonberg, L., & Astedt, B. (1975). On some late effects of bilateral oophorectomy in the age range 15-30 years. *Acta Obstet. Gynecol. Scan., 54*, 449.

Jose, C. J., Barton, J. L., & Perez-Cruet, J. (1979). Hyponatremic seizures in psychiatric patients. *Biological Psychiatry, 14*, 839.

Kalager, T., Brubakk, D., & Bassoe, H. (1978). Cardiac performance in patients with anorexia nervosa. *Cardiology, 63*, 1-4.

Kassirer, J., & Schwartz, W. (1966). Selective HCl depletion in normal man. *American Journal of Medicine, 40*, 10.

Kemmann, E., Pasquale, S. A., & Skaf, R. (1983). Amenorrhea associated with carotenemia. *Journal of the American Medical Association, 249*, 926-929.

Keys, A., Brozek, J., Henschel, A., Mickelson, O., & Taylor, H. L. (1950). *The biology of human*

starvation. Minneapolis: University of Minnesota Press.
Kim, Y., & Michael, A. F. (1975). Hypocomplementemia in anorexia nervosa. *Journal of Pediatrics, 87,* 582-585.
Klahr, S., & Alleyne, G. A. O. (1973). Effects of chronic protein-malnutrition on the kidney. *Kidney International, 3,* 129-141.
Klinefelter, H. F. (1965). Hypercholesterolemia in anorexia nervosa. *Journal of Clinical Endocrinology, 25,* 1520-1521.
Lacey, J. H., Hart, G., Crisp, A. H., & Kirkwood, B. A. (1979). Weight and skeletal maturation: A study of radiological and chronological age in an anorexia nervosa population. *Postgraduate Medicine, 55,* 381-385.
Lampert, F., & Lau, B. (1976). Bone marrow hypoplasia in anorexia nervosa. *European Journal of Pediatrics, 124,* 65-71.
Levin, P. A., Falko, J. M., Dixon, K., Gallup, E. M., & Saunders, W. (1980). Benign parotid enlargement in bulimia. *Annals of Internal Medicine, 93,* 827-829.
Levine, H. J., Isner, J. M., Salem, D. N. (1982). Primary versus secondary mitral valve prolapse: Clinical features and implications. *Clinical Cardiology, 5,* 371-375.
Lindsay, R., Aitkin, J. M., Anderson, J. B., Hart, D. M., Macdonald, E. B., & Carke, A. C. (1976). Long-term prevention of postmenopausal osteoporosis by oestrogen. *Lancet, 1,* 1038.
Macaron, C., Schneider, G., & Ertel, N. H. (1975). The starved kidney: A defect in renal concentrating ability. *Metabolism, 24,* 457-459.
Mant, M. J., & Faragher, B. S. (1972). The haematology of anorexia nervosa. *British Journal of Haematology, 23,* 737-749.
Marshall, W. A., & Tanner, J. M. (1969). Variations in the pattern of pubertal changes in girls. *Archives of Disease in Childhood, 44,* 291.
Mecklenburg, R. S., Loriaux, D. L., Thompson, R. H., Andersen, A. E., & Lipsett, M. B. (1974). Hypothalamic dysfunction in patients with anorexia nervosa. *Medicine, 53,* 147-159.
Mitchell, J. E., & Gillum, R. (1980). Weight dependent arrhythmia in a patient with anorexia nervosa. *American Journal of Psychiatry, 137,* 377-378.
Mollison, P. L. (1946). Observations on cases of starvation at Belsen. *British Medical Journal, 1,* 4.
Mordasini, R., Klose, G., & Greten, H. (1978). Secondary type II hyperlipoproteinemia in patients with anorexia nervosa. *Metabolism, 27,* 71-78.
Nestel, P. J. (1974). Cholesterol metabolism in anorexia nervosa and hypercholesterolemia. *Journal of Clinical Endocrinology and Metabolism, 38,* 325-327.
Palmblad, J., Fohlin, L., & Lunstrom, M. (1977). Anorexia nervosa and polymorphonuclear granulocyte reactions. *Scand Journal of Haematology, 19,* 334-342.
Pearson, H. A. (1967). Marrow hypoplasia in anorexia nervosa. *Journal of Pediatrics, 71,* 211-215.
Pertschuk, M. J., Crosby, L. O., Barot, L., & Mullen, J. L. (1982). Immunocompetency in anorexia nervosa. *American Journal of Clinical Nutrition, 35,* 968-972.
Powers, P. S., Malone, J. I., & Duncan, J. A. (1983). Anorexia nervosa and diabetes mellitus. *Journal of Clinical Psychiatry, 44,* 133-135.
Prader, A., Tanner, J. M., & von Harnack, G. A. (1963). Catch-up growth following illness or starvation. *Journal of Pediatrics, 62,* 646-659.
Pyle, R. L., Mitchell, J. E., Eckert, E. E., Halvorson, P. A., Neuman, P. A., Goff, G. M. (1983). The incidence of bulimia in freshman college students. *The International Journal of Eating Disorders, 2,* 75-85.
Rampling, D. (1982). Acute pancreatitis in anorexia nervosa. *Med J. Austra, 2,* 194-5.
Roland, J. M., & Bhanji, S (1982). Anorexia nervosa occurring in patients with diabetes mellitus. *Postgraduate Medical Journal, 58,* 354-356.
Russell, G. F. M., & Bruce, J. T. (1966). Impaired water diuresis in patients with anorexia nervosa. *American Journal of Medicine, 40,* 38-48.
Safai-Kutti, S., & Kutti, J. (1984). Zinc and anorexia nervosa. *Annals of Internal Medicine, 100,* 318.
Saleh, J. W., & Lebwohl, P. (1980). Metoclopramide-induced gastric emptying in patients with anorexia nervosa. *American Journal of Gastroenterology, 74,* 127-132.

Saul, S. H., Dekker, A., & Watson, C. G. (1981). Acute gastric dilatation with infarction and perforation. Report of fatal outcome in patient with anorexia nervosa. *GUT, 22,* 978-983.

Schleimer, K. Anorexia nervosa in *Nutrition* in *Adolescence.* Maribou Symposium, June 14, 1980, pp. 67-71.

Schoettle, U. G. (1979). Pancreatitis: A complication, a concomitant or a cause of an anorexia nervosa-like syndrome. *Journal of the American Academy of Child Psychiatry, 18,* 384-390.

Schott, G. D. (1979). Anorexia nervosa presenting as foot drop. *Postgraduate Medicine, 55,* 58-60.

Sein, P., Searson, S., Nicol, A. R., & Hall, K. (1981). Anorexia nervosa and pseudo-atrophy of the brain (letter). *British Journal of Psychiatry, 139,* 257-258.

Sheriden, P. H., & Collins, M. (1983). Potentially life-threatening hypophosphatemia in anorexia nervosa. *Journal of Adolescent Health Care, 4,* 44-46.

Sherman, B. M., Halmi, K. A., & Zamudio, R. (1975). LH & FSH response to gonadotropin-releasing hormone in anorexia nervosa: Effect of nutritional rehabilitation. *Journal of Clinical Endocrinology and Metabolism, 41,* 135.

Simonson, E., Henschel, A., & Keys, A. (1948). The electrocardiogram of man in semistarvation and subsequent rehabilitation. *Am Heart J, 35,* 584-602.

Soman, V. R., & Felig, P. (1980). Insulin binding to monocytes and insulin sensitivity in anorexia nervosa. *American Journal of Medicine, 68,* 66-72.

Stege, P., Visco-Dangler, L., & Rye, L. (1982). Anorexia nervosa: Review including oral and dental manifestations. *Journal of the American Dental Association, 104,* 648-652.

Thomsen, K. (1978). Zinc, liver cirrhosis and anorexia nervosa. *Acta Dermatovener* (Stockholm), *58,* 283.

Thurston, J., & Marks, P. (1974). Electrocardiographic abnormalities in patients with anorexia nervosa. *British Heart Journal, 36,* 719-723.

Tur, A. F. (1944). Electrocardiographic observations in malnutrition. *Alimentary Dystrophy and Avitaminosis.* Leningrad: Institute I. P. Pavlov, pp. 80-87.

Vigersky, R. A. (1977). *Anorexia nervosa.* New York: Raven Press.

Vigersky, R. A., Andersen, A. E., Thompson, R. H., & Loriaux, D. L. (1977). Hypothalamic dysfunction in secondary amenorrhea associated with simple weight loss. *New England Journal of Medicine, 297,* 1141-1145.

Wachslicht-Rodbard, H., Gross, H. A., Rodbard, D., Ebert, M. H., & Roth, J. (1979). Increased insulin binding to erythrocytes in anorexia nervosa. *New England Journal of Medicine, 300,* 882-887.

Wallace, M., Richards, P., Chesser, E., & Wrong, O. (1968). Persistent alkalosis and hypokalaemia caused by surreptitious vomiting. *Quarterly Journal of Medicine, 37,* 577.

Warren, M. P., & VandeWiele, R. L. (1973). Clinical and metabolic features of anorexia nervosa. *American Journal of Obstetrics and Gynecology, 117,* 435-449.

Watt, J. (1977). Benign parotid swellings: a review. *Proceedings of the Royal Society of Medicine, 70,* 483-486.

Wesselius, C. L., & Anderson, G. (1982). A case study of a male with anorexia nervosa and low testosterone levels. *Journal of Clinical Psychiatry, 43,* 428-429.

Wigley, R. D. (1960). Potassium deficiency in anorexia nervosa with reference to renal tubular vacuolation. *British Medical Journal, 2,* 110-113.

Williams, R. H. (Ed.). (1981). *Textbook of endocrinology.* Philadelphia: W. B. Saunders.

Wolff, H. P., Vecsei, P., Kruck, F., et al. (1968). Psychiatric disturbance leading to potassium depletion, sodium depletion, raised plasma renin concentration and secondary hyperaldosteronism. *Lancet, 1,* 257-261.

Chapter 2

Nutritional Aspects of Anorexia Nervosa and Bulimia

Johanna Dwyer

INTRODUCTION

The purposes of this chapter are threefold. I first review the range of nutrition-related effects that are seen in anorexia nervosa and eating disorders associated with it. This is followed by a review of nutritional screening and assessment procedures. The chapter concludes with a brief guide to the dietary aspects of treatment.

Anorexia Nervosa and Appetite

Appetite is a desire for certain bodily satisfactions such as the sustenance provided by food to satisfy the natural physiological needs of the body (Bolles, 1980). That is, appetite is a mental want related to a bodily need. In the past few decades it has become clear that in addition to physiological factors such as metabolic deficit or illness, appetite is dependent on psychological factors such as learning, palatability, selection pressures, feeding strategies, and emotion, as well as cultural factors such as social pressures not to eat too much (Bolles, 1980). Moreover, lack of appetite is only one of many factors which are associated with failure to eat. For example, many individuals on reduc-

---

The assistance of salary support from the Culpepper Foundation to Dr. Dwyer which covered part of the research for preparing this chapter is acknowledged with appreciation, as are the helpful comments of Ms. Carol Stollar, R.D., M. Ed., on treatment and the editorial assistance of Glenda Brown.

ing diets consciously restrain themselves from eating, even though they are hungry, in order to lose weight.

The term *anorexia nervosa* means a nervous loss of appetite. In this sense, the name of the syndrome is a misnomer because in actuality those afflicted by it do *not* necessarily suffer from lack of appetite, although they deliberately and willfully limit their food intake in spite of frequently overwhelming desires to eat. The failure to eat goes hand in hand with other behavioral changes. Those suffering from the condition become preoccupied with food and adopt ritualistic practices concerning eating. Individuals who were previously thought of by their parents as "good," compliant, successful, and gratifying children become angry, distrustful, negativistic, and stubborn. They claim not to need help and care, and insist on their right to eat as they wish and to be as thin as they want to be. In fact, they often are proud of the rigid discipline over eating and the food rituals they impose on themselves, as if their visible weight loss gives them the sense of effectiveness and control in at least this one area of their lives. Table 1 presents some of the commonly used signs and symptoms for recognizing the disorder.

The Heterogeneity of Anorexia Nervosa

One of the most exciting developments in the past decade of research on anorexia nervosa has been better characterization of other syndromes which are sometimes associated with it and alter its manifestations, such as bulimia, vomiting, and laxative and diuretic abuse (Beumont, George & Smart, 1976; Casper, Ekert, Halmi, Goldberg, & Davis, 1980; Johnson, Thompson, & Schwartz, 1982; Russell, 1979). They may occur singly but often appear together, leading to synergistic adverse effects. Correction of the complications produced by these abnormalities before they become serious has helped to reduce mortality from the disease. Each will be discussed briefly below.

Bulimia in Anorexia Nervosa

Patients with the classical form of anorexia nervosa are sometimes called starvers or restricters. They lose weight by constantly fasting or eating very small amounts of food. Others, known as bulimic anorexics, gorgers, purger/vomiters, or bulimarexics, also fast or eat very small amounts of food, but they periodically (e.g., several times a week) indulge in binge eating during which they gorge themselves (Casper et al., 1980).

Because most bulimics conceal their behavior, it is less obvious than the anorexia nervosa itself, which has more clear-cut physical signs as it progresses. Bulimia occurs in as many as half of the patients who suffer from anorexia nervosa (Fairburn, 1984). A minority of such patients also use

Table 1
Diagnostic Criteria for Anorexia Nervosa

Age	10–40 years (onset of illness between 10 and 30)
Weight Loss	At least 25% of original body weight and/or 15% below usual weight for age and height.
Attitudes	Distorted attitudes toward eating food and weight that override hunger, admonitions, reassurances or threats and are evidenced by: • denial of illness and failure to recognize nutritional needs • apparent enjoyment in losing weight • desired body image of extreme thinness and a terror of fatness, distorted body image • unusual hoarding or handling of food, food rituals
Signs	One or more of these are usually present: • lanugo hair (downy pelage) • bradycardia (pulse at rest 60/minute or less) • hypothermia (36.1°C or less) • bulimic episodes (rapid consumption of a large amount of food in a short period of time, usually 2 hours or less) • vomiting (self-induced)
Other Common Findings	• periods of overactivity • no known medical illness accounting for anorexia or weight loss (or bulimia if it is present) • No other major psychiatric disorder (e.g., major affective disorder or schizophrenia) • amenorrhea of at least 3 months' duration (if post-menarcheal) • abuse of laxatives or diuretics may also be present • inconspicuous eating high calorie, easily ingested foods during binges which patient feels unable to stop voluntarily, which are terminated by sleep, social interruptions, abdominal pain or self-induced vomiting, and which are followed by self-deprecating thoughts, depressed moods • previous attempts to lose weight in past by strict reducing diet, self-induced vomiting, laxatives, or diuretics

Adapted from Casper et al., 1980; Fairburn, 1984; Feighner et al., 1972; with additions by the author.

vomiting, laxatives, or diuretics to control their weight (Fairburn, 1984).

Bulimic and restricting anorexia nervosa patients differ in many respects that are relevant to their nutritional therapy. Patients with bulimic anorexia nervosa are more likely to have histories of intense family conflict, premorbid obesity, and stressful events in the period preceding the onset of their illness than are those who consistently restrict their intakes (Strober, 1984). They are more outgoing and extroverted, report a stronger appetite, vomit more frequently, are more likely to be anxious, depressed, or guilty, more frequently report body-related complaints, and exhibit greater interpersonal sensitivity (Casper et al., 1980). Impulsive behaviors such as the use of alcohol for sedative effects, use of anorexic drugs and street drugs, stealing, self-mutilation, suicide attempts, and addiction proneness are also more common among them. Even after recovery to normal weight, the bulimia frequently persists (Fairburn, 1984; Fairburn & Cooper, 1982).

Whether the bulimic form of anorexia nervosa is simply a subtype of the anorexia or an "end stage" in the natural history of the disease representing a more severe and chronic form with a particularly poor prognosis is still being debated (Garfinkel, Moldovsky, & Garner, 1980). Even with vomiting and the use of laxatives, bulimic anorexics rarely reach weights as low as the fasters. However, their long-term outcomes are poorer because of the presence of problems such as mood disorders and harmful impulsive behaviors such as suicide attempts and alcoholism.

Vomiting and Anorexia Nervosa

Vomiting is another purposeful manipulation of body functions used to accelerate weight loss. A number of patients who suffer from the bulimic type of anorexia nervosa also engage in self-induced vomiting and laxative use after they gorge. In fact, they may plan to do so before they overeat. However, there are also fasters with anorexia nervosa who indulge in vomiting without gorging.

Laxative Abuse in Anorexia Nervosa

The range of bowel movement frequency in normal people is very large: from three times daily to three times weekly. The general population in this country has many misconceptions about what constitutes constipation and anorexia nervosa patients are no exception.

Laxative abuse is relatively uncommon among patients who suffer from the form of anorexia nervosa that involves starvation alone. However, these patients are often bothered because their usual frequency of defecation is less than it was prior to their illness. This is to be expected in view of their restricted intake of food and fluids, as well as the general slowing of metabolic processes which ensues as starvation progresses. They often suffer from constipation and may occasionally use laxatives to correct it.

Laxative abuse is more common among bulimic anorexics, for whom it appears to serve both psychological purposes associated with purging after a binge and weight reduction purposes.

Diuretic Abuse in Anorexia Nervosa

In the hopes of losing still more weight or of correcting the postural hypotension which often ensues in anorexia nervosa, patients may resort to diuretic abuse. Again, this is more common among bulimic anorexics.

NUTRITION-RELATED EFFECTS

Physical Effects of Starvation

The physiological abnormalities of anorexia nervosa are many but are identical to those occurring in simple starvation when weight loss reaches a similar extent (Felig, 1979; Garfinkel & Garner, 1982; Keys, Brozek, Henschel, Mickelson, & Taylor, 1950; Meguid, Collier, & Howard, 1981; Vigersky, Anderson, Thompson, & Loriaux, 1977).

The most striking physical effect of anorexia nervosa is the loss of weight from levels which are usual for the individual. The most frequently used criterion for diagnosis is that weight loss is 25% or more, but occasionally individuals who have lost lesser amounts are afflicted with the disorder. Any loss over 25% from a normal starting weight places the patient at high risk from the nutritional standpoint; when losses approach 40–50% or body weight reaches 70 pounds, they are usually incompatible with survival unless heroic measures such as tube feeding or total parenteral nutrition can be employed.

Total weight loss is a poor index of the risks of emaciation. Those who are normally obese or plump can withstand greater losses than those whose usual weights are low. Rates of weight loss combined with total loss are better correlated with emaciation, because the composition of weight loss changes as starvation progresses from a mixture which is largely fat with lesser amounts of protein and water to one which consists largely of lean tissue, as body fat reserves are depleted. Very rapid losses are a sign that lean tissue, which is high in protein and water but low in energy, is being lost. A thousand-calorie deficit early on in starvation when body fat is the predominant tissue being lost may cause a weight loss of only about a third of a pound, while a similar deficit after prolonged starvation, when fat reserves have been depleted and only lean tissue is left to catabolize, may lead to a loss of a pound or more. Since rapid weight loss signals the loss of lean tissue or of large amounts of fluid, thus leading to possible electrolyte imbalances, it is a sign of impending danger in patients suffering from anorexia nervosa.

In chronic starvation many physiological changes take place as the body attempts to conserve lean body mass and to use its energy reserves as parsimoniously as possible. These include a variety of endocrine changes which bring about decreases in resting metabolism and obligatory energy outputs to minimize energy expenditure. Other shifts also take place which lead to the preferential utilization of ketone bodies by brain and muscle tissue instead of glucose, thus slowing protein catabolism. However, some obligatory bodily losses of about three grams of nitrogen continue each day. This is the equivalent of 20 grams of body protein or about 100 grams of lean tissue. Therefore, loss of lean tissue is inexorable and inevitable if starvation continues for a long time, and ultimately it alone may prove to be fatal.

These losses of lean tissue have profound pathological effects (Cahill, 1970; Cahill, Aoki, & Rossini, 1979; Halmi & Falk, 1981). When body protein is depleted to 30-50%, respiratory muscle function is often impaired, predisposing the patient to respiratory infections and pneumonia. Extreme emaciation may also give rise to cardiac muscle wasting and cardiac abnormalities (Sours et al., 1981). The endocrine changes of starvation result in diuresis with dramatic downward shifts in fluid balances early in its course. The kidney eventually adjusts to starvation by conserving sodium and potassium but, when profound emaciation ensues, edema may result because it is impossible to synthesize enough of the serum proteins such as albumins to maintain normal fluid balance. Edema may also result upon refeeding, especially with carbohydrates, owing to extensive sodium retention (DeFronzo, 1981; Kolanowski, 1981).

Those who consume large amounts of protein while extremely emaciated often exhibit very high blood urea concentrations since renal excretory capacity in the emaciated state is insufficient to rid the body of all of this protein breakdown product (Fohlin, 1977; Richards & Brown, 1975). Psychological changes include dysphoria, depression, difficulties in concentration, sleep disorders, and preoccupations with thoughts about food and eating also accelerate as starvation progresses (Keys et al., 1950). These in turn may spur the anorexic to even greater efforts to abstain from eating.

Given these physiological realities, it is understandable that the major causes of death in anorexia nervosa include extreme emaciation, suicide, and cardiac events (Hsu, 1980; Schwartz & Thompson, 1981).

Patients who run especially high risks of death are suicidal, very emaciated patients with electrolyte abnormalities or cardiovascular irregularities. Other signs of grave problems are marked hypothermia (less than 95°F), hypotension (especially with postural hypotension, since these patients are more prone to cardiovascular collapse), toxic encephalopathy, abnormal biochemistries such as low serum potassium, hypoglycemia, absence of ketonuria in the face of starvation, or electrocardiographic abnormalities.

Nutritional Consequences of Other Behavioral Abnormalities in Anorexia Nervosa

Self-induced vomiting. The medical consequences of self-induced vomiting are many. The acidic vomit damages the enamel of the teeth and also the gums, leading to severe dental problems. These are the single most common complications of the behavior. Both vomiting and the excessive use of fruit juices or other acid beverages to quench thirst produce an acid environment in the oral cavity (Hellstrom, 1977). The dehydration caused by starvation or the use of laxatives, diuretics, and antidepressant drugs causes decreased salivation and viscid saliva (Schlemier, 1980). The result is a special type of erosion of the teeth called perimylolysis, with the damage being greatest on the inner surface of the teeth where the tongue rubs against the teeth and bathes them in the vomitus which is retained on the tongue between the filiform papillae. The distinctive caries near the gums are due to these same factors.

Regurgitation of acid also leads to irritation of the esophagus, a persistent sore throat, irritated or infected salivary glands (which often result in a chipmunk-like appearance), hiatus hernia, dehydration, and electrolyte imbalance. Eventually the individual may become so habituated to vomiting after eating that it can no longer be controlled, resulting in social problems.

Laxative abuse. Abuse of laxatives can alter electrolyte balance, cause loss of normal intestinal muscle action, and lead to intestinal inflammation, urinary problems and kidney failure (Curry, 1982).

Diuretic abuse. One major reason for concern about use of diuretics, as well as frequent vomiting and laxatives, when they are present in anorexia nervosa is that all of these behaviors increase outputs of potassium (Kutz, Eckert, & Gebott, 1972; Schwartz & Relman, 1953; Wallace, Richards, Chesser, et al., 1968).

Because virtually all (e.g., 98%) of the potassium in the body is intracellular, potassium deficiency draws down these intracellular stores and ratios of intra- to extracellular potassium change with extracellular concentrations usually dropping to a greater extent than intracellular concentrations. It is thought that abnormalities seen among hypokalemic, potassium deficient patients, such as those of cardiac electrical conduction, skeletal muscle weakness, and intestinal ileus, result from changes in these ratios (Johnson & Catinchi, 1978).

Even when it does not result in arrhythmias or cause other serious metabolic problems, diuretic-induced hypokalemia often leads the patient to feel extremely weak; this may add to the lassitude already common in the anorexic patient and make it difficult for the patient to attend to the tasks of daily living.

There is unanimity among experts that severe hypokalemia is a potent health hazard. The dangers of the type of moderate hypokalemia which accompanies the administration of many diuretics are considered to be great by some experts (Maffly, 1976), while others are not so impressed (Kassirer & Harrington, 1977; Ramsay, Boyle, & Ramsay, 1977). However, diuretic abuse which often involves use of very large doses of these medications is likely to be more hazardous, especially if patients are health professionals or have access to the more potent diuretics available only by prescription.

Because of their already weakened state and low potassium intakes, even without the use of diuretics anorexia nervosa patients are already at high risk of potassium deficiency. Conditions such as gastrointestinal disorders like diarrhea or renal problems as well as self-induced vomiting may further deplete potassium to the point that its lack becomes life-threatening (Wallace et al., 1968).

Unfortunately, diuretic-abuse-induced hypokalemia is not predictable in its occurrence. It is likely that the longer-acting diuretics are likely to produce continuing kaliuretic effects and thus to be the most dangerous (Araoye, Change, Khatri et al., 1978), but state of health, level of dietary intake, and other modulating factors may also be involved.

Depending upon the dose and type of diuretic which is abused, the risks of hypokalemia and other adverse reactions vary. Recent references summarize the major side effects which have been noted, and they are described more briefly below (Katz et al., 1972; Orderda & West, 1982).

The thiazide diuretics cause increased secretion of potassium in the distal convoluted tubule of the kidney, resulting in potassium depletion. Therefore, it is with use of thiazide diuretics that hypokalemia, which often leads to hypochloremic alkalosis, is most likely to be seen among anorexic patients.

The mercurial diuretics act by inhibiting active chloride and sodium reabsorption transport in the ascending limb of Henle's loop and at the distal convoluted tubule. They can result in marked increases in chloride excretion which can result in hypochloremic alkalosis. In recent years more potent, so-called loop diuretics have become popular because they can be administered orally. These include ethacrynic acid and furosemide. Both are potent, short-acting diuretics which inhibit tubular reabsorption of sodium chloride in the diluting (ascending) segment of the loop of Henle, with the result that both potassium excretion is enhanced and from 20–30% of the filtered load of sodium chloride is excreted. Misuse or chronic use of these drugs may give rise to hypochloremic hypokalemic alkalosis, as well as contraction of extracellular volume, orthostatic hypotension, and azotemia. Misuse can cause a profound and dangerous diuresis in a patient suffering from anorexia nervosa.

Spironolactone and triamterene are potassium-sparing agents and relatively weak diuretics which can enhance the action of the thiazide and loop diuretics, while counteracting some of their negative kaliuretic effects. They increase urinary losses of sodium and decrease potassium excretion. Their major side effect is hyperkalemia in patients suffering from renal failure.

When an anorexic patient is discovered to be abusing diuretics, great care must be taken in correcting the potassium deficiency and in repleting body stores. If patients are repleted too fast, hyperkalemia, which is also life-threatening, may develop. For this reason no more than 20 mEq of KCl per hour are administered if intravenous routes are used.

Psychological Effects of Starvation

At least two different types of psychological problems must be dealt with in anorexia nervosa. First are the biologically generated difficulties due to the starvation and malnutrition. With realimentation, these problems begin to disappear. These will be discussed below. Second are the psychodynamic problems which are often masked by the starvation-related difficulties but do not go away upon refeeding or with weight gain. These are discussed in other chapters in the context of the psychiatric treatment of the disorder.

Biologically generated psychiatric difficulties are most apparent in classical anorexia nervosa in which the patient constantly restricts her food intake to near starvation levels. In prolonged starvation emotional changes develop directly as a result of emaciation. These include depression, irritability, difficulties in concentration, a preoccupation with food and eating, insomnia, and hyperactivity. Previously cheerful individuals become irritable, quarrelsome, and depressed. They are apathetic and lethargic when they are faced with the tasks of daily life and find that it takes a great amount of willpower to perform even the simplest job. Hyperactivity sometimes includes frantic or ritualized exercise and involves considerable amounts of energy expenditure; in other cases it manifests simply as excessive busyness or inability to concentrate. When physically demanding activities are performed in this debilitated state, enormous efforts of concentration are necessary since the body's natural inclination in starvation is toward a slowing down of all voluntary activity.

Patients with anorexia nervosa remain as intelligent as they ever were, but their thoughts tend to narrow and to be focused on food. In spite of their extreme hunger, when they are served a meal, they often dawdle, are finicky, eat odd combinations, and toy with the food for a long time before they eat it. They often develop rituals around food and are preoccupied by them.

The combination of the psychological difficulties associated with starvation and the underlying problems which led to the disorder in the first place are insupportable for some patients, and this may account for the fact that suicides rank among the major causes of death among anorexia nervosa patients.

Starvation-related psychological changes do not disappear immediately upon refeeding. It often takes several months before they subside, and it is not until weights begin to approach normal levels that all of the weight-loss-induced mental changes subside. However, even then the paranoid-delusional-like state in which the organizing principle is the defense against being fat must be dealt with, and it is not until this is done that the distorted body image of the anorexic returns to normal.

Dieting as a Trigger for Anorexia Nervosa and Bulimia

The question of whether dieting to lose weight is a cause or merely a manifestation of anorexia nervosa frequently arises when the etiology and pathogenesis of these disorders are considered. Present evidence suggests that it is simplistic to regard dieting as necessary and sufficient in itself to cause anorexia. However, the mind sets, attitudes, and behaviors associated with dieting may predispose individuals to develop these disorders. It is difficult to recognize when this common preoccupation of adolescents and young adults becomes an all-encompassing obsession, since so many in this age group exhibit similar behaviors on a periodic basis.

Current ideals of feminine beauty held by both males and females favor the attainment and maintenance of leanness (Dwyer, Feldman, Seltzer, & Mayer, 1969; Nylander, 1971). Studies of the dimensions of *Playboy* centerfold photographs, the dimensions of winners of the Miss America pageant, as well as references to reducing diets in magazines, show that the lean body type is increasingly favored (see Schwartz, Thompson, & Johnson, this volume).

There is abundant evidence that dieting to lose weight is increasingly common at all ages but particularly among adolescent females in American society (Dwyer, 1980a; Dwyer, Feldman, & Mayer, 1970). Unusual diets which often combine weight reduction, vegetarianism, or other eating practices are also prevalent (Dwyer, 1980a, 1982). Many individuals who do not regard themselves as dieting nevertheless engage in restrained eating, and their food intake is under conscious control (Dwyer & Mayer, 1970).

At the same time, food is inexpensive, abundant, heavily advertised and marketed, widely available, and the centerpiece of much American social life; and labor-saving devices favor sedentary living. In spite of the lip service paid to physical activity and the growing popularity of certain activities such as jogging, recent surveys reveal that adolescent females as a group are so sedentary that, in order to maintain energy balance, their calorie intakes must be several hundred calories below the current Recommended Dietary Allowances (Dwyer, 1980b).

Recent studies have also implicated weight reduction efforts with various eating disorders. Restrictive reducing diets often precede the onset of binges in bulimic individuals (Johnson, 1982). Members of occupational groups in which leanness is particularly advantageous, such as ballet dancers and models, often exhibit many of the symptoms of anorexia nervosa (Crisp, 1970).

Vomiting is a means of controlling weight without the necessity of constantly submitting to the constraints of restrained eating habits. Laxative abuse also achieves rapid, albeit temporary, drops in weight. Both are now known to be more common than was previously thought among nondieting adolescents and young adults (Johnson, 1982). The use of medications for health and emotional problems is of course also extremely common in the larger society, and abuse of both over-the-counter and prescription drugs is hardly unique to those whose aim is weight reduction.

In recent years the mass media and social pressures have emphasized the desirability of vigorous, competitive, individual sports such as jogging and swimming for females as well as males. These are often practiced so religiously that they go beyond enjoyment to the very limits of endurance, and an increasing number of studies have found anorexia-nervosa-like symptoms among those who do so (Feicht et al., 1978; Garner & Garfinkel, 1978; Smith, 1980).

Thus, the larger environment, social pressures, cultural ideals, ingestion-related practices and attitudes, levels of physical activity, and attitudes toward medication favor thinness regardless of how it is achieved. Dieting, bulimia, and other eating disorders are prevalent enough so that those who engage in them do not stand out as strikingly different or unusual, nor do they suffer from social stigma.

However, the epidemiology of the syndromes also reveals that, in addition to behavioral manifestations characteristic of eating disorders, other factors set individuals suffering from classical anorexia and bulimic anorexia nervosa apart from their peers who abuse diets, laxatives, or indulge in self-induced vomiting (Johnson, 1982). Therefore, while it makes sense for the health professional to delve further for other signs and symptoms when a patient's history suggests an extreme distortion of body image, ever downward shifting targets of weight, or an unusual dedication to dieting, there is little reason to suspect this diagnosis without additional corroborating evidence if dieting alone is present and weight is within normal limits.

NUTRITIONAL ASSESSMENT

The purpose of nutritional assessment is to discover what the patient's present intake-related characteristics are, to make eating-related observations which may be helpful in psychotherapy, to reassure the patient that her proposed intake will not be allowed to get out of control and that it will be nutritious, and to develop an appropriate plan for dietary treatment which must include control over eating as well as weight gain.

Although anorexic or bulimic patients usually pay lip service to the notion that they should eat more, they are unable to do so without guidance and they are usually unaware of the part undernutrition plays in their diseases. A laissez-faire attitude on the part of the therapist, which involves letting patients proceed in eating at their own pace, will result in constant evasions, and a stable or declining weight, as well as inhibiting psychotherapy. It is most effective for the psychotherapist and primary physician to collaborate with a physician specially skilled in clinical nutrition or a registered dietitian in order to make the nutritional assessment and implement the nutritional care plan. Previous nutritional experience in handling these patients is critical. They are extraordinarily resistant to treatment and may attempt to play one therapist off against another. The nutritionist's involvement is especially critical in the early phases of treatment when starvation-related signs and symptoms are so pronounced that they themselves constitute a medical problem and contribute to psychopathology.

Determining Food Intake: Diet History

The purpose of the dietary assessment is to discover previous and present practices which have led to the weight loss and malnutrition. Patient reports of current intakes are notoriously unreliable. Even so they furnish enough baseline data to demonstrate why undernutrition is present and to suggest how intakes may be gradually changed to improve the situation. The process of revelation also makes the patient document behaviors which previously have been denied. This is a necessary although not sufficient step toward dietary change.

Table 2 summarizes some helpful questions for gaining more information on the history of weight and dieting. It is helpful to get a picture of not only current patterns of eating (which may show extreme variation in day-to-day intake), but also the kinds of weight reduction techniques which the patient used in the past, and any previous trouble with weight and eating.

The best way to ascertain food intake is by direct observation or by monitoring of intakes and outputs. However, this is rarely possible except on an inpatient basis. For outpatients, 24-hour recalls or dietary histories will provide some indications of intakes of energy and other nutrients. It is especially important to probe about foods eaten as opposed to foods served, about portion sizes (which are often miniscule), and about behaviors such as self-induced vomiting or laxative abuse which may affect absorption. Information on meal or snack frequency, food likes and dislikes, may also be helpful in later planning a diet for the patient.

Table 2
Weight/Height Questions for Patients to Distinguish Between Usual and Unusual Preoccupations with Dieting and Weight Loss

---

How much do you want to weigh now?
Why do you want to weigh this much?
What is the highest weight you have ever weighed?
How did you lose to your present weight from that weight?
How do you plan to lose weight to get to your target weight?
Can you tell me how much time a day you spend thinking about food, losing weight, dieting, how you look and so forth?
How do you feel about being fat? Do you think you are fat now?
Do other people say things about your being fat? Who are they? Have they said such things in the past? Who were these people?
Do you have a regular menstrual period each month? If no, when did your period stop?
What would you say your major eating problems are?
Tell me the kinds of ways that your eating problems influenced your
- life
- work
- day to day life outside of work
- the way you feel about yourself
- personal relations

Which of your eating problems bothers you the most?

Once a picture of current regular intake has been obtained, the energy and protein intake levels should be calculated using a table of food composition (Pennington & Church, 1980) or a microcomputer program (Dwyer & Suitor, 1984). It may also be helpful to calculate intakes for micronutrients which appear from observing the diet to be low. This information is shared with the patient and a specific, modest dietary change to add a small amount of calories per day (e.g., 100–200 calories) is suggested. The patient is then informed that additional dietary assessment will be necessary: she will then be required to weigh and measure all foods eaten and to note any other behaviors (exercise, binging, vomiting, laxative use, etc.) which may affect food intake. Food records are provided which are to be filled in immediately after the food is ingested at each meal on each day. They are to be mailed in prior to the next dietary interview for further analysis. If "perfect" records are provided which are filled in with exactly the same pen or pencil, it is likely that directions have not been followed. Either the records have been filled in long after the meals have been eaten or they have been fabricated altogether. In any event calculations of energy, protein, and micronutrients should be made. If they are widely different from previous intakes, this should be noted and the patient informed. Records that the patient brings in can be further cross-checked by asking for an oral recollection of intake after the records have been given to the nutritionist. This is especially useful when it is suspected that the patient is not keeping food records as directed.

Other Eating-Related Disorders and Practices in Anorexia Nervosa

Because some patients, especially those who are bulimic, have very irregular eating habits and often engage in self-induced vomiting, laxative, and diuretic use, it is important to obtain additional information on these behaviors. The questions in Table 3 related to binge eating and those in Table 4 on vomiting, laxatives, and diuretics are helpful in these regards.

Weight

Accurate weights taken under standard conditions (e.g., light clothing with nothing in the pockets, shoes off) on a beam balance are preferable, since changes in weight are critical in detecting improvement or decline. Weights provided by patients should not be used. Patients should be weighed at every visit to the office.

Table 3
Questions on Binge Eating for Patients

Do you binge?
Do you feel this is a problem?
Why?
How often do you binge?
What happens (usually) during the binge?
  Do you eat very fast?
  What kinds of foods do you eat?
  Do you eat very large amounts of food?
  Do you vomit and then go back and eat more?
  How long does it last?
When did you first start binging?
How do you feel before a binge?
  Is there anything particular which triggers the binge?
How do you feel during the binge?
What do you do after the binge?
Are there any steps you try to take to avoid binging or to limit the binge once it starts?

Table 4
Useful Questions for Patients on Laxatives and Vomiting

Laxatives:
  How often do you normally have a bowel movement? How would you describe your movements?
  How often did you usually have bowel movements before you started using laxatives?
  Is constipation a problem for you?
  Do you use laxatives? How often, what kind, how much? Where do you get them?
  When did you first start using laxatives?
  Why do you think you need a laxative?
  Are there any other reasons why you use laxatives?
  How do you feel after taking laxatives?
  Have you noticed any effects you did not want from using the laxatives?
  Are there any special times or events when you use laxatives?
  Have you ever tried to stop using laxatives? If so, what happened when you did?
Diuretics: Questions are similar to those related to laxatives except for the first three items.
Vomiting
  Is vomiting a problem for you?
  Do you ever use any drugs such as ipecac to help you vomit?
  Do you gag yourself or tickle your throat to vomit?
  How do you feel before you vomit? After you vomit?
  What feelings or events cause you to vomit?
  When did you first make yourself vomit?
  How often do you vomit?
  Why do you vomit?
  Do you vomit after meals or binges or only after eating certain kinds of foods?
  When was the last time you made yourself vomit?
  How do you feel after you vomit?
  Are there any methods you have discovered to keep yourself from wanting to vomit or from vomiting even if you feel like doing so?

Laboratory and Clinical Information

Biochemical tests and clinical observations provide additional data which will help to determine areas representing special problems for patients. For example, low serum potassiums may confirm that low food intakes, self-induced vomiting, and diuretic abuse may be reaching dangerous levels. Abnormal electrocardiograms may indicate electrolyte imbalances or wasting of the cardiac muscle. For this reason it is essential to review all data and for all providers of care in a particular case to confer to make sure that all of the problems found will be addressed in the treatment plan.

Setting Weight Targets

While it is helpful to get the patient's view on weight range targets, more objective assessments are needed as well. Rough guides to appropriate weight ranges can be obtained from tables of desirable weight for height issued by insurance companies. These ranges, adjusted in accordance with the physician's judgment and past weight histories, represent a target to aim for over the long term. Usually 90% of ideal weight for height and sex is reasonable. Psychological, physical, and hormonal recovery are rarely complete until the patient achieves at least 85% of ideal weight, and in many instances psychological recovery requires even greater gains.

It is also important to assess realistic expectations for weight gain and the best means to achieve them. If weight is dropping rapidly, biochemical values indicate problems, weight has already dropped to close to 40% or 50% of desirable levels, or another illness is also present which complicates treatment, the physician may have little recourse except special tube feeding techniques or intravenous hyperalimentation (Dwyer & O'Donnell, 1982). These techniques require an experienced nutritional support team to carry them out. Weight gain expectations in such cases will need to be individually established. Because special enteral and parenteral routes of feeding are totally under the control of the therapist and the issue of control of food intake is central in anorexia nervosa and related disorders, use of these therapies may complicate later psychotherapy. For these reasons they are avoided, except in life-threatening situations.

For patients who are otherwise healthy and able to eat by mouth at the outset of treatment, the first objective should be to stop weight loss. Once weight has been stabilized, goals of a quarter or a half-pound per week are reasonable. Target weight ranges take months or years to achieve.

Once the problems that the patient is experiencing have been defined, it is important to explain how these have come about and how they are related to nutrition. This sets the stage for the treatment or intervention phase of the program.

NUTRITIONAL TREATMENTS

The goals of diet therapy are to assist the patient in reestablishing normal dietary patterns and food-related behaviors, to help stop weight loss, to gain an appropriate weight which, once it has been reached, can be controlled, to avoid the metabolic consequences of the anorexia nervosa or bulimia, and to keep the patient in psychotherapy so that the underlying disorder can be addressed. If another disease such as diabetes mellitus is also present, appropriate dietary and other adjustments must also be made.

In order to achieve these objectives a nutritional care plan must be formulated. The components of such a plan are described in this section.

Special Routes of Alimentation

Medical necessity is primary in determining whether, at the outset of treatment, enteral or parenteral means of alimentation should be employed. All of the considerations which enter into making this judgment are beyond the scope of this review, but have been well discussed in several recent articles (Blackburn & Harvey, 1982; Dwyer & O'Donnell, 1982; Pertschuk, Crosby, & Mullen, 1983). Regardless of the route chosen, careful nutritional assessment and the formulation of a nutritional rehabilitation plan are important aspects of treatment. Improvements in nutritional treatment have been partially responsible for the lower mortality rates from the disorder today (Schwabe, Lippe, Chang, Pops, & Yager, 1981). Particular attention must be devoted to the nutritional care plan of the very emaciated patient (McBurney & Wilmore, 1981).

The route of administration should be as simple as possible given the nutritional status of this kind of patient. Total parenteral nutrition by central vein is an expensive procedure which carries its own considerable risks and therefore it is reserved only for very ill or very emaciated (e.g., 40-50% of normal weight) patients. Constant nursing care and careful monitoring by a nutritional support team are mandatory since problems of manipulation, pulling out the catheters, and turning down the flows on the solutions being dripped into the veins are more frequent among anorexics than among patients on parenteral nutrition for other disorders. In spite of these problems, total parenteral nutrition either by central or peripheral vein can be life-saving for the extremely debilitated patient, and it represents an advance in therapy unavailable until the past decade.

Common indications for feedings by fine bore nasogastric tube include considerable emaciation (e.g., 25% of normal weight), resistance to the nutritional care plan (such as manipulation of weight by water loading, weights hidden in the pockets, refusal to eat, refusal to maintain serum potassium levels within normal limits, hiding of food and weight loss), presence of another disease or condition which requires a special route of feeding, or any other situation which the physician feels imperils life. Patients must be carefully monitored since some will resist by attempting to pull out the tube or to stop flow from the tube into the gut. As the patient begins to stabilize her weight and then to gain, mixed oral/nasogastric feedings can be instituted so that the patient can gradually be weaned away from the tube.

Consultation with a physician who is expert in nutritional support is advisable whenever special enteral or parenteral routes are being considered, and can also be helpful when oral alimentation is being considered. These individuals specialize in nutritional rehabilitation, which is the anorexic's most immediate problem. The available options with respect to alimentation strategies are changing so rapidly that expert advice is well worth the time.

Fortunately, many patients exhibit lesser degrees of emaciation which do not require special routes of alimentation. The remainder of this section will focus on oral routes of alimentation, since these are the most common, with emphasis on treatment in outpatient settings. Recent follow-up studies show that outcomes are positive in both classical anorexia nervosa and bulimarexic patients with early intervention and long-term continuity of ambulatory management (Morgan, Purgold, & Welbourne, 1983).

Individualization

Anorexia nervosa is a heterogeneous disorder. It follows that no single dietary treatment will work for all such patients. The diet plan must be individualized to address the specific problem areas, likes and dislikes, and patterns of each patient so as to minimize potential barriers to adherence. The process of achieving trust and the patient's commitment to adhere to the diet plan is always time-consuming, often taking between one and two hours per session. It is also extremely challenging and often frustrating to the provider, since progress is usually very slow. Even careful explanations of the medical consequences of the disorder and the need for change rarely produce desired behaviors. In part, this is because the anorexic does not feel sick and therefore does not feel in need of help or that therapy has something to offer.

In order to develop rapport with the patient, it is important to cast the dietary counseling sessions as collaborative inquiries into how food is being used as a way of coping with internal or external events, not as psychiatric interviews. A great deal of patience and the ability to accept the patient's beliefs as genuine for her even if they are counterproductive are critical characteristics for nutritionists involved in anorexia nervosa treatment.

Motivation

Poor motivation is often present. It may help to begin with a description of starvation-related symptoms such as difficulties in concentration, sleep, fatigue, and preoccupation with thoughts about food and eating which may be bothering the patient and which can partially be relieved by action on the nutritional front. Motivation is further increased by a frank discussion of both the advantages and disadvantages of change, but several sessions may be necessary before the patient agrees to try to gain weight or focus on a reasonable target weight range (Garfinkel & Garner, 1982; Garner & Bemis, 1982).

The nutritionist must also be highly motivated, since nutritional recovery from anorexia nervosa often requires months. In one study of hospitalized patients, even after two months of successful refeeding total body nitrogen had still not reached normal levels (Russell, Prendergast, Darby, Garfinkel, Whitwell, & Jeejeebhov, 1983). Chronic low weight and scanty menstruation also persist for many months, especially among those with longstanding, preexisting illness, previous personality difficulties, or disturbed and hostile relationships with relatives (Hsu, 1980; Morgan, Purgold, & Welbourne, 1983; Slade, 1982).

How Anorexics Avoid Eating

Since the core of the nutritional treatment plan is to increase voluntary food intake, the therapist must be aware of how anorexics avoid eating. They resist persuasion, reassurances, admonitions, and even outright threats to eat. They avoid situations in which they have to eat; they dawdle at the dining table; and they claim that they are not hungry or that the food is unappealing. Their reported food intakes are sometimes grossly overestimated and may be completely without a connection to reality. In other instances, foods which were served to them rather than foods actually eaten are reported. Therefore, dietary histories and even food records, particularly those obtained from patients who have not been carefully instructed on how to keep them in advance, cannot be relied upon.

If patients are fed under supervision, more accurate estimates of intake can be obtained; but even under such circumstances patients have been known to palm food off their trays for later disposal or to procrastinate with the assurance they will eat later but then throw the food away. After they have eaten, they may induce vomiting. Others attempt to compensate for increased energy intakes by increasing their energy outputs by exercises, pacing, walking, and the like. Patients who are being fed by tube or intravenously may try to pull out these sources of alimentation. Early in treatment patients may insist on using the lowest of all possible caloric values in food tables when they are involved in planning their diets, and refuse to eat even one calorie over the agreed upon amount. When their records fall short of the treatment plan, they may claim that their stomach was upset or that they were suffering from a virus and thus were unable to eat.

Patients often attempt to bargain with care providers for improvements in laboratory values rather than weight. They will sometimes drink large amounts of fluid, avoid defecation and urination, wear several layers of clothing and carry heavy objects in their pockets prior to being weighed in the hope that, if they can demonstrate weight gain, they will not be prescribed additional calories in their diets. If this fails, they may drop out of treatment if they are in an outpatient treatment facility or sign themselves out if they are in the hospital.

Because patients dislike direct confrontations about eating, the fortress of defenses against weight gain may not be immediately apparent to the therapist during nutritional counseling. The patient gives outward assurances of understanding the problem and how to correct it; therefore, the therapist often assumes that adherence to the prescribed diet will be forthcoming. The extraordinary resistance becomes evident, however, if, instead of planning and discussing with the patient in the counseling session what she will eat, the nutritionist offers a series of foods the patient has previously claimed to be acceptable and asks her to eat a small morsel. Often such a task will engender outright refusal and, if the therapist persists in insisting that at least a taste be taken, the patient may become hostile or dissolve into tears.

Establishing Energy Needs

The diet history and food pattern data will provide some indication of the level of energy intake. It must be corrected in the case of bulimic anorexics, for energy which was vomited and thus never absorbed. Activity records may reveal that energy outputs are also considerable. Total weight lost, the rate at which weight is being lost, and biochemical values all provide some reality checks of energy intake estimates and also other deficits which need to be remedied. Even if diets are sufficient in protein, when energy intakes do not cover bodily needs the protein will be catabolized and, therefore, some degree of protein calorie malnutrition rather than simply marasmus is likely to be present.

An estimate of energy needs is also needed. Basal energy needs can be estimated using tables which are widely available (Wilmore, 1977). Additional and variable amounts of energy will be needed for physical activity; these, too, can be approximated using standard references. Over and above these needs are the extra rations of energy and protein necessary to rebuild lean body mass and fat stores and to restore a normal body composition. Since the very thought of weight gain engenders extreme fear in most anorexic patients, it is best to begin with a goal of stopping weight loss. For most patients this can be achieved with a daily intake of about 1200 calories. If energy intakes are set higher at first, patients may be so frightened that they will drop out of therapy. It is also important early in treatment to restrict the level of physical activity if the patient is known to be doing a good deal of pacing back and forth, walking, jogging, or other exercises, since these activities increase energy expenditures considerably. If the patient is hospitalized, nurse-supervised eating can be helpful in assuring that food is actually eaten, but surveillance must be close. For the bulimic anorexic, it is usually not possible to stop binging, self-induced vomiting, and laxative abuse completely, but it may be possible to decrease its frequency.

Meal Plans

In addition to assuring that energy intakes are sufficient to stop weight loss and initiate weight gain, there are other nutritional considerations. The diet should provide liberal amounts of protein, vitamins, and minerals to meet normal needs and to permit restoration of lean body mass. Recommendations on protein levels vary: 1.5-2 grams per kilogram should be more than adequate for these purposes. A vitamin mineral supplement which approximates the Recommended Dietary Allowances may be helpful in assuring that micronutrient needs are met; very large megadose amounts (some five to 10 times the Recommended Allowances) are not necessary and may be harmful.

Many anorexics avoid choosing foods they prefer or enjoy because they fear they will lack the control to stop eating if they do so. Others choose foods they can eat quickly so that they can get eating over with. These points must be kept in mind in helping them plan their diets. If assurances about control are provided and demonstrated by the use of very specific menu plans, weighing and measuring foods, and calculating energy intakes, they can be gradually coaxed into choosing more palatable diets.

Another difficulty many anorexics have is that they feel full after eating only small amounts of food. Because fullness sometimes triggers self-induced vomiting in bulimic anorexics, it is especially important to space feedings with this population, and to include small snacks throughout the day and evening rather than focusing only on three meals per day. The use of foods high in caloric density and low in bulk or liquids with these same properties can also be helpful in these respects.

More rapid progress can often be made by the judicious use of nutritional supplements which are particularly high in nutrient density but low in volume, in addition to usual foods.

Variety needs emphasis in meal planning. Most anorexics eat very monotonous diets because they fear the calorie contents of new foods. Extending food variety gradually, with instruction about energy contributions from each new food, is therefore important.

Various food guides such as the Basic Four or the American Dietetic Association (1981) Food Exchange Lists are helpful in planning menus. However, exchanges are somewhat imprecise in the exact caloric contents of one food as opposed to another within each category. These differences in calories are trivial from the standpoint of diet planning for normal individuals but are disturbing to the anorexic who is obsessed with the avoidance of weight gain, fatness, and calories. Most patients feel more secure if actual menus specifying precisely what food shall be eaten in exactly what amount are provided to them for each day.

Patient Involvement in Monitoring Food Intake

Patients' fears can be further allayed by giving them a weighing scale, household measurement utensils, and a standard table of food composition which they can check to assure themselves that energy intakes are in fact exactly what was specified in the diet plan (Pennington & Church, 1980). In addition to easing their anxieties, these steps will help them to realize what a standard portion of food is. Many anorexics have become accustomed to eating bird-like portions; if left to their own devices on an outpatient basis, they will contend that they are following the menu plan if they are eating these tiny portions.

Another advantage of a food table is that it provides rather precise estimates of the calories and other nutrients in many foods. Thus, the fear of eating foods which are new to the patient and which have previously been avoided (in part because of the unknown number of calories they contain) can be lessened. Anorexics are interested in the nutrient composition of foods, so providing them with a standard food table staves off arguments about the exact energy contribution of various foods. Most anorexics have their own calorie-counting books or tables, which are usually abbreviated popular versions of standard food tables, and the energy values provided in them may differ from those in more authoritative sources. When both the therapist and the patient use the same standard of reference for calories, disagreements are avoided. Food composition tables permit outpatients to eat out without undue fear since they can analyze menus in restaurants and elsewhere away from home.

The final reason for having the patient participate in weighing, measuring, recording, and calculating her energy intakes is that involvement in diet planning may in itself be therapeutic in encouraging greater adherence to diet and involving the patient in monitoring improvement. Ultimately, the patient must learn to control her food intake, with health considerations predominating. These self-monitoring procedures described above help her to practice doing this. Self-monitoring and recording of eating patterns, bulimic episodes and energy outputs, abuse of laxatives, self-induced vomiting, and diuretic intake are also important in bulimarexic patients who have special problems in one or more of these areas.

Monitoring Weight

Patient monitoring of intake is not an end of nutritional rehabilitation in itself but rather a means to achieve it. Changes in weight and laboratory values provide more direct evidence that progress is being made. While improvements in eating patterns such as inclusion of more variety, decreased bulimic and vomiting episodes, less use of laxatives and diuretics, and changes for the better in laboratory values should be acknowledged by the therapist, they are not a substitute for or alternative to weight gain. Both the therapist and the patient need to keep the goal of small increments in weight as the target, and the greatest amount of praise should be reserved for improvements in this area.

It is often helpful to reassure the patient, especially at first, that what is being strived for in the therapeutic diet is rehabilitation of the depleted lean body mass. This is reflected by changes in both laboratory values and in pounds, which should be pointed out by the therapist in order to reassure the patient that all the weight being gained is not simply fat. It is also important to emphasize that, especially if the patient is very dehydrated and emaciated at the outset of treatment, some weight gain may ensue simply as a result of rehydration rather than because of other changes in body composition. While an understanding of the biology of nutritional rehabilitation and changes in body composition which occur during refeeding is not enough in and of itself to overcome the formidable defenses the anorexic patient has against weight gain, it may serve to allay fears to some extent.

Weight gain is a key indicator of progress, so it is important that the patient be weighed on an accurate scale, preferably the same scale on each visit. Scales in health care facilities vary considerably in their accuracy, and if different scales are used for each weighing, the small increments in weight gain which are to be expected each week are often obscured by variability due to the measuring apparatus. Occasionally early on in rehabilitation, owing to expansion of the extracellular fluid, electrolyte retention, or repletion of glycogen stores, the dehydrated patient will experience gains of several pounds over the course of the week. The patient must be reassured that this is "false," (e.g., fluid weight gain), that gains in the future will be only a small fraction of this initial gain, and that this is a one-time occurrence owing to changes in water balance.

Progression in Energy Intakes and Weight Gain

A reasonable expectation for weight gain is between .25 and .50 pounds per week. The increments in energy intake which are necessary to achieve this vary because the energy composition of weight gain differs as the tissue of gain changes. However, at first, increases of 100-200 calories per day (which provide from 700-1400 calories extra over the week) will be adequate to permit gains of this magnitude, since lean body mass is being restored and in some instances the patient is being rehydrated. Increments of 100-200 calories when usual intakes are 800-1200 calories or even less to begin with are small quantitatively speaking, but very large as a proportion of the intakes the patient is accustomed to. Similar increments later in therapy are proportionately smaller. From the psychological standpoint these differences are extremely important. The nutritionist or physician must be careful not to attempt to increase energy intakes very rapidly at first, or patient resistance and nonadherence will ensue.

Bulimic anorexics also need reassurances that even if they can reduce the frequency of self-induced vomiting only slightly this is progress. They also need instructions that after they do binge they should immediately return to their usual meal plan and eat the next scheduled meal. This procedure is more likely to break the pathological chain of binging, vomiting, and fasting than is an attempt to make up the binge by vomiting or by missing several meals thereafter.

Any positive change should be noticed and remarked upon by all the professionals involved in a patient's treatment. Relapses or lack of progress must not trigger recriminations, but rather be attacked as a puzzling problem which patient and nutritionist must tackle jointly together.

It cannot be emphasized enough that the usual course of rehabilitation among anorexics is very slow — clear-cut indicators of progress often take months rather than weeks, and weight plateaus are common. Also, attitudes to and relationships with the therapist often fluctuate greatly over the course of treatment. It often seems that rapport between the patient and the therapist worsens as the patient begins to get better. At first, the debilitated patient is often overcompliant — that is, she is perfectly willing to accept the physician's or nutritionist's interpretations of what is wrong with her diets or food intake but without changing anything. As nutritional rehabilitation and psychotherapy progress, the outward cooperation and compliance of the patient with the nutritionist's instructions often give way to criticism, negativism, and later to open hostility on the patient's part. The therapist needs to understand that this is a sign of progress, not failure in the patient's path toward wellness. When the patient passes from the phase of polite, feigned agreement to rebellion and an overt expression of her opinion that she is different and that the remedies will not work for her, this is a good, not a bad sign. The therapist can then enlist the patient's help in planning strategies together which both parties can agree *will* work for her.

Dealing with Nonadherence

Once the possibility of some undiagnosed illness has been ruled out, lack of progress in terms of weight gain must be dealt with in a straightforward and matter-of-fact manner. A direct question, "What are you doing to prevent weight gain?" will sometimes provide the answer, particularly if it involves exercise. In other cases, such as self-induced vomiting, patients will not be forthright in revealing their methods or they may in fact not be conscious of how they are doing it. If the patient is hospitalized, the failure to gain weight is treated differently depending upon the therapist's particular theoretical orientation, as well as the patient's state of inanition and emaciation. In some settings, restoration of privileges to use commons rooms, to watch television, or the like are made contingent on weight gain. In others, behavior modification techniques are not employed but the patient is placed on a supervised eating schedule.

Manipulative behavior on the patient's part associated with dietary noncompliance often takes the form of attempts to turn various members of the treatment team against each other. It is extremely important for the psychotherapist to be informed of suspected nonadherence to the dietary regimen and for the psychotherapist to confront the patient about it—it is not a matter the dietitian alone can deal with.

The therapist must remember in dealing with manipulative behavior on the part of the patient that it is a sign not of willful malevolence on the part of the patient but rather of the patient's desperation and frustration. If it is seriously destructive, the patient must be put under surveillance.

If the patient is very emaciated, lack of progress or losses in weight may be the signal for hospitalization if treatment is on an outpatient basis, or for a special route of feeding if the patient is already hospitalized.

Special Considerations in Bulimic Anorexia Nervosa

Bulimic anorexia nervosa patients are especially resistant to treatment and they often take longer to motivate. Their binging makes them especially fearful that they will be unable to stop eating voluntarily once they start, and thus they require special reassurances and more specific assistance to become convinced that their weight will not be allowed to get out of control or to exceed agreed upon targets if they follow prescribed routines.

Fairburn (1984) employs a three-stage treatment for bulimic anorexia nervosa patients. The first stage involves several visits per week and lasts at least six weeks and often longer. Its objective is to disrupt the starving and gorging syndrome. Patients complete food records daily to monitor their intakes, intakes they regard as excessive, vomiting, laxative use, and weights. They are provided with a meal plan to follow regardless of their hunger to overcome the starving/gorging cycle and are given behavior modification hints to help them adhere to the plan. They are also asked to develop lists of pleasurable activities which do not involve eating to pursue when they feel their sense of control is poor.

Patients are informed about the sequelae of bulimia, diuretics, self-induced vomiting, and laxatives, as well as of starvation, depending on which of these behaviors is involved; and a gradual phase-out is recommended. Structuring of time and eating activities to allow little free time often helps in controlling laxative abuse after binging.

Gradual weight gain by whatever means possible is emphasized as a nonnegotiable target behavior. Occasional joint interviews with those who live and eat with the patient in order to discuss the problem and its treatment and their role are scheduled.

It is extraordinarily difficult for patients who have fallen into a pattern of self-induced vomiting to give it up altogether, but if they can decrease its frequency considerably, binging can often be brought under control. The laxative abuser requires psychological and medical help, as well as nutritional advice (Oster, Materson, & Rogers, 1980). The goal is to gradually decrease and to finally eliminate the frequency of laxative use. Laxative-abusing patients need to understand that such abuse is a poor way to lose weight, that it can in itself lead to difficulties with gastric motility, constipation, and a variety of fluid and electrolyte problems including hypokalemia, hypocalcemia, and hypermagnesemia. In some bulimic anorexics large amounts of laxatives are used to "purge" the system following a binge. The goal is a gradual phase-out of both binging and the laxative abuse which follows it. Decreasing the laxative abuse can help to decrease binging.

During stage two of treating the bulimic anorexia nervosa patient, the goal is to continue to lessen the frequency of bulimic episodes while continuing gradual (e.g., 1kg/week) weight gain. Weekly appointments for several months may be necessary (Fairburn, 1984). Diet therapy can be handled by a nutritionist, but psychotherapy should be left to those with special expertise in this area. The meal plans prescribed in stage one are modified as appropriate to assure calorie levels are sufficient for weight gain. If dietary restraint or not eating for long periods during the day (particularly if a binge has occurred recently) is present, special attention is devoted to adhering to the prescribed meal and snack pattern. Also, many anorexics avoid "fattening" foods except during binges, when they feel out of control. In order to break down the connection between these foods and lack of control, patients are asked to prepare lists of enjoyable foods which are avoided and small amounts of these foods are incorporated into the meal plan schedules. They also continue to write down problem episodes in eating as in other aspects of life. Training in problem-solving and cognitive restructuring of abnormal attitudes toward body shape, weight, food, and eating are also included. These are best dealt with by the psychotherapist, while the nutritionist concentrates on monitoring adherence to behavioral instructions involving food, diet, and weight gain. The nutritionist can also encourage the patient to accept that she is an inaccurate judge of her body weight and shape, and to continue to follow the regimen in spite of her perceptions.

In the final stage of Fairburn's (1984) treatment for the bulimic type of anorexia nervosa, visits are scheduled at biweekly intervals with the psychotherapist. The goal is to assure that weight gain continues and that the direction of change is maintained in spite of occasional episodes of poor control. When the patient feels ready, a typed maintenance plan is provided and arrangements for extended followup are made.

Previously Treated Patients

Individuals who have been treated and failed to respond in the past are especially difficult to deal with (Holmgren, Sohlberg, Berg, Johansson, Norring, & Rosmark, 1984). Usually they are older and live apart from their parents; their lives are so completely devoted to accommodating the ritual demands of continuing emaciation and bulimia that their behaviors are well hidden from public view. They are often skeptical that any treatment can help them.

It is unlikely that such severely chronic patients will yield to outpatient therapies because their life-styles and environments are so well adapted to the syndrome. Hospitalization in a special unit is appropriate. Holmgren et al. (1984) have recently described excellent results using environmental manipulation, behavior therapy, and nutritional rehabilitation in such an inpatient setting. The strategy is to demonstrate that an eating control system which is less cumbersome and more effective than the patient has devised exists and will work for her. Once trust has been gained, the patient is gradually trained to control her own food intake.

Constipation and Other Gastrointestinal Complaints

The recovering anorexic often complains of constipation, gas, and stomach pains. Bulimic anorexics who have used large amounts of laxatives after binges may also experience constipation as the frequency of laxative abuse declines. All of these patients need to be told that, as food intakes increase, food choices improve, laxatives are abandoned, and bowel control is relearned, the constipation will disappear spontaneously (Orderda & West, 1977). An alternative treatment for constipation should also be discussed.

The first measure to stress from the dietary standpoint is that increases in food intake will be helpful in and of themselves. Then, patients also need to recognize that foods high in dietary fiber (which incidentally are not particularly high in calories) are particularly helpful. High fiber foods include whole grain breads and cereals, raw vegetables, legumes, and fruits with the skins. As the fiber content of the diet increases, stool bulk and softness will increase since the fiber itself holds water and stimulates the growth of the gut flora, which also pass out into the feces. Foods high in fiber are preferable to dietary fiber supplements such as bran because it is virtually impossible for patients to consume enough naturally occurring fiber to cause intestinal obstruction. If the patient takes very large doses of wheat bran or other fiber supplements without sufficient fluids, it is possible for such difficulties to arise.

The third keystone of dietary treatment of constipation is for the patient to take plenty of fluids each day (e.g., four to six eight-ounce glasses of water per day), in addition to fluids taken with meals.

Patients who have been addicted to laxatives need retraining to respond to the urge to defecate rather than to ignore it. Setting a regular pattern for elimination and taking time to relax aids in getting habits readjusted. Exercise, especially that using the abdominal muscles, can improve muscle tone, which aids in propulsion of the feces and as part of a regular exercise program physical activity itself may help to reduce emotional stress-related effects on defecation.

Finally, the patient needs to realize that continued laxative use will sustain rather than inhibit constipation. This is particularly true when the stimulant laxatives such as the anthraquinones (e.g., castor oil or Bisacodyl) are used; they empty the entire colon and thus discourage the return of normal function because there is nothing to evacuate the next day.

CONCLUSION

The connections between anorexia nervosa and nutrition are several. Abnormal food-related behaviors are nutritional signs of the disease. From the medical standpoint, the losses of fat and weight and many other physiological changes are accounted for primarily by undernutrition; physical rehabilitation is dependent upon appropriate nutritional therapy and reeducation of appetite. Other physiological effects sometimes seen in bulimic anorexia, such as those stemming from excessive use of laxatives, diuretics, or self-induced vomiting, also result from disruption of normal function of the gastrointestinal tract and are correctable when the patient is retrained to facilitate normal alimentation and elimination without hindrance.

The psychiatric symptoms of the disorder are also largely food, eating, and body-image-related, and concern fears that loss of control in eating will lead to fatness or powerlessness in other parts of life. As the starvation of anorexia nervosa progresses, emotional changes directly related to starvation itself dominate the other psychiatric problems. Psychiatric treatment is ineffective in dealing with the emotional aspects of the illness until the physiological difficulties are dealt with. Nutritional rehabilitation, therefore, plays an important role in treatment of some of the medical and psychological problems which are secondary to the starvation resulting in anorexia nervosa, and as such it is an essential part of its treatment. However, ultimate restoration and maintenance of normal weight and function are impossible without psychiatric treatment of the underlying psychological disorder (Schwartz & Thompson, 1981).

REFERENCES

American Dietetic Association. (1981). *Handbook of clinical dietetics*. New Haven, CT: Yale University Press.

Araoye, M. A., Change, M. Y., Khatri, I. M., et al. (1978). Furosimide compared with hydrochloride long-term treatment for hypertension. *Journal of the American Medical Association, 240*, 1863.

Beumont, P. J. V., George, P. C. W., & Smart, D. E. (1976). Dieters and vomiters and purgers in anorexia nervosa. *Psychological Medicine, 6*, 617-622.

Blackburn, G. L., & Harvey, K. B. (1982). Nutritional assessment as a routine in clinical medicine. *Postgraduate Medicine, 71*, 46-63.

Bolles, R. C. (1980). Historical note on the term appetite. *Appetite, 1*, 306.

Cahill, G. F. (1970). Starvation in man. *New England Journal of Medicine, 282*, 668-675.

Cahill, G. F., Aoki, T. T., & Rossini, A. A. (1979). Metabolism in obesity and anorexia nervosa. In R. J. Wurtman & J. J. Wurtman (Eds.), *Nutrition and the brain* (pp. 1-70). New York: Raven Press.

Casper, R. C., Ekert, E. D., Halmi, K. A., Goldberg, S. C., & Davis, J. M. (1980). Bulimia: Its incidence and clinical importance in patients with anorexia nervosa. *Archives of General Psychiatry, 37*, 1030-1035.

Crisp, A. H. (1970). Premorbid factors in adult disorders of weight, with particular reference to primary anorexia nervosa (weight phobia). *Journal of Psychosomatic Research, 14*, 1-22.

Curry, C. E. (1982). Laxative products. In *American Pharmaceutical Association, Handbook of nonprescription drugs* (pp. 69-92). Washington, DC: American Pharmaceutical Association.

DeFronzo, R. A. (1981). Insulin and renal sodium handling: Clinical implications. *International Journal of Obesity, 5*, 93-104.

Dwyer, J. T. (1980a). Sixteen popular diets. Brief nutritional analyses. In A. J. Stunkard (Ed.), *Obesity*. Philadelphia: W. C. Saunders.

Dwyer, J. (1980b). Patient-oriented perspectives on management of obesity-related problems of adolescents. In M. Mehlman (Ed.), *Advances in human nutrition* (pp. 263-304). Park Forest, IL:Pathotox Publishers.

Dwyer, J. T. (1982). Vegetarian, "health," and "junk" foods. In D. Paige (Ed.), *Manual of clinical nutrition* (pp. 1-23). Pleasantville, NJ: Nutrition Publications.

Dwyer, J. T., Feldman, J. J., & Mayer, J. (1970). The social psychology of dieting. *Journal of Health and Social Behavior, 11*(4), 269-287.

Dwyer, J. T., Feldman, J. J., Seltzer, C. C., & Mayer, J. (1969). Adolescent attitudes toward weight and appearance. *Journal of Nutrition and Education, 1*(2), 14-19.
Dwyer, J. T., & Mayer, J. (1970). Potential dieters: Who are they? Attitudes toward weight and dieting behavior. *JADA, 56,* 510-514.
Dwyer, J. T., & O'Donnell, T. (1982). Nutrition. In M. E. Molitch (Ed.), *Medical management of the surgical patient.* Philadelphia: Davis.
Dwyer, J. T., & Suitor, C. W. (1984, March). Caveat emptor: Assessing needs, evaluating computer options: Evaluating mail order and microcomputer diet analysis programs. *Journal of the American Dental Association, 84*(3), 302-312.
Fairburn, C. G. (1984). Bulimia: Its epidemiology and management. In A. J. Stunkard & E. Stellar (Eds.), *Eating and its disorders* (pp. 235-256). New York: Raven Press.
Fairburn, C. G., & Cooper, P. J. (1982). Self-induced vomiting and bulimia nervosa: An undetected problem? *British Medical Journal, 284,* 1153-1155.
Feicht, C. B., Johnson, T. S., Martin, B. J., Sparks, K. E., & Wagner, W. W. (1978). Secondary amenorrhea in athletes. *Lancet, 2,* 1145-1166.
Feighner, J. P., Robins, E., Fuze, S. B., Woodruff, R. A., Winokur, G., & Munoz, R. (1972). Diagnostic criteria for use in psychiatric research. *Archives of General Psychiatry, 26,* 57-63.
Felig, P. (1979). Starvation. In L. J. DeGroot, G. F. Cahill, L. O'Diel, J. Martini, J. Potts, D. H. Nelson, E. Steinberger, & A. J. Wingard (Eds.), *Endocrinology, Vol. 3* (pp. 1927-1940). New York: Grune & Stratton.
Fohlin, L. (1977). Anorexia nervosa. Body composition, cardiovascular and renal function in adolescent patients with anorexia nervosa. *Acta Paediatrica Scandinavica* (Suppl.), *268,* 1-50.
Garfinkel, P. E., & Garner, D. M. (1982). *Anorexia nervosa: A multidimensional perspective.* New York: Brunner/Mazel.
Garfinkel, P. E., Moldovsky, H., & Garner, D. M. (1980). The heterogeneity of anorexia nervosa: Bulimia as a distinct subgroup. *Archives of General Psychiatry, 37,* 1036-1040.
Garner, D. M., & Bemis, K. M. (1982). A cognitive-behavioral approach to anorexia nervosa. *Cognitive Therapy and Research, 6,* 123-150.
Garner, D. M., & Garfinkel, P. E. (1978). Sociocultural factors in anorexia nervosa. *Lancet, 2,* 674.
Halmi, K. A., & Falk, J. R. (1981). Common physiologic changes in anorexia nervosa. *International Journal of Eating Disorders, 1*(1), 16-27.
Hellstrom, I. (1977). Oral complications in anorexia nervosa. *Scandinavian Journal of Dental Research, 85,* 71.
Holmgren, S., Sohlberg, S., Berg, E., Johansson, B. M., Norring, C., & Rosmark, B. (1984). Phase 1 treatment for the chronic and previously treated anorexia bulimia nervosa patient. *International Journal of Eating Disorders, 3,* 17-36.
Hsu, L. K. G. (1980). Outcome of anorexia nervosa: A review of the literature (1954 to 1978). *Archives of General Psychiatry, 37,* 1041-1043.
Johnson, C. (1982). Anorexia nervosa and bulimia. In T. J. Coates, A. C. Petersen, & C. Perry (Eds.), *Promoting adolescent health: A dialog on research and practice* (pp. 397-412). New York: Academic Press.
Johnson, C., Thompson, M., & Schwartz, D. (1983). Anorexia nervosa and bulimia: An overview. In W. J. Burns & J. V. LaVigne (Eds.), *Review of pediatric psychology, Vol. 1.* New York: Grune & Stratton.
Johnson, C. D., & Catinchi, F. M. (1978). The prominent electrocardiographic conduction aspects of hypokalemia in a patient with periodic paralysis. *American Heart Journal, 95,* 359.
Kassirer, J. P., & Harrington, J. T. (1977). Diuretics and potassium metabolism: A reassessment of the need, effectiveness and safety of potassium therapy. *Kidney International, 11,* 505.
Katz, F. H., Eckert, R. C., & Gebott, M. D. (1972). Hypokalemia caused by surreptitious self-administration of diuretics. *Annals of Internal Medicine, 76,* 85.
Keys, A., Brozek, J., Henschel, A., Mickelson, O., & Taylor, H. L. (1950). *The biology of human starvation* (2 volumes). Minneapolis: University of Minnesota Press.
Kolanowski, J. (1981). Influence of insulin and glucogen on sodium balance in obese subjects during fasting and refeeding. *International Journal of Obesity, 5,* 105-114.

Maffly, R. H. (1976). How to avoid complications of potent diuretics. *Journal of the American Medical Association, 235*, 2526.

McBurney, M., & Wilmore, D. W. (1981). Rational decision making in nutritional care. *Surgery Clinics of North America, 61*, 571-581.

Meguid, M. M., Collier, M. D., & Howard, L. J. (1981). Uncomplicated and stressed starvation. *Surgery Clinics of North America, 61*, 529-543.

Morgan, H. G., Purgold, J., & Welbourne, J. (1983). Management and outcome in anorexia nervosa. A standardized prognostic study. *British Journal of Psychiatry, 143*, 282-287.

Nylander, I. (1971). The feeling of being fat and dieting in a school population. *Acta Sociomedica Scandinavica, 3*, 17-26.

Orderda, G. M., & West, S. (1982). Emetic and antiemetic products. In *American Pharmaceutical Association, Handbook of nonprescription drugs*, (pp. 93-106). Washington, DC: American Pharmaceutical Association.

Oster, J. R., Materson, B. J., & Rogers, A. I. (1980). Laxative abuse syndrome. *American Journal of Gastroenterology, 74*, 451-458.

Pennington, A., & Church, H. N. (1980). *Bowes and Church's food values of portions commonly used* (1st edition). Philadelphia: J.B. Lippincott.

Pertschuk, M. J., Crosby, L. O., & Mullen, J. L. (1983). Current psychiatric therapies. In J. H. Masseman (Ed.), *Total parenteral nutrition in anorexia nervosa*. Philadelphia: W.B. Saunders.

Ramsay, L. E., Boyle, P., & Ramsay, M. H. (1977). Factors influencing serum potassium in treated hypertension. *Quarterly Journal of Medicine, 46*, 401.

Richards, P., & Brown, C. L. (1975). Urea metabolism in an azotemic woman with normal renal function. *Lancet*, (August 2), 207-209.

Russell, G. F. M. (1979). Bulimia nervosa: An ominous variant of anorexia nervosa. *Psychological Medicine, 9*, 429-448.

Russell, D. M., Prendergast, P. J., Darby, P. L., Garfinkel, P. E., Whitwell, J., & Jeejeebhou, K. N. (1983). A comparison between muscle function and body composition in anorexia nervosa: The effect of refeeding. *American Journal of Clinical Nutrition, 38*, 229-237.

Schlemier, K. (1980). Anorexia nervosa. Supplement nr. 18 till *Naringsforskning*, p. 67-71, Stockholm.

Schwabe, A. D., Lippe, B. M., Chang, J., Pops, M. A., and Yager, J. (1981). Anorexia nervosa. *Annals of Internal Medicine, 94*, 371-381.

Schwartz, D. M., & Thompson, M. D. (1981). Do anorectics get well? Current research and future needs. *American Journal of Psychiatry, 138*, 319-323.

Schwartz, W. B., & Relman, A. S. (1953). Metabolic and renal studies in chronic potassium depletion resulting from overuse of laxatives. *Journal of Clinical Investigation, 32*, 258.

Slade, P. (1982). Towards a functional analysis of anorexia nervosa and bulimia nervosa. *British Journal of Clinical Psychology, 21*, 167-169.

Smith, N. J. (1980). Excessive weight loss and food aversion in athletes simulating anorexia nervosa. *Pediatrics, 66*, 139.

Sours, H. E., Frattali, V. P., Brand, C. D., Feldman, R. A., Forbes, A. L., Swanson, R. C., & Paris, A. L. (1981). Sudden death associated with very low calorie weight reduction regimens. *American Journal of Clinical Nutrition, 34*, 453-461.

Strober, M. (1984). Stressful life events associated with bulimia in anorexia nervosa: Empirical findings and theoretical speculations. *International Journal of Eating Disorders, 3*, 3-16.

Vigersky, R. A., Anderson, A. E., Thompson, R. H., & Loriaux, D. H. (1977). Hypothalamic dysfunction in secondary amenorrhea associated with simple weight loss. *New England Journal of Medicine, 297*, 1141-1145.

Wallace, M., Richards, P., Chesser, E., et al. (1968). Persistent alkalosis and hypokalemia caused by surreptitious vomiting. *Quarterly Journal of Medicine, 37*, 577.

Wilmore, D. W. (1977). *The metabolic management of the critically ill* (Appendix: Metabolic support plan, pp. 1-21). New York: Plenum Medical Book Co.

Chapter 3

Neuroendocrine Aspects of Eating Disorders

Paul M. Copeland

This chapter has a dual focus. Primarily, it will review the changes in the hypothalamic-pituitary axes found in anorexia nervosa and bulimia. The second focus follows from the first: It will explore these neuroendocrine changes in a search for clues of a possible biological basis for eating disorders.

The neuroendocrine changes in anorexia nervosa have been extensively investigated; the study of bulimia is far more rudimentary. The changes observed in anorexia nervosa may be considered to represent a combination of the effects of starvation and the effects of "psychic stress." Psychic stress may be nonspecific or it may be intimately linked to the cause of anorexia nervosa. Nonspecific psychic stress may be the cause of several neuroendocrine abnormalities, e.g., elevated cortisol production. On the other hand, some of the neuroendocrine changes may result from specific alterations which predispose to anorexia nervosa or bulimia.

The neuroendocrine abnormalities unique to anorexia nervosa may be obscured by the neuroendocrine effects of starvation. It is especially important to explore the neuroendocrine alterations which differentiate anorexia nervosa from starvation alone. Within these distinctive changes may reside abnormalities which reflect a biological predisposition to eating disorders. Considered in turn will be neuroendocrine alterations which are shared with starvation (appetite regulation, thyroid hormones, growth hormone, temperature regulation, antidiuretic hormone) and neuroendocrine alterations in which differences occur between anorexia nervosa and starvation alone (gonadotropins, adrenocortical hormones). Neuroendocrine alterations in bulimia will be reviewed for each group of hormones. Finally, the central nervous system neurotransmitter changes which may contribute to anorexia nervosa and bulimia will be discussed.

APPETITE REGULATION

Binge-eating occurs in 50% of patients with anorexia nervosa and is, of course, the major symptom of bulimia (Garfinkel, Moldofsky, & Garner, 1980). Binge-eating may at first glance appear to be a purely psychiatric symptom; however, its occurrence with the prolonged dieting of anorexia nervosa suggests an underlying change provoked by starvation. Binge-eating in anorexia nervosa is likely a hypothalamically-triggered response to the stress of self-imposed dieting. Bulimia in anorexia nervosa may be viewed as a "breaking through" of uncontrolled appetite.

Binge-eating is well-described in experimental starvation. Near the end of World War II, Keys studied a group of conscientious objectors who volunteered for a prolonged period of experimental starvation (Keys, Brozek, Henschel, Mickelson, & Taylor, 1950). They were subjected to a near-starvation diet for 24 weeks. Many of the psychological changes they reported resemble those seen in anorexia nervosa. The men experienced an increased preoccupation with food. Food became the main topic of conversation. It dominated their daydreams. When they read or watched movies, they were struck by how often food was mentioned. They began reading cookbooks and collected recipes. Some men talked of changing careers and becoming cooks. Like patients with anorexia nervosa who prepare food for others while denying it to themselves, these starved men focused their attention on food. After the 24 weeks of semi-starvation, there were 12 weeks of refeeding during which the amounts of food were still limited. After those 12 weeks, there was another 12-week period of observation during which food was unrestricted. During this period many of the men began binging:

> The men frequently found it difficult to stop eating. No. 20 "stuffs himself until he is bursting at the seams, to the point of being nearly sick," and still he felt hungry; No. 120 reported that he had to discipline himself to keep from eating so much as to become ill; No. 1 ate until he was uncomfortably full; and subject No. 30 had so little control over the mechanics of "piling it in" that he simply had to stay away from food, because he could not find a point of satiation even when he was "full to the gills." (Keys et al., 1950, pp. 846–847)

The parallels to the bulimic behavior of some patients with anorexia nervosa are evident. For many anorexics, the stress of rigid dieting precipitates bulimia. The stress of dieting also appears to be an initiator of bulimic behavior in many patients with normal-weight bulimia.

The binge-eating behaviors in anorexia nervosa and normal-weight bulimia are likely parts of a continuum. The anorexic bulimics and the normal-weight bulimics may differ in the starvation threshold at which binging behavior is precipitated. Both anorexic and normal-weight bulimics share behavioral characteristics (e.g., impulsivity) absent in "pure restricter" anorexics (Casper, Eckert, Halmi, Goldberg, & Davis, 1980; Garfinkel et al., 1980).

Bulimic and non-bulimic anorexics have neuroendocrine differences which may establish their degree of predisposition to binging. Differences in cerebrospinal fluid serotonin metabolites have been described (see section on Central Nervous System Neurotransmitters). Thus, while appetite regulation is not the principal abnormality in anorexia nervosa, the consequences of starvation may be manifested by disorders in appetite regulation.

THYROID HORMONES

Alterations in the hypothalamic-pituitary-thyroid axis in anorexia nervosa closely resemble those seen in starvation alone. Both conditions manifest changes categorized as the euthyroid sick state (Wartofsky & Burman, 1982). Normally, the thyroid gland produces thyroxine (T_4) and triiodothyronine (T_3). Metabolically, T_3 is the more active hormone. Approximately 35-40% of the T_4 is converted by monodeiodination to T_3. This peripheral conversion produces 80-90% of all circulating T_3. In starvation, anorexia nervosa, and other euthyroid sick states, the peripheral conversion of T_4 to T_3 is decreased. Serum T_3 levels are low in anorexia nervosa (Croxson & Ibbertson, 1977; Moshang, Parks, Baker, Vaid, et al., 1975). Clinically, patients with anorexia nervosa have many symptoms and signs suggestive of hypothyroidism: dry skin, bradycardia, hypothermia, constipation, delayed Achilles tendon reflex relaxation time, and low basal metabolic rate. To some extent, the low T_3 may be contributing to these symptoms; however, patients with anorexia nervosa should not be regarded as hypothyroid and should not be given thyroid supplement. The decreased T_3 levels may be viewed as the "wisdom of the body" in protecting against relative hypermetabolism in the starved state (Moshang & Utiger, 1977). Decreased T_3 levels may be protective against accelerated protein breakdown.

Serum T_4 levels may also be slightly lowered in anorexia nervosa (Croxson & Ibbertson, 1977). This finding, like the low T_3 level, also should not lead to the interpretation that the patient is hypothyroid (Wartofsky & Burman, 1982). The active component of T_4, the dialyzable free T_4, is usually normal. Free T_4 is in equilibrium with T_4 bound to serum proteins. Most T_4 is bound to T_4-binding globulin. Measures of T_4-binding globulin, while occasionally low, are usually normal in anorexia nervosa. It would be predicted that a low total T_4 and normal T_4-binding globulin would yield a low free T_4. The paradox may be explained by a circulating substance (probably a fatty acid) that inhibits the binding of T_4 to T_4-binding globulin. This inhibitor has been detected in the sera of patients with other euthyroid sick syndromes (Chopra, Huang, Hurd, Boredo, & Solomon, 1984).

The low T_3 and occasionally low T_4 in patients with anorexia nervosa poses the problem of distinguishing this euthyroid sick state from true hypothyroidism. Three clinically useful means of achieving this discrimination are:

1) Reverse T_3 levels are increased in anorexia nervosa (Leslie, Isaacs, Gomez, Raggatt, & Bayliss, 1978). Normally T_4 may be monodeiodinated either to the active hormone T_3 (5'-deiodinase), or to the metabolically inactive reverse T_3 (5-deiodinase). Unlike T_3, the production rate of reverse T_3 is not changed in the euthyroid sick state. Rather, the clearance rate of reverse T_3 decreases and, therefore, reverse T_3 levels increase. Reverse T_3 levels are elevated in anorexia nervosa while the levels are low in hypothyroidism. The elevated reverse T_3 levels can reliably distinguish the thyroid abnormalities of anorexia nervosa from true hypothyroidism.
2) $T_3 : T_4$ ratios are decreased in anorexia nervosa (Croxson & Ibbertson, 1977). As discussed above, T_4 to T_3 conversion is decreased in anorexia nervosa. In hypothyroidism, T_3 levels are relatively preserved. A low $T_3 : T_4$ ratio, like a high reverse T_3, is characteristic of anorexia nervosa and is not observed with primary, secondary (pituitary failure), or tertiary (hypothalamic failure) hypothyroidism.
3) Thyroid-stimulating hormone (TSH) levels are normal or low in anorexia nervosa (Moshang et al., 1975). These levels distinguish anorexia nervosa from primary hypothyroidism where TSH levels are high. TSH levels will not discriminate patients with anorexia nervosa from those with pituitary or hypothalamic failure.

The hypothalamic alterations in the control of TSH secretion appear to be similar in anorexia nervosa and in fasting. In fasting, the TSH response to thyrotropin-releasing hormone (TRH) is blunted (Wartofsky & Burman, 1982). In anorexia nervosa, the response is blunted or delayed (Casper & Frohman, 1982). The mechanism of these alterations is not clear. In rats, TSH levels suppressed by starvation can be increased by anti-somatostatin serum (DeRuyter, Burman, Wartofsky, & Smallridge, 1984). Whether somatostatin plays a role in the altered TSH responses of anorexia nervosa remains to be determined.

With recovery of caloric intake and weight gain, serum T_3 levels in anorexics rise toward normal (Croxson & Ibbertson, 1977; Leslie et al., 1978). In one series of 13 anorexics, in four of the patients T_3 levels rose above the normal range (Moore & Mills, 1979). This overshoot may contribute to the observed increases in caloric expenditure after initial weight gain (Kaye, Gwirtsman, George, & Ebert, 1984; Pertschuk, Crosby, & Mullen, 1983). Increased noradrenergic activity with refeeding may also contribute to increased caloric expenditure (Kaye et al., 1984). A plateau in weight gain, therefore, should not be regarded as signaling diminished food intake.

Thyroid hormone levels are generally normal in bulimia. Studies have reported a blunted TSH response to TRH in some bulimics (Gwirtsman, Roy-Byrne, Yager, & Gerner, 1983). This change may reflect temporary caloric restriction; however, it also resembles the response observed in many patients with major depression. A blunted TSH response to TRH has been cited as a neuroendocrine feature which links bulimia and affective illness. Nonsuppression of cortisol by dexamethasone is the other major neuroendocrine similarity between bulimia and affective illness; it will be considered in the discussion of adrenocortical hormones.

GROWTH HORMONE

Another neuroendocrine abnormality shared by starvation and anorexia nervosa is an elevated growth hormone level (Casper, Davis, & Pandey, 1977). Growth hormone normally acts by stimulating the production of somatomedin C. Somatomedin C is responsible for the growth-promoting action of growth hormone. Somatomedin C levels are low in anorexia nervosa and in starvation (Clemmons, Klibanski, Underwood, & McArthur, 1981; Frankel & Jenkins, 1977; Hintz, Suskind, Amatayakul, Thanangkul, & Olson, 1976; Phillips & Vassilopoulou-Sellin, 1979). Somatomedin C exerts feedback inhibition on growth hormone secretion through actions in both the hypothalamus and the pituitary (Berelowitz, Szabo, Frohman, Firestone, et al., 1981; Tannenbaum, Guyda, & Posner, 1983). Growth hormone levels are very sensitive to recent caloric intake (Brown, Garfinkel, Jeuniewic, Moldofsky, & Stancer, 1977). When anorexics begin to eat again, growth hormone levels fall within a few days. Even before weight has changed, improved caloric intake will decrease growth hormone levels. Upon refeeding, patients consuming more than 1500 calories per day had significantly lower growth hormone levels than those who continued to eat less than 1500 calories per day (Brown et al., 1977).

An abnormal sensitivity of growth hormone-secreting cells to TRH has been described both in anorexia nervosa and in starvation. Whereas normally there is no growth hormone change in response to TRH, anorexic and starved patients manifest a growth hormone elevation in response to TRH (Gold, Pottash, Sweeney, Martin, & Davies, 1980). Recent data show that increased exposure to hypothalamic growth hormone-releasing factor can induce such an elevation (Borgers, Uskavitch, Kaiser, Cronin, et al., 1983). With the fall in somatomedin C levels in starvation and anorexia nervosa, the secretion of growth hormone-releasing factor would be expected to increase. Such an increase may produce the abnormal response of growth hormone to TRH.

One study reported that four of six normal weight bulimics appeared to have an abnormal growth hormone response to TRH (Mitchell & Bantle, 1983). Baseline growth hormone values in this study were insufficiently stable to define a significant increase in growth hormone. Normal pulsations in growth hormone may account for the variability. The lack of a saline placebo test also makes interpretation of a response difficult since growth hormone levels are known to increase in response to psychological stress. Possible growth hormone abnormalities in bulimia require further investigation.

TEMPERATURE REGULATION

Temperature regulation is diminished both in patients with anorexia nervosa and in patients with weight loss who do not have the psychiatric features of anorexia nervosa (Vigersky, Andersen, Thompson, & Loriaux, 1977). That is, both groups of patients have difficulty maintaining normal body temperature in a hot or cold environment. There is a failure to shiver in response to a cold environment. The lack of shivering suggests the phenomenon is a central, probably hypothalamic defect, rather than a result of decreased fat insulation.

ANTIDIURETIC HORMONE (VASOPRESSIN)

Several abnormal features of vasopressin release have been observed in patients with anorexia nervosa at low weights. Abnormalities of the posterior pituitary secretion of vasopressin include both hypo-responsiveness to osmotic stimuli and erratic secretion unrelated to osmolarity (Gold, Kaye, Robertson, & Ebert, 1983; Vigersky & Loriaux, 1977). Normally, plasma vasopressin increases smoothly in reponse to increasing plasma osmolarity. Vasopressin acts upon the kidney to retain water which compensates for increased plasma osmolarity or decreased plasma volume. People who lack vasopressin have diabetes insipidus and are unable to conserve water appropriately. They develop tremendously increased urination and thirst.

About 25% of patients with anorexia nervosa or substantial simple weight loss develop partial diabetes insipidus (Gold et al., 1983; Vigersky & Loriaux, 1977). This mild abnormality is probably caused by a hypo-responsiveness of vasopressin to osmotic stimuli. The mild abnormality generally does not cause clinical symptoms. Anorexics often have slightly increased urination and thirst but these changes may not be caused by diminished vasopressin secretion. Many anorexics drink a large amount of caffeinated beverages which exert a diuretic effect (Oliver, 1984).

The study of plasma vasopressin response to osmotic stimuli has produced more tantalizing results with regard to a possible neuroendocrine defect in anorexia nervosa (Gold et al., 1983). This study showed a highly unusual erratic response of vasopressin to a salt infusion in anorexics while at low weight. Whereas in normal individuals plasma vasopressin levels progressively increase with hypertonic sodium chloride infusion, three of four low-weight anorexics showed erratic peaks of vasopressin unrelated to plasma sodium concentrations. While other factors such as declines in blood pressure, nausea, pain, or anxiety may provoke vasopressin secretion, the experimenters found no evidence of these stimuli. In a longitudinal follow-up study, the erratic vasopressin response persisted for at least one month after weight was restored to normal. It did not disappear until six months after weight recovery. It is not yet known whether the erratic response is unique to anorexia nervosa. Parallel studies have not been reported in simple weight loss. In addition to these abnormalities in the posterior pituitary secretion of vasopressin, and thereby in plasma vasopressin levels, cerebrospinal fluid (CSF) vasopressin levels are elevated in anorexia nervosa (Gold et al., 1983). Vasopressin in the CSF emanates from a source distinct from that for peripheral plasma vasopressin (Reppert, Artman, Swami-Nathan, & Fisher, 1981). Whereas plasma vasopressin originates in the paraventricular and supraoptic nuclei of the hypothalamus and is transported to the posterior pituitary gland, the major source of CSF vasopressin is the suprachiasmatic nucleus of the hypothalamus. This source is regulated independently from the sources of peripheral plasma vasopressin. In anorexia nervosa, levels of CSF vasopressin frequently remain elevated even six months after weight recovery (Gold et al., 1983). This prolonged elevation may simply represent a lag in the restoration of normal levels. Alternatively, elevated brain vasopressin levels may be a "trait" as opposed to "state" marker, signaling a predisposition to anorexia nervosa.

GONADOTROPINS

The observed abnormalities of gonadotropin secretion in anorexia nervosa are largely shared by those in simple starvation. Both conditions manifest hypogonadism and amenorrhea on a hypothalamic basis. There are, however, some important differences in the ontogeny of the abnormalities: In anorexia nervosa, the amenorrhea has its onset prior to food restriction or weight loss in up to 25% of patients (Fries, 1977). In addition, there is a delay in the recovery of menses: Women who lose weight without the psychiatric features of anorexia nervosa generally regain menses when they increase their weight above the 10th percentile for height, but about 15% of patients with anorexia nervosa fail to regain menses for months to years after achieving a normal weight (Frisch & McArthur, 1974; Hsu, Crisp, & Harding, 1979). Plasma gonadotropin levels are low in patients with anorexia nervosa. There is a loss of normal luteinizing hormone (LH) and follicle-stimulating hormone (FSH) pulsations (Boyar, Katz, Finkelstein, Kapen, Weiner, Weitzman, & Hellman, 1974). The pattern may resemble that of prepuberty with a complete absence of normal LH and FSH pulsations or it may resemble early puberty with only sleep-related pulsations (Katz, Boyar, Roffwarg, & Weiner, 1978). Testing with single boluses of luteinizing hormone releasing hormone (LHRH) gives variable results which depend upon the degree of weight recovery (Palmer, Crisp, Mackinnon, Franklin, et al., 1975; Sherman, Halmi, & Zamudio, 1975). At very low weights, anorexic females have a markedly blunted LH and a slightly blunted FSH response. These responses resemble those of prepuberty. At intermediate degrees of weight recovery the gonadotropin responses can be normal or even supra-normal.

The immature LH secretory pattern seen in anorexics at low weights often persists after weight recovery. These patients frequently have a persistence of abnormal eating attitudes or even of bulimic behavior (Halmi & Falk, 1983; Katz et al., 1978). Among patients at the Eating Disorders Clinic of the Massachusetts General Hospital, 38% of normal-weight bulimics with a history of anorexia nervosa had continued amenorrhea despite their restored weight (Copeland, Ridgway, Pepose, & Herzog, 1984).

The clinical picture of amenorrhea in anorexia nervosa is a low estrogen state (Warren & VandeWeile, 1975). In the clinical evaluation, patients with profound weight loss do not have a menstrual flow when given progestins. This lack of progestin withdrawal bleeding reflects a failure of endometrial proliferation in the low estrogen state. The clinical implications of the low estrogen state include an increased risk of osteoporosis. There is no correlation, however, between the degree of osteoporosis and a single measurement of the magnitude of estrogen deficiency (Rigotti, Nussbaum, Herzog, & Neer, 1984). In addition to decreased estrogen, other factors contributing to osteoporosis probably include nutritional inadequacy (producing its impact perhaps via protein depletion and low somatomedin C levels) and high cortisol levels. The risk of osteoporosis is even greater among anorexics who are less physically active (Rigotti et al., 1984). Estrogen replacement therapy should be considered for amenorrheic anorexic patients with a documented low bone density.

With weight restoration and return of menses, normal fertility is usually achieved. Some weight-recovered anorexics who remain amenorrheic will regain menstruation and fertility with clomiphene therapy (Marshall & Fraser, 1971). Clomiphene, an estrogen receptor blocker, can produce a surge in gonadotropin secretion and trigger ovulation. Ovulation can also be induced by pulsatile administration of luteinizing hormone-releasing hormone (LHRH) (Marshall & Kelch, 1979). The success of this approach demonstrates that the locus of the abnormal gonadotropin secretion is hypothalamic and that the pituitary gland is intrinsically normal. Clinically, clomiphene therapy and pulsatile LHRH therapy should be reserved for those patients close to ideal body weight who have made a substantial psychiatric recovery.

Males with anorexia nervosa are also hypogonadal. They are generally impotent and have decreased libido. As in the females, the FSH response to LHRH is relatively preserved even at lower body weights while the LH response is blunted or absent at very low weights. The LH response progresses to a hyper-response at intermediately low weights of about 100-110 pounds. With full weight recovery the responses become normal.

The mechanism by which weight loss disrupts LHRH secretion is unclear. The source of the neuroendocrine dysfunction in the control of LHRH secretion largely remains to be identified. One possible candidate is increased endogenous opioid activity. Opioids will diminish LHRH pulsations in normal women. Increased opioid tone can disrupt LHRH secretion; in fact, this mechanism probably accounts for the diminished gonadotropin secretion in hyperprolactinemia. Infusion of naloxone, an opiate antagonist, elicits pulsations of LH in patients with hyperprolactinemia (Grossman, Moult, McIntyre, et al., 1982). Naloxone infusions are also effective in increasing LH levels in a subset of patients with anorexia nervosa (Baranowska, Rozbicka, Jeske, & Abdel-Fattah, 1984). Among a group of 11 anorexics for whom naloxone raised LH levels, in all but two patients the amenorrhea preceded weight loss. Among 14 other anorexics, who had an equivalent body weight deficit, naloxone infusion did not change LH levels. In all but two patients of this latter group, amenorrhea first appeared with weight loss. Therefore, increased endogenous opioids may mediate amenorrhea which precedes weight loss but do not appear to influence weight-loss-induced decreases in LH secretion.

A possible role of central dopaminergic activity in LHRH secretion has been subject to conflicting interpretations (Buvat, Lemaire, Buvat-Herpaut, Lepretre, & Fourlinnie, 1983; Halmi, Owen, Lasley, & Stokes, 1983). Halmi et al. (1983) suggest that a decreased prolactin response to the dopamine antagonist, chlorpromazine, indicates a deficiency in dopaminergic function. Conversely, Buvat et al. (1983) note that another dopamine antagonist, pimozide, produced an increased gonadotropin response to LHRH. They suggest increased dopaminergic activity may inhibit LH secretion in anorexia nervosa.

Not only is the central nervous system mechanism yet to be determined for weight-loss-related amenorrhea, but the peripheral signal by which low body weight triggers the central change is unknown. One candidate which has received attention is hypercarotenemia (Frumar, Meldrum, & Judd, 1979). Amenorrhea has been noted in normal-weight women who had excessive dietary intake of carotene in vegetables (Kemmann, Pasquale, & Skaf, 1983). They had high serum levels of carotene. When their diet was modified to reduce carotene intake, their serum levels fell and menses were restored. Patients with anorexia nervosa also commonly have elevated serum carotene levels (Silverman, 1983). The elevation cannot be attributed to excessive carotene intake. Possibly, the low T_3 levels and functional hypothyroidism contribute to these increased carotene levels (see section on Thyroid Hormones). Carotene levels are increased in true thyroidal hypothyroidism as well. Patients with anorexia nervosa who have frankly elevated serum carotene levels have significantly lower T_3 and T_4 levels than anorexics who have normal serum carotene levels (Curran-Celentano, Erdman, Nelson, & Grater, 1984). Whether "normal" serum carotene levels in a subset of anorexics actually represent elevated levels for the particular individual's physiology remains to be determined. The mechanism by which carotenemia might produce amenorrhea is unknown. More direct prospective tests of this hypothesis are needed.

Amenorrhea is also prevalent among patients with normal-weight bulimia. The origin of the amenorrhea is unknown but has been ascribed to alternate periods of binging and fasting accompanied by inadequate nutrition (Warren, 1983). This speculation requires additional evidence. Another factor which appears to contribute to amenorrhea in normal-weight bulimia is a past history of weight loss. A study at the Massachusetts General Hospital showed that even among bulimics without a prior history of diagnosable anorexia nervosa, those with amenorrhea at the time of evaluation had significantly lower past standard weight (percent ideal body weight) nadirs than those with regular menses (Copeland et al., 1984). Whereas only 41% of normal weight bulimics with regular menses had a standard weight nadir below 0.92, a substantial 87% of those with amenorrhea had nadirs below this level. Amenorrheic bulimics without a history of weight loss either exercised excessively or had the onset of amenorrhea following a stressful life transition. The amenorrheic bulimic patients with the intermediately low past weights (standard weight between 0.75 and 0.92) never met the weight loss criteria for anorexia nervosa; yet, they probably form part of a group Russell has termed "cryptic" anorexia nervosa (Russell, 1984). Cryptic anorexics possess many of the dieting concerns and body image distortions of anorexics, but do not have as obvious a pursuit of weight loss. Their intermediate low weights, however, may provoke amenorrhea which can persist, as it does in many anorexics, after a degree of weight recovery.

ADRENOCORTICAL HORMONES

Changes in the hypothalamic-pituitary-adrenal axis in anorexia nervosa differ distinctly from those of starvation alone. The increased cortisol production rate in anorexia nervosa contrasts sharply from the decreased cortisol production rate in malnutrition (Beitins, Kowarski, Migeon, & Graham, 1975; Doerr, Fichter, Pirke, & Lund, 1980). The elevated cortisol production rate is a feature shared with endogenous depression although not all patients with anorexia nervosa are easily classified as depressed.

The overall picture of the hypothalamic-pituitary-adrenal axis in anorexia nervosa appears to represent a combination of the effects of starvation and of some other "psychic stress" factor. Ambient cortisol levels are elevated in anorexia nervosa (Walsh, Katz, Levin, Kream, et al., 1978). This increase is a result of both an increased production rate and a decreased clearance of cortisol. The decreased clearance may be ascribed to the T_3 hypothyroidism of starvation (Boyar, Hellman, Roffwarg, Katz, et al., 1977). Liver metabolism of cortisol is slowed in starvation. Administration of T_3 restores cortisol clearance toward normal.

Starvation, however, does not account for the increased cortisol production rate. As assessed by radioactive tracer techniques, patients with protein-calorie malnutrition have a decreased cortisol production rate (Smith, Bledsoe, & Chhetri, 1975). The rate increases to normal after refeeding. In anorexia nervosa, however, the cortisol production rate decreases toward normal with initiation of weight gain. A reflection of the increased cortisol production rate in anorexia nervosa is the increased excretion of urinary free cortisol (Walsh et al., 1978). Urinary free cortisol is an excellent measure of cortisol secretion since the plasma-binding capacity for cortisol is readily exceeded at high levels and the excess is excreted by the kidney.

In addition to an overall increase in cortisol production rate, there is often a loss of the diurnal variation in cortisol secretion (Boyar et al., 1977; Doerr et al., 1980). Normally cortisol is secreted in more frequent and higher amplitude pulses in the early morning hours. Peak secretion usually occurs between 0400 and 0800 hours. There is an evening, and especially a late night, trough. Many patients with anorexia nervosa lack diurnal variation in cortisol levels and have persistent high levels with more frequent secretory pulses (Doerr et al., 1980). A similar lack of diurnal variation has been noted in patients with endogenous depression. With weight recovery, the anorexics attain normal diurnal variation. The cortisol production rate also declines toward normal (Walsh, Katz, Levin, et al., 1981).

Patients with anorexia nervosa have been noted to have increased cortisol levels after the noon meal (Doerr et al., 1980). The phenomenon has also been reported in normal persons (Ishizuka, Quigley, & Yen, 1983). A controlled study found no difference in meal-related cortisol secretion between bulimics and normals (Copeland, Herzog, Carr, Klibanski, & MacLaughlin, in preparation). It is unlikely that cortisol responses to meals account for the abnormalities of the hypothalamic-pituitary-adrenal axis in eating disordered patients.

The secretion of cortisol is regulated by adrenal cortical activity which is influenced by adrenocorticotropic hormone (ACTH) from the pituitary. ACTH secretion, in turn, is influenced by the secretion of corticotropin-releasing factor (CRF) and other substances secreted into the hypothalamic-pituitary portal vessels. Vasopressin is one substance secreted by the hypothalamus that is a potent stimulus to ACTH secretion and acts synergistically with CRF to release ACTH. ACTH secretion is regulated by feedback inhibition by glucocorticoids at both hypothalamic and pituitary sites. Decreased sensitivity to glucocorticoid inhibition is suggested by diminished ability of the synthetic glucocorticoid, dexamethasone, to suppress cortisol secretion. Incomplete suppression of cortisol by dexamethasone is practically the rule among patients with anorexia nervosa (Gwirtsman & Gerner, 1981). Incomplete dexamethasone suppression of cortisol is not unique to anorexia nervosa and occurs, albeit less consistently, in several psychiatric illnesses. The mechanism of this dexamethasone nonsuppression, however, may differ among the various conditions.

Weight loss itself can shift a normal dexamethasone suppression test to an abnormal test. Some obese persons who are placed on low calorie diets will develop incomplete suppression by dexamethasone after a few weeks of weight loss (Edelstein, Roy-Byrne, Fawzy, & Dornfield, 1983). Another study found weight loss in normal volunteers caused an increased number of positive dexamethasone suppression tests (Berger, Krieg, & Pirke, 1982). This study was somewhat unusual for its high percentage of abnormal baseline tests. In depressed patients, some studies have found a correlation of weight loss and abnormal dexamethasone suppression tests (Berger, Doerr, Lund, Bronisch, & Von Zerssen, 1982), but other studies have disputed the correlation (Coppen, Harwood, & Wood, 1984). It is not known if the weight loss causes increased hypothalamic-pituitary-adrenal axis activity. Alternatively, weight loss may diminish dexamethasone absorption or increase its clearance while decreasing the clearance of cortisol. Studies using urinary free cortisol as a reflection of adrenal activity have not been reported.

In summary, alterations in the hypothalamic-pituitary-adrenal axis in anorexia nervosa include an increased cortisol production rate, an abnormal diurnal variation of cortisol secretion, and a decreased sensitivity to suppression by dexamethasone. These phenomena may be accounted for by a variety of possible mechanisms: 1) an increased secretion of CRF or of vasopressin from the hypothalamus; 2) an increased pituitary sensitivity to CRF causing increased ACTH secretion; 3) an increased adrenal responsiveness to ACTH; 4) an intrinsic increased adrenal activity or increased responsiveness to a non-ACTH factor. In addition to these mechanisms, the abnormal dexamethasone suppression test may be caused by a decreased absorption (a gut abnormality) or an increased clearance (hepatic enzyme alteration) of dexamethasone. We will now consider the evidence for each of these possible mechanisms.

1) There are no direct measurements of endogenous CRF in anorexia nervosa. The possibility of increased CRF production "makes sense" from an *a priori* viewpoint. In psychiatric illness, central nervous system stressors may produce a nonspecific response provoking increased secretion of CRF. Levels of CRF are significantly increased in the cerebrospinal fluid (CSF) of patients with major depression (Nemeroff et al., 1984). Abnormalities of vasopressin secretion are well-described in anorexia nervosa (see section on Antidiuretic Hormone). The increased CSF vasopressin levels may reflect increased hypothalamic secretion of vasopressin. Vasopressin can act synergistically with CRF to stimulate ACTH release.

2) An increased pituitary sensitivity to CRF may be a consequence of increased stimulation by CRF or it may reflect an intrinsic pituitary abnormality. Preliminary evidence suggests the changes in ACTH response to CRF in anorexia nervosa may be different from those in endogenous depression. While patients with either disorder manifest high cortisol levels, the ACTH response to CRF is blunted in depression but may be slightly accentuated in anorexia nervosa (Kaye & Gold, 1984). The blunted response in depression is consistent with feedback inhibition by endogenous cortisol at the pituitary. The possibly accentuated response in anorexia nervosa would suggest the pituitary is either relatively resistant to cortisol or stimulated by another factor which preserves the response to CRF.

3) Patients with anorexia nervosa have increased adrenal sensitivity to ACTH. This increased sensitivity may be a consequence of a trophic change induced by increased ACTH stimulation or it may represent an independent adrenal alteration. It is not known whether the increased sensitivity to ACTH accounts for the increased cortisol production rate or for dexamethasone nonsuppression. More studies of ambient ACTH and cortisol levels would be needed to pinpoint increased adrenal responsiveness to ACTH as the source of these abnormalities.

4) Besides increased sensitivity to ACTH, increased cortisol production may result from intrinsic increased adrenal activity or increased responsiveness to a non-ACTH factor. In normal humans, morning pulses of cortisol are

not necessarily triggered by pulses of ACTH (Fehm, Klein, Holl, & Voigt, 1984). There may be increased cortisol secretion stimulated by a neural or humoral factor other than ACTH. Other evidence of an ACTH-independent stimulus for cortisol secretion comes from studies of dexamethasone suppression. Escape of cortisol levels from dexamethasone suppression in patients with endogenous depression (Fang, Tricou, Robertson, & Meltzer, 1981) and with bulimia (Copeland et al., in preparation) can occur without corresponding elevations in ACTH levels. These findings suggest that in these disorders ACTH may not be the trigger for the increased cortisol levels.

Dexamethasone suppression tests are abnormal in about 50% of patients with bulimia (Hudson, Pope, Jonas, Laffer, et al., 1983). The possible mechanisms for the abnormality are similar to those outlined for anorexia nervosa. Like patients with anorexia nervosa and with endogenous depression, bulimics also have higher integrated ambient cortisol levels (Copeland et al., in preparation). Cortisol clearance has not been studied in these patients, but an increased cortisol production rate is a more likely mechanism for the higher levels.

Adrenal androgen secretion is diminished in anorexia nervosa. Historically, decreased 17-ketosteroids excretion was described 30 years ago (Perloff, Lasche, Nodine, Schneebert, & Vieillard, 1954). Unlike cortisol metabolites, however, decreased excretion of adrenal metabolites does not only reflect decreased clearance rates. Plasma levels of dehydroepiandrosterone sulfate (DHEA-S), the major secreted adrenal androgen, are also decreased at low weights (Zumoff, Walsh, Katz, et al., 1983). In view of the increased cortisol production in these patients, it is evident that adrenal synthesis is shunted away from androgen production. A decreased activity of the enzyme 17,20-lyase may explain this shift. This enzyme catalyzes the conversion of 17-hydroxypregnenolone to DHEA. Alternatively, there may be a decreased secretion of the putative adrenal-androgen stimulating hormone. This unidentified factor secreted from the pituitary has been invoked to explain the independent secretion of adrenal androgens and cortisol in normal physiology.

CENTRAL NERVOUS SYSTEM NEUROTRANSMITTERS

Many central nervous system (CNS) neurotransmitters have been implicated in control of appetite and weight. Among these neurotransmitters, norepinephrine, serotonin, and opioids have been found to have intriguing abnormalities which may explain either the pathogenesis or manifestations of anorexia nervosa. The guiding hypotheses in this work are: 1) A neurochemical change may predispose a person to anorexia nervosa or bulimia; and

2) The self-imposed starvation may itself lead to neuroendocrine changes. These changes may foster other behaviors, e.g., binge-eating.

Norepinephrine

Hypothalamic norepinephrine has a profound effect on eating behavior in rats. Instillation of physiologic concentrations of norepinephrine into the paraventricular nucleus of the medial hypothalamus initiates feeding behavior in rats (Leibowitz, 1980). The animals prefer carbohydrate-rich foods and eat larger than normal meals. Alpha-adrenergic blocking agents can prevent this effect of norepinephrine on feeding. To illustrate the complexity of the neurohumoral mechanisms, it should be noted that there is also a lateral hypothalamic beta-adrenergic system that inhibits feeding behavior.

Starvation also has substantial effects on hypothalamic norepinephrine. Multiple lines of evidence suggest secretion of medial hypothalamic norepinephrine increases with starvation. The turnover rate of norepinephrine increases in the medial hypothalamus (Leibowitz, 1980). There is also a downregulation of alpha-adrenergic receptors in the paraventricular nucleus which decreases sensitivity to the actions of norepinephrine in this region. This downregulation probably reflects the increased exposure of receptors to the secreted norepinephrine.

This medial hypothalamic noradrenergic system has been invoked to explain some of the phenomena of anorexia nervosa and bulimia. It has been proposed that anorexics have a deficiency of hypothalamic noradrenergic activity which predisposes them to decreased food intake (Leibowitz, 1984). One must consider, though, that anorexia nervosa is not truly a disorder of appetite, but rather of weight regulation. Some anorexics, however, develop a misperception of satiety and feel full quickly. While this phenomenon likely relates to their decreased gastric emptying (Saleh & Lebwohl, 1980), a central nervous system component may also be involved.

Alterations of noradrenergic physiology in starvation may also explain binge eating. With food deprivation, there is increased secretion of norepinephrine in the medial hypothalamus. As the deprivation is prolonged, the norepinephrine may trigger an episode of binge eating. Bulimia is observed in about 50% of anorexics, and this mechanism would account for its high prevalence. It would also explain the frequent onset of bulimia in normal weight individuals during a prolonged phase of dieting.

Direct investigation of noradrenergic function in eating disorders has revealed several abnormalities which may pertain to the hypotheses discussed above. Studies of urinary excretion of norepinephrine metabolites have consistently shown evidence of reduced norepinephrine turnover in underweight patients with anorexia nervosa (Gerner & Gwirtsman, 1981). These studies, however, are limited in that 3-methoxy, 4-hydroxy-phenylglycol (MHPG) is measured as a reflection of central norepinephrine turnover. While much of the urinary MHPG is derived from central norepinephrine, the majority is a metabolite of peripheral norepinephrine. Peripheral norepinephrine largely comes from the sympathetic nervous system. Sympathetic nervous system norepinephrine turnover is well-known to decrease with dietary restriction. Therefore, MHPG cannot be regarded as definitively identifying a central nervous system change. Measurement of cerebrospinal fluid (CSF) norepinephrine or MHPG shows no change in underweight anorexics or in the same patients soon after weight recovery (Kaye, Gwirtsman, Jimerson, Ebert, et al., 1984). Nevertheless, an abnormality in central noradrenergic neurons may still be an etiologic factor in anorexia nervosa. After long-term weight recovery (20 ± 7 months) anorexics had a 50% decrease in CSF norepinephrine levels compared to controls (Kaye, Ebert, Raleigh, & Lake, 1984). The apparently normal levels at low weights and after short-term weight recovery may be a consequence of alterations in alpha-receptor sensitivity.

Using the growth hormone response to clonidine as a reflection of alpha-2-receptor sensitivity, Kaye, Gwirtsman, George, & Ebert (1984) have suggested that there is an up-regulation of alpha-2-receptors in underweight anorexics and a down-regulation after short-term weight restoration. They conclude that noradrenergic abnormalities exist at all stages of anorexia nervosa. One problem with this analysis is that growth hormone secretion is drastically affected by caloric intake (Brown et al., 1977). Thus, at low weights increased growth hormone release may reflect decreased somatomedin C production associated with starvation. The decreased growth hormone secretion with weight restoration may reflect recovery of somatomedin C secretion. Other probes of alpha receptor sensitivity are needed before conclusions may be reached with regard to a hypothesized pervasive abnormality in CNS noradrenergic physiology in anorexia nervosa.

Studies of central noradrenergic activity have not yet been reported in normal-weight bulimics. Clinically, imipramine, a tricyclic antidepressant which inhibits norepinephrine reuptake, has been successful in decreasing binging behavior (Pope, Hudson, Jonas, & Yurgelun-Todd, 1983). The effectiveness in controlling binging of an agent which increases synaptic norepinephrine concentrations underscores the primitiveness of our understanding of the CNS mechanisms that operate in eating disorders. It seems paradoxical that an agent which increases effective norepinephrine concentrations prevents binging. One explanatory model is that continuous exposure to norepinephrine, achieved by uptake blockade, produces down-regulation of alpha-adrenergic receptors. This down-regulation would decrease sensitivity to pulses of norepinephrine. Such a model emphasizes the differences between continuous and pulsatile exposure to a neurotransmitter.

5-Hydroxytryptamine (Serotonin)

Increased central nervous system serotonin produces satiety in a variety of animal models. Serotonin also reduces appetite for carbohydrates. Levels of the major serotonin metabolite, 5-hydroxyindoleacetic acid (5-HIAA), are decreased in the CSF of underweight anorexics; however, like other amine metabolites (e.g., homovanillic acid, a dopamine metabolite), low CSF levels return to normal with weight recovery (Kaye, Ebert, Raleigh, & Lake 1984).

A more promising finding in the serotonergic system is in the differentiation of "pure restricter" anorexics from bulimic anorexics. Studies have used probenecid to block the egress of 5-HIAA from the CSF. Accumulation of 5-HIAA after probenecid treatment reflects the metabolic turnover rate of serotonin. In anorexics after weight recovery, the differences between the post-probenecid and pre-probenecid 5-HIAA levels were greater among pure restricter than bulimic anorexics (Kaye, Ebert, Gwirtsman, & Weiss, 1984). The presumed lower turnover of serotonin in the bulimic anorexics may reflect a diminished satiety mechanism which predisposes to binging.

Antagonism of serotonin appears to stimulate appetite. Cyproheptadine, a serotonin antagonist, will increase eating in normal people. Cyproheptadine has been used with moderate success to increase food intake in patients with anorexia nervosa (Halmi, Eckert, & Falk, 1982).

Opioids and Other Peptides

Increased hypothalamic opioid activity is associated with increased feeding in laboratory animals. In genetically obese rats and mice, increased feeding can be blocked by the opioid antagonist, naloxone (Margules, Moisset, Lewis, Shibuya, & Pert, 1978). High doses of naloxone reduced meal size in obese humans (Atkinson, 1982). Also, infusion of the opioid, beta-endorphin, in the medial hypothalamus of rats stimulates feeding behavior. The feeding response elicited by beta-endorphin is dependent on intact alpha-adrenergic receptors (Leibowitz & Hor, 1982). This dependency suggests that the alpha-adrenergic system is the final common pathway for the effects of beta-endorphin on feeding.

Opioid activity is increased in the CSF in underweight anorexics (Kaye, Pickar, Naber, & Ebert, 1982). The levels are restored to normal with weight recovery. The increased levels in the starved state may contribute to the propensity for binging behavior. Studies of opioid activity in the CSF have not yet been reported for normal-weight bulimics.

Other peptide neurotransmitters, such as cholecystokinin (Crawley, Rojas-Ramirez, & Mendelson, 1982) and bombesin (West, Williams, Braget, & Woods, 1982) can produce satiety in animals and humans. As yet, abnormalities of these peptides have not been shown in patients with eating disorders.

CONCLUSION

The neuroendocrine alterations of anorexia nervosa represent a combination of the effects of starvation and the effects of specific psychoneuroendocrine abnormalities. These latter abnormalities may provide clues for the etiology of anorexia nervosa. Peripheral hormonal abnormalities in gonadotropins, adrenocortical hormones and, perhaps, vasopressin may indicate neuroendocrine alterations specific to anorexia nervosa. Tracing the central nervous system origin of these abnormalities may provide insights into the factors which predispose individuals to anorexia nervosa.

Similarly, patients with bulimia manifest abnormalities in several hypothalamic-pituitary axes. Ovarian function, cortisol secretion, and thyrotropin responses to thyrotropin-releasing hormone can be abnormal in bulimics. Bulimics may have an exaggerated central nervous system response to the stress of food restriction that predisposes them to binge eating. A deficiency in serotonin secretion is a possible mechanism for this predisposition. Possible abnormalities in norepinephrine, opioids, or other neurotransmitters merit additional investigation.

REFERENCES

Atkinson, R. L. (1982). Naloxone decreased food intake in obese humans. *Journal of Clinical Endocrinology and Metabolism, 55,* 196-198.

Baranowska, B., Rozbicka, G., Jeske, W., & Abdel-Fattah, M. H. (1984). The role of endogenous opiates in the mechanism of inhibited luteinizing hormone (LH) secretion in women with anorexia nervosa: The effect of naloxone on LH, follicle-stimulating hormone, prolactin, and beta-endorphin secretion. *Journal of Clinical Endocrinology and Metabolism, 59,* 412-416.

Beitins, I. Z., Kowarski, A., Migeon, C. J., & Graham, C. G. (1975). Adrenal function in normal infants and in marasmus and kwashiorkor. *Journal of Pediatrics, 86,* 302-308.

Berelowitz, M., Szabo, M., Frohman, L. A., Firestone, S., Chu, L., & Hintz, R. L. (1981). Somatomedin-C mediated growth hormone negative feedback by effects on both the hypothalamus and the pituitary. *Science, 212,* 1279-1281.

Berger, M., Doerr, P., Lund, R., Bronisch, T., & Von Zerssen, D. (1982). Neuroendocrinological and neurophysiological studies in major depressive disorders: Are there biological markers for the endogenous subtype? *Biological Psychiatry, 17,* 1217-1242.

Berger, M., Krieg, C., & Pirke, K. M. (1982). Is the positive dexamethasone test in depressed patients a consequence of weight loss? *Neuroendocrinology Letters, 4,* 177.

Borgers, J. L. C., Uskavitch, D. R., Kaiser, D. L., Cronin, M. J., Evans, W. S., & Thorner, M. O. (1983). Human pancreatic growth hormone-releasing factor-40 (hpGRF-40) allows stimulation of GH release by TRH. *Endocrinology, 113,* 1519-1521.

Boyar, R. M., Hellman, L. D., Roffwarg, H., Katz, J., Zumoff, B., O'Connor, J., Bradlow, H. L., & Fukushima, D. K. (1977). Cortisol secretion and metabolism in anorexia nervosa. *New England Journal of Medicine, 269,* 190-193.

Boyar, R. M., Katz, J., Finkelstein, J. W., Kapen, S., Weiner, H., Weitzman, E. D., & Hellman, L. (1974). Anorexia nervosa: Immaturity of the 24-hour luteinizing hormone secretory pattern. *New England Journal of Medicine, 291*, 861-865.

Brown, G. M., Garfinkel, P. E., Jeuniewic, N., Modolfsky, H., & Stancer, H. C. (1977). Endocrine profiles in anorexia nervosa. In R. Vigersky (Ed.), *Anorexia nervosa* (pp. 123-135). New York: Raven Press.

Buvat, J., Lemaire, A., Buvat-Herbaut, M., Lepretre, P., & Fourlinnie, J. C. (1983). Psychoneuroendocrine investigations in 115 cases of female anorexia nervosa at the time of their maximum emaciation. *International Journal of Eating Disorders, 2*, 117-128.

Casper, R. C., Davis, J. M., & Pandey, C. N. (1977). The effect of nutritional status and weight changes in hypothalamic function tests in anorexia nervosa. In R. Vigersky (Ed.), *Anorexia nervosa* (pp. 137-140). New York: Raven Press.

Casper, R. C., Eckert, E. D., Halmi, K. A., Goldberg, S. C., & Davis, J. M. (1980). Bulimia: Its incidence and clinical importance in patients with anorexia nervosa. *Archives of General Psychiatry, 37*, 1030-1035.

Casper, R. C., & Frohman, L. A. (1982). Delayed TSH release in anorexia nervosa following injection of thyrotropin-releasing hormone (TRH). *Psychoneuroendocrinology, 7*, 59-68.

Chopra, I. S., Huang, T., Hurd, R. E., Beredo, A., & Solomon, D. H. (1984). A competitive ligand binding assay for measurement of thyroid hormone-binding inhibitor in serum and tissues. *Journal of Clinical Endocrinology and Metabolism, 58*, 619-628.

Clemmons, D. R., Klibanski, A., Underwood, L. E., McArthur, J. W., Ridgway, E. C., Beitins, I. Z., & Van Wyk, J. J. (1981). Reduction of plasma immunoreactive somatomedin C during fasting in humans. *Journal of Clinical Endocrinology Metabolism, 53*, 1247-1250.

Copeland, P. M., Herzog, D. B., Carr, D. B., Klibanski, A., & MacLaughlin, R. A. (in preparation). Effect of dexamethasone on meal-related cortisol and prolactin secretion in bulimics and normals.

Copeland, P. M., Ridgway, E., Pepose, M., & Herzog, D. B. (1984). Amenorrhea in bulimia. (Abstr. 122) First Int'l Conference on Eating Disorders, New York, April 1984.

Coppen, A., Harwood, J., & Wood, K. (1984). Depression, weight loss and the dexamethasone suppression test. *British Journal of Psychiatry, 145*, 88-90.

Crawley, J. N., Rojas-Ramirez, J. A., & Mendelson, W. B. (1982). The role of central and peripheral cholecystokinin in mediating appetitive behaviors. *Peptides, 3*, 535-538.

Croxson, M. S., & Ibbertson, H. K. (1977). Low serum triiodothyronine (T_3) and hypothyroidism in anorexia nervosa. *Journal of Clinical Endocrinology and Metabolism, 44*, 167-174.

Curran-Celentano, J., Erdman, J. W., Nelson, R. A., & Grater, S. J. E. (1984). Thyroid hormone in anorexia nervosa with and without hypercarotenemia. (Abstr. 11) First Int'l Conference on Eating Disorders, New York, April 1984.

DeRuyter, H., Burman, K. D., Wartofsky, L., & Smallridge, R. C. (1984). Thyrotropin secretion in starved rats is enhanced by somatostatin antiserum. *Hormone and Metabolic Research, 16*, 92-96.

Doerr, P., Fichter, M., Pirke, K. M., & Lund, R. (1980). Relationship between weight gain and hypothalamic-pituitary-adrenal function in patients with anorexia nervosa. *Journal of Steroid Biochemistry, 13*, 529-537.

Edelstein, C. K., Roy-Byrne, P., Fawzy, F. I., & Dornfield, L. (1983). Effects of weight loss on the dexamethasone suppression test. *American Journal of Psychiatry, 104*, 338-341.

Fang, V. S., Tricou, B. J., Robertson, A., & Meltzer, H. Y. (1981). Plasma ACTH and cortisol levels in depressed patients: Relation to dexamethasone suppression test. *Life Science, 29*, 931-938.

Fehm, H. L., Klein, E., Holl, R., & Voigt, K. H. (1984). Evidence for extrapituitary mechanisms mediating the morning peak of plasma cortisol in man. *Journal of Clinical Endocrinology and Metabolism, 58*, 410-414.

Frankel, R. J., & Jenkins, J. S. (1975). Hypothalamic-pituitary function in anorexia nervosa. *Acta Endocrinologica, 78*, 209-221.

Fries, H. (1977). Studies on secondary amenorrhea, anorectic behavior, and body-image perception: Importance for the early recognition of anorexia nervosa. In R. Vigersky (Ed.), *Anorexia nervosa* (pp. 163-176). New York: Raven Press.

Frisch, R. E., & McArthur, J. W. (1974). Menstrual cycles: Fatness as a determinant of minimum weight for height necessary for their maintenance or onset. *Science, 185*, 949-951.
Frumar, A. M., Meldrum, D. R., Judd, H. L. (1979). Hypercarotenemia in hypothalamic amenorrhea. *Fertility and Sterility, 32*, 261-264.
Garfinkel, P. E., Moldofsky, H., & Garner, D. M. (1980). The heterogeneity of anorexia nervosa. *Archives of General Psychiatry, 37*, 1036-1040.
Gerner, R. H., & Gwirtsman, H. E. (1981). Abnormalities of dexamethasone suppression test and urinary MHPG in anorexia nervosa. *American Journal of Psychiatry, 138*, 650-653.
Gold, P. W., Kaye, W., Robertson, G. L., & Ebert, M. (1983). Abnormalities in plasma and cerebrospinal-fluid arginine vasopressin in patients with anorexia nervosa. *New England Journal of Medicine, 308*, 1117-1123.
Gold, M. S., Pottash, A. L. C., Sweeney, D. R., Martin, D. M., & Davies, R. K. (1980). Further evidence of hypothalamic-pituitary dysfunction in anorexia nervosa. *American Journal of Psychiatry, 137*, 101-102.
Grossman, A., Moult, P. F. A., McIntyre, H., et al. (1982). Opiate mediation of amenorrhea in hyperprolactinaemia and in weight loss-related amenorrhea. *Clinical Endocrinology, 17*, 379-388.
Gwirtsman, J. E., & Gerner, R. H. (1981). Neurochemical abnormalities in anorexia nervosa: Similarities to affective disorders. *Biological Psychiatry, 16*, 991-995.
Gwirtsman, H. E., Roy-Byrne, P., Yager, J., & Gerner, R. H. (1983). Neuroendocrine abnormalities in bulimia. *American Journal of Psychiatry, 140*, 559-563.
Halmi, K. A., Eckert, E., & Falk, J. R. (1982). Cyproheptadine for anorexia nervosa. *Lancet, 1*, 1357-1358.
Halmi, K. A., & Falk, J. R. (1983). Behavioral and dietary discriminators of menstrual function in anorexia nervosa. In P. L. Darby, P. E. Garfinkel, D. M. Garner, & D. V. Coscina (Eds.), *Anorexia nervosa: Recent developments in research* (pp. 323-329). New York: Alan R. Liss.
Halmi, K. A., Owen, W. P., Lasley, E., & Stokes, P. (1983). Dopaminergic regulation in anorexia nervosa. *International Journal of Eating Disorders, 2*, 129-133.
Hintz, R. L., Suskind, R., Amatayakul, K. Thanangkul, O., & Olson, R. (1976). Plasma somatomedin and growth hormone values in children with protein-calorie malnutrition. *Journal of Pediatrics, 92*, 153-156.
Hsu, L. K. G., Crisp, A. H., & Harding, B. (1979). Outcome of anorexia nervosa. *Lancet, 1*, 61-65.
Hudson, J. I., Pope, H. G., Jonas, J. M., Laffer, P. S., Hudson, M. S., & Melby, J. C. (1983). Hypothalamic-pituitary-adrenal axis hyperactivity in bulimia. *Psychiatry Research, 8*, 111-117.
Ishizuka, B., Quigley, M. E., & Yen, S. S. C. (1983). Pituitary hormone release in response to food ingestion: Evidence for neuroendocrine signals from gut to brain. *Journal of Clinical Endocrinology and Metabolism, 57*, 1111-1116.
Katz, J. L., Boyar, R., Roffwarg, H., & Weiner, H. (1978). Weight and circadian luteinizing hormone secretory pattern in anorexia nervosa. *Psychosomatic Medicine, 40*, 547-567.
Kaye, W. H., Ebert, M. H., Gwirtsman, H. E., & Weiss, S. R. (1984). Differences in brain serotonergic metabolism between nonbulimic and bulimic patients with anorexia nervosa. *American Journal of Psychiatry, 141*, 1598-1601.
Kaye, W. H., Ebert, M. H., Raleigh, M., & Lake, C. R. (1984). Abnormalities in CNS monoamine metabolism in anorexia nervosa. *Archives of General Psychiatry, 41*, 350-355.
Kaye, W. H., & Gold, P. W. Personal communication. (1984).
Kaye, W. H., Gwirtsman, H. E., George, E. T., & Ebert, M. H. (1984). Altered energy efficiency may affect weight maintenance in anorexia nervosa. (Abstr. 140) First Int'l Conference on Eating Disorders, New York, April 1984.
Kaye, W. H., Gwirtsman, H. E., Jimerson, D. C., Ebert, M. H., Lake, C. R., & George T. (1984). Altered adrenergic functional activity found in underweight and weight recovered anorectics. (Abstr. 139) First Int'l Conference on Eating Disorders, New York, April 1984.
Kaye, W. H., Pickar, D., Naber, D., & Ebert, M. H. (1982). Cerebrospinal fluid opioid activity in anorexia nervosa. *American Journal of Psychiatry, 139*, 643-645.
Kemmann, E., Pasquale, S. A., & Skaf, R. (1983). Amenorrhea associated with carotenemia. *Journal of the American Medical Association, 249*, 926-929.

Keys, A., Brozek, J., Henschel, A., Mickelson, O., & Taylor, H. L. (1950). *The biology of human starvation*. Minneapolis: University of Minnesota Press.
Leibowitz, S. F. (1980). Neurochemical systems of the hypothalamus: Control of feeding and drinking behavior and water-electrolyte excretion. In P. J. Morgane & J. Panskepp (Eds.), *Behavioral studies of the hypothalamus* (pp. 299-437). New York: Marcel Dekker.
Leibowitz, S. F. (1984). Noradrenergic function in the medial hypothalamus: Potential relation to anorexia nervosa and bulimia. In K. M. Pirke & D. Ploog (Eds.), *The psychobiology of anorexia nervosa*. Berlin: Springer-Verlag, pp. 35-45.
Leibowitz, S. F., & Hor, L. (1982). Endorphinergic and α-noradrenergic systems in the paraventricular nucleus: Effects on eating behavior. *Peptides, 3*, 421-428.
Leslie, R. D. G., Isaacs, A. J., Gomez, J., Raggatt, P. R., & Bayliss, R. (1978). Hypothalamo-pituitary-thyroid function in anorexia nervosa: Influence of weight gain. *British Medical Journal, 2*, 256-258.
Margules, D. L., Moisset, B., Lewis, M. J., Shibuya, H., & Pert, C. B. (1978). Beta-endorphin is associated with overeating in genetically obese mice (ob/ob) and rats (fa/fa). *Science, 202*, 988-991.
Marshall, J. C., & Fraser, T. R. (1971). Amenorrhea in anorexia nervosa: Assessment and treatment with clomiphene citrate. *British Medical Journal, 4*, 590-592.
Marshall, J. C., & Kelch, R. P. (1979). Low dose pulsatile gonadotropin-releasing hormone in anorexia nervosa: A model of human pubertal development. *Journal of Clinical Endocrinology and Metabolism, 49*, 712-718.
Mitchell, J. E., & Bantle, J. P. (1983). Metabolic and endocrine investigations in women of normal weight with the bulimia syndrome. *Biological Psychiatry, 18*, 355-365.
Moore, R., & Mills, I. H. (1979). Serum T_3 and T_4 levels in patients with anorexia nervosa showing transient hyperthyroidism during weight gain. *Clinical Endocrinology, 10*, 443-449.
Moshang, T., Jr., Parks, J. S., Baker, L., Vaid, V., Utiger, R. D., Bongiovanni, A. M., & Snyder, P. J. (1975). Low serum triiodothyronine in patients with anorexia nervosa. *Journal of Clinical Endocrinology and Metabolism, 40*, 470-473.
Moshang, T., Jr., & Utiger, R. D. (1977). Low triiodothyronine euthyroidism in anorexia nervosa. In R. Vigersky (Ed.), *Anorexia nervosa* (pp. 263-270). New York: Raven Press.
Nemeroff, C. B., Widerlöv, E., Bissette, G., Walléns, H., Karlsson, I., Eklund, K., Kilts, C. D., Loosen, P. T., & Vale, W. (1984). Elevated concentration of CSF corticotropin-releasing factor-like immunoreactivity in depressed patients. *Science, 226*, 1342-1344.
Oliver, M. A. (1984). *Caffeine consumption in anorexia nervosa*. Unpublished doctoral dissertation. MCH Institute of Health Professions.
Palmer, R. L., Crisp, A. H., Mackinnon, P. C. B., Franklin, M., Bonnar, J., & Wheeler, M. (1975). Pituitary sensitivity to 50 μg LH/FSH-RH in subjects with anorexia nervosa in acute and recovery stages. *British Medical Journal, 1*, 179-182.
Perloff, W. H., Lasche, E. M., Nodine, J. H., Schneebert, N. G., & Vieillard, C. B. (1954). The starvation state and functional hypopituitarism. *Journal of the American Medical Association, 155*, 1307-1313.
Pertschuk, M. J., Crosby, L. O., Mullen, J. L. (1983). Nonlinearity of weight gain and nutrition intake in anorexia nervosa. In P. L. Darby, P. E. Garfinkel, D. M. Garner, & D. V. Coscina (Eds.), *Anorexia nervosa: Recent developments in research* (pp. 301-310). New York: Alan R. Liss.
Phillips, L. S., & Vassilopoulou-Sellin, R. (1979). Nutritional regulation of somatomedin. *American Journal of Clinical Nutrition, 32*, 1082-1096.
Pope, H. G., Hudson, J. L., Jonas, J. M., & Yurgelun-Todd, D. (1983). Bulimia treated with imipramine: A placebo-controlled double-blind study. *American Journal of Psychiatry, 140*, 554-558.
Reppert, S. M., Artman, H., Swami-Nathan, S., & Fisher, D. A. (1981). Vasopressin exhibits a daily rhythm in CSF but not in blood. *Science, 213*, 1256-1257.
Rigotti, N. A., Nussbaum, S. R., Herzog, D. B., & Neer, R. M. (1984). Osteoporosis in women with anorexia nervosa. *New England Journal of Medicine, 311*, 1601-1606.
Russell, G. F. M. (1984). Bulimia nervosa. First Int'l. Conference on Eating Disorders, New York, April 1984.
Saleh, J. W., & Lebwohl, P. (1980). Metoclopramide-induced gastric emptying in patients with

anorexia nervosa. *American Journal of Gastroenterology, 74*, 127-132.

Sherman, D. M., Halmi, K. A., & Zamudio, R. (1975). LH and FSH response to gonadotropin-releasing hormone in anorexia nervosa: Effect of nutritional rehabilitation. *Journal of Clinical Endocrinology and Metabolism, 41*, 135-142.

Silverman, J. A. (1983). Anorexia nervosa: Clinical and metabolic observations. *International Journal of Eating Disorders, 2*, 159-166.

Smith, S. R., Bledsoe, T., & Chhetri, M. K. (1975). Cortisol metabolism and the pituitary-adrenal axis in adults with protein-calorie malnutrition. *Journal of Clinical Endocrinology and Metabolism, 40*, 43-52.

Tannenbaum, G. S., Guyda, H. J., & Posner, P. I. (1983). Insulin-like growth factors: A role in growth hormone negative feedback and body weight regulation via brain. *Science, 220*, 77-79.

Vigersky, R. A., Andersen, A. E., Thompson, R. H., & Loriaux, D. L. (1977). Hypothalamic dysfunction in secondary amenorrhea associated with simple weight loss. *New England Journal of Medicine, 297*, 1141-1145.

Vigersky, R. A., & Loriaux, D. L. (1977). Anorexia nervosa as a model of hypothalamic dysfunction. In R. A. Vigersky (Ed.), *Anorexia nervosa* (pp. 109-121). New York: Raven Press.

Walsh, B. T., Katz, J. L., Levin, J., Kream, J., Fukushima, K. K., Hellman, L. D., Weiner, H., & Zumoff, B. (1978). Adrenal activity in anorexia nervosa. *Psychosomatic Medicine, 40*, 499-506.

Walsh, B. T., Katz, J. L., Levin, J., et al. (1981). The production rate of cortisol declines during recovery from anorexia nervosa. *Journal of Clinical Endocrinology and Metabolism, 53*, 203-205.

Warren, M. P. (1983). Effects of undernutrition on reproductive function in the human. *Endocrine Reviews, 4*, 363-377.

Warren, M. P., & VandeWeile, R. L. (1975). Clinical and metabolic features of anorexia nervosa. *American Journal of Obstetrics and Gynecology, 117*, 435-449.

Wartofsky, L., & Burman, K. D. (1982). Alterations in thyroid function in patients with systemic illness: The "euthyroid sick syndrome." *Endocrine Reviews, 3*, 164-217.

West, D. B., Williams, R. H., Braget, D. J., & Woods, S. C. (1982). Bombesin reduces food intake of normal and hypothalamically obese rats and lowers body weight when given chronically. *Peptides, 3*, 61-67.

Wheeler, M. J., Crisp, A. H., Hsu, L. K. G., & Chen, C. N. (1983). Reproductive hormone changes during weight gain in male anorectics. *Clinical Endocrinology, 18*, 423-429.

Zumoff, B., Walsh, B. T., Katz, J. L., et al. (1983). Subnormal plasma deyhydroisoandrosterone to cortisol ratio in anorexia nervosa: A second hormonal parameter of ontogenic regression. *Journal of Clinical Endocrinology and Metabolism, 56*, 668-672.

Chapter 4

Biological Treatments of Eating Disorders

*Harrison Pope and
James Hudson*

BACKGROUND: THE NEED FOR AN EFFECTIVE THERAPY

Many therapeutic techniques—psychodynamic, familial, group, and behavioral—have been proposed for anorexia nervosa and bulimia, and each has been reported effective in certain patients. However, none has yet been shown to be effective in a *controlled* study, that is, a study which compares one group of patients receiving the therapy to a matched control group which receives a "placebo" treatment. Since anorexia nervosa and bulimia can both remit spontaneously (Hsu, 1980; Pope & Hudson, 1984), such a control group is required to demonstrate that improvement with a given therapy is significantly greater than that which might occur simply as a result of the natural course of the illness.

For many treatment techniques, even the number of available uncontrolled studies remains small. We have been unable to find any formal study—controlled or uncontrolled—of any specific psychodynamic therapy for either anorexia nervosa or bulimia. One large uncontrolled study of family therapy of anorexia nervosa has appeared, reporting excellent results (Liebman, Minuchin, & Baker, 1974; Minuchin, Rosman, & Baker, 1978). However, many of the patients studied may have had a good prognosis to begin with (Pope & Hudson, 1984), some had not lost enough weight to meet the American Psychiatric Association's (1980) criteria for anorexia nervosa, and about half had simultaneously received hospital treatment, which has been reported to produce good short-term results by itself (Pierloot, Vandereycken, & Verhaest, 1982; Russell, 1981). Thus it is difficult to ascertain how much of the observed improvement was attributable to the family therapy itself, and how much to other factors. Similarly, two uncontrolled studies of group therapy (Boskind-Lodahl & White, 1978; White & Boskind-White, 1981), both with bulimics, have also reported good results, but were retrospective and only partially quantitative. Also, the patients studied may have been unusually eager to change their behavior (Pope & Hudson, 1984), which makes it difficult to evaluate the results in the absence of a control group.

Behavior therapy of anorexia nervosa has generated four controlled studies to date (Eckert, Goldberg, Halmi, Casper, & Davis, 1979; Garfinkel, Moldofsky, & Garner, 1977; Pertschuk, 1977; Wulliemier, Rossel, & Sinclair, 1975); the first of these reported a slight advantage for behavior therapy (Wulliemier et al.; 1975), but three subsequent larger studies (Eckert et al., 1979; Garfinkel et al., 1977; Pertschuk, 1977)—one employing two-to-three-year follow-up—failed to demonstrate any advantage of behavior therapy over ordinary hospital treatment. No controlled studies of behavior therapy of bulimia are yet available; a single uncontrolled study (Fairburn, 1981) reported excellent results in nine patients, but represents only a retrospective observation.

In summary, most research on treatment of the eating disorders remains inconclusive. In fact, a recent review of outcome studies of anorexia nervosa (Agras & Kraemer, 1984) concluded that there has been no significant advance in its treatment, demonstrable in improved outcome, in the past 50 years! Given the failure of years of research to produce improved treatment, it is perhaps not surprising that recent biological therapies have aroused increasing interest. Although many of the available biological studies are preliminary, a review suggests that they may offer the possibility of a significant advance in the treatment of eating disorders. The following review is not exhaustive, but emphasizes those treatments which have been extensively studied or which have shown promise in initial studies.

TWO EARLIER BIOLOGICAL THERAPIES

Two drugs—cyproheptadine (Periactin) for anorexia nervosa and phenytoin (Dilantin) for bulimia—represented the first biological treatments to be subjected to controlled trials. Both have produced equivocal results.

Cyproheptadine is an appetite stimulant. Although there does not seem to be any clear evidence in the literature that patients with anorexia nervosa *lack* an appetite (more likely, they have a phobia-like fear of eating and gaining weight [Crisp & Bhat, 1982]), various researchers have conjectured that appetite stimulation might improve treatment of the disorder. The first controlled study of cyproheptadine, in Peru, found that 10 anorexic patients given cyproheptadine gained significantly more weight than 10 who received inert placebo pills (Zubiate, 1970). Since this study was both placebo-controlled and blind, its results appeared promising. But two larger subsequent studies in the United States (Goldberg, Halmi, Eckert, Casper, & Davis, 1979; Vigersky & Loriaux, 1977) — also placebo-controlled and blind — have both failed to find cyproheptadine effective. Thus, the evidence currently weighs against cyproheptadine. However, another controlled study, using higher doses of cyproheptadine than had previously been given, has tentatively reported more promising results (Halmi, 1982).

When all the facts are in, it may be that cyproheptadine will prove at least partially effective for some cases of anorexia nervosa. However, it seems unlikely that the drug will revolutionize treatment; even if it does help to promote weight gain for some anorexic patients, an appetite stimulant would seem unlikely to allay most patients' fears of eating and weight gain, or the depression which is almost ubiquitous in anorexia nervosa (Hendren, 1983). Also, it should be remembered that 50% of anorexic patients display bulimic symptoms (Garfinkel, Moldofsky, & Garner, 1980; Casper, Eckert, Halmi, Goldberg, & Davis, 1980); an appetite stimulant might exacerbate, rather than reduce, the urge to binge. Thus, for the present, it seems best to remain skeptical of cyproheptadine, pending further data.

Phenytoin, by contrast, is an anticonvulsant. It was proposed as a treatment for bulimia on the theory that eating binges might represent a form of seizure disorder. The compulsive, "automatic" nature of binge eating resembles the automatic behavior seen in psychomotor epilepsy, and some observers felt that they could perceive specific abnormalities on the electroencephalograms of bulimic patients (Green & Rau, 1974). Thus phenytoin — a drug with very few side effects in most individuals — seemed appropriate to try. The early results were spectacular: in an initial study, nine of 10 bulimic patients responded (Green & Rau, 1974). But the study was nonblind and uncontrolled; as discussed earlier, uncontrolled reports must be viewed with great caution. In this case, such skepticism proved well-founded: in an excellent placebo-controlled double-blind study (Wermuth, Davis, Hollister, & Stunkard, 1977) stimulated by the earlier findings, only 42% of 19 patients showed a moderate or marked response to phenytoin, and of four marked responders followed long-term, two relapsed despite continuing to take the drug. Furthermore, no correlation was found between EEG abnormalities and response to phenytoin in this study. Perhaps as a result of these unpromising findings, no further studies of phenytoin have appeared, to our knowledge, in the six years since the double-blind study was published. Between 1975 and the present, we have tried phenytoin in about 10 bulimic patients without success (Pope & Hudson, 1984).

THE MAJOR AFFECTIVE DISORDER THEORY

An emerging biological theory of the eating disorders, supported by an increasing body of evidence, proposes that both anorexia nervosa and bulimia may be closely related to major affective disorder. Major affective disorder is a group of severe disorders of mood, including manic depressive illness (bipolar disorder) and major depression (American Psychiatric Association, 1980). Major affective disorder is now widely recognized as a biological illness (or family of illnesses): It displays a strong hereditary component (Mendlewicz & Rainer, 1977; Nurnberger & Gershon, 1982; Pope & Hudson, 1984), appears to be associated with a number of biochemical abnormalities demonstrable on laboratory tests (Carroll, Feinberg, Greden, et al., 1981; Carter, Reveley, Sandler, et al., 1980; Kirkegaard, 1981; Kupfer, Foster, Coble, et al., 1978; Pope & Hudson, 1984), and responds to a number of biological treatments, including lithium carbonate (Goodwin, 1979) and antidepressant medications (Klein, Gittelman, Quitkin, et al., 1980). The depression seen in major affective disorder is thus quite different from ordinary "situational" or "reactive" depression: The former is hereditary, probably unrelated to environmental events, and readily treatable with medications; the latter presumably lacks a genetic or biochemical basis, generally occurs in response to environmental stresses, and usually does not respond to antidepressants.

For those who are unfamiliar with antidepressant medications, it is important to emphasize this final point: Most antidepressant drugs have essentially no effect in normal individuals or in ordinary "situational" depressions. For example, if a normal individual were to take imipramine (Tofranil), amitriptyline (Elavil), or a similar antidepressant for several weeks, he or she would notice no euphoric or stimulant effect; all that would likely be noticeable would be a dry mouth, some constipation, and perhaps some lightheadedness or sleepiness. On the other hand, if an individual with major depression were to take such a drug, dramatic relief of the symptoms would typically occur after approximately three weeks of treatment.

In other words, antidepressants are somewhat analogous to antibiotics: If a healthy person takes penicillin, he or she feels no better; but if an individual with pneumonia takes penicillin, pronounced relief may occur. The fact that antidepressants are effective in major depression, but ineffective in normal individuals or in most individuals with situational depressions, is further evidence that major depression is a biological disorder, and that drug treatment perhaps corrects an underlying "chemical imbalance." The drug does *not* merely "cover over" the depression with a euphoric or tranquilizing effect.

In summary, then, major affective disorder has been extensively studied;

portions of its biochemistry and genetics are understood, and many specific treatments for it have been discovered. If it were found that the eating disorders were closely related to major affective disorder, we could promptly bring a great deal of existing theoretical and practical knowledge to bear on their treatment. What is the evidence?

Five lines of evidence suggest a link between the eating disorders and major affective disorder. First, the symptoms of major depression, and sometimes even the symptoms of manic depressive illness, are frequently reported in anorexia nervosa and bulimia (Barcai, 1977; Cantwell, Sturzenberger, Burroughs, Salkin, & Green, 1977; Casper et al., 1980; Eckert, Goldberg, & Halmi, 1982; Garfinkel et al., 1980; Hendren, 1983; Hudson, Pope, Jonas, et al., 1983c; Kron, Katz, Gorsynski, & Weiner, 1978; Pope & Hudson, 1984). In the past, it was often conjectured that depressive symptoms might simply be a reaction to the eating disorder itself: patients with anorexia nervosa and bulimia would seem bound to be depressed by their symptoms. However, data from our laboratory (Hudson et al., 1983c) and others suggest that this theory cannot explain the observations: About half of our anorexic and bulimic patients were found to have developed major depression at least one year *before* the onset of their eating disorder symptoms.

A second line of evidence — outcome studies — reinforces this conclusion: Anorexic patients have often been found to display depressive symptoms on follow-up, even at times when their eating disorder was in remission (Cantwell et al., 1977; Hsu, Crisp, & Harding, 1979; Hudson et al., 1983c; Pertschuk, 1977). Since this depression cannot easily be explained as a reaction to weight loss or other anorexic symptoms, it again suggests a possible relationship between the eating disorders and major affective disorder.

Third, compelling evidence is presented by a number of family history studies (Cantwell et al., 1977; Gershon, Hamovit, Schreiber, et al., 1982; Hudson, Pope, Jonas, et al., 1983a; Winokur, March, & Mendels, 1980). These studies have all found that anorexic and bulimic patients frequently have a positive family history of major depression and/or bipolar disorder. For example, in a recent study from our group (Hudson et al., 1983a), the prevalence of major affective disorder in the first-degree relatives of anorexic and bulimic patients was not significantly different from that found in the families of manic depressive patients, but was much greater than that found in the families of comparison groups of patients with schizophrenia and with borderline personality disorder. It is very difficult to explain this finding other than with the hypothesis that anorexia nervosa and bulimia are closely related to major affective disorder.

The phenomenologic, follow-up, and genetic evidence receives further support from a fourth, more tentative body of data: laboratory studies. Two tests — the dexamethasone suppression test (Carroll et al., 1981) and the thyrotropin-releasing hormone stimulation test (Kirkegaard, 1981)—have both been reported to be positive in many patients with major affective disorder, but infrequently positive in medically healthy patients with psychiatric disorders unrelated to major affective disorder. Interestingly, both of these tests are also positive in bulimia (Hudson, Pope, Jonas, et al., 1983b; Roy-Byrne, Gwirtsman, Yager, et al., 1982) with about the same frequency as in major depression. The bulk of these findings cannot be explained by the stress of binge eating or by body weight (since the bulimic patients studied were all within ±15% of normal weight) (Hudson et al., 1983b). If further study upholds the specificity of these tests, the findings would again favor the possibility that bulimia may be linked to major affective disorder.

Comparable laboratory studies of anorexia nervosa are less reliable, because weight loss itself may affect the test results (Carroll et al., 1981; Smith, Bledsoe, & Chetri, 1975). However, even in anorexic patients, the laboratory findings cannot be entirely explained on the basis of weight loss (Walsh et al., 1981).

Perhaps most intriguing is the fifth line of evidence: Anorexia nervosa and bulimia appear to respond to the same medications that are effective in the treatment of major affective disorder. This will be presented in detail in the section below; in brief, the treatment response findings support the findings of the four previous indices listed above.

Thus, in contrast to the often limited empirical data available to support many other popular theories of the eating disorders, the major affective disorder theory rests on the internally consistent findings of five lines of validating evidence: phenomenology, follow-up, family history, laboratory tests, and treatment response.

ANTIDEPRESSANT TREATMENT OF ANOREXIA NERVOSA

Given the above findings, one might expect to find a sizable literature on treatment of anorexia nervosa with antidepressants. Surprisingly, although there exist a number of uncontrolled reports of successful treatment with tricyclic antidepressants (Mills, 1976; Moore, 1977; Needleman & Waber, 1976, 1977; White & Schnaultz, 1977), such as imipramine and amitriptyline, there exists only one controlled study, using 50 milligrams per day of the antidepressant clomipramine—and this study found negative results (Lacey & Crisp, 1980).

Upon review, however, the reasons for this seem clear. Most of the studies tried antidepressant drugs for their appetite-stimulating properties, rather than for their antidepressant properties. As a result, low doses of antidepressants— well below the range required for a true antidepressant effect—were generally used. This may account for the failure of clomipramine in the controlled study; with clomipramine and similar tricyclic antidepressants, doses of three to four milligrams per kilogram of body weight are frequently required to produce an antidepressant effect, particularly in younger patients, who metabolize the drugs rapidly (Klein et al., 1980). Thus, an anorexic patient weighing only 88 pounds might require as much as 120-160 milligrams per day of a tricyclic antidepressant to achieve adequate antidepressant blood levels. To our knowledge, a controlled study using such doses has not yet been performed; the results would be of great interest.

There is another problem with tricyclic antidepressants: Their side effects may often be quite annoying, particularly in an emaciated patient. In our experience, anticholinergic side effects, such as dry mouth, blurred vision, constipation, and memory lapses, have been particularly bothersome to anorexic patients, making adequate blood levels difficult to achieve (Pope & Hudson, 1984). This may limit the potential usefulness of the tricyclics in anorexia nervosa even though, on theoretical grounds, we might predict that they would be effective.

Fortunately, two antidepressant medications unrelated to tricyclics, called trazodone (Desyrel) and tranylcypromine (Parnate), create much less pronounced anticholinergic side effects. This makes it much easier for the patient to raise the dose to an adequate level. In our initial experience with six anorexic patients, previously resistant to all other treatment, three displayed a moderate or marked response to trazodone or tranylcypromine within eight weeks; not only did they display a 15%-40% increase in body weight, but they described a marked decrease in their fears of eating and preoccupation with weight. This observation, although encouraging, is of course uncontrolled and thus subject to the same *caveats* raised earlier in this review. We have now initiated a controlled and blind study with these agents in anorexia nervosa in order to address the issue in a more rigorous manner.

One other finding is of interest: Lithium carbonate, a drug used primarily to treat manic depressive illness and recurrent major depression, may also be effective in anorexia nervosa. Encouraged by the dramatic results reported in an uncontrolled trial with two anorexic patients (Barcai, 1977), researchers at the National Institute of Mental Health recently initiated a placebo-controlled double-blind study of lithium in anorexia nervosa (Gross, Ebert, & Faden, 1981). The methodology was sound, and the results were encouraging—the study found a statistically significant difference between the weight gain of eight anorexic patients on lithium as compared to eight patients on placebo. The lithium-treated patients also improved on other measures of eating behavior, and these differences became apparent after only three to four weeks of treatment. However, the findings must be interpreted with caution, since the patients in the lithium group tended to weigh more and eat more than the placebo patients even *before* they began to take lithium. Thus, further studies with lithium are needed to assess its usefulness in anorexia nervosa.

In summary, preliminary results with antidepressants and lithium carbonate in anorexia nervosa appear encouraging, particularly in view of the fact that improvement is described within a matter of weeks, rather than after months or years as in some other treatments. However, additional blind and controlled studies, using other antidepressant agents, larger patient samples, and longer observation periods, are required to test more thoroughly the effectiveness of these agents.

ANTIDEPRESSANT TREATMENT OF BULIMIA

Successful treatment of bulimia with antidepressants was first reported in 1978 by Rich, who described a woman whose binge eating disappeared upon treatment with phenelzine, reappeared when phenelzine was withdrawn, and again remitted when phenelzine was resumed. However, with the exception of one other anecdotal report (Shader, 1982), no other observations of antidepressant treatment in bulimia appeared until 1982, when our group published an uncontrolled study of eight patients (Pope & Hudson, 1982). Six of these patients, who had displayed chronic bulimic symptoms for as much as four years prior to treatment, displayed a moderate (greater than 50%) or marked (greater than 90%) reduction in their frequency of binging after a few weeks of treatment with tricyclic antidepressants. Although the study was uncontrolled, the rapid improvement in these patients, some of whom had failed to control their bulimia despite many previous courses of therapy, suggested that antidepressants might represent a significant advance in the treatment of the disorder.

Only two months later, even more impressive results were reported from another center: Walsh and his colleagues described complete or nearly complete remissions of bulimic symptoms in six patients treated with antidepressants of the monoamine oxidase inhibitor family (Walsh, Stewart, Wright, et al., 1982). Although again uncontrolled, the observations seemed unlikely to be due to chance: the six women had been binge eating for three to 15 years, some as often as five times a day, before treatment. The disappearance of such longstanding symptoms after a few weeks of drug treatment seems most unlikely to be attributable to a coincidental spontaneous remission.

Both in our study and the study of Walsh and colleagues, the antidepressants seemed to do much more than reduce the number of binges. Both personal reports (Pope & Hudson, 1982) and test scores (Walsh et al., 1982) revealed a marked decrease in preoccupation with food, obsessions about body weight, depression, and other symptoms characteristic of the bulimic syndrome.

In early 1983, three further uncontrolled reports (Jonas, Hudson, & Pope, 1983; Mendels, 1983; Roy-Byrne, Gwirtsman, Edelstein, et al., 1983), all reporting improvement in some or all of the patients treated, have appeared. The rapid accumulation of positive findings in the literature has strengthened the case for antidepressant treatment of bulimia, but has also highlighted the need for controlled studies. Fortunately, five such studies have now appeared.

The first of these (Sabine, Yonace, Farrington, et al., 1983), in England, used a placebo-controlled, double-blind design to test the antidepressant drug mianserin in bulimia. Surprisingly, *both* the mianserin group *and* the placebo group improved markedly on a number of measures, including measures of depression, anxiety, eating attitudes, and a "bulimia rating scale." Despite this improvement, the actual frequency of binges did not change in either of the groups.

It is difficult to interpret the curious results obtained in this study. The marked improvement in the placebo group suggests that the placebo patients were benefited in some way simply by their periodic encounters with the members of the research group. The researchers stress that their contact did not in any way resemble "insight-directed psychotherapy," and conjecture that the mere act of seeking help for a distressing condition may have contributed to the placebo patients' improvement. This contrasts sharply with the reports of bulimic patients in other studies: They often describe multiple attempts at many different types of therapy, usually with repeated failure to control their symptoms (Pope & Hudson, 1984). Thus, the patients in the mianserin-placebo study may have represented an unusual group, much more responsive to brief professional contact than is ordinarily described.

There remains the question of why binge frequency did not improve in either group, despite the improvement on several related indices. If antidepressants are effective in bulimia, why did mianserin not reduce the binging behavior itself?

Several possibilities present themselves. First, the dose of mianserin used — 60 mg a day — was smaller than that required by some other investigators to produce an antidepressant effect. A recent American study, for example, required doses of up to 150 mg a day to relieve depressive symptoms (McGrath, Quitkin, Stewart, et al., 1981).

Second, even allowing that 60 mg a day were an adequate dose, it is not clear that patients with frequent self-induced vomiting or laxative abuse would retain the full dose of the drug. Since blood levels of mianserin were not measured, there is no way to exclude this possibility.

Third, assuming that the dose was adequate and that patients were not inadvertently purging some or all of the medication, it may be that mianserin is simply less effective in bulimia than are tricyclic antidepressants or monoamine oxidase inhibitors. But it would be difficult to assess this possibility without a further study, using higher doses of mianserin, providing some assurance that the drug was not lost through purging, and—most important—using subjects with sufficiently severe and refractory cases of bulimia that they would be unlikely to improve merely on the basis of a few contacts with the research team and a dose of placebo pills! Pending such data, it is perhaps premature to decide for or against the effectiveness of mianserin.

In some ways, the mianserin results are not very relevant to American readers, since the drug is not available in this country; the Food and Drug Administration is apparently still awaiting further evidence of its effectiveness and safety. However, our group has recently published a placebo-controlled, double-blind study (Pope, Hudson, Jonas, et al., 1983) of bulimic patients, using imipramine, a long-established antidepressant that has been available in this country for more than 25 years. Since imipramine is a readily available drug, widely used in American psychiatric practice, we will present the results of this study in somewhat greater detail.

We recruited 22 subjects who met the American Psychiatric Association's DSM-III (1980) criteria for bulimia. In addition we required that each subject have been ill for at least one year, and currently be experiencing at least two binges per week, each followed by vomiting or laxative abuse. But these were only minimum criteria; the subjects actually averaged about 1.4 binges per *day*, and they displayed an average duration of illness of more than seven years; some had been binge eating for as long as 14 or 16 years. Most had tried many previous forms of therapy, including psychotherapy, group therapy, behavior therapy, and in some cases, even hospitalization—all with no lasting effect. In short, the subjects suffered from severe and refractory cases of bulimia—seemingly unlikely to improve after a few office visits, or with a few placebo pills.

The subjects were randomized to treatment with imipramine (11 subjects) or placebo (11 subjects). Identical capsules containing 50 milligrams of imipramine or inert placebo were given to each subject, with instructions to gradually raise the dose to four capsules at bedtime. Neither the subjects nor the investigators were aware of whether imipramine or placebo was being administered. A research assistant, also blind to the treatment received, rated each subject at the beginning of the study and after two, four, and six weeks, using a number of indices: frequency of binges, the Hamilton Depression Rating Scale (Hamilton, 1960) intensity of binges, preoccupation with food, self-control with relation to food, and subjective overall improvement.

During the six weeks of the study, three subjects had to be withdrawn. Two developed rashes and itchiness; both proved to be on imipramine. A third became discouraged that she was not improving and took an overdose of her pills. Fortunately, she proved to be on placebo. These three patients were subsequently treated with other antidepressants, separately from the study, on an open (non-blind) basis.

Some of the subjects thought that they could guess which treatment they were receiving. But they were not as accurate as they suspected: Two women complained of dry mouth, annoying lightheadedness, and sedation, and were quite convinced that they were receiving imipramine. However, neither of them experienced any decrease in their urge to binge. At the end of the six weeks, it turned out that both had been on placebo.

The results of the study are shown in the six graphs in Figure 1. Imipramine

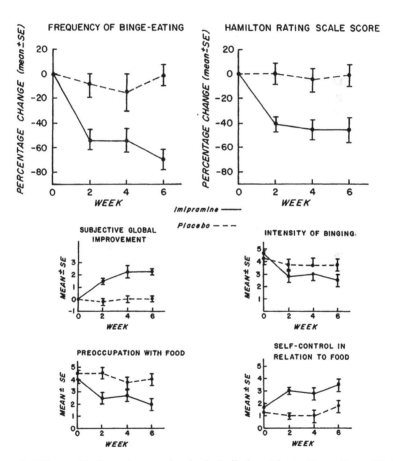

Figure 1. Effects of imipramine vs. placebo in bulimic subjects. (From Pope, Hudson, Jonas, et al., 1983. Copyright 1983, the American Psychiatric Association. Reprinted by permission.)

subjects experienced, on the average, a 70% reduction in the frequency of their binges. And, unlike the subjects in the British study, described above, our placebo subjects showed virtually no improvement at all. Similarly, the imipramine subjects improved about 50% on the Hamilton Depression Scale, as compared to almost no change with placebo recipients. Both of these differences were statistically significant (specifically, by the Wilcoxon rank sum test, two-tailed, $p < .01$ and $p < .02$ for these comparisons, respectively).

The four smaller graphs also show a marked superiority of imipramine to placebo. The imipramine subjects did not merely experience a reduction in the frequency of their binges; they also had less intense binges, felt less preoccupied with food, felt more self-control with relation to food, and described much greater feelings of overall improvement. Three of these differences were also statistically significant ($p < .05$ or better), and the fourth almost reached significance ($p = 0.06$).

Long-term follow-up of the study subjects provides further evidence for antidepressant effectiveness, as shown in Table 1 on the following page. Subjects with a good response to imipramine were maintained on imipramine; those with a poor response, or with annoying side effects, were switched to other antidepressants. In all, of the 20 subjects followed long-term, 18 (90%) experienced at least a 50% reduction in their binge eating with antidepressants; seven (35%) experienced an essentially complete disappearance of their binges. This improvement had persisted for follow-up periods of up to eight months at the time that the table was constructed; at the time of this writing, several of the patients have now maintained their improvement for more than two years (see below).

In summary, this study provides persuasive evidence that antidepressants are rapidly effective in many cases of bulimia, and indirect evidence for the hypothesis that bulimia is related to major affective disorder. Of course, we would emphasize that the results are hardly spectacular. Although 90% of subjects improved, only about one third of subjects experienced an essentially complete remission of their bulimic behavior. On the other hand, it should be recalled that these subjects had chronic cases of bulimia, refractory to multiple previous therapeutic attempts over years of time. Therefore, even a 35% rate of remission, over the space of a few weeks, is gratifying in such a severely ill population.

In the 14 months since our placebo-controlled double-blind study appeared, three new placebo-controlled double-blind studies have been performed, and all have produced positive results. In the first of these, Walsh and his associates at Columbia University performed a placebo-controlled double-blind study using the antidepressant medication phenelzine (Nardil) (Walsh, Stewart, Roose, et al., 1984). In a sample of 25 subjects, they found a highly significant difference between phenelzine and placebo, both on measures of frequency of binge eating and on associated measures of eating disorder and

Table 1
Follow-Up Data on Study Patients

	Subject	Medication	Response[a]	Follow-up interval (mo.)[b]
imipramine group	1	imipramine	+++	8
		desipramine	+++	
	2	imipramine	++	6
	3	imipramine	++	5[c]
	4	imipramine	++	2[c]
		trazodone	++	
	5	imipramine	0	
		tranylcypromine	+++	5
	6	imipramine	+	
		trazodone	+	6
		phenelzine	+	
	7	imipramine	+++	5[d]
	8	imipramine	++	2[c]
	9	imipramine	+	4[d]
placebo group	1	imipramine	++	3[c]
	2	imipramine	0	
		trazodone + lithium	0	6
		buproprion	0	
	3	imipramine	0	
		trazodone	0	
		tranylcylpromine	0	6
		phenelzine	0	
	4	tranylcypromine	+++	3
	5	imipramine	+++	6[d]
	6	imipramine	+	2[c]
		desipramine		
	7	trazodone	++	
		phenelzine	++	4
	8	imipramine	+++	5
	9	(declined treatment)		
	10	imipramine	+	1[c]
Subjects excluded during the study period (see text)	1	tranylcypromine	+++	7
		phenelzine	+++	
	2	(declined treatment)		
	3	nortriptyline	+	7

[a]Responses: 0: less than 50% decrease in binge frequency
              +: more than 50% decrease in binge frequency
              ++: more than 75% decrease in binge frequency
              +++: complete remission of binges for one month or more
[b]Follow-up interval represents time that response has been maintained or time until patient was lost to follow-up.
[c]Lost to follow-up.
[d]The three subjects marked "d" recently experimented with stopping their imipramine for various reasons. They relapsed to original levels of binge-eating within 1-12 weeks, and have all chosen to resume imipramine.
(From Pope, Hudson, Jonas, et al., 1983. Copyright 1983, the American Psychiatric Association. Reprinted by permission.)

depression. Many of the subjects experienced a complete remission of their bulimia by the end of the study period. However, it is important to emphasize that not all of the subjects were able to complete the study, since some experienced pronounced hypotension (lightheadedness) on phenelzine, and thus were not able to take an adequate dose of the drug.

In the second study, at the Mayo Clinic (Hughes, Wells, & Cunningham, 1984), Hughes and his associates used desipramine (Norpramin), a medication closely related to imipramine, the drug used in our own placebo-controlled double-blind study, described above. The results with desipramine were particularly impressive; 15 (68%) of the 22 subjects in this study experienced a complete remission of their bulimic symptoms within 10 weeks of starting treatment. As in our own study and that of Walsh and colleagues, the subjects reported marked improvement in other symptoms of eating disorder and in symptoms of depression.

One of the most important findings of the Mayo Clinic study was the need for testing plasma levels (blood levels) of antidepressant medication in order to be sure that these were in the therapeutic range. When Hughes and associates tested their subjects, they found that 10 had desipramine plasma levels below the probable therapeutic range. Four of these subjects were already in remission from their bulimia, and therefore were not given dosage adjustment. However, the other six subjects had their dosage adjusted upward, and four then went on to experience a remission of their bulimia. This finding indicates how important it is to adjust dosage using plasma levels; had Hughes and associates not tested plasma levels and adjusted dosage, they would have considerably underestimated the true effectiveness of desipramine in treating bulimia.

In the third study, Mitchell and associates at the University of Minnesota used another tricyclic antidepressant, amitriptyline (Elavil) (Mitchell & Groat, in press). They also tested blood levels, but on only eight of the 16 patients who were receiving amitriptyline. When the blood levels were analyzed, it was found that one patient had level of zero—suggesting that possibly she was not taking her medication at all—and three other patients had plasma levels which were probably below the therapeutic range for amitriptyline. Unfortunately, the authors measured these levels near the end of the study period, so that it was not possible for them to correct the dosage to achieve adequate plasma levels in the manner of the Hughes et al. study described above. This is a potentially important limitation, which may have seriously compromised the apparent efficacy of amitriptyline in this study. Yet, in spite of this, amitriptyline still emerged as significantly superior to placebo on the Hamilton Rating Scale for depression, and was also superior to placebo (although not reaching statistical significance) on all of the four measures of eating behavior. On two of these measures, the results approached statistical significance ($p < .1$) in favor of an amitriptyline effect.

Finally, it should be noted that in none of these studies was any psychotherapy administered. In the University of Minnesota study, there was some attempt to encourage subjects to reduce their binge eating and to praise them for improvement; beyond this, however, none of the studies used any sort of intervention other than medication.

The combined results of these several carefully controlled studies produce a very strong case for the effectiveness of antidepressant treatment in bulimia. At this point, antidepressant treatment remains the only treatment for bulimia that has been shown to be effective in placebo-controlled studies.

One question still remains open: How well do antidepressants perform over the long term? Is there a tendency for some patients to gradually relapse over the passage of time, or is the improvement maintained? Can patients eventually stop their antidepressants without relapsing? Recently, our group addressed these questions by performing a two-year follow-up of the patients treated in our original placebo-controlled double-blind study with imipramine (Pope, Hudson, & Jonas, 1984). Of the 20 patients who received antidepressants either during or immediately after the study, 11 are still being followed at two years. Of these, eight (73%) are in remission from their bulimic symptoms. None of these has received any form of psychotherapy, group therapy, or family therapy during the follow-up interval; medication has remained their only treatment. It is also of interest to note that three of the eight have been able to discontinue their medication, without a recurrence of bulimia, at various times during the follow-up interval; one was able to stop her medication after six-and-a-half months, another after nine months, and another after 23 months. The others are still on medication. Of the remaining three subject followed up for two years, one is currently markedly improved (see above for a definition of this and other terms), one is moderately improved, and one is unimproved. The unimproved subject, interestingly enough, is the only subject who stopped taking antidepressant medications against our recommendations. After stopping trazodone, her bulimia returned to its original frequency.

Nine additional subjects from the study were lost to follow-up at various times during the two-year interval. Two of these were also in remission at the time that they were lost to follow-up, and seven showed either moderate or marked improvement as of last follow-up. Pooling the total group of 20 subjects and rating their symptoms at the time that they were last seen, we find that a total of 10 (50%) were in remission, nine (45%) were moderately improved or markedly improved, and only one (5%) — the subject who discontinued her medication as described above — was unimproved.

It is important to point out, however, that the mere measure of improvement in frequency of binge eating may not reflect the overall well-being of the subject. For example, in a recent study of group therapy in bulimia (Lacey, 1983), a majority of the patients were able to stop binge eating, but their overall level of depression *rose* by about 50% during the course of the treatment. This indicates the importance of assessing levels of depression, as well as changes in eating behavior, in all treatment studies. In our follow-up study, we tested for depression by administering the Hamilton Depression Rating Scale (Hamilton, 1960) to all of our subjects who were still available for follow-up at two years. They displayed a highly significant decrease in their depressive symptoms, with Hamilton scores even lower, on the average, than those that they had exhibited at the end of the double-blind study in 1982.

In summary, both in acute treatment and on long-term follow-up, antidepressant medications have been found highly effective for bulimic patients. Most importantly, antidepressants appear effective not just for the symptoms of binge eating, but for the whole patient. In the studies reviewed above, patients have reported a marked decrease in depression, in preoccupation with food and body weight, and in other distressing symptoms associated with bulimia.

CONCLUSIONS AND RECOMMENDATIONS

The present state of the evidence can be summarized as follows:

1) Given that no previous therapies for anorexia nervosa and bulimia have been demonstrated effective in controlled studies (i.e., studies using a simultaneous control group receiving a "placebo" treatment), biological therapies represent an important and potentially fruitful area of current research.

2) Appetite stimulants such as cyproheptadine appear at best of limited value in anorexia nervosa. However, cyproheptadine may be useful, and conceivably may even have antidepressant effects, in certain individual patients (Halmi, 1982).

3) The anticonvulsant phenytoin may be effective in a limited number of cases of bulimia, but appears ineffective in a majority of cases.

4) A promising recent theory is that anorexia nervosa and bulimia may be closely related to major affective disorder. This theory predicts that the eating disorders might respond to antidepressants or lithium carbonate.

5) Preliminary data favor the possibility that antidepressants and lithium carbonate may be of value in at least some patients with anorexia nervosa. However, the evidence remains too tentative to permit firm conclusions.

6) More extensive evidence exists for the case of bulimia; four placebo-controlled double-blind studies with tricyclic antidepressants and monoamine oxidase inhibitors have found these agents highly effective for bulimia, particularly when care is taken to ensure an adequate plasma level of medication. Many patients treated with antidepressants experience a remission of their bulimic symptoms without ancillary psychotherapy. The beneficial ef-

fects of antidepressants appear to persist — or even improve — on long-term follow-up.

Although it is premature to make specific recommendations for the pharmacological treatment of anorexic patients, it appears that in bulimic patients antidepressant trials are warranted. In our current practice, we recommend imipramine or desipramine, with *monitoring of blood levels* to be certain that the drug is in the therapeutic range, for a trial of three to four weeks at therapeutic levels (Pope, Hudson, & Jonas, 1983). If this fails, and if the patient can follow the required dietary precautions, a trial of a monoamine oxidose inhibitor, with *monitoring of platelet monoamine oxidase levels* to ensure adequate dosage, may often produce rapid benefit. Occasionally, patients who have failed to respond to both types of agents will respond to trazodone, lithium carbonate, carbamazepine, or other agents. Given the availability of antidepressant treatment, the fact that it does not interfere with other therapeutic modalities, and the often rapid improvement which may occur, there is rarely a reason to deny a trial of these agents to a bulimic patient.

However, the evidence remains in its early stages. Further research into the biological basis and pharmacological treatment of the eating disorders — particularly, we would suggest, further treatment studies with antidepressants, lithium carbonate, and other thymoleptic agents — offers the hope of greatly improved treatment of these often chronic and refractory conditions.

REFERENCES

Agras, W., & Kraemer, H. (1984). Anorexia nervosa: Treatment and outcome. In A. J. Stunkard & E. Stellar (Eds.), *Eating and its disorders* (pp. 193-207). New York: Raven Press.

American Psychiatric Association. (1980). *Diagnostic and statistical manual of mental disorders*, 3rd ed. (DSM-III). Washington, D.C.: American Psychiatric Association.

Barcai, A. (1977). Lithium in adult anorexia nervosa. *Acta Psychiatrica Scandinavica, 55*, 97-101.

Boskind-Lodahl, M., & White, W. C. (1978). The definition and treatment of bulimarexia in college women — A pilot study. *Journal of the American College Health Association, 27*, 84-86.

Cantwell, D. P., Sturzenberger, S., Burroughs, J., Salkin, B., & Green, J. K. (1977). Anorexia nervosa: An affective disorder? *Archives of General Psychiatry, 34*, 1087-1093.

Carroll, B. J., Feinberg, M., Greden, J. F., et al. (1981). A specific laboratory test for the diagnosis of melancholia: Standardization, validation, and clinical utility. *Archives of General Psychiatry, 38*, 15-22.

Carter, S. M., Reveley, M. A., Sandler, M., et al. (1980). Decreased urinary output of conjugated tyramine is associated with lifetime vulnerability to depressive illness. *Psychiatry Research, 3*, 13-21.

Casper, R. C., Eckert, E. D., Halmi, K. A., Goldberg, S. C., & Davis, J. M. (1980). Bulimia: Its incidence and clinical importance in patients with anorexia nervosa. *Archives of General Psychiatry, 37*, 1030-1035.

Crisp, A. H., & Bhat, A. V. (1982). "Personality" and anorexia nervosa — the phobic avoidance stance: Its origins and symptomatology. *Psychotherapy and Psychosomatics, 38*, 178-200.

Eckert, E. D., Goldberg, S. C., & Halmi, K. A. (1982). Depression in anorexia nervosa. *Psychological Medicine, 12*, 115-122.

Eckert, E. D., Goldberg, S. C., Halmi, K. A., Casper, R. E., & Davis, J. M. (1979). Behavior therapy in anorexia nervosa. *British Journal of Psychiatry, 134*, 55-59.

Fairburn, C. G. (1981). A cognitive behavioral approach to the management of bulimia. *Psychological Medicine, 11*, 707-711.

Garfinkel, P. E., Moldofsky, H., & Garner, D. M. (1977). The outcome of anorexia nervosa: Significance of clinical features, body image, and behavior modification. In R. A. Vigersky (Ed.), *Anorexia nervosa* (pp. 315-329). New York: Raven Press.

Garfinkel, P. E., Moldofsky, M., & Garner, D. M. (1980). The heterogeneity of anorexia nervosa: Bulimia as a distinct subgroup. *Archives of General Psychiatry, 37*, 1036-1040.

Gershon, E. S., Hamovit, J. R., Schreiber, J. L., et al. (1982). *Anorexia nervosa and major affective disorders associated in families: A preliminary report.* Presented at the Annual Meeting of the American Psychopathological Association, New York. March 1.

Goldberg, S. C., Halmi, K. A., Eckert, E. D., Casper, R. C., & Davis, J. M. (1979). Cyproheptadine in anorexia nervosa. *British Journal of Psychiatry, 134*, 67-70.

Goodwin, F. K. (Ed.). (1979). The lithium ion: Impact on treatment and research. *Archives of General Psychiatry, 36*, 833-916.

Green, R. S., & Rau, J. H. (1974). Treatment of compulsive eating disturbances with anticonvulsant medication. *American Journal of Psychiatry, 131*, 428-432.

Gross, H. A., Ebert, M. H., & Faden, V. B. (1981). A double-blind controlled trial of lithium carbonate in anorexia nervosa. *Journal of Clinical Psychopharmacology, 1*, 376-381.

Halmi, K. A. (1982). Cyproheptadine for anorexia nervosa. *Lancet, 1*, 1357-1358.

Hamilton, M. (1960). A rating scale for depression. *Journal of Neurology, Neurosurgery, and Psychiatry, 23*, 56-62.

Hendren, R. L. (1983). Depression in anorexia nervosa. *Journal of the American Academy of Child Psychiatry, 22*, 59-62.

Hsu, L. K. G. (1980). Outcome of anorexia nervosa: A review of the literature (1954 to 1978). *Archives of General Psychiatry, 37*, 1041-1046.

Hsu, L. K. G., Crisp, A. H., Harding, B. (1979). Outcome of anorexia nervosa. *Lancet, 1*, 61-65.

Hudson, J. I., Pope, H. G., Jr., Jonas, J. M., et al. (1983a). Family history study of anorexia nervosa and bulimia. *British Journal of Psychiatry, 142*, 133-138.

Hudson, J. I., Pope, H. G., Jr., Jonas, J. M., et al. (1983b). Hypothalamic-pituitary-adrenal axis hyperactivity in bulimia. *Psychiatry Research, 8*, 111-117.

Hudson, J. I., Pope, H. G., Jr., Jonas, J. M., et al. (1983c). Phenomenologic relationship of eating disorders to major affective disorder. *Psychiatry Research, 9*, 345-354.

Hughes, P. L., Wells, L. A., & Cunningham, C. J. (1984, May). *Controlled trial using desipramine for bulimia.* Presented at the Annual Meeting of the American Psychiatric Association, Los Angeles.

Jonas, J. M., Hudson, J. I., & Pope, H. G., Jr. (1983). Treatment of bulimia with monoamine oxidase inhibitors (letter). *Journal of Clinical Psychopharmacology, 3*, 59-60.

Kirkegaard, C. (1981). The thyrotropin response to thyrotropin-releasing hormone in endogenous depression. *Psychoneuroendocrinology, 6*, 189-212.

Klein, D. F., Gittelman, R., Quitkin, F., et al. (1980). *Diagnosis and drug treatment of psychiatric disorders: Adults and children* (2nd ed.). Baltimore: Williams & Wilkins.

Kron, L., Katz, J. L., Gorsynski, G., & Weiner, H. (1978). Hyperactivity in anorexia nervosa: A fundamental clinical feature. *Comprehensive Psychiatry, 19*, 433-440.

Kupfer, D. J., Foster, F. G., Coble, P., et al. (1978). The application of EEG sleep for the differential diagnosis of affective disorders. *American Journal of Psychiatry, 135*, 69-74.

Lacey, J. H. (1983). Bulimia nervosa, binge eating, and psychogenic vomiting: A controlled treatment study and long-term outcome. *British Medical Journal, 286*, 1609-1613.

Lacey, J. H., & Crisp, A. H. (1980). Hunger, food intake, and weight: The impact of clomipramine on a refeeding anorexia nervosa population. *Postgraduate Medical Journal, 56*, 79-85.

Liebman, R., Minuchin, S., & Baker, L. (1974). An integrated treatment program for anorexia nervosa. *American Journal of Psychiatry, 131*, 432-436.

McGrath, P. J., Quitkin, F. M., Stewart, J. W. et al. (1981). An open clinical trial of mianserin. *American Journal of Psychiatry, 138*, 530-532.

Mendels, J. (1983). Eating disorders and antidepressants (letter). *Journal of Clinical Psychopharmacology, 3*, 59.

Mendlewicz, J., & Rainer, J. (1977). Adoption study supporting genetic transmission in manic depressive illness. *Nature, 268*, 327-329.

Mills, I. H. (1976). Amitriptyline therapy in anorexia nervosa (letter). *Lancet, 2*, 687.

Minuchin, S., Rosman, B. L., & Baker, L. (1978). *Psychosomatic families: Anorexia nervosa in context.* Cambridge, MA: Harvard University Press.

Mitchell, J. E., & Groat, R. (In press). A placebo-controlled double-blind trial of amitriptyline in bulimia. *Journal of Clinical Psychopharmacology.*

Moore, D. C. (1977). Amitriptyline therapy in anorexia nervosa nervosa. *American Journal of Psychiatry, 134*, 1303-1304.

Needleman, H. L., & Waber, D. (1976). Amitriptyline therapy in patients with anorexia nervosa (letter). *Lancet, 2*, 580.

Needleman, H. L., & Waber, D. (1977). Amitriptyline in anorexia nervosa. In R. A. Vigersky (Ed.), *Anorexia nervosa* (pp. 357-362). New York: Raven Press.

Nurnberger, J. I., & Gershon, E. S. (1982). Genetics. In E. S. Paykel (Ed.), *Handbook of affective disorders.* New York: Guilford Press.

Pertschuk, M. J. (1977). Behavior therapy: Extended follow-up. In R. A. Vigersky (Ed.), *Anorexia nervosa* (pp. 305-314). New York: Raven Press.

Pierloot, R., Vandereycken, W., & Verhaest, S. (1982). An inpatient treatment program for anorexia nervosa patients. *Acta Psychiatrica Scandinavica, 66*, 1-8.

Pope, H. G., Jr., & Hudson, J. I. (1982). Treatment of bulimia with antidepressants. *Psychopharmacology, 78*, 167-179.

Pope, H. G., & Hudson, J. I. (1984). *New hope for binge eaters.* New York: Harper and Row.

Pope, H. G., Jr., Hudson, J. I., Jonas, J. M. (1983). Antidepressant treatment of bulimia: Preliminary experience and practical recommendations. *Journal of Clinical Psychopharmacology, 3*, 274-281.

Pope, H. G., Jr., Hudson, J. I., & Jonas, J. M. (1983). Antidepressant treatment of bulimia: A research update. Presented at the Annual Meeting of the American Psychiatric Association, Los Angeles.

Pope, H. G., Jr., Hudson, J. I., Jonas, J. M., et al. (1983). Bulimia treated with imipramine: A placebo-controlled double-blind study. *American Journal of Psychiatry, 140*, 554-558.

Rich, C. L. (1978). Self-induced vomiting: Psychiatric considerations. *Journal of the American Medical Association, 239*, 2688-2689.

Roy-Byrne, P., Gwirtsman, H., Edelstein, C. K., et al. (1983). Eating disorders and antidepressants (letter). *Journal of Clinical Psychopharmacology, 3*, 60-61.

Roy-Byrne, P., Gwirtsman, H., Yager, J., et al. (1982, May). Neuroendocrine tests in bulimia. Paper presented at the Annual Meeting of the American Psychiatric Association, Toronto, Canada.

Russell, G. F. M. (1981). The current treatment of anorexia nervosa. *British Journal of Psychiatry, 138*, 164-166.

Sabine, E. J., Yonace, A., Farrington, A. J., et al. (1983). Bulimia nervosa: A placebo-controlled double-blind therapeutic trial of mianserin. *British Journal of Clinical Pharmacology, 15*, 195S-202S.

Shader, R. I. (1982). The psychiatrist as mind sweeper. *Journal of Clinical Psychopharmacology, 2*, 233-234.

Smith, S. R., Bledsoe, T., & Chetri, M. K. (1975). Cortisol metabolism and the pituitary-adrenal axis in adults with protein-calorie malnutrition. *Journal of Clinical Endocrinology and Metabolism, 40*, 43-52.

Vigersky, R. A., & Loriaux, D. L. (1977). The effect of cyproheptadine in anorexia nervosa: A double-blind trial. In R. A. Vigersky (Ed.), *Anorexia nervosa* (pp. 349-356). New York: Raven Press.

Walsh, B. T., Katz, J. L., Levin, J., Kream, J., Fukushima, D. K., Hellman, L. D., Weiner, H., & Zumoff, B. (1981). The production rate of cortisol declines during recovery from

anorexia nervosa. *Journal of Clinical Endocrinology and Metabolism, 53,* 203-205.
Walsh, B. T., Stewart, J. W., Roose, S. P., et al. (1984). Treatment of bulimia with phenelzine: A double-blind placebo-controlled study. *Archives of General Psychiatry, 41,* 1105-1109.
Walsh, B. T., Stewart, J. W., Wright, L., et al. (1982). Treatment of bulimia with monoamine oxidase inhibitors. *American Journal of Psychiatry, 139,* 1629-1630.
Wermuth, B. M., Davis, K. L., Hollister, L. E., & Stunkard, A. K. (1977). Phenytoin treatment of the binge-eating syndrome. *American Journal of Psychiatry, 134,* 1249-1253.
White, J. H., & Schnaultz, N. L. (1977). Successful treatment of anorexia nervosa with imipramine. *Diseases of the Nervous System, 38,* 567-568.
White, W. C., & Boskind-White, M. (1981). An experiential-behavioral approach to the treatment of bulimarexia. *Psychotherapy: Theory, Research, and Practice, 4,* 501-507.
Winokur, A., March, V., & Mendels, J. (1980). Primary affective disorder in relatives of patients with anorexia nervosa. *American Journal of Psychiatry, 137,* 695-698.
Wulliemier, F., Rossel, F., & Sinclair, K. (1975). La thérapie comportementale de l'anorexie nervose. *Journal of Psychosomatic Research, 19,* 267-272.
Zubiate, T. N. (1970). Tratamiento de la anorexia nervosa con una associacion cyproheptadine-vitaminas. *Revista Médica de la Caja Nacional de Segura Social, 19,* 147-153.

Part II

Sociocultural Perspective

Chapter 5

Anorexia Nervosa and Bulimia: The Sociocultural Context

Donald M. Schwartz, Michael G. Thompson, and Craig L. Johnson

Our society's longstanding preoccupation with sex and sexual matters is being challenged by a new cultural obsession: The relentless pursuit of thinness. Ours is an age fixated on food and bodies. A 1978 Nielson survey showed that 45% of all U.S. households have somebody dieting during the course of the year. Fifty-six percent of all women 24–54 years of age diet. And of women who diet, 76% acknowledge doing so for cosmetic rather than health reasons. Concerns about diet and exercise have shifted from a growing leisure time hobby to a national obsession. We believe that one effect of this change, and other changes in our culture, has been an increase in women suffering from eating disorders. This includes an increase in the incidence of anorexia nervosa, as well as the more newly identified problems of relatively normal weight women who binge eat and then employ extreme forms of weight control, including vomiting and laxative abuse.

The potential effects of an increase in eating disorders is reason for concern. The destructive impact on individuals of these disorders continues to be documented by those who research and treat them. Recent trends suggest that more and more young women, and perhaps young men, will be afflicted by these problems. This chapter is based on the assertion that the apparent increase in anorexia nervosa and related eating disorders is the result of forces at work in the culture which direct girls and women in distress toward this

---

This work was supported in part by George and Tina Barr and the Biomedical Research Support Grant. It is reprinted with permission from the *International Journal of Eating Disorders*, Vol. 1, No. 3, 1982, published by Van Nostrand Reinhold Company, Inc.

particular solution. The anthropologist, Clyde Kluckholn (1984), wrote: "Every culture has its pet mental disturbances." We are worried that eating disorders are becoming the pet mental disturbance of affluent cultures in general and America in particular. Especially at risk are certain vulnerable groups of adolescent girls and young adult women.

The focus of this chapter is on the interplay between sociocultural forces and personality, specifically psychopathology, as a way of explaining the increase in contemporary women suffering from eating disorders. To pave the way to that discussion we must first confront three questions:

1) Is there really a change in the culture's preoccupation with food and thinness?
2) Is there really an increase in anorexia nervosa and other related eating disorders?
3) What are our current theories of the etiology of eating disorders and why are they inadequate in explaining the increase in this phenomenon?

THE CULTURE'S PREOCCUPATION WITH FOOD AND THINNESS

In her review of the movie "Who Is Killing the Great Chefs of Europe?" which starred the corpulent Robert Morley, Pauline Kael of the *New Yorker* wrote:

> Guilt-ridden, diet-conscious American audiences may be in a unique position to laugh at the food fixation of this movie. "Great Chefs" comes at a time when the generation that protested Vietnam has become health-food minded and their younger siblings are becoming vegetarians. Guilt about ingestion has become a national political issue. (Kael, 1978)

From a more clinically scientific perspective Hilde Bruch, in the preface to her 1978 book, *The Golden Cage*, spoke to both the increase in anorexia and her speculation about the role of sociocultural forces in explaining that increase. Dr. Bruch wrote that anorexia nervosa has increased markedly in the last 15 to 20 years and that

> . . . one might speak of an epidemic illness, only there is no contagious agent; the spread must be attributed to psychosociological factors. . . . I am inclined to relate it to the enormous emphasis that fashion places on slimness. . . . (Bruch, 1978)

Until recently, systematic, empirical studies documenting a shift in the culture's preoccupation with thinness were virtually nonexistent. Wallechinsky, Wallace, and Wallace (1977) provided a nonscientific but nonetheless systematic piece of evidence supporting the notion of a shift in the culture toward slim, thin-hipped women. These authors reported in their *Book of Lists* that each of the 3500 yearly visitors to Madame Tussaud's London waxworks is asked to note who he/she thinks is the most beautiful woman in the world. Since 1970 Elizabeth Taylor has fallen steadily from the top of the list and Twiggy, surely an idealized anorexic, has ascended. Twiggy first made the top five in 1974. By 1976 she ranked number one.

Garner, Garfinkel, and ourselves (1980) looked in several different areas for evidence that cultural norms surrounding ideal weight and real population changes both reflected a tendency toward greater thinness. As exemplars of "ideal" feminine beauty we studied Playboy Magazine Playmate centerfolds, and contestants and winners of the Miss America Pageant from 1959 through 1978. Within each group we looked for changes across the 20 years as well as contrasts between these cultural prototypes of feminine beauty and population norms. We found that in both groups mean weights were significantly less than corresponding population means published by the Society of Actuaries for each year. Thus, women selected as exemplars of feminine beauty were consistently thinner than the actual norms for comparable women in the population. Secondly, within each of the two groups when age and height were controlled, weight declined across the 20-year period which was studied. Ideal shapes for women became progressively thinner over the 20 years. Interestingly, there were no differences in weight between Miss America contestants and actual winners until 1970, after which winners' weights were consistently less than the average weight of all contestants.

These findings were particularly striking when compared to the actual weights of women in the population at large. When comparing the actuarial norms from 1959 with those of 1979, the average weight of women under 30 (when height is controlled) is consistently several pounds heavier in 1979 than in 1959. This is the age group from which most or all Playboy playmates and Miss America contestants are likely to come. Thus, our findings cannot be explained simply as a reflection of a decrease in average body weights over the 20-year period studied.

In the same study, evidence was sought for a parallel increase in the culture's interest in and attention to dieting. The number of feature articles on dieting and weight loss from six major women's magazines were reviewed for the same 20-year period covered by the Playboy and Miss America surveys. A regression analysis showed a significant and systematic increase over the 20 years. The mean number of articles for the first decade was 17.1, compared to 29.6 for the second decade. Again, this is a significant increase in the number of diet articles in the last 10 years (Garner et al., 1980).

This work gives strong support to the assertion that there has been an upsurge in cultural interest and attention to weight and diet. The other side of society's approval of abstinence and thinness is its revulsion for obesity and excessive eating. We know of no work which documents a shift in the culture's norms and attitudes in this domain. Wooley & Wooley (1979) have compiled an impressive array of existing studies which document the stigma and hatred directed toward obesity in childhood. They introduce their literature review by observing:

> The child whose build is socially "deviant" comes early in life to be regarded by others as responsible for his/her "condition" and deserving of social disapproval, and, sooner or later, is subjected to pressures to restrict food intake in order to "correct" his/her condition. Failure to do so is seen as a "weakness," "wanting to be fat," or even as a masochistic desire for rejection. (Wooley & Wooley, 1979)

Their conclusion following the review is equally terse and pessimistic:

> These studies document the hatred of obese children by other children and by adults. The impact this hatred has on the individual child is probably irreversible. It is not only the obese child who suffers from this hatred; anti-fat attitudes learned in childhood no doubt become the basis for self-hatred among those who become overweight at later ages, and a source of anxiety and self-doubt for anyone fearful of becoming overweight. (Wooley & Wooley, 1979).

Wooley and colleagues not only document the opprobium which society visits on the obese, but they also confirm and explore how that social dynamic affects women much more than men. Again, these authors review an impressive array of articles to support their assertion that:

> Studies of attitudes toward endomorphic children reveal that children of both sexes, and of all body builds, adopt the prevailing negative stereotypes associated with endomorphy. However, at later ages, beginning with adolescence, females are more affected than males by this prejudicial climate. (Wooley & Wooley, 1979)

This is an extremely important differentiation. Any etiological theory about eating disorders must be comprehensive enough to answer two questions: Why the increase in recent years? Why the disproportionate number of women rather than men affected by this problem? The Wooley review strongly supports the idea that a sociocultural model may offer the best answer to these two questions, most especially the second question.

EVIDENCE OF AN INCREASE IN ANOREXIA AND RELATED EATING DISORDERS

Nathaniel Apter, a senior clinical psychiatrist at Michael Reese Hospital, remarked that when he was chairman of the Department of Psychiatry at the University of Chicago, in the 1950s, a case of primary anorexia nervosa was so rare that medical students and psychiatric residents were told they would be unlikely to see more than a few cases across an entire lifetime of practice. Now he notes it is not uncommon to find five or six cases at one time on the units at Michael Reese. Despite these repeated anecdotal observations by senior clinicians, proving a real increase in anorexia is not that easy. While there is considerable evidence to suggest such an increase, there are also significant arguments to be made that the increase is more *apparent* than real. A careful examination and possible refutation of these arguments are beyond the scope of this paper; however, before reviewing evidence that anorexia and related eating disorders are on the rise, the contrary arguments should at least be noted. They are:

1) The increase could be due to better record-keeping and reporting.
2) The increase could be due to an absolute increase in the number of adolescents — the product of the baby boom following World War II.
3) The increase could be a function of an increase in interest in anorexia by professionals and the lay public. Neither popular media nor professional journals, unfortunately, are immune to a "fad" effect.
4) The increase could be a function of the fact that individuals and centers specializing in treatment of anorexia may confuse the increase in numbers of referrals, due to public reputation, with actual increases in the disorder.

It is true that the epidemiological baseline data available from 10-15 years ago can never unequivocally answer the question. Twenty years from now, perhaps, if adequate baseline data are being collected presently, we may "know" definitely whether anorexia and related disorders are increasing. Notwithstanding these cautions, however, there is considerable preliminary evidence ranging from clinical impressions to larger empirical studies which strongly support the idea that these eating disorders are indeed on the rise. Further, even if, in the unlikely event that the more conservative arguments turn out to be true (that is, that the apparent rise in incidence is an artifact of statistics or record keeping), it would still be useful to ask why there has been such an upturn in interest and attention to eating disorders in both the professional and lay community.

What is the evidence that anorexia is increasing? First of all, the leading authorities in the field of anorexia seem to agree that there has been an increase. Bruch, again, writes that it has become a common problem in high schools and colleges. The growing concern resulted in the first international, interdisciplinary conference being held in Maryland in 1976. There was a conference on anorexia in Montreal in 1979, and a second international conference in Toronto in 1981. Secondly, there is at least some empirical evidence that anorexia is increasing. Theander's (1970) retrospective follow-up study, covering a period of 30 years, found that the annual incidence of cases for the entire period was 2.4 cases per 1 million population. However, during the last 10 years of the period studied, from 1951 to 1961, the annual incidence was 4.5 cases, or approximately double the rate for the entire life span. Theander, himself, was reluctant to infer that there was a real increase; rather, he attributed it to increased reporting and awareness.

Kendell and co-workers' (1973) case register survey in Scotland, suburban London, and upper New York State revealed an increased incidence in all three locales. Though case records of mental health clinics and psychiatric hospitals are one of the most accurate methods of establishing actual incidence, epidemiological investigators agree that only a small percentage of primary anorexics are counted through such case register studies. Thus, Kendell's figure of 16 cases annually per 1 million population may be conservatively low.

In recent years, investigators have looked more closely at target populations in which anorexia is likely to be found in a natural setting: namely, in girls' schools. In 1976, Crisp, Palmer, and Kalucy investigated nine girls' schools in England (seven private and two public schools) and found a prevalence of one severe case of primary anorexia nervosa in approximately every 200 girls under the age of 16 in private schools, one in 100 among girls ages 16-18 in private schools, and one in 250 of all adolescent girls, attending both public and private schools. Nylander (1971) has concluded that the disorder is present in quite definite and severe form in one of every 150 Scandinavian adolescent women. Lacey (1979) in England, estimates that 7% of adolescent girls suffer from anorexia.

If we take a conservative figure from the anorexia outcome literature that one third to one half of anorexics never recover, and we extrapolate from these data, we are led to conclude—using Nylander's figures or Crisp's, respectively—that one in 450 or one in 750 adult women is afflicted for life with chronic primary anorexia, or with some severe anorexic symptoms.

The final piece of evidence for an increasing incidence of anorexia is the tremendous growth of the literature on anorexia. Up until 1950 there were perhaps 250 cases—usually individual case reports—described in the literature. There are now perhaps 5000 patients reported on in studies ranging in sample size from 20-350 anorexics.

Thus, there is no small amount of evidence whose cumulative effect is to support the assertion that anorexia nervosa is increasing in incidence. This evidence does not even begin to shed light on the relatively newly identified phenomena of anorexia-like behavior, attitudes and lifestyle of otherwise normal weight women. The depth and extent of these problems has only come to the attention of clinicians and researchers in the past few years. There is little or no epidemiological data with respect to this problem in the present, much less a bank of historical documentation with which to make comparisons. There are few who are not struck, however, by the epidemic proportions of this behavior now that the surface has been scratched.

CURRENT THEORIES OF THE ETIOLOGY OF EATING DISORDERS

There are three major theories of the etiology of anorexia nervosa. The first set of theories which can roughly be called ego psychological, argue that anorexia is a function of an impaired child-maternal environment in the early years of a child's life. Palazzoli (1974) suggests that due to arbitrary and unempathic mothering, the child splits off the inner representation of the mother, which remains unintegrated throughout the characteristically compliant childhood of the anorexic. At puberty, however, the girl's body begins to grow more round, and is experienced concretely by the girl as the return—the potentially overwhelming return—of the archaic mother at the expense of the self. Palazzoli calls this "intrapersonal paranoia." Bruch's theory suggests that, again, due to arbitrary mothering, which demands compliance from the child in the face of natural bodily impulses (primarily hunger), the child fails to develop any ego structures which allow her to accurately perceive internal cues of hunger and satiation. For both Bruch and Palazzoli, anorexia is an effort—a last deperate effort—to gain perfect control over the body as a way of regaining control of self and personhood.

The issue of control is central also to family systems theories about anorexia nervosa. Minuchin (1970) has found that anorexic families tend to be superficially nice and good, while covertly they are deeply enmeshed, overprotective, rigid, and unable to meet or manage conflict. For the potentially anorexic child, loyalty and protection take precedence over autonomy and self-realization. The child's autonomy is curtailed by the intrusive concern and overprotection of other family members. Large areas of her psychological and bodily functioning remain the subject of others' interest and control long after they should have been autonomous.

The third major area of etiological theory is organic and proposes that there is some primary endocrinological defect or trigger which precipitates the illness.

What can these three theories contribute to our understanding relative to the increasing incidence of the disorder? The answer is: *little, perhaps nothing at all*. Taking each theory at a time and applying it to the phenomenon of increased prevalence result in a kind of logical absurdity.

For example, if indeed anorexia is primarily or only a result of arbitrary mothering, then one must infer that for some reason there has been an increased incidence of warping, unempathic mothering in the western world. One can speculate about the breakdown of the family, the rising divorce rate, and other factors, but it would be pointless to do so. The factors involved in the multitude of subtle mother-infant interactions are too complicated to be spoken about in sweeping, general ways. The same is true of family systems theories. Do we really have an epidemic of enmeshed, overprotective families in this country? Organic theories similarly fail us in explaining a social phenomenon.

To attempt to make any linear theory of causation account for as complicated a phenomenon as the increase of anorexia nervosa in western society is, in one sense, to set up a straw man who is easily knocked down. It has long been recognized that a multiplicity of factors are involved in the disorder. That is why anorexia nervosa has been thought to be a paradigmatic, psychosomatic illness. However, even the psychosomatic models that have been offered, including the Kaufman and Heiman model (1964), seriously underplay the role of sociocultural forces in shaping the form and symptom picture of anorexia nervosa.

We would like to suggest that anorexia nervosa is the *final common pathway* of a number of etiological factors, and that the influence of social phenomena are not only an important part of this etiology, but may be *the* part that can explain the possible rise in the incidence. Just as coronary heart disease is the physical illness of a land of abundance, anorexia nervosa may be a parallel psychological illness. The risk factor model offers an appealing framework for understanding the possible causes of anorexia, particularly for assessing the sociocultural contribution. Finally, it is an explanatory model which is also comprehensive enough to allow for the incorporation of etiological factors offered by traditional theories of anorexia.

A RISK FACTOR MODEL FOR ANOREXIA AND RELATED EATING DISORDERS

In coronary heart disease, it is recognized that there are a number of risk factors from different domains: physical (e.g., the natural production of serum cholesterol), dietary (intake of fats), lifestyle, behavioral (smoking), and psychological (A versus B personalities). Any one factor increases the likelihood of coronary heart disease. Having two or more factors raises the risk exponentially rather than additively.

What are the risk factors for anorexia nervosa? We know from the theories just reviewed that there are a number of definable risks: an impairment in the maternal environment, a particular pattern of family interactions, and perhaps some predisposing endocrine factor. To this we can add some sociocultural factors. You are more at risk if you are white, middle or upper-class, and come from a high-achieving family. We suspect further that if you live in a culture where the roles of women are complex, conflicting, and in change, and these pressures exist in a milieu which emphasizes a high positive value on slimness and a negative value on obesity, you are at a greater risk for anorexia. However, we are not yet in a position to say which of these factors is of greater or lesser import. We presume that in some cases of anorexia, the early life traumas and familial factors have proportionately a greater share in producing the disorder, and in other cases sociocultural pressures may have a greater share. But we do not know how to identify or weigh the different contributions of different factors—or whether that is even possible or relevant.

Before going on we must stop for a minute and confront a difficult diagnostic problem. Anorexia nervosa is a severe and intractable disorder, which has aspects that are developmentally primitive. Bruch's psychological criteria for anorexia highlight these deeply rooted psychological difficulties. She has presented these three criteria: 1) inability to perceive internal body cues; 2) delusional body image; and 3) a paralyzing sense of ineffectiveness (the cornerstone of her psychological diagnosis of true primary anorexia nervosa). If we suggest that there are some anorexics in whom sociocultural factors play a larger part than early traumas, are we still speaking of primary anorexia nervosa? Or, are we speaking of a more superficial disorder? This is a crucial question, which Bruch herself raises when she used the term psychosociological epidemic.

What we are suggesting is that there are many pathways to the eventual shape of an emotional disorder. The particular form which the pathological adaptation takes may be a direct function of the trauma itself. When food regulation, for example, becomes caught up in the content of overly negligent or overly intrusive parenting, any number of anorexogenic preconditions may develop: failure to learn to experience and perceive the normal psychological cues of satiation and hunger, and the use of food control as an attempt to achieve autonomy and separation from parents are two examples that come readily to mind.

At the same time, the course of the eventual disorder, its form and content, may not necessarily be set in the early life of the infant. Rather, the early life trauma may establish a general disposition toward emotional difficulty in later life, the exact form of which may be shaped by factors and events separated from the early life of the child with respect to time, place, and character. This seems particularly true of the newer cases of anorexia and anorexia-like syndromes. The cultural influence in affluent western society stresses the importance of weight control and thinness as a desirable state in contemporary women, and reviles a failure to do so. Such cultural contents become swept up as symptoms, especially when they overlap some of the underlying motives in a predisposed individual. For example, the pursuit of thinness through the rigid adherence to diet and weight sanctions smoothly fits the underlying needs of someone who is emotionally conflicted around the issues of self-esteem regulation, or autonomy, or control over separation. A similar collusion between contemporary cultural influences and psychopathology can be seen in the rise in the importance of television content in the delusions and hallucinations of schizophrenic patients, and perhaps also in the upsurge in violence against public figures by those suffering from explosive character disorders.

THE BORDER BETWEEN SOCIOCULTURAL FORCES, PERSONALITY AND BEHAVIOR

Perhaps the most challenging question is how does the culture actually influence the parameters of psychology? A psychiatric symptom represents a form of life adaptation which makes a psychological statement. It is a way of coping and yet it may be a sign of distress. Elements in the culture determine in part both the coping value and the signaling value of a given symptom. It does this in two ways: by defining what is desirable, and by defining what is obscene or taboo. The "relentless pursuit of thinness" that we find in anorexics—which has so often been called a "caricature" of what society considers beautiful—is an example of the former. Anorexic girls do believe that what they are doing does in fact make them more desirable and more attractive.

Similarly, anorexics avoid that which our culture has defined as repulsive and taboo. Crisp (1974) has called anorexia a "fat phobia." He captures part of the anorexic's intense need to resist those impulses which our fitness-conscious society has branded evil: gluttony and culinary abandon.

We are not accustomed to think of mental disorders as political issues, or as cultural by-products. Therefore, it is useful to consider the analogy of classical conversion hysteria, about which Freud wrote in his early career. This, too, was a disease found almost exclusively in women. It, too, mimicked certain social roles—particularly fragility and helplessness—that women of that day were supposed to fill. There is a striking parallel between the "belle indifférence" of the classical conversion hysteria and the denial of emaciation found in many anorexics. The hysteric was often quite indifferent to the limb paralysis which was the symptom masking some underlying conflict. Freud would consider a symptom such as a hand paralysis to be a conflict, masking the urge to masturbate, for example. We now know that Freud was only partially correct. However, we see in the anorexic how the emaciation often denies the intense bulimic urges, and that the symptoms take a socially acceptable form—dietary and weight consciousness. The anorexic, in her relentless pursuit of thinness, attempts both to satisfy society's demands and to deny or temporize powerful internal needs.

We are not suggesting that anorexia is the modern day form of hysteria, but that both may be emotional disorders whose form and content were and are heavily influenced by the sociocultural context in which they are observed.

This does not seem too ambitious a statement. Both involve the formation of symptoms whose function is to signal distress while symbolizing the underlying wish or impulse. The particular taboo impulse in each case appears to be determined by the norms of the time. The hysteria analogy for anorexia is so apt, precisely because we can see, in retrospect, how the sexually repressive atmosphere of the culture influenced the formation of hysterical symptoms. There remain many countries in the world — among them the Moslem countries — where classical conversion hysterias are still extremely common and where sexuality is still highly repressed. By contrast, such disorders are much rarer in the western world.

TOWARD A SOCIAL-PSYCHOLOGICAL MODEL OF LIFE ADAPTATIONS

The risk factor model offers a comprehensive framework for understanding the various etiological factors which contribute to the disorder of anorexia nervosa and related eating disorders. It is a model which helps explain why anorexia and eating disorders may be on the increase. Importantly, this approach integrates traditional notions of the etiology of these conditions without denying the relevance of recent sociocultural shifts which are particularly helpful in explaining the increase. As a means of integrating these various ideas, we offer a schematic which suggests the precedence and interplay between the several forces and factors determining any life adaptation. Any originality in Figure 1 lies in the organization and construction of the schematic itself. The ideas which underlie it have been prominent for decades. Freud (1916) wrote of three complementary series of forces which shaped adult behavior and personality: 1) biological disposition; 2) early life trauma; and 3) present day stress. A similar approach was utilized by Talcott Parsons (1960) in his monolithic attempt to develop a unified theory of the social sciences. Jacob Getzels (1963) developed a sociocultural theory and model for schools which has influenced educators for several generations. His model, in particular, was useful in the construction of the schematic presented here.

Figure 1 organizes the various factors which we believe contribute to an anorexic life adjustment. The model is designed to conceptualize the variety of relationships possible between these numerous factors and to suggest possible directions of causation. It helps explain how anorexia, either in its primary form or in less malignant form, may be a life adaptation which can be reached by numerous routes. The model also offers a way of organizing present research and pointing to neglected areas currently in need of investigation.

Finally, this approach suggests how, in time, a risk factor equation might successfully be applied to anorexia nervosa, as well as to other psychiatric syndromes. Risk factor models in mental illness tend to fall into two types. The first are models which permit predictions about prognosis (that is, outcome),

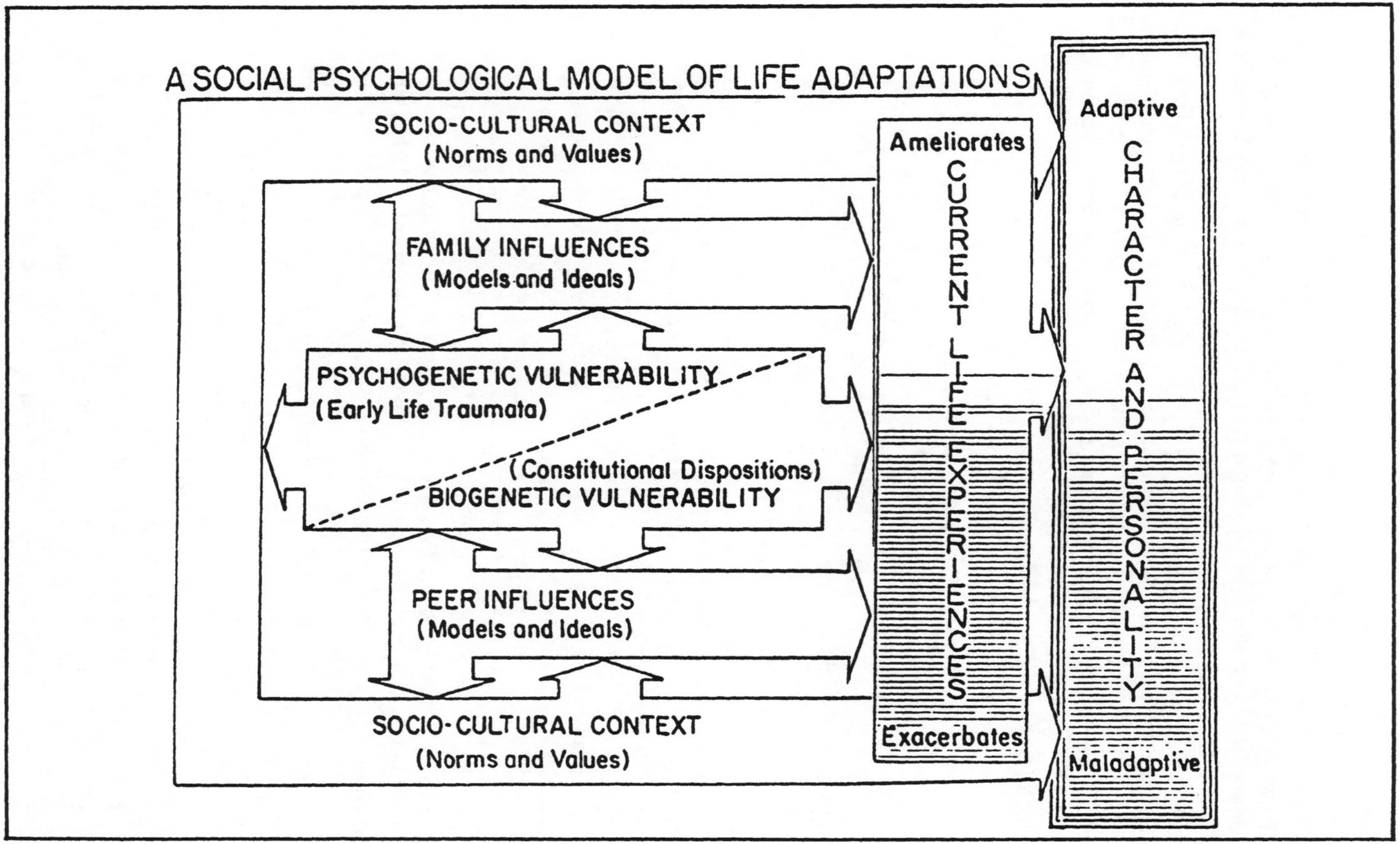
A SOCIAL PSYCHOLOGICAL MODEL OF LIFE ADAPTATIONS
SOCIO-CULTURAL CONTEXT
(Norms and Values)
FAMILY INFLUENCES
(Models and Ideals)
PSYCHOGENETIC VULNERABILITY
(Early Life Traumata)
(Constitutional Dispositions)
BIOGENETIC VULNERABILITY
PEER INFLUENCES
(Models and Ideals)
SOCIO-CULTURAL CONTEXT
(Norms and Values)
Ameliorates
CURRENT LIFE EXPERIENCES
Exacerbates
Adaptive
CHARACTER AND PERSONALITY
Maladaptive

Figure 1.

once someone has been diagnosed as having a given disorder. Such prognostic factors have been identified in both schizophrenia and in anorexia (Crisp, Kalucy, Lacey, & Harding, 1977; Garfinkel & Garner, 1982; Halmi, Goldberg, Eckert, Casper, & Davis, 1977; Stephens, 1970; Stephens & Astrup, 1963; Vaillant, 1963).

The second type of risk factor model is one which attempts to predict who is at high risk premorbidly for developing anorexia nervosa, given a set of predisposing factors. In the field of heart disease this would be the difference between predicting who is likely to recover from heart disease after a first episode versus a more epidemiological model which attempts to predict who is at risk for developing heart disease in a given culture before the onset of a coronary event. It is this broader type of model that we are developing here.

The model presents a conceptual way of understanding an individual's present form of life adaptation in the world. Life adaptation includes the more enduring internal factors which we generally think of as character and personality. These are what depth psychologists call psychic structure and the personologists call personality traits. Life adaptation also includes the more or less consistent patterns of behavior which an individual displays across time and across situations. This side of the life adaptation equation, an individual's behavior, is shaped by his current life situation. Whether an individual's more or less enduring way of being in the world finds easy or difficult expression depends on the environment in which the person finds (or in some cases puts) him- or herself. The current life situation determines whether the person is likely to find his or her way of being in the world as successful or unsuccessful. When someone's way of understanding, experiencing, and behaving in the world is less successful, stress is unavoidable. Such stress is inevitably uncomfortable and can lead to the extremes of symptoms and emotional disorders on the one hand, or adaptive growth and change on the other hand. Which outcome is likely depends largely on the extent and breadth of internal strength and structure which already exists within the individual. In the model, this role of current life experiences is expressed in the large vertical element just to the left of that representing character and personality.

The horizontal elements which occupy the left side of the model express the role of early developmental factors in shaping the present form of an individual's character and personality. A first, most prominent influence in whether an individual is at risk for a restricted and less adaptive internal character is the presence of some constitutional diathesis, an innate disposition which makes the individual vulnerable to psychological distress. Such diatheses have been proposed for a number of emotional disorders and at several different levels, depending on the perspective of the investigator. These range from cellular explanations for manic depressive illness, such as a dysfunction in the capacity to pump lithium out of the cell, to behavioral explanations for schizophrenia in the early molding behavior of the neonate which elicits, in turn, certain maladaptive mothering responses. Here we can only make a glancing reference to the myriad possibilities for potential constitutional diatheses to the later development of anorexia nervosa. First, there is the possibility of neural deficits or endocrine anomalies affecting the normal reflex of hunger and satiation in the neonate. At the behavioral level we might ask if there are certain behavioral anomalies around feeding that might elicit or interact with inappropriate responses from the mother as the principal shaper of early eating behaviors and the learning which develops from that interaction.

A second prominent influence in whether an individual is at risk is the occurrence of one or more early life traumata which then makes the individual psychologically vulnerable to later life distress. As with constitutional dispositions, the possibilities for psychological traumata are numerous and vary according to the perspective of the theorist or investigator. For anorexia nervosa we might speculate the potential consequence of a physical trauma, such as an undetected pyloric stenosis, in interfering with the early learning that leads to psychological correlates to the physiological hunger and satiation reflexes. At another perspective we have already suggested the potential anorexogenic implications when early food regulation becomes caught up in the content of overly negligent or overly intrusive parenting. Such parenting would at a sufficient degree and frequency constitute a psychogenetic vulnerability to later life psychopathology in general, and to an eating disturbance in particular.

These most primary influences on character are continually in transaction with the several other forces at work on the individual in the environment. In Figure 1 these are broken down into the proximal influences of family and peers, and the more distal influences of society and culture. These forces may transmute or intensify the effects of constitutional disposition and/or early life traumata both during the formative years, when character is most malleable, and later, when character is fairly well established. This is why the model expresses the idea that early developmental factors of all kinds may have a direct and/or indirect effect on current life adaptation. For example, we might imagine an individual predisposed from the earliest kinds of factors to regulate self-esteem through food and weight controls consistent with our understanding of anorexic or anorexic-like character. Let us imagine such a person were raised in an environment of family and friends who not only tolerated such behavior but also admired the norms and values of a general culture which held in high esteem thinness and athleticism in women, especially in such sublimated forms as dance or modeling. The result might be an individual in whom there was a comfortable fit between innate character and the childhood and adolescent environment in which that character was nourished and developed. Grant further that such a person was able to develop sufficient skills to be a professional dancer or model, within the general sociocultural context which valued such skills, then the final adaptation would be highly successful. How successful or unsuccessful any current life adaptation is depends on the fit between the person's present character, the current life experiences he/she is able to have or make available, and how well the interaction between these two produces something which is valued in the culture in which it is occurring. In our example of the ballet dancer, such a character is only successfully adaptive when it is able to find and utilize current life experiences which are consonant with that character and in a sociocultural context which places a high value on the outcome of such a fit between character (and skills) and life opportunity.

IMPLICATIONS FOR RESEARCH: IMPORTANT FIRST EFFORTS

Figure 1 suggests numerous ways to an anorexic-like lifestyle. At one extreme are individuals whose life adjustment is set in earliest life by constitutional and/or early developmental trauma. These are the individuals with classical and deep-seated anorexia and who conform to our most traditional ideas about the disorder and its etiology. These are people who we might suspect would make an anorexic life adjustment no matter what the cultural press and forces toward food, eating, body size, and weight. At the other extreme are those whose eating problems seem to be a direct function of specific factors and forces in the contemporary culture. While these might (or might not) be individuals who in any culture are more vulnerable to stress and more likely to react to that stress with some kind of emotional problem or symptom, the form and content of that reaction can be seen as a direct function of the cultural forces at work at the time. These, we suggest, are the individuals who are most likely to develop what Kluckholn (1954) referred to as "a culture's pet mental disturbance." More important, these are the individuals who constitute that group which we believe accounts for the rising incidence in anorexia and related eating problems.

If we believe that the sociocultural milieu affects the shape and adaptive value of psychological symptomatology, then we must begin to research the sociocultural milieu. When we study anorexics only in the hospital or in outpatient offices, we are ignoring the context in which the disorder grows. Studies outside clinical settings and which focus on the milieu as well as the individual are almost nonexistent. In closing, we would like to review a few of those studies already conducted or underway which do attempt to explore the sociocultural context of anorexia nervosa.

The several primarily epidemiological studies noted in an earlier section (Crisp et al., 1976; Lacey 1979; Nylander, 1971) are, by inference, of this type. By studying populations of middle-class female adolescents who are particularly vulnerable to peer and media cultural forces, these authors are offering indirect evidence with respect to the role of sociocultural press and the incidence of eating disorders. The first study specifically designed to demonstrate that a vocational or social press can induce anorexia or anorexic-like behavior was a study of ballet dancers and models by Garner and Garfinkel (1978). They developed a small questionnaire covering anorexic thought and behavior, which they entitled the Eating Attitudes Test. They gave it to anorexics, normals, and ballerinas. They found the normals scored around 16, anorexics scored around 58, and ballerinas scored directly between them on anorexic attitudes and behavior. Their mean EAT scores were 25. Each of the groups was, statistically, significantly distinct from one another. Garner and Garfinkel found seven women diagnosable as having primary anorexia nervosa in the ballet company. They concluded that people with high scores on the EAT measure were overrepresented in ballet companies, and that this means either that such companies attract anorexics, or that anorexiform behavior—and perhaps true anorexia nervosa—can be induced by vocational pressure.

In an effort to explore further the spectrum of eating disorders, the authors investigated anorexic-like symptomatology in otherwise normal college women (Thompson & Schwartz, 1981). The study was conducted at a local private college that attracts women from upper-middle- and middle-class homes. Initially we interviewed a sample of 25 women who are currently anorexic, using the Feighner diagnostic research criteria. Having obtained a "true" anorexic comparison group, we went to the college and screened women in classrooms using Garner and Garfinkel's EAT measure. We screened a total of 125 women. We found that fully a quarter of them scored higher on the measure than Garner and Garfinkel's ballet students, indicating extremely high levels of body preoccupation, and anorexic-like symptomatology. Excluding those women who were more than or less than 10% over or under average body weight for height and age, we interviewed and tested the remainder. These 25 women were called the normal "high-problem" group. Finally, for purposes of comparison, we interviewed 25 women who reported virtually no problems at all with eating. The three groups: anorexic, "high-problem," and "no-problem" were then compared.

We did not locate any women with primary anorexia among the women we screened. Though we knew that there were at least three on campus, they did not fall in the sample. What we did encounter was an extraordinary amount of eating disorder pathology in the "high-problem group." For example, we rated 54% of our primary anorexics as habitually binge eating to a moderate or severe degree. Fifty-two percent of our "high-problem" group were moderate to severe bingers. Only 23% of the no-problem group reported moderate binging.

Forty-eight percent of our anorexic sample practiced self-induced vomiting for purposes of weight control. Fifty-two percent—that is, 13 of 25 women in the "high-problem" group—practiced self-induced vomiting regularly as a method of weight control. If we consider these women as a percentage of the entire sample we screened, we conclude that 10% of women at a private, co-educational college practice weight control by regular self-induced vomiting. Extrapolating from those laxative abusers we found, we estimate that 3% attempt to control weight with periodic laxative abuse.

Perhaps we could convey the extent and power of the anorexic-like symptomatology we found by saying that if we were to disguise the tapes of these interviews, it would be almost impossible to distinguish the primary anorexic subjects from many of the normal women with anorexic-like symptoms. They speak the same way of their bodies, their food worries, their exhausting battles with the impulse to eat. Oftentimes these preoccupations become a life focus. For example, we found that most self-induced vomiters have another self-induced vomiter as their "closest friend." Problem-free women had often never heard of or never met a self-induced vomiter. We are impressed by the tendency of some normally-functioning, normal-weight women to organize their thinking, their emotional distress, and their social lives around anorexic-like concerns. Only one woman out of the 25 in the high-problem group was in treatment of any kind.

This study, like that of Garner and Garfinkel (1978), reveals a whole universe of women important to our understanding of the relationship between the culture and the increase of women with primary anorexia nervosa and related eating disorders. It is in the study of more "high-problem" normal populations that future research can help us understand the sociocultural contributions to this disorder. In turn, these first studies which document widespread anorexia-like phenomena, at least in ballet companies and college women, raise important research questions about this group. Most obvious is what is the relation of this group, if any, to primary anorexia nervosa.

SUMMARY

In this chapter we have posed and partially answered a series of questions: 1) Is there a change in the culture's press toward eating and thinness? 2) Are anorexia and related disorders increasing? 3) To what extent do existing theories explain the increase? 4) What kinds of expanded theory and research can help explain the increased incidence and prevalence of anorexia and related eating disorders? Finally, we have pointed to the kinds of research just now being done, and which must be done in the future to better understand the rise in this disorder and the contribution of sociocultural factors to that rise.

REFERENCES

Bruch, H. (1978). *The golden cage: The enigma of anorexia nervosa.* Cambridge: Harvard University Press.
Crisp, A. H. (1974). Primary anorexia nervosa or adolescent weight phobia. *Practitioner, 212,* 525-535.
Crisp, A. H., Palmer, R. L., & Kalucy, R. S. (1976). How common is anorexia nervosa? A prevalence study. *British Journal of Psychiatry, 128,* 549-554.
Crisp, A. H., Kalucy, R. S., Lacey, J. H., & Harding, B. (1977). The long-term prognosis in anorexia nervosa: Some factors predictive of outcome. In R. A. Vigersky (Ed.), *Anorexia nervosa.* New York: Raven Press.
Freud, S. (1916-1917). Introductory lectures on psychoanalysis. *Standard Edition,* (Vols. 15 & 16). London: Hogarth Press, 1961, 1963.
Garner, D. M., & Garfinkel, P. E. (1978). Sociocultural factors in anorexia nervosa. *The Lancet* (Sept.) *2,* 674.
Garner, D. M., Garfinkel, P. E., Schwartz, D., & Thompson, M. (1980). Cultural expectations of thinness in women. *Psychological Reports, 47,* 483-491.
Getzels, J. W. (1963). Conflict and role behavior in the educational setting. In W. Charters, J. & N. L. Gage (Eds.), *Readings in the social psychology of education.* Boston: Bacon and Allyn.
Halmi, K., Goldberg, S. C., Eckert, E., Casper, R., & Davis, J. M. (1977). *Pre-treatment evaluation in anorexia nervosa.* New York: Raven Press.
Kael, P. (1978). Great chefs of Europe, Book Review. *New Yorker.*
Kaufman, M. R., Heiman, M. (Eds.). (1964). *Evolution of psychosomatic concepts.* New York: International Universities Press.
Kendell, R. E., Hall, D. J., Hailey, A., & Babigian, H. M. (1973). The epidemiology of anorexia nervosa. *Psychological Medicine, 3,* 200-203.
Kluckholn, C. (1954). *Mirror for man.* New York: McGraw Hill.
Lacey, J. (1979). Personal communication to Vivian Meehan.
Minuchin, S. (1970). The use of an ecological framework in the treatment of a child. In E. J. Anthony & C. Koupernik (Eds.), *The child in his family.* New York: Wiley.
Nielsen, A. C. (1979). Who's dieting and why? Chicago, IL: A. C. Nielsen Co., Research Department.
Nylander, T. (1971). The feeling of being fat and dieting in a school population. *Acta Sociomedica Scandinavica, 3,* 17-26.
Palazzoli, M. S. (1974). *Self-starvation.* (A. Pomerans, Trans.) London: Chaucer.
Parsons, T. (1960). *Structure and process in modern society.* New York: Free Press.
Stephens, J. H. (1970). Long-term course and prognosis in schizophrenia. *Seminars in Psychiatry, 2,* 464-484.
Stephens, J. H., & Astrup, C. (1963). Prognosis in process and non-process schizophrenia. *American Journal of Psychiatry, 119,* 945-953.
Theander, S. (1970). Anorexia nervosa: A psychiatric investigation of 94 female patients. *Acta Psychiatrica Scandinavica Supplementum, 214,* 1-194. Copenhagen: Munksgaard.
Thompson, M., & Schwartz, D. (1981). Life adjustment of women with anorexia nervosa and anorexic-like behavior. *International Journal of Eating Disorders, 2,* 47-60.
Vaillant, G. E. (1963). Prospective prediction of schizophrenic remission. *Archives of General Psychiatry, 120,* 367-375.
Wallechinsky, D., Wallace, I., & Wallace, A. (1977). *Book of lists.* New York: William Morrow.
Wooley, S., & Wooley, O. (1979). Obesity and women—I. A closer look at the facts. *Women's Studies Int. Quart., 2,* 69-79.

Chapter 6

Bulimarexia:
A Sociocultural Perspective

Marlene Boskind-White

Bulimarexia, the binge-purge syndrome in which women typically consume inordinate amounts of food and later purge via self-induced vomiting, laxatives or extreme fasting, was introduced to the professional literature in 1978 (Boskind-Lodahl & White, 1978). At the time of our initial research at Cornell University, the diagnostic category *bulimia* was devoid of any reference to purging. More important, bulimia was described as a rare disorder, which, like anorexia nervosa, was overwhelmingly interpreted and managed within the boundaries of psychoanalytic theory. Many of the co-eds who responded to our initial outreach efforts had been previously labeled anorexic by therapists. Most found the clinical description of the emaciated anorexic foreign and frightening and were unwilling or unable to identify with this diagnostic entity. We therefore introduced the term bulimarexia in order to distinguish the binge-purge syndrome from anorexia and bulimia as defined in DSM-II.*

From the outset we were dismayed and astonished at the tremendous response to our publications. Thousands of women responded to our early work, readily revealing their binge-purge behavior. Their pain and shame were overwhelming as they bemoaned their wasted talents, interrupted relationships, and significant medical problems.

Current research indicates that bulimarexia is increasing rapidly. Estimates among college students range from 3.8% (Stangler & Printz, 1980) to 13% (Halmi, Falk, & Schwartz, 1981). In a massive survey regarding women's at-

---
*The reader should consult our book (Boskind-White & White, 1983) for a complete analysis of etiological, familial, and physiological factors associated with bulimarexia.

titudes about their bodies and food, *Glamour* magazine (February, 1984) polled 33,000 women and found that 41% of the respondents felt moderately unhappy or very unhappy with their bodies. Furthermore, only 25% were heavier than they should have been, while 30% were below recently established norms for their height and weight. When asked to describe how they felt about specific parts of their bodies, a majority were either "dissatisfied" or "ashamed of" their stomach, hips, and thighs. The authors observed, "What we see is a steadily growing cultural bias—almost no woman, of whatever size, feels she's thin enough" (p. 198). The majority of these women (80%) felt they had to be slim to be attractive to men. The survey also revealed an intense degree of desperation about weight control with a suprising number of respondents using potentially dangerous substances such as diet pills (50%), liquid formula diets (27%), and diuretics (18%). Eighteen percent "sometimes" or "often" used laxatives for weight loss; 45% had tried fasting or starving; and 15% had turned to self-induced vomiting. Thus, bulimarexia is indeed prevalent among young women today.

In the last few years, public awareness of bulimarexia has increased significantly. Anorexia Aid Societies throughout the country have provided an effective means of support for desperate women, their parents, and other loved ones. Self-help groups have been generated so that national networks have been established, often under the guidance and leadership of women who have overcome this pervasive habit. Such women become role models for others; they share valuable insights and offer concrete suggestions stemming from their struggles and successes. Through these kinds of supportive, awareness-expanding experiences, many women have been able to gain a more balanced perspective about their bodies and the stifling aspects of the "feminine role" assigned to women by society.

Universities and colleges across the country have begun outreach intervention and preventative programs, educational seminars, and lectures, as well as group and individual psychotherapy for bulimarexics. Today therapists are much more informed about these problems because of the sudden proliferation of articles in journals. Over the past seven years we have trained over 100 professionals in our group therapy workshops alone.

Medical journals are slowly beginning to publish articles about this pervasive habit and its medical ramifications. Despite these obvious gains, however, certain appalling facts remain. Today, an enormous population of women, young and old, are obsessed with bodily perfection and extreme standards of slimness and food. These destructive pursuits typically vitiate many lives. Sadly, the women we have worked with spend inordinate amounts of time obsessing about food and their bodies and have little time and energy to grow, pursue goals, and develop qualities necessary for psychological survival in today's changing society. Their dialogue is replete with "I used to's."

Equally frightening is the major threat to women's health resulting from binging and purging. These behaviors, when prolonged, may be potentially life threatening: Women run the risk of cancer, cardiac arrest, renal failure, kidney and liver damage (Boskind-White & White, 1983). Because of severe energy crises in metabolism, lethargy and depression are often consequences which can lead to suicide.

Pessimistic statements regarding prognosis in bulimarexia not only are unwarranted, but also tend to demotivate and reinforce secrecy and deception among those struggling to overcome the illness. More effective treatment methods are clearly needed. However, gloomy appraisals of treatment enhance feelings of learned helplessness and hopelessness — major stumbling blocks to successful treatment.Bulimarexia is not a disease; it is a *learned habit* fostered by an insidious socialization process which prepares women to accept weakness, sickness, and victimization. Since these attitudes and behaviors are learned, they can be *unlearned*. We have found the prognosis for bulimarexic women to be good in general, primarily because they are bright, talented, and capable. Although many have not been helped by traditional forms of therapy, they respond quite positively to a group format, as evidenced by a recent outcome study (see Chapter 13). This chapter will illuminate the role of sociocultural factors in the etiology of bulimarexia.

In late 1966, a 17-year-old 5'6" 97-pound nymphet from England, Lesley Hornby Armstrong, nicknamed *Twiggy,* burst upon the American fashion scene and draped her emaciated 31"-22"-32" skeleton over the pages of *Seventeen* and *Vogue.* Created in part by slick opportunistic promotion, Twiggy became an overnight sensation. Thousands of young American women began to pattern their clothes, makeup, hairstyle, and body after her.

Today, many experts in the field of eating disorders point an accusing finger at Twiggy and connect her appearance with the appalling increase of diagnosed cases of anorexia nervosa and bulimarexia. To support this view, they remind us that the first outbreak of these disorders occurred during the flapper era which emphasized slimness as stylish and desirable (Beuf, Dglugash, & Eininger, 1976). However, while most of these experts deplore the social attitudes that apparently established Twiggy's emaciated body type as ideal, few examine these social factors within their treatment programs. Psychoanalysts, in particular, have a difficult time acknowledging cultural themes, since they have emphasized unconscious conflicts about sexuality, pregnancy wishes (bulimia), or fears of oral impregnation (anorexia) as primary to the etiology of eating disorders. Cultural factors are therefore viewed as secondary to the working through of these intrapsychic conflicts. Some contemporary clinicians have disregarded these traditional interpretations in favor of a theory holding toxic mother-child relationships responsible (Bruch, 1973). Thus, they encourage and reinforce examining the *inner space* of the child and her family rather than acknowledging *outer* cultural pressures and historical themes.

Can it be that Twiggy, single-handedly, established the trend in body type that has relentlessly persisted over 15 years, or are there other more relevant historical and psychosocial pressures which propel young women like lemmings to the sea?

Responses to these questions are broad and varied. It is simplistic to examine a cultural phenomenon such as Twiggy in isolation. Attention must be devoted to the type of role that was desired for women during fat and thin eras, the prevailing economic conditions at the time, and those beliefs and attitudes about themselves and society which enticed women to embrace a particular body type.

The next part of this chapter addresses the paradoxical historical and cultural themes contributing to today's obsession with slimness. The last part focuses on relevant psychosocial pressures influencing women from the 1940s to the present. An examination of the conditioning histories of our mothers and grandmothers serves to illuminate the shocking persistence and prevalence of eating disorders among contemporary women.

THIN VERSUS FAT

Garland (1970) suggests that it is myopic to study one body type in opposition to another. Rather, she emphasizes that modified versions of extreme body types have often been desired simultaneously within cultures. For example, the Greeks emphasized slimness, beauty, and seductiveness in their wives and daughters. However, some of their goddesses were glorified as "mother earth" with solid, powerful, massive bodies and expressions of serenity, dignity, and nobility. In the 1930s the slim body of the 1920s persisted despite Mae West's voluptuousness displayed on the silent screen. Today, in spite of the fact that reed-slim figures prevail, Playboy centerfolds continue to present a curvaceous (albeit slimmer) counterpart to Marilyn Monroe.

Until Victorian times a woman's body had been expected to reflect a "mother-earth" image. As long as her primary identity was tied to the role of mother, moderate plumpness was tolerated and became symbolic of fertility, health, and the ability to survive. During the Victorian era, however, fat and thin were appropriate within the same body. During the early 1900s the ideal woman grew older and more matronly. As Lurie (1981) points out, the Victorian woman typically was the mother of many children in a society that defined her role as skilled domestic manager and tutor. During this period, necklines plunged and women looked more seductive. Lace-layered breasts, petticoats, bows, and padded corsets initiated the bustle and hour-glass shape which was becoming stylish. Women wore cumbersome, painful outfits throughout the year, often fainting from the heat or pain resulting from welts and cracked ribs. The tiny waist, created by rigid lacing, exaggerated breasts and hips, making the female torso appear regal, erect, and statuesque. In contrast to this older womanly ideal, young, undeveloped women appeared gaunt, pale, and fragile, thus creating another Victorian stereotype—the weak, timid, delicate, shrinking violet. This hour-glass shape and the immature, fragile ideal did not however render fatness a sin. Bulk in men personified power, authority, and wealth, while plump women were considered sexually desirable.

The inhibiting and restrictive dress and body required in the Victorian era arose in response to the creation of a new kind of American middle-class woman. Home and family were seen as separate from the world of work and money. As Hymowitz and Weissman (1978) point out, for the first time in America a class of women emerged who were supported by their husbands. No longer partners, they had become dependent. Prior to this era women were often viewed as strong, brave, daring, hardy, and adventurous. In 1710, one such woman in Virginia was described as showing

> nothing of ruggedness or immodesty in her carriage, yet she will carry a gun in the woods and kill deer, turkeys, etc., shoot down wild cattle, catch and tye hogs, knock down trees with an ax and perform the most manful exercises as well as most men in these parts. (quoted in Hymowitz & Weissman, 1978, p. 4)

By the 1800s these qualities were becoming exclusively masculine and women's roles were being sharply redefined.

RICH VERSUS POOR

With the first great influx of European immigrants following the Victorian era, a robust female form increasingly came to be associated with being old, lower class, and intellectually inferior. Soon slimness among women became the hallmark of wealth and status. The embryonic haute couture emerged in full force to cater to the demands of the wealthy for extravagant, lavish fashions. If their models were slim, it was because this was the new womanly ideal espoused by the upper class. Pragmatic designers were anxious to sell their creations, and fabrics "hung" better on slender forms, displaying workmanship to the best possible advantage. Thus, during the early 1900s high status clothes, combined with a slender torso, became major criteria for distinguishing upper- and lower-class women.

Poor immigrants, on the other hand, remembered too well the privations of poverty and the ravages of desire. For them fat and eating continued to be associated with health and prosperity. The availability of food in the new world was a welcome contrast to their frugal backgrounds. Fattening, low-nutrient foods such as starches and sweets were cheaper and more readily available than meats and fresh fruits. Thus, in the new affluent society that was emerging, the upper classes no longer needed to display their wealth in the form of excess adipose tissue. As pointed out by Bruch (1973), "there comes a time in having socially arrived that one no longer needs to demonstrate one's leisure class status" (p. 348).

Furthermore, 19th century industrialization provided young girls with new opportunities. They flocked to the mill towns to sign up for work for a variety of reasons, as indicated in the following account:

> One girl who sits at my right hand at the table is in the factory because she hates her mother-in-law. . . . The one next to her has a wealthy father, but like many of our country farmers he is very penierious and he wishes his daughters to maintain themselves. . . . The next has a "well-off" mother, but she is very pious and will not buy her daughter so many pretty gowns and collars and ribbons as she likes. . . . The next one has a horror of domestic service. The next one has left a good home because her lover, who has gone on a whaling voyage, wishes to be married when he returns, and she would like more money than her father will give her. (quoted in Hymowitz & Weissman, 1978, p. 124).

Mill work provided many girls of the lower and middle classes with a chance at the new-found American dream of transcending poverty. They nurtured the hope of finding properous middle-class husbands who would support them in a ladylike, dependent style. A majority spent their hard-earned wages buying fashionable clothing so that at church and other social functions no one could detect a difference in social status (Hymowitz & Weissman, 1978, p. 127). Thus, clothing and the body type that were emulated by the upper classes soon filtered down to lower- and middle-class girls who were aspiring to greater social and economic status.

The social class distinctions between rich/slim and poor/fat that began in the Victorian era continues with a vengeance today. Studies conducted in the 1950s through the 1980s revealed that obesity occurred seven times more frequently among lower-class than upper-class women (Goldblatt, Moore, & Stunkard, 1973). Furthermore, obesity among women who dropped in social status was greater than among those who were upwardly mobile. The longer a woman's family had been in the U.S., the less likely she was to be obese (Moore, Stunkard, & Srole, 1962).

Silverstone (1969) suggests that it is not the tendency to become fat but the concern with being overweight which distinguishes the lower from the upper classes. Bruch (1973) also points out that there exists a subculture in the lower socioeconomic groups in which emphasis on appearance, with slenderness as the only valued body configuration, is not paramount. This seemed to be true of the black culture, at least until recently. Black women depicted in TV programs over the last few years are often overweight and yet still project power, competence, and integrity. More importantly, all had relationships with men who loved and respected them in spite of their bulk. We are currently subjecting this hypothesis to closer scrutiny.

YOUNG VERSUS OLD

Madge Garland, a Professor of Fashion Design, points out that fashion changes often follow great political and social upheavals, while in a static society dress tends to change very little (Garland, 1970). This was certainly true in the early 1900s. When World War I had ended, the children of the Victorian nouveaux riches had grown up and begun to sense their economic power. Well-informed women also had access to a new birth control device—the diaphragm. Jazz music and clothes came to reflect the new values of a wealthy, youthful minority. For the first time in American history, a generation of college-age men and women had money, leisure time, prestige, and power. A prevailing stereotype of the flapper is that she was both emancipated and immoral. However, as Hymowitz and Weissman (1978) suggest, her emancipation was more apparent than real. Although she got rid of her corsets and cut her hair, she bound her breasts to make herself flat! Thus, the "new style" was just another form of female conformity. In 1920 only two cosmetic firms saw a profit. In 1927, 18,000 cosmetic enterprises paid taxes (Allen, 1959, p. 73). The flapper's "freedom" thus signified an escalation in the war to attract men. A woman was supposed to *look* sexy, free, and available. In actuality, however, she was not available until after marriage. A woman who was aware of the diaphragm was really not supposed to use it until she was a wife (Hymowitz & Weissman, 1978, p. 292).

The slimness of flapper women has also been exaggerated. Although their skirts were shorter, little in the way of flesh was revealed because of thick stockings. Women wore loose, smocklike dresses that were waistless, and their oversized floor-length coats made it almost impossible to assess their shape. Thus, the flaws in a woman's body were still hidden from the world.

As in the Victorian era, young middle-class girls began to embrace the upper-class ideal of body and clothes. Now, in addition to factory work, women were becoming governesses, typists, and sales clerks. They wanted to wear clothes that suited their new endeavors, and rags-to-riches designers such as Chanel made high fashion out of realistic working-girl clothes as women flocked to buy these cheap, mass-produced copies of the originals. Although young women of the 1920s embraced a slimmer ideal of womanhood, older women, in general, refused. They viewed the flapper era as a passing phase, one of immaturity and frivolousness, and thus they waited for a return to normality in dress. They did not have long to wait. The depression put an end to such youthful irreverence and brought forth a more serious and sophisticated male and female ideal. Body shape was modified for both men and women, with a heavier, fuller look desired. Breasts and curves returned to favor in the 1930s primarily because of the revealing draped dresses with long tight sleeves that became the hallmark of many designers. Women were still slender and often went braless because of plunging necklines and bare backs.

The 1940s saw a mimicking of the Victorian shape with Dior's padded shoulders, a swollen upper body, and a pinched waist. More than a few fashion experts maintain that this was a sign of women's desire to return to the shelter of the suburbs after World War II complicated the serious work of being wives and mothers. Although there were many changes in fashion between the 1930s and 1950s, models continued to be depicted as sophisticated, worldly-looking women in their thirties. It was once again the era of the mature woman. Sex goddesses such as Rita Hayworth and Betty Grable revealed ample breasts, rounded derrières, and long legs to the accompanying leers, cheers, and gestures of admiring men.

In the mid-1950s society and fashion continued to encourage maturity, but now a new trend emerged. The babies of the post-World War II baby boom had grown into teenagers and their clothers began to suggest a new form of liberation. Bobby socks, saddle shoes, jeans, and loose sweaters became the trademark of a growing but still embryonic youth movement. As in the flapper era, the word "liberation" was exaggerated. In the 1950s women no longer wore corsets or bound their breasts, but harnessed themselves in girdles and tight-fitting bras. Furthermore, their minds were still ruled by traditional romantic fantasies of love, rescue, and surrender.

In the 1960s mass communication networks which originated during World War II, along with newly introduced jet service to Europe, began to erase regional and social differences in the U.S.A. The "pop decade" had arrived. It was in England that this second youthful revolution began. Suddenly cultural values stopped filtering down from the wealthy to the masses. New ideas and talent began to arise within the working classes, the pop underground, and young aspiring English designers. For the first time in English history, working class youth had money to spend. One half of Britain's youth had dropped out of school at 15 because they were unable to continue their education in class-restricted schools which only the wealthy could afford. They were holding down jobs, turning their backs on parental dictates, and spending their money on what they wanted—clothes, music, and other forms of entertainment. Their heroes, such as Terence Stamp, Michael Caine, The Beatles, Tom Jones, and Twiggy, came from solid, working-class backgrounds.

Paris was displaced by London as the capital of women's fashions and Kings Road and Carnaby Street became household words. In the U.S.A., as in England, one half of the population was under 25, and by 1964 one fourth of the nation's families earned $10,000 or more a year. We were a young nation reared in prosperity with installment buying; teenagers began to actualize the American dream of earning and spending more money (Bender, 1967, pp. 25-32).

Twiggy arrived in the U.S.A. in 1966. Exaggerated youthfulness and wide-eyed, long-legged, innocent asexuality were personified by this child model. She looked like a pre-adolescent, the most prominent age group at that time in the U.S.A. Thousands of women began to emulate her body type, starving themselves in the process, primarily because their former models, the older women of our society, were bound up by their roles as suburban traditional housewives. Soon, however, these women, too, began to experience the pop generation, and a behavior contagion took hold. Older women were also experiencing a fear of aging and were devalued more than at any time in history. Their fear of aging, combined with the youthfulness around them, was creating a particularly insidious form of anxiety. This anxiety was further heightened by the fact that women's bodies were more visible than at any other time in American history. Only small, perfectly formed, ungirdled women could go braless and miniskirted. In fact, even young women of normal weight were unattractive by these distorted standards. Thousands of women with more matronly figures were thereby swept into a dangerous pursuit of slimness in order to conform to the current fashion ideal.

Thus, unlike the flapper era, older women did not resist but rather embraced the values of the teenage elite, equating power with money and slimness. And if they accepted absurd fashion, it was only because they had been conditioned to the absurdity of life in general and were eagerly abandoning themselves to the lie of the Feminine Mystique.

In 1965, after reviewing the haute couture collection in Europe, fashion writer Eugenia Sheppard pointed out that shapely legs were out of fashion and the new ideal was that of a petite, underdeveloped girl with no calf. Most of the prominent designers followed suit in an attempt to revitalize the fashion industry, which had fallen on hard times as a result of the proliferation of boutiques. These designers, too, began to appeal to youth by draping their clothes on adolescent bodies. This trend further reinforced extreme slimness in older women and caused Bess Myerson, the shapely Miss America of 1947, to comment: "We used to dress like Jackie Kennedy. Now we're dressing like Caroline."

FEMININE VERSUS MASCULINE

Chernin (1981) suggests that in times of oppression and war women are permitted to look voluptuous, whereas in times of greater freedom they revert to looking like boys. Were flappers, with their boyish bobbed hair, emulating men? When women begin to feel a sense of personal power, do they embrace an exaggerated form of masculinity? Lurie (1981) points out that flappers did not look like men, rather they looked like *little girls*. Their bee-stung mouth, squeaky voice, and bobbed hair resembled a small child's. Liberation was therefore more fantasy than reality. Perhaps these women were not attempting to break out of their role. They may have wanted less inhibiting clothes primarily because they were interested in comfort and attracting men.

The Twiggy look has also been equated with the desire for women to mimic men and their power (Chernin, 1981). However, what is typically lost sight of is the fact that the 1960s was the "unisex" decade. If girls looked like boys, then boys looked like girls. The long thick bangs of the Beatles soon gave way to long flowing locks and jewelry worn by Hippies. From the rear it was often impossible to determine a young person's gender. And if the trousers worn by women in the 1960s seemed to imply freedom once again, Lurie (1981) reminds us that pointed shoes with their stiletto heels, platform shoes, and clogs represent a

> series of more or less successful campaigns to force, flatter or bribe women back into uncomfortable and awkward styles, not only for the purpose of vicarious ostentation and security of sexual ownership, but also and increasingly in order to handicap them in professional competition with men. The hobble skirt, the girdle, the top heavy hats of the teens and forties, the embarrassingly short dresses of the twenties and the sixties all have aided this war effort. Today its most effective strategic devices are fashionable footwear and the demand for slimness. (p. 227)

Embracing a "rejection of femininity and a desire for masculinity" theory often leads experts to attribute the contemporary obsession with slimness to the "homosexual influence" within fashion houses. Marilyn Bender, a fashion writer for the *New York Times*, has addressed this myth admirably. She does not deny that some designers are homosexuals but points out that many of them design very feminine clothes, while many heterosexual designers produce masculine designs for women (Bender, 1967, p. 36). Since the early 1900s there have always been a few designers who dress women in men's clothes. In posters Marlene Dietrich looks out at us in tails, tie, and top hat, while Dior's version of the trousered suit in the 1960s is decked with a peaked Jules-et-Jim men's hat. The look, however, rather than masculine, is blatantly provocative, coquettish, and seductive. Once again "traditional" women with "traditional" beliefs are simply dressed in new clothes.

In the last 20 years in particular, feminists have introjected the belief that men prefer thin women; thus women, in order to please and attract men, pursue slimness.

The hypothesis that men prefer Twiggy's thinness is at best uninformed. After years of questioning hundreds of men about such preferences, we have as yet to encounter a single one who insisted that Twiggy was "his" ideal. Bo Derek is far more apropos. Women began to emulate Twiggy and were not particularly interested in what men had to say. The fact that they subscribed to semi-starvation and asexual bodies is a tragic statement about the pliability of women in general and their desperate need for approval and acceptance in particular. Lacking a firm and secure sense of identity, they struggled and starved to emulate the identity of this young, successful emaciate. The old adage, "No woman can be too young and too attractive" was rewritten. Thinness was equated with youth, beauty, and survival. The diet industry leapt to the occasion with one eye on the almighty dollar and the other on the psychology of women. Cashing in on women's gullibility, self-consciousness, uncertainty, and anxiety, the new fad diets promised love, male approval, and magical solutions to the problems of life. It did not matter what men said; most women believed what they had been sold by the media.

Today, these erroneous beliefs continue to be attributed to men despite a plethora of research to the contrary. Men are more likely to be attracted to a woman's face (especially her eyes) than to her body (Oregon State Survey, 1976).

HEALTH VERSUS DISEASE

American culture, although a melting pot of nationalities, has always been substantially influenced by Protestantism. As Beuf et al. (1976) point out, the Puritan traits of goodness and moral fiber became synonymous with the thin person, whose very appearance was a walking testimony to a life lived in moderation, void of self-indulgence. By comparison, the heavier person was viewed as indulgent, selfish, and lacking willpower. If the Puritans viewed fat as evil, the Freudian impact in the 1930s and 1940s added some new dimensions. The heavier person was said to be infantile and a victim of frustrated sexual impulses (Beuf et al., 1976). Medical opinion and new trends denouncing overweight during the last two decades added ammunition to these psychological indictments. With time, nutrition and a balanced diet were lost in the deluge of medical hypotheses linking overweight to a variety of disease processes. An overreaction to fat has been the tragic result. Beuf et al. (1976), looking at copies of the *New England Journal of Medicine* between 1968 and 1976, found articles stressing overweight outnumbered articles mentioning anorexia nervosa as a problem at a rate of six to one. The emphasis in these articles was overwhelmingly on weight control, with little attention to or importance placed on nutrition or under-eating disorders.

DEPENDENCE VERSUS INDEPENDENCE

In the 1970s another significant societal event occurred: the unprecedented prolongation of education. Men began attending graduate school and avoiding early marriages. Birth control and abortion took care of thousands of babies that in earlier decades would have resulted in some desperate marriages. Keniston (1971) labeled this phenomenon a new stage of adolescent/adult life, one typified by a sense of worthlessness and lack of definition—a psychological no man's land. Such a phenomenon would have been more appropriately labeled a "no woman's land," since women in particular were unprepared for making this adjustment. In the past, attending college provided women with a sense of security, especially since most women "knew" marriage would follow on the heels of college. Suddenly women were expected to do something with their educations. They could no longer hide behind their fear of success nor make protestations of unequal opportunities. Men were expecting women to become economic partners. The country was in a recession and many husbands were no longer able to be the only breadwinner. Many were asking for help as new jobs and careers became available to women. Discrimination suits were starting to have an impact. Universities and other organizations began actively recruiting women. Ehrenreich and English (1979) pointed out that women in the 1970s were experiencing an ambiguous and frustrating form of liberation:

> After the old dependency came the new insecurity of shifting relationships. . . . A competitive work world, unstable marriages—an insecurity from which no woman could count herself "safe" and settled. There was a sense of being adrift, but now there was no one to turn to. . . . (Ehrenreich & English, 1979, p. 228)

Women were alone and on their own more than at any time in American history. In spite of their growing sisterhood and feminist camaraderie, socialization had taught them to be passive, fragile, and frightened of competitiveness. They were unprepared to take care of themselves both psychologically and economically. Divorce had become commonplace. Attracting a man was still the primary pursuit of most women; however, they were now expected to spend longer periods of time on their own—waiting, plotting, and competing with other women for the attentions of men.

Today women are expected to pursue a career as well as motherhood and wifehood. Despite their lack of experience in coping with criticism, rejection, and confrontation, they are expected to compete with men in the marketplace.

Feminist slogans such as "Do it on your own" further fan the fires of perfectionism.

Apparently, conforming to the unrealistic, dangerous, stereotypical image of femininity in order to attract a man is still the primary pursuit of most women; even the well-educated liberated women of the 1980s are susceptible. It is our thesis, therefore, that the current emphasis on unrealistic slimness, which has dominated women for almost 20 years, has more to do with the etiology of bulimarexia than any other single factor. The media, dependent as it is upon women as consumers, continues to encourage the chic image commensurate with the bulimarexic mentality. For now, along with her mind and fantasies, the bulimarexic's body must fit a mold that is unhealthy and virtually impossible to maintain. Those women who do so must experience an absolute, obsessional vigilance over their diet and body. They have little time to develop other talents. Once there, they are typically disillusioned to find that the absurd ideal of slimness which they have tortured themselves to attain has not resulted in the social success and fulfillment for which they have yearned. It is therefore not coincidental that the uniquely feminine disorder, bulimarexia, has become even more widespread in the 1980s.

REFERENCES

Allen, F. (1959). *Only yesterday.* New York: Harper.
Bender, M. (1967). *The beautiful people.* New York: Coward-McCann.
Beuf, A., Dglugash, R., & Eininger, E. (1976). *Anorexia nervosa: A sociocultural approach.* Working paper, University of Pennsylvania, Philadelphia, PA.
Boskind-Lodahl, M., & White, W., Jr. (1978). The definition and treatment of bulimarexia in college women—A pilot study. *Journal of American College Health Association, 27*,(2), 27-29.
Boskind-White, M., & White, W. C., Jr. (1983). *Bulimarexia: The binge purge cycle.* New York: W. W. Norton.
Bruch, H. (1973). *Eating disorders: Obesity, anorexia nervosa and the person within.* New York: Basic Books.
Chernin, K. (1981). *The obsession: Reflections on the tyranny of slenderness.* New York: Harper & Row.
Ehrenreich, B., & English, D. (1979). *For her own good: 150 years of the experts' advice to women.* New York: Anchor Books.
Feeling fat in a thin society. (1984, February). *Glamour,* p. 198.
Garland, M. (1970). *The changing form of fashion.* New York: Praeger.
Goldblatt, P. B., Moore, M. E., & Stunkard, A. J. (1973). Social factors in obesity. In N. Krell (Ed.), *The psychology of obesity.* Springfield, IL: Charles C Thomas.
Halmi, K. A., Falk, J. R., & Schwartz, E. (1981). Binge-eating and vomiting: A survey of a college population. *Psychological Medicine, 11,* 697-706.
Hymowitz, C., & Weissman, M. (1978). *A history of women in America.* New York: Bantam Books.
Keniston, K. (1971). *Youth and dissent: The rise of the new opposition.* New York: Harcourt, Brace, Jovanovich.
Lurie, A. (1981). *The language of clothes.* New York: Random House.
Moore, M. E., Stunkard, A. J., & Srole, L. B. (1962, September). Obesity, social class and mental illness. *Journal of the American Medical Association, 181,* 962-966.

Oregon State Survey. Reported in the *Sunday Bulletin*, Philadelphia, PA, January 24, 1976, p. 20.
Silverstone, J. T. (1968). Psychological aspects of obesity. *Proceedings of the Royal Society of Medicine, 61,* 371-375.
Stangler, R. S., & Printz, A. M. (1980). DSM III: Psychiatric diagnosis in a university population. *American Journal of Psychiatry, 137,* 937-940.

Chapter 7

Visibility/Invisibility: Social Considerations in Anorexia Nervosa — A Feminist Perspective

Susie Orbach

INTRODUCTION

My treatment approach, rooted in a feminist consciousness, was developed during my work with anorexic women at The Women's Therapy Centre in London. It begins with a respect for the woman and her symptom by charging her with the responsibility for maintaining a minimum weight during our work together. For the anorexic, the issue of control is fundamental. Her life seems to depend on it, and her daily experience is of doing battle to maintain that control. Since the main arena of struggle between herself and those with whom she interacts is her body and her food, acknowledging and respecting that indeed she can and does have the control and it shall not be taken from her creates a space transcending the syndrome in which she can be related to. This does not mean that I ignore it, but rather that the therapy relationship is not defined in terms of food and weight management. Since the anorexic's own experience of self may well have been reduced to such a vision, not focusing on the anorexia potentially expands her horizon and makes it possible for her to have the even more troublesome aspects of her emotional life come to the fore. In addition, this approach has several useful treatment effects because, for the first time, the anorexic can relax somewhat. Her need to be in charge of her own food has been recognized. Perhaps the more hidden and invisible aspects of her problem will be recognized too. When she is seen as a person who has rights and needs rather than a recalcitrant patient who has to be pacified, the therapy has the chance to meet the client's evolving needs.

The most obvious part about the anorexic's struggle is her need to be thin, and her *success* at achieving this. The anorexic is able to transform her body dramatically. She becomes *so* small in fact that she loses the minimum amount of body weight at which she will menstruate. What she does eat—or to be more precise, the food she permits in her body—is so minimal and so controlled that her body becomes literally starved of nutrients. She develops a cluster of physical symptoms: Her extremities become sensitive to cold; she cannot sleep much and becomes an early riser; and eventually a soft downy hair grows all over her body to keep her warm. In other words, the anorexic is involved in a serious and successful transformation of her body. She has fantasized that everything in her life would be better if she were thin, but sadly, although she actually attains this state of thinness, the achievement itself brings little of what it promises. A transformation then occurs in the thrust and in the meaning of the symptom. The anorexic now becomes utterly caught up in maintaining the various schemes she has devised to minimize the threatening influence of the food she consumes.

While the anorexic fears taking in food for herself, she feels the need to be around it. Not eating does not provide relief from thinking about food; in fact, she thinks about it constantly, measures and weighs in her mind what she can and cannot have, and, in a desperate attempt to get physically close to the food, she becomes involved in preparing food for others, especially desserts. She shows deep concern for the food needs of those close to her. In this way her own desire for food is partially met through the process of projective identification. She gives to others what she so craves herself. This kind of response will be usual whether or not the anorexia contains bulimic features. Some anorexic women binge on extremely large quantities of food frequently, as often as twice a day. They feel tortured about having given in to the eating and so the act of eating is only contemplated and carried out with the intention of bringing up the food.

There are many misconceptions about anorexia nervosa. Practitioners are often frightened, bewildered, or repulsed by the problem and as a result they are loath to try and understand it from the point of view of the person who is suffering from it. Out of that fear then comes ignorance, which spurs the development of theories and treatment models resting on the practitioners' prejudices rather than the clients' needs. I think it is fair to say that it is only since the advent of the Women's Liberation Movement that it has been really possible for women to say in their own words what it means to be a female in 20th-century society. Only now can we begin to truly understand what eating problems in general and anorexia specifically are all about, and, as practitioners, help individual women find different solutions to the very real life problems and the inter- and intrapsychic dilemmas they are trying to address through this symptom.

BODY IMAGE AND WOMEN'S RELATIONSHIP TO FOOD

A commonly held view of anorexia is that it represents the female's refusal to be an adult. It is perceived as a disorder of puberty, an attempt to remain a little girl, a denial of femininity. If we examine the implications of this interpretation we can see that it has two aspects that distinctly infantilize the woman. Seen as a child, the client becomes less of a threat and the meaning of her symptom is delegitimized. Her behavior is unacceptable and must be dealt with; her opinions can be discounted because they are immature. The most progressive of practitioners work within this model to one extent or another and are then caught in a dilemma as they become engaged in a power struggle with a very persistent, tenacious person. They become enmeshed in a paradox. On the one hand, they view the anorexic as weak and childlike, and, on the other, she is experienced as behaving in a willful, crafty, sneaky, and intransigent manner, relentless about getting what she wants and therefore so hard to deal with that she must be controlled. In talking with doctors one gets the impression that they are involved in a power struggle over who is going to control the anorexic's body. Force-feeding, enforced bed rest, and forcing women to be taken by wheelchair to the toilet and to be supervised once there may seem benevolent ("the patient is weak," etc.), but these measures in reality reflect a kind of subtle rape of the female body, an intrusion so brutal and invasive that in seeking an explanation I am forced to posit men's need, albeit unconscious, to control women.

Behind the notion that this is a disorder of puberty lies another unquestioned assumption. Grown-up femininity is assumed to be unproblematic. The anorexic's refusal to accept her role is, per se, pathological, not an extremely complicated response to a confusing social role.

The Women's Liberation Movement has provided a totally new context for looking at women's relationship to both food and their bodies. Pre-feminist analyses or approaches that ignore feminism suffer, then, from not being able to comprehend why women are involved in such a complicated and, in the case of anorexia, savage struggle with food and body image. In not being able to comprehend the anorexia (or compulsive eating and bulimia for that matter) practitioners throw up their arms in despair and disgust while mechanically "treating" the sufferer as though she were an offending object. They try to get her to be the "right size," to look like a "real woman," to eat nicely, and to give no offense. Thus, by dismissal or by dispensing their treatment, they unwittingly reinforce the perpetuation of the symptom. They become part of the problem rather than part of the solution.

I always find myself using harsh words about conventional practitioners who work with anorexics because I am moved to rage every time I meet yet another woman who tells stories of humiliation in being force-fed and psychologically manipulated. I am reminded of the suffragettes on hunger strikes in jail in England, and the political authorities exercising their right to control women's bodies and women's protest by restraining them and forcing food down them.

Today, in civilized hospitals in the United States, catheters are thrust into anorexic women's necks. Yet, like the hunger striker, the anorexic is starving, she is longing to eat, she is desperate for food. Like the hunger striker, she is in protest against her conditions. Like the hunger striker, she has taken as her weapon a refusal to eat. *Not* eating is her survival tool.

Feminism allows us to hear in a new way the stories of women who suffer with anorexia. It recasts the terrain on which psychological inquiry is based. As feminists we take as our starting point that women are oppressed in this society, that our psychology reflects a preparation for this and rebellion against it, that our psychologies are gender specific (Baker Miller, 1983; Chodorow, 1978; Eichenbaum & Orbach, 1983), and that each individual psyche embodies an ensemble of patriarchal social relations.

If we reflect on the meaning of food, fatness, thinness, and femininity, we see that these words conjure up many-layered pictures of social practices we are all involved in and affected by. Women's relationship to food, their bodies, and femininity is at once extremely complex and extremely simple (Orbach, 1978; 1982). Two imperatives underlie it which in turn become highly elaborated.

The first of these is that throughout history we know the female form as an object of pleasure for men. Although the fashion in what is considered desirable has varied over time and from culture to culture—fattening sheds for pubescent girls in Africa, the Western obsession with slimness since the late 1950s—the important point to be made is that a woman's body is viewed as a central aspect of her existence and the individual woman's ability to adapt it to the current norm, whatever that may be, plays a role in her sense of well-being and in her relation to herself.

Each year the shop mannequins displaying women's clothes on plaster bodies are shaved down so that the new fashions can be presented on this year's skinnier model (Glass, 1980). Prepubescent girls now display women's clothes in the advertisements. Women's breasts and hips are supposed to get smaller and smaller giving them an increasingly elongated state. Women strive to emulate the new image as they are promised in its wake love, happiness, success, and wealth.

One's commonsense feeling that these mythical but nevertheless desirable qualities do not accompany slimness is overridden by the mass of media persuasion which stresses the necessity of slimness to a woman's survival. Such messages become insinuated into each woman's experience of self and find their expression in each woman's relationship to her body. Women tend to live outside their bodies, judging them, evaluating them, looking at themselves to see whether they can mirror the received images of femininity. A woman's body is never all right as it is. It can always be improved. A woman's legs, hair, bust, skin, and cellulite are all in danger of being unseemly unless attended to in a feminine way. A woman's body is the beneficiary of hours of attention, worry, and fretting. Women constantly try to mediate the grueling effects of body insecurity. This preoccupation is both a hidden and a public state of affairs. Women accept, at some level, the importance of looking a particular way. Obsession with the body is a permitted form of self-expression and self-involvement for women. But this publicly sanctioned private activity hides the deeply anguished relationship that so many women have to their bodies.

Another crucial aspect of women's social role, whose underbelly lay invisible before the Women's Liberation Movement helped us to see more clearly, is the paradoxical relationship of women to food and feeding. Each woman experiences important aspects of her identity and well-being deriving from an ability to nurture and feed others. Women of today have grown up knowing that one day they would shape their family's feeding. It has been, traditionally, the female who is responsible for shopping and cooking, for knowing just what each family member likes, and for making arrangements to satisfy those various food needs. Whether or not women work outside the home or share the domestic labor with their partners, women still *feel* that feeding others is a part of what they should be doing. When women attempt to divorce themselves from the kitchen, they can feel guilty and experience loss. When a woman gives up this aspect of her social role it can *feel* like a loss of an aspect of self.

At the same time as women are aware of their responsibility and desire to feed others, they come to know that food has an altogether different meaning for them. Consider the shocking and cruel fact that a woman comes to experience this same food which she gives to others with love and caring, food which is the mechanism for conveying so many emotional nuances, an expression of nurturance and bonding, as somehow dangerous to herself. Women read daily in any newspaper or magazine how they must tether their impulses towards this very same food. They must restrain their desires for the cakes they bake for others and satisfy themselves with a water-packed tuna salad with all the trimmings. Diet, deprive, deny is the message women receive. Even more sinister, they must pretend that the cottage cheese and melon is as pleasurable as a grilled cheese sandwich for lunch. For the woman, then, food becomes a potential enemy and a threat.

ANOREXIA AS A POSSIBLE SOLUTION

Having made these general remarks about women's relationship to food and body image, I will now consider anorexia as one of the possible outcomes facing a woman as a consequence of being raised in such a context. Like the meaning of the symptom itself, anorexia has been barely visible. It is seen as a new and frightening disorder. Until very recently institutes, training programs, and graduate schools did not include study of it in their curriculum. Along with this advent of interest in anorexia have developed numerous prejudices, e.g., it is morbid, it is untreatable, it is a disorder of the prepubescent girl, it affects girls from upper-middle class families, it indicates a pre-incestuous father-daughter relationship, it shows up in high achievers, it is a flight from full genital sexuality, and so on. The anorexic women that I have seen do not conform to these pictures. They have ranged from 17 to 60. They were not dragged to therapy but came themselves, even if with enormous hesitancy and fear. They have been from working class backgrounds and middle income groups. They include mothers and a grandmother. Their life experience is various but they all share a tortured relationship to their bodies and food.

The most outstanding feature that presents itself to me as a therapist on meeting an anorexic is the importance of secrecy. She is not able to show herself or to show that she has a problem. She is not able to do this because from her point of view the anorexia is *not* the problem, it is *the solution*. While everyone can see her anorexia, no one can see the person behind the anorexia. She is invisible and unknowable to herself and to others. What is visible to the outsider is some of the brutal deprivation in which she engages. Her diminished body causes an observer to wince in pain and wonder uncomprehendingly. What is visible to the anorexic herself is something quite different. Whereas we see her wasting away and disappearing, she feels herself to be strong for *she is in the process of creating, of making out of herself, a new person, one whom she can admire, from whom she can gain a little self-esteem*.

This new person, however, is in a precarious position. The anorexic is in danger of evaporating and making visible her vulnerable opposite: the despairing, anguished, needy person who lives deep within her. For this reason she becomes ever more secretive, ever more vigilant, and increasingly caught up in intricate routines and regulations in the dual attempt to (a) construct a barrier between the world and her vulnerable inner self and (b) reinforce the notion that she is strong, impenetrable, and untouchable. Viewed from this vantage point, we can see that the secrecy is not "manipulative" or "willful" per se. It is, rather, the woman's attempt to have something for herself, something she can feel good about and hold onto. The anorexia, the denial, the fulfilling of more and more arduous physical tasks represent her capacity to achieve and be successful.

THE NEED FOR CONTROL: SUCCESS AND SECURITY

This raises the following questions. Why is success so necessary, why is it judged in these terms, and why must it be approached in such a stealthy way? This need for the anorexic to have something uniquely her own and something that she alone fashions arises because she feels that throughout her life she has been on a path shaped by others. Who *she* is has been ignored and dismissed. She hasn't had a chance to develop herself. The anorexic has responded to the desires of others and tried to fit herself to their projections. She is not able to live this way anymore. She'll "do her own thing" at any cost. She turns to her body which becomes the arena for struggle. Treating it as an enemy, she wrestles with it, trying to dominate it by denying its needs. She puts all of her energy into trying to conquer her body, control it, and have it submit to her will. She will be *active* in relation to it. Paradoxically, and tragically, in this struggle with her body, she perpetuates the very denial of self that she is fighting against. But in the process she gains a measure of self-respect and peace for she has shown herself and the world that she can be more in charge of her own life than anyone else.

On the one hand the anorexia is about being thin, very, very thin. The woman expresses in her body image her confusion about how much space she may take up in the world. Although she looks extremely frail, she feels herself to be strong, to have defeated the exigencies of the body, to have overcome its human limits. Her 70-pound body can run eight miles a day and work out for hours on the exercise machines. She doesn't need food, she doesn't need to respond to the unseemly appetites of the ordinary female body. While others consider her pathetic and in need of help, her self-image is one of which she is proud. She feels strong and impenetrable. The question this raises is why she needs to live without a body or relate to her body as something to be so very tightly controlled and challenged.

The anorexic's body is symbolically linked to her emotional needs. If she can get control over her body, then perhaps she can get control over her neediness — that dreaded cost of femininity. She submits her body to rigorous discipline to divert her from her feelings. She experiences her emotional life, particularly her needs and conflicts, as an attack on herself and thus she attempts to control these feelings so that she will not be devoured by them. She tries to gain control over her body and mind by creating a new person out of herself. In other words, she rejects her needy, hungry, and yearning self and sets up incredibly tough standards that the new self will achieve. This is the meaning of her rigorous diet and exercise regimen during which, for example, she may touch her toes 3000 times a day in order to justify a half-hour's rest. She strives to become perfectly admirable and, in turn, the submission to the exercises creates a protective psychic and physical boundary, shielding her from her human vulnerability and limitations. She feels a strength for she has become someone with neither needs nor appetites.

What are these dreadful needs from which she has to escape? And what is it that the anorexic has so failed at that she feels relentlessly impelled to correct? The anorexic woman has absorbed from early on, only more intensely, the very same message that all girls receive during their passage towards femininity. She has understood that she must shape her life in the image of others. She must be concerned with and attend to the needs of others. As she develops, she must negotiate her own needs, desires, and impulses in an environment filled with emotional detours and cultural obstacles. Somewhere she has understood the danger and the impossibility of living and being for herself. A client, Roberta, tells me of knowing she always had to wake up with a smile. It was imperative that she fulfill her parents' projections. Any expression of pain was illegitimate and terrifying to the family. Roberta was denied the right to develop a capacity to deal with distress, conflict, or even ordinary unhappiness. Uncomfortable feelings were to be hidden. They were *felt* to be obscene, vulgar and overwhelming. They must not be exposed. In denying herself food and concomitantly developing an ever increasing series of daily tasks to be accomplished, Roberta is attempting to suppress her needy side, assuaging the guilt that these aspects of self engender while policing her emotional life. As she brutally denies herself, she is reassured and temporarily soothed by her success at keeping her inner experience from view.

But this kind of socialization is very costly. Roberta has identified needs of any sort with being all wrong. She feels her needs are bad. She feels she is bad. She is always trying to make reparations, to rid herself of ugly appetites and wants.

Roberta and her anorexic sisters are caught up in a struggle to try to reshape themselves physically and emotionally. Roberta has little faith in her environment, so she withdraws from it. Inside of her head, hours and hours are spent caught up in the obsession. Not only does she reconstruct her body, but she also creates an entire internal world which makes ordinary social intercourse difficult. Any anxiety, indeed any feeling *that touches her*, gets immediately channeled into the obsession. She thinks about how much she ate, how she will avoid eating for the next several days, and how much better she will feel once she has constructed a plan. In other words, she is distracted and soothed by her obsession, where all things work out satisfactorily. She knows the ups and downs of such thoughts intimately. She confronts the anxiety eating creates by resolving not to. She feels relief and is energized by her renewed commitment to vigilance. But tragically, she is only further away from the distressing feelings that trigger the obsessing in the first place. The feelings are neither experienced directly nor digested, and so the idea is fed and reinforced that she cannot cope with upsetting feelings. The gap between her spontaneous needs and her ability to respond to them grows ever wider.

IMPLICATIONS FOR CLINICAL INTERVENTIONS

I will now explore how the features of control, secrecy, and the need for success shape certain clinical interventions that are both possible and useful. It should be noted that the therapist needs to maintain a delicate balance between recognizing the strength that is bound up in the anorexia—that is, in the defense—at the same time as she is relating to the person *behind* the anorexia. In my clinical experience I find the anorexic bringing two distinct selves into the therapy session. The easiest to meet, the most visible and seemingly engaged, is what I call the anorexic defense, the part of her that reveals no need. The other self is as yet embryonic, underdeveloped, and unrecognized by the woman herself.

As I have previously noted, it is important for the therapist to acknowledge both the strength that is manifested in the anorexic defense and its source, for while the aim of the therapy will be ultimately to help the inner self emerge, the client has no sense of her own strength or potency beyond the symptom. As we have seen, she is in retreat from an inner sense of weakness and fragility and she needs our help in integrating the anorexia with her own creative reservoir of strength. At the same time it is essential that the therapist not get too caught up in the anorexia itself, but rather, relate to the emotional chaos and terror that lurk behind it.

This can be a tenuous balancing act, for one feature of the anorexia is that the woman becomes fantastically secretive about it. She shuns discussions of her body size (except to say that she needs to lose weight) and is extremely cagey about her eating habits. She often reassures people that she has just eaten, inventing whole meals in the process. She finds it extremely hard to acknowledge that she has a food problem, and when forced to sit at a lunch or a dinner table with others, an anorexic moves the food around the plate, buries it in napkins, or under salad leaves. She desperately wants to have the food but will not submit to her desire for it. She is involved in an elaborate fiction about both her food and her body.

The therapist's job is to provide what Winnicott (1965) calls a holding relationship so that the felt-to-be-despised, needy, and hungry person can safely emerge and accept the therapeutic relationship. Sometimes it seems to me that the building of such an alliance is an art. A kind of sensitivity and attention to the smallest details are required, as in all successful art forms. This particular therapy relationship requires much delicacy because the inner self is so fragile. There is little chance of the inner despair emerging if the self-esteem gained from the defensive posture is not recognized and validated.

Above all, then, the anorexic is most scared of her needs surfacing, catching her unawares and rendering her helpless. She has only contempt for the needy "little girl" inside who has been deprived for so long. She will find it very hard to accept that the therapist could value her and not be repulsed by the exposure of the "little girl." So the building of the therapy relationship will be a sensitive process strewn with resistance and "premature recovery." The woman longs desperately to collapse and relinquish her routines in this new relationship but is caught in a dilemma because she does not yet experience a self that exists outside the parameters of her anorexia.

The anorexia works as a defense against dependency needs. Like many women raised in our society, her psyche has been influenced in a particular way. Her dependency needs and her desires for initiation and autonomy were thwarted in her early relationship with mother. From early on mother discouraged her daughter from expecting that her emotional needs would be met or that she could be active in the world. Unconsciously, mother pushed her away and encouraged her to take care of herself by burying her needs and desires. These needs and desires come to be experienced as overwhelming or wrong; thus, she feels emotionally unentitled and undeserving (Eichenbaum & Orbach, 1983).

In the therapy, this creates particular obstacles to what the woman most needs to do, but is ever so reluctant to allow: to feel a reliance on the therapist, to recognize her desire to be dependent, and to feel the therapist being there for her. It is only as her dependency needs become visible that she can experience them as being acceptable. Then the shame attached to them can dissipate, the needs themselves can be addressed, and the possibility emerges that the vulnerable little girl hidden inside can begin to be nurtured and integrated. This, of course, is easier said than done for a central feature of a female's psychology is the shielding from view of her dependency needs and their conversion into a caring for others.

In all of my experiences with anorexic women a similar set of feelings is aroused in me. I experience myself trying to connect with one who has never truly related. There is little sense of a person to relate to. Rather, there is a highly defended and developed persona perched on stilts, lacking inner relatedness and a sense of being. The woman attempts to protect me and herself from her inner despair and hopelessness. She has no confidence that either of us can tolerate the depression and futility that she feels. When she is able to expose it, she is flooded with guilt and horror for what has been made visible. She anticipates rejection and has a hard time when it isn't forthcoming. She may retreat from these feelings of acceptance. It may feel to the therapist as though the client is attempting to control the therapy relationship just as she controls her food. There is a temptation for the therapist to feel excluded.

If this description of therapy with an anorexic seems quite difficult, that is because it *is* demanding. But part of why it is so hard is because her brutality towards herself arouses in me strong feelings of compassion on which it is inappropriate to act. Raised as a woman, I have all sorts of urges to look after her, to attend to her needs, to nurture her.

With a compulsive eater, interventions are felt to be soothing and palatable. The anorexic, given her negative experiences with "taking in" from the environment, is mired in such an intransigent need-denying state that interpretations I make must be absolutely on target and non-invasive. Hence, I have to exercise a certain amount of restraint, concentrating on being as precise and accurate as possible when I try to reflect back what I have understood. We can only meet if I truly empathize with her experience and follow her initiations.

CONCLUSION

If we look at an anorexic's behavior symbolically, we can see that she has shaped for herself a particularly extreme, intense, and rebellious relationship vis-à-vis the various struggles all women face. She has changed her body dramatically. She has become smaller and smaller as today's culture demands, but so small that her body becomes an indictment against the idealized feminine sexuality of today's society. She has agreed to take up only a little space in the world, but at the same time, her body state evokes immense interest on the part of others and she becomes a focus for their attention. In other words, her invisibility clamors for recognition. We cannot avert our gaze.

In controlling her food so very tightly she is caricaturing the message beamed at all women. However, she will not be the passive victim of the diet doctor or weight watchers, for *she* is in charge and *active* in relation to the suppression of her bodily needs. And in denying her needs—as women are so often reminded to do—she creates a person who will not impose on or ask for things from others. Thus, she excels as the "good girl." At the same time she steadfastly attempts to meet those needs in a most persistent and tenacious manner. Her anorexia is a paradoxical embodiment of stereotyped femininity and its very opposite.

REFERENCES

Baker Miller, J. (1983). *Towards a new psychology of women*. Boston: Beacon Press.
Chodorow, N. (1978). *The reproduction of mothering: Psychoanalysis and the sociology of gender*. Berkeley: University of California Press.
Eichenbaum, L., & Orbach, S. (1983). *Understanding women: A feminist and psychoanalytic approach*. New York: Basic Books.
Eichenbaum, L., & Orbach, S. (1983). *What do women want? Exploding the myth of dependency*. New York: Coward, McCann.
Glass, D. D. (1980). *Facts & figures, a man alive*. London: BBC-TV.
Orbach, S. (1978). *Fat is a feminist issue*. New York: Paddington Press.
Orbach, S. (1982). *Fat is a feminist issue*. New York: Berkley Books.
Winnicott, D. W. (1965). *The maturational processes and the facilitating environment*. London: International Universities Press.

Part III

Psychological Perspective

Chapter 8

Long-Term Dynamic Group Therapy with Bulimic Patients: A Clinical Discussion

W. Nicholson Browning

This chapter will present and discuss clinical experience of long-term group therapy with bulimic patients gained during the past 21 months at the Mass. General Hospital.*

These groups were intended to be run in long-term, dynamically-oriented treatment format. In this regard, they differ from most of the group work described to date, which has been largely oriented toward behavioral treatment in short-term formats. Several assumptions underlie dynamic group psychotherapy for these patients:

1) Bulimia in normal weight women, as well as in underweight women and previously anorexic women, represents a psychiatric disorder with significant impairment of functioning. This group treatment approach, therefore, focuses on broad aspects of functioning rather than on symptom control alone.
2) A major aspect of bulimia is the shame and attendant secretiveness which surround the symptom. We believe there is value in the opportunity to share the experience with other patients with similar problems.
3) Bulimic patients have significant disturbances in object relations which may be effectively identified and treated in group therapy.

This report discusses work in progress and is not intended to be a definitive statement about the therapy of this disorder. In the following section, I will

---

*I am also indebted to Dale Sokolov and Donna Miller who generously shared their experiences running similar groups.

discuss two aspects of bulimia in detail: 1) the secondary autonomy of the compulsion; and 2) the characterological quality of the false self (Winnicott's notion), found in many, if not all, bulimic patients. In the next section, I will discuss some observations concerning the seemingly unique dynamics of group therapy with bulimic patients. Specifically, these observations include:

1) The problem of adequately assessing these patients' motivation for treatment.
2) The prolonged phase of affiliation which seems to typify these groups.
3) The avoidance of direct affect.
4) The significance of dependency issues.

Finally, I will describe the use of two active techniques which depart from more traditional, nondirective group psychotherapy methods.

THE DISORDER

The Secondary Autonomy of the Compulsion

Obsessional symptoms such as binge eating tend to become secondarily autonomous, that is, to become independent of the conflicts for which the symptom was initially an emblem and a remedy.

The binging cycle typically begins during late adolescence or young adult life. Usually the beginning is quiet; the patient overeats and remonstrates with herself the next day: "Diet today; don't get carried away like that again." Initially, there is no fear, no sense of a shark just beneath the water's smooth surface. But the overeating grows more significant; there is something compelling about it; a sense of driven excitement begins to attend episodes of overeating and with it comes anxiety.

We might presume that the excitement of accompanying anxiety indicates the process of a symptom in formation in the psychoanalytic sense. We would misunderstand the situation, in my view, were we to assume (along with the patient) that the anxiety which has begun to accompany episodes of binging is congruent with the fear of gaining weight. While this is the conscious experience of most patients, the excitement and anxiety are the signals of the many unwelcome and unacceptable feelings and impulses, which are beginning to take up symbolic residence in this driven activity. This inference will be elaborated later in the chapter.

Without exception, bulimic women value self-control. They are uncomfortable with the excitement which is part of the frenzied experience of binging. Like dictatorships, they look suspiciously at activities that seem to have some autonomy. A means of retaining a sense of control must be imposed. Appetite must not be trusted — it is an enemy and must be suppressed. They may struggle for a time trying to deny their appetite, to quiet its incessant importuning. But nothing will silence its voice, until a new discovery occurs: They can purge; they can fool their appetite by feeding their mouths but not their bodies. By vomiting, laxative abuse, or compulsive exercise, they can relax their vigilance against appetite. Often this solution initially appears as a blessing: Perhaps this will be a convenient method to manage the disagreeable chore of staying thin.

Thus, an apparently stable truce may develop. The insurgent impulse will tolerate this secret expression because its effects can be undone by vomiting, exercise, or other means. Such a truce may be relatively comfortable for a prolonged period and may contribute to (although not entirely explain) the long delay between the development of bulimia and the request for treatment. The undoing has reestablished a sense of control over impulse and the anxiety is quieted.

Usually, however, the truce is ultimately unstable. There is a metamorphosis through which the psychological trick to undo the force of appetite comes to possess a controlling power of its own. Vomiting no longer produces a sense of relief; this too has become part of the compulsion. The patient no longer is able to feel that she has escaped the controlling power of her appetite; that power now resides in the entire cycle. She no longer experiences herself as choosing to vomit (or to exercise); she *has* to vomit. Once again, she has lost the sense of autonomy. This experience produces shame, horror, and sometimes panic.

For a time, while the binge lasts, the state of consciousness is altered. Inner tension abates. The bulimic has given in; so she can relax her vigilance. Eating — the act and the immediate feeling it produces — generates an anesthesia. For a short merciful period there is no feeling, only lethargy. The wretched aftermath will come, but it is rarely there during or immediately after the binge.

The last act in the cycle is the purge. For many patients, vomiting is physically easy but emotionally awful. They feel ashamed and humiliated; purging becomes a punishment for the excesses of eating.

In patients for whom control is so enormously important, the loss of control is frightening. If it can happen once, it can occur again. If it can happen with food, then it can occur with any impulse. If it can happen slightly, then it could easily occur in an overwhelming way. There is an aspect of magical thinking which is extremely important in the dynamics of this symptom. These patients have, in their efforts at self-control, not allowed themselves to tolerate their mental representation of unacceptable impulses. Consequently, once the desire to eat is present, the sense of having control is lost. There is little appreciation for the difference between impulse and action. Sins in the mind rank with sins in deed.

This helps explain why bulimic patients are caught in such a frustrating cycle. They cannot win; as soon as they think about eating, there seems so little point in struggling. Why struggle when they are already defeated? So they eat and deliver the message of failure to themselves over and over again. Their only defense is to hope somehow not to be afflicted with the impulse again. They are thus in a position analogous to the man who is told, "You will be shot if you think of the word elephant. Do not think elephant!" It is impossible. The longer the time that has passed since the instruction, the greater the tension. Inevitably, the cascade of events will start again, and it begins with the forbidden impulse.*

This self-sustaining cycle contributes, of course, to a reluctance to seek treatment and to these patients' reluctance to discuss the symptom even when they are in therapy. They suffer from the magical notion that if they do not mention the problem, perhaps it will vanish.

Thus it can be understood how the symptom can become part of a vicious cycle which can perpetuate itself independently of the conflicts which give rise to it. The argument, though not fully developed here, is presented to highlight the patients' experience. We will return to this point when discussing the technical aspects of the group treatment.

The Characterological Feature of the False Self

Frequently, bulimic patients are perfectionistic. In the areas they believe are significant, nothing must be wrong. This trait reflects an anxiety when things are not just as they should be, more than it does a real concern for any particular product or activity. It is, therefore, more closely associated with anxiety about imperfection, and gives rise to the desire to be in control and anxiety lest that control falter.

The internal dynamics of this desire for perfect self-control are best understood by reference to Winnicott's notion of a "false self." The false self is the persona constructed and presented to the world in order to satisfy significant others. It is false because genuine impulses and feelings are not permitted expression, even mental expression. For this reason, Winnicott (1975) says, "The false self cannot . . . experience life or feel real" (p. 297).

Bruch (1979) has beautifully described the family circumstances in which

---

*Otto Fenichel (1945) discusses the phenomenon of the magical powers of words and thoughts in his chapter on obsessions and compulsions: "Words can kill or resurrect. They can perform miracles or turn time back. . . . Because words and thoughts are believed to have such real effects, they are also dangerous" (p. 296).

this false self develops in anorexic patients. Bulimic patients, like anorexic patients, feel they must please their parents perfectly. The parents may be generous, attentive, and even perfectionistic in their parenting. Their children, prior to the development of eating disorders, feel they must be grateful and pleased in order not to hurt their parents. They do not feel permitted to express or even experience the aggression that normally facilitates healthy separation and individuation. The children come to feel that their parents' self — their parents' internal integrity — is a responsibility they bear directly. They experience themselves as their parents' self-objects. It is as though an imaginary bargain has been struck early in development: In order to assure themselves of love and nurturance, these patients have "agreed" to become what they believe their parents expect and need them to be. This is the false self.

With its construction comes an immediate and curious problem for future development. The false self cannot be truly loved or emotionally nourished. Praise and affection, no matter how genuine, no longer apply to the true self, which is now hidden and largely unconscious. Praise and affection belong instead to this imaginary construction. The development of genuine self-esteem and self-confidence is blocked, no matter how outstanding the patients' accomplishments might be. As Winnicott (1975) states, "The false self may achieve a deceptive false integrity" (p. 297). But this is a brittle construction. It can be seen that the false self stands in a protective relationship to the true self, bargaining, as it were, for what Winnicott calls "good-enough mothering." In the cyclical alternation between binging and reform, the bulimic patient is trapped in the self-perpetuating oscillation between expressions of need coming from the true self, and the fear of abandoning the protective false self. Therapy, whatever the modality, must encourage and nurture the expressions of genuine affects which reside in the true self. This necessarily requires the tolerance of considerable anxiety and dependence.

This hypothesis concerning an aspect of the character of many bulimic patients helps expain why the symptom typically emerges in late adolescence or early adult life when the critical developmental task is the formation of a coherent ego-identity.

The construction of the false self has been hypothesized to be a means of securing parental love and approval. I have also argued that the bargain has been unfortunate for the child because she is forever in the position of receiving love which must be without nourishment because it is always the false self which is being fed. The true self, then, is in the position of endlessly waiting for the time when it will be remembered and rewarded. Leaving home presents a crisis, because the bargain becomes permanently a losing one; the situation will never correct. True identification with a genuinely nourishing parent, which becomes an affirming and approving introject, has not occurred and perhaps never will, and this makes leaving home frightening indeed. This hypothesis also suggests why the symptom is so closely associated with depressive symptomatology.

GROUP THERAPY

My discussion of group therapy with bulimic patients derives largely from my own experience over approximately 21 months in the Eating Disorders Unit at Mass. General Hospital, and from discussion with the other therapists leading groups there.

The therapy groups were all constructed along rather traditional lines: Each consisted of five to eight members and met for 90 minutes weekly. Members were referred for group therapy following an extensive intake procedure (about eight hours, including complete psychological testing, nutritional history and evaluation, comprehensive past history, and psychiatric interview). New members typically met once or twice with the group leader prior to joining the groups. All groups were led by individual leaders.

Observations About Group Dynamics

1) *Bulimic patients often generate unwarranted optimism in the therapist seeing them for the first time.* These patients are adept at telling you what you want to hear, and may seem to be better candidates for group therapy than they actually are. All of our groups had trouble forming: Patients who were apparently enthusiastic and eager came to one or two meetings and then dropped out, even when a clear contract about announcing and discussing departures had been agreed upon. It is therefore important that careful evaluation and discussion of motivation must precede acceptance into group treatment.

2) *The period of affiliation is, as might be anticipated from the dynamics of these patients, prolonged and difficult.* There is an initial period of excitement, pleasure, and relief as they share their symptoms with one another. This is often the first time they have talked about the symptom to anyone other than a therapist. So there may be a tremendous relief from the sense of isolation and shame. One woman exclaimed,

> This is incredible. I'm looking around this room and all of you are doing the same thing I am, and you all look like normal people! I thought anyone who did this was incredibly weird.

Bulimic patients experience their symptom passively, as something which happens to them and over which they are powerless. There is a corresponding passivity in the transference to the therapist: There is a strong wish that therapy will provide a key or solution through which they will regain control. This makes the therapy difficult for most bulimic patients because, while they struggle to be "good patients," they feel increasingly frustrated that they are not being cured—that somehow they are not "getting it." They most frequently conceal this disappointment or show it in depressive actions such as missed meetings, becoming silent, or dropping out of the group. Early on in the group meetings, it is particularly difficult for the group to express disappointment in or hostility towards the therapist.

In my experience, there was usually someone in the role of group skeptic who doubted that she could be treated. Inevitably this position provoked a compliant and therapist-supporting posture from the other group members, who would reassure the skeptic that she should not be discouraged. But the bitter resentment that the therapist was withholding the answers was far more difficult for the group to express. A mythology that therapy was a sort of necessary ordeal emerged in my group. According to this notion, you had to keep coming to the group no matter how frustrated and confused you felt. The therapist knew what was the matter, but could not tell you. Somehow you had to learn the secret for yourself. As some of the patients improved, they began to belong to the elect—the inner circle in which the answers were known, but could not be spoken. This magical idea survived despite repeated confrontations and challenges.

The following interchange occurred between the therapist and one woman, after she had been in the group for about eight months and demonstrates the ambivalent dependence which is such a strong theme in these groups.

Patient: I know you can't tell what we should do. I know we have to figure it out for ourselves. But it's very frustrating sometimes.
Therapist: The group feels I'm withholding something.
Patient: Oh no. I mean, I know you can't tell us. I know that wouldn't do any good.
Therapist: It isn't easy to be angry with someone you think has the answers you need.
Another patient: "I don't think she [the first patient] is angry. We're angry at ourselves.

3) *Another characteristic aspect of working with bulimic patients in groups is the avoidance of direct expression of affect.* For some time in the group these patients are not likely to experience affect arising out of interpersonal exchange; the group remains a remote and intellectualized experience. Almost without fail in my experience, the first affects permitted direct expression by each member in the group were depressive feelings relating to loneliness, abandonment, and unworthiness. Since these feelings are related to such

strong longings and have been experienced as dystonic wishes which must be suppressed, their expression changes the patient's relationship to the group and arouses anxiety. The group's acceptance and tolerance of these wishes, however, also promote genuine bonding. One very quiet and inhibited woman said after 11 months,

> You know, it's funny, but coming here is very important to me. I feel it's the only place in my life where I can be myself. I don't know why really, but I feel like I can say anything here and it will be all right. I guess this is the only place I have ever felt that.

4) *The capacity to tolerate dependency within the group is always accompanied with the capacity to be less secretive outside the group.* As a patient became more affectively expressive and dependent in the group, group members urged her to be less secretive about her symptoms elsewhere. Many patients had either not told or had grossly minimized their symptoms to very important other people in their lives, such as boyfriends, parents, and individual therapists. Usually, patients felt some relief from oppressive shame and humiliation after they had explained their symptoms to people they were close to. After telling her boyfriend, one patient said,

> It was amazing. I mean, he hardly batted an eye. I was so scared he would be so disgusted he would never want to see me again. But he didn't even think it was a very big deal. He said he used to do the same thing in high school when he was training for wrestling.

Expressing genuine disappointment and anger with the therapist is both more difficult and more important than expressing loneliness and dependency. Most of these patients, as described previously, unconsciously believe that they must earn love and approval by perfect behavior, even perfect thinking. The expression of hostility and dissatisfaction is therefore especially conflicted and frightening because of the fear of rejection. One patient fell in love with a very sympathetic and warm man in the course of therapy. Despite his repeated reassurances to her, and despite his accommodation to her many difficult requests (which were probably all tests of his devotion), she remained irrationally convinced that he would throw her over as soon as he "really understood" what she was like. She recognized her conviction was irrational, but she could not shake it. When I asked her how she dealt with the same sort of feeling in relation to me, she looked surprised and said that feeling just didn't come up in therapy:

> I mean I don't even think about it. This is professional. You could be replaced. I mean, you know, you could replace me if you wanted to; and I guess I could replace you. I mean, I wouldn't want to, but you know, this isn't personal.

Winnicott relates this phase of the therapy to earlier failures of empathetic parenting ("of good-enough mothering"). He says,

> These failures of empathy had a disruptive effect at the time, and a treatment of the kind I am describing has gone a long way when the patient is able to take an example of original failure and to be angry about it. Only when the patient reaches this point, however, can there be the beginning of reality testing. (1975, p. 298)

Winnicott makes a special point of relating this aspect of treating patients presenting a false self to the patients' reaction to what he calls the therapist's failures of understanding and empathy. According to Winnicott, even minor failures of understanding on the part of the therapist or of the group will become the seed around which old pain and disappointment will be precipitated. This is without question the most difficult aspect of group therapy with bulimic patients. It is quite difficult to perceive when bulimic patients are hurt or misunderstood; often they have very little awareness of it themselves. Moreover, even when it is clear, they are most alarmed and would much prefer to politely overlook it. This is, of course, easier for the therapist and for the group, and is an error I have fallen into repeatedly. Nevertheless, let me offer a more hopeful example which illustrates a more productive chain of events.

A patient in my group began by wondering whether therapy could really be of any use. I interpreted her concern about whether a therapist could take care of her as related to her uncertainty about whether her parents could take care of her. This patient began to sob as she described how she had believed for a long time that her family was perfect and that she herself had tried to make it so; but when she was in high school, her mother became overtly paranoid. Food had to be specially prepared; school and friends were not to be trusted. The patient tried even harder to satisfy her mother. Her father was blank and seemed not to notice. Remarkably enough, this was the first time she had made a connection between these events and the onset of her bulimia, which began shortly after she realized her mother was seriously disturbed. This example is intended only to illustrate the associational link between disappointment in the therapy and anger and disappointment with the primary objects.

Although the situation briefly presented here led to some very useful work, disappointments in the group's failures which were not taken up or even perceived have, I believe, been the major reason for premature termination. In every instance where I have been able to interview the patient after the termination, the patient has felt the group was probably worthwhile, but that she could probably not be helped there. Not one of these prematurely terminating patients could acknowledge directly her anger and disappointment with the group or with the therapist, although it seemed clearly present in every case.

ACTIVE TECHNIQUES

Psychodramatic Reenactment

In the discussion above, I have referred to the difficulty most bulimic patients have in recognizing and expressing affects and have related this to Winnicott's idea of the false self. Group members repeatedly described life events of obvious significance to them without significant feeling. After what seemed to me a reasonable amount of trust had formed in the group, I began to ask the members if they could present some of these episodes through psychodramatic reenactment. This request was always made with the proviso that they should be sure they felt entirely comfortable presenting material in this fashion, and that they should stop immediately if they felt uncomfortable with the approach. Anyone who declined was thanked for respecting her own limits.

An example will best illustrate how this technique was introduced. A college student who had been in the group for about seven months described being home for a holiday. She told the group again how wonderful her family was and how much she enjoyed being with them. So it seemed strange to her that, although she had enjoyed the visit, her bulimia had become much worse while she was there. She puzzled with the group about this for a while without being able to figure anything out. During the discussion her affect was quizzical, but bland. I suggested to her that she might be able to discover something if she were to dramatically reconstruct a significant image she had about the vacation. She was doubtful, but agreeable. She decided to examine a period of time which preceded a binge. She reenacted lying in bed in the morning, having just awakened and heard her mother, who she knew was the only other person in the house, moving about in the kitchen. After a short while, she heard the kitchen door close as her mother left for work. This scene was reconstructed with as much detail as the patient could supply. With the sound of the door closing in the reenactment, she suddenly experienced the tremendous sense of loneliness and sadness that this sound triggered. She realized at once that the sound had repeatedly triggered binges during the visit and that the obsession had served to shield her from this powerful and painful emotion.

This very simple reenactment led to a very productive string of associations for this patient. She was able to remember her sense that she was always a disappointment to her parents and unable to please them, and finally her conviction that they had always wanted a boy. She was able to feel angry with her mother for her subtly critical attitude. It was ultimately a source of significant relief to notice the myriad ways in which she tried to please her parents and others by trying to be things she was not.

I cannot, of course, say that these associations would not have come to the fore without the psychodramatic reconstruction. Nevertheless, it is clear that such reenactment has been immensely useful in recovering and utilizing affects that otherwise remain very hazy and uncertain in these patients' experience. The criticism that these patients will comply with these specific suggestions in an effort to please the therapist can only be offset, in my experience, by the strength of the chain of associations which follows so frequently from the technique described here, and from the tremendous subjective sense of relief that nearly always accompanies such an exploration. It seems more useful to consider that if strong and genuine affect is *not* uncovered in this fashion, then either the experience being explored is not significant *or* the patient may be simply being compliant.

Finally, following Moreno's prescription about the use of the group with psychodramatic methods, the therapist should ask the group members to share their associations from their own personal experience, rather than to comment critically or psychologize. It is extremely important not to abandon the member who has just taken a risk. Sharing personal experience says, "Yes, I also have felt something like that."

Paradoxical Prescriptions

The second active technique I have used relates to the secondary autonomy of the binge/purge cycle. It is borrowed from paradoxical prescriptions as used in some forms of strategic family therapy. Let me give an example. When I fet that some progress had been made in understanding the conflicts which had given rise to the symptoms, and when a reasonably sound working alliance had been established, I suggested to a particular group member that she might be prepared to make a major effort to do something about her symptom. The answer was an enthusiastic yes. Did she feel ready even if it might require a significant effort? Definitely yes. Would she be willing to make that effort even if it meant possibly gaining some weight? Here she paused and expressed her uncertainty by saying perhaps. When I suggested that "perhaps" hardly represented a real seriousness of purpose, she responded, "All right, definitely. What is the effort?" I asked her to review exactly what she had eaten in the past week or two, including the binges. I then asked her to agree in the group to: 1) eat three normal meals daily, even if this was somewhat annoying or difficult; and 2) to decide then and there that she would binge just as many times as she had during the preceding weeks on whatever she would choose.

The suggestion provoked surprise and alarm even with patients who had heard it before. With more or less difficulty, the patient to whom the suggestion was made would agree. In the course of making the decision, however, the illusion that every binge is going to be the last is thrown into sharp relief. The incredulity with which the suggestion is received betrays the partially conscious conviction held by bulimics that next week they will not binge anymore. This was just as true when the symptom had been present for years. In the discussion about whether the group members should try the suggestion or not, they agreed that in fact they probably would *not* stop in the next week. Relinquishing that illusion usually afforded some relief. When patients agree to this suggestion, a curious affect emerges: on every occasion shock has given way to wry puzzlement and a sort of playful curiosity. Tension somehow seems to lessen, and a more relaxed disposition emerges.

One patient returned the week after undertaking this agreement and said, "I'm really sorry. I couldn't do it. I felt too good and I just couldn't make myself binge. I didn't want to." I said that since she did make an agreement, I thought she should try to follow through on it. Perhaps she could make an agreement which allowed for some flexibility: She would be allowed to cheat by skipping one of the binges she had promised and she would be allowed to skip one breakfast. She agreed. After several weeks she was binging once weekly, but wanted to have the option to skip that. Reluctantly, I agreed she might skip it for a week. She binged rarely for the eight months after that.

Asking the patient to deliberately choose to have the symptom places her in a curious, puzzling, but helpful predicament. First, the negotiation requires confrontation with the debilitating illusion that she must stop at once. It is some relief to abandon this position. Second, the negotiation requires allowing the possibility of gaining some weight. This also affords some relief, although it also generates some anxiety. Third, and most important, the agreement robs the obsession of some of its power. If the patient does binge, she is no longer breaking her own internal prohibitions; she is instead following the instructions of her doctor. The damage to her self-esteem is consequently lessened. If she does not binge, as was the case with the patient described, then she is no longer symptomatic. The destructive, self-reinforcing, secondarily autonomous cycle is interrupted in either case.

In eight cases in which I have made use of this instruction, there was no instance of the symptom worsening, and in every case but one (in which I think I made the suggestion prematurely), the patient no longer felt so fearfully out of control.

Both of the active techniques described here have the disadvantage of making the therapist more central and of reinforcing the magical expectations about how therapy is to proceed. I suspect, but have no way of knowing for certain, that magical passive transference may be more likely with a male therapist anyway. The image of the slender and sexy woman who will successfully snare men that is promoted by the media and advertising industry certainly reinforces this idea. Nevertheless, it is my impression that both of these active techniques are on balance useful adjuncts to traditional dynamic group therapy.

Psychodramatic enactment of significant events promotes the experience and recognition of important affects which otherwise remain obscured behind the false self. Sharing of those affects within the group stimulates bonding between members and promotes introspective searching for similar shared feelings in an atmosphere of tolerant acceptance. Prescription of the symptom loosens the self-reinforcing and self-esteem damaging cycle that makes this such a difficult disorder to bear and to treat.

REFERENCES

Boskind-White, M., & White, W. C. (1983). *Bulimarexia: The binge-purge cycle*. New York: W. W. Norton.

Bruch, H. (1979). Family background in eating disorders. In E. J. Anthony & C. Koupernik (Eds.), *The child in his family, Vol. 1*. Melbourne, FL: Krieger.

Fenichel, O. (1945). *The psychoanalytic theory of neurosis*. New York: W. W. Norton.

Winnicott, D. W. (1975). Clinical varieties of transference. In *Collected papers: Through paediatrics to psychoanalysis*. London: Hogarth Press.

Chapter 9

Psychotherapeutic Partnering: An Approach to the Treatment of Anorexia Nervosa and Bulimia

*April Benson and
Linda Futterman*

Collaboration in psychotherapy is discussed only sporadically in either the psychological literature or psychotherapy training programs. While informal collaborations between colleagues treating members of the same family are common, rarely are these formalized or made part of the total treatment approach. For the past several years, the authors have functioned as psychotherapeutic partners with a variety of anorexic and bulimic patients and families. What began as an informal sharing of information with each other about our respective work with members of the same family has evolved over time into a treatment approach that employs both collaborative and conjoint psychotherapy, with regular meetings between us to discuss our work in these cases.

Our patients, anorexics and bulimics, were females between the ages of 13 and 23 at the time of intake. All but one was living at home when treatment began. This report is an attempt to describe our method in detail, and to discuss the various issues that arise and need to be successfully negotiated for this form of therapeutic intervention to be effective.

We believe that working collaboratively with a therapeutic partner on these difficult cases has assets for both patients and therapists. The old adage about two heads being better than one is apropos. The partners are not only sharing information about each member of the family, but also collaborating in their efforts to understand both the intrapsychic and interpersonal worlds of the patient and family. We help each other to manage the intense countertransference reactions which are so easily evoked by these patients and families. The patients and their families benefit from a smoothly functioning therapeutic team, experienced in treating patients with these particular problems.

The peer supervision and active support between the two therapists transform what can be a debilitating, frustrating experience into an exciting, rewarding professional challenge.

Among those who practice psychotherapy with anorexic and bulimic patients, it is now widely agreed that successful treatment includes some form of intervention with significant others in the patient's environment. The form this intervention takes varies as a function of the therapist's theoretical orientation, his or her therapeutic skill, and the particular situation. In our work we view the individual patient, the parents, and the family unit as distinct participants in the development and maintenance of these disorders. As a result, we use a multidimensional framework in each case, intervening with individual, parent, and family in accordance with the specific needs of the situation. One therapist assumes primary responsibility for work with the individual patient and the other assumes primary responsibility for work with the parent or parents. Either both therapists together or the child's therapist herself is involved when the family is the unit of intervention, depending upon the circumstances. The section on family treatment will address this further.

We include ourselves among the many therapists who see internal and external, intrapsychic and interactional as interrelated, interdependent spheres. Theoretically, we have both been heavily influenced by developmental object relations theory and self psychology and share the technical perspective that the therapist treating these disorders must take an active, authoritative role. We set appropriate external limits when the arrested intrapsychic structure of the patients and/or the problematic nature of the family's functioning necessitates the use of this analytic parameter. We believe that the unusual combination of our collaborative work and the multidimensional nature of the treatment itself have led to the positive results we have had thus far. Our technique has developed organically over time, and is continually modified as we learn from our therapeutic results.

HISTORY

Psychodynamic approaches to the treatment of anorexia and bulimia have paralleled both the evolution of psychoanalytic theory and the development of psychotherapeutic technique. In the first published reports of psychotherapeutic treatment for anorexia nervosa (Grote & Meng, 1934; Lorand, 1943; Waller, Kaufman, & Deutsch, 1940), the treatment of choice was classical psychoanalysis. The patient was seen individually several times a week and the parents were seen only for an initial history-taking session.

By the early 1950s, child analysts in England and the United States had come to appreciate the role of parental psychopathology in the development of childhood disorders. They saw that despite the successful analysis of underlying conflicts, the patient's progress was severely limited if the family environment was unchanged.

One of the earliest forms of work which included direct parental involvement in the treatment was that of Sperling (1950). She began to include mothers in the treatment of adolescent anorexics, as she had done previously in the psychoanalytic treatment of younger children. Whether she did a full analysis with the mother or engaged in occasional contact depended upon the pathology of the daughter and/or mother.

Another early treatment which bore some resemblance to the approach we are advocating was reported by Berlin, Boatman, Sheimo, and Szurek (1951). These clinicians described a case of collaborative psychotherapy with a hospitalized anorexic and her parents. The adolescent, her mother, and her father were seen individually in treatment by three different therapists. All three therapists saw the same supervisor and there were some supervisory sessions attended by all three therapists. This is one of the few reports in the literature that describes the simultaneous treatment of three principal family members and the only account in the literature, to our knowledge, that describes this type of process with an anorexia nervosa patient.

The following problems illustrate some of the potential pitfalls of the collaborative process. The therapists (Berlin et al.) did not know each other well, they were defensive with each other, and they were reluctant to share information. The unresolved competitiveness among them led to disunity within the treatment team. As a result, work with the entire family suffered. In addition, the almost exclusive intrapsychic focus both in the sessions and in the supervision occluded from view many of the interpersonal dynamics operative within the family.

More recent advances in psychotherapy have both deepened the understanding of the intrapsychic elements of anorexia and bulimia and extended the treatment of these disorders into a wider interpersonal field. Developmental object relations theory and self psychology have afforded an enlarged intrapsychic perspective, making the borderline and narcissistic pathology in these patients more understandable. The rise of interpersonal thinking and the growing popularity of communication and systems theories have expanded the investigation to include the patient's immediate interpersonal environment, the family. The most prevalent forms of outpatient treatment for these disorders all involve significant family members in the treatment, to varying degrees and in varying contexts. What follows is a summary of the positions of some of the current experts.

A wealth of clinical experience with these patients and their families has convinced Bruch that inasmuch as the development of anorexia nervosa is so closely related to abnormal patterns of family interaction, successful treatment always involves resolution of the underlying family problems. Despite the claims of family therapists, Bruch has not been convinced that family therapy by itself offers any advantage or is even feasible for this disorder. She states in a 1982 review article:

> The stagnating patterns of family interaction must be clarified and unlocked, but this alone is not enough: Regardless of what the family contribution to the illness has been in the past, the patient has integrated the abnormal patterns and misconceptions, and only individual intensive psychotherapy can correct the underlying erroneous assumptions that are the precondition for the self-deceptive pseudosolution. (p. 307)

With a young hospitalized patient, Bruch does see the parents and child in family sessions during hospitalization, so that by the time the child comes home there has been some rearrangement in the psychological interaction in the family. In these family sessions, Bruch gives the parents simple recommendations which establish firm boundaries between subsystems within the family. She also utilizes these meetings with the family to state therapeutic goals, gain the family as allies and evaluate the family interaction, and then often refers the marital couple for conjoint therapy. According to Bruch, it is not enough for the therapist to enlist the parents' cooperation; the therapist must also help the parents to permit a change and to find their own satisfactions in order to be able to let go of their child. With older adolescents or young adults, the work with the family is just as important, even if the patient is living away from home.

According to Sours (1980), the optimal therapeutic approach for the anorexic depends on "a genetic-structural assessment, the level of her fixation and regression, the primitiveness of her defenses, the extent of the family's pathology and her ego assets. . . " (p. 370). Just as there is no unitary concept of anorexia nervosa, there is no unitary treatment for anorexia nervosa. Sours believes that anorexics who have been symptomatic longer than one year require individual treatment. Especially after the anorexic has made a solid alliance in individual treatment, conjoint marital therapy for the parents is advisable. The parents usually need therapy beyond what family treatment can provide, and Sours has found that some parents decide in conjoint treatment to enter individual therapy.

Sours' perspective is shared by Wilson, a psychoanalyst whose work in psychosomatic disorders grew out of his association with Sperling. Although not explicitly stated in his 1980 article, "The Family Psychological Profile in Anorexia Nervosa Patients," Wilson advises collaborative treatment of the anorexic's parents and intensive analytic psychotherapy for the anorexic or bulimic. Wilson sees the parents first, enlists their aid as allies in the treatment, and then refers one or both of the parents to a colleague. The form and nature of the collaboration between the two therapists is not specifically addressed in Wilson's writings. He is opposed to having the same therapist treat the adolescent and parents, in that the developing child will mistrust the therapist, who becomes identified too closely with the judging parent. When the anorexic patient refuses or resists treatment, preliminary therapy of the parent can lead to a healthy treatment motivation in the anorexic adolescent, who is then referred to a colleague.

Nurturant-authoritative therapy, the theoretical model of Steven Levenkron (see his chapter later in this volume), places the therapist at the center of the patient's life during the illness. He views the illness as a hypothetical parent to the sufferer and offers himself as a better parent. According to Levenkron, the parents of the anorexic have failed to provide the necessary nurturance and strength to their child. Instead, there has been an " . . . implicit reversal of dependency" between parent and child, with the child assuming the role of supporting the parents emotionally. The treatment affords a corrective emotional experience, with the therapist providing what has been lacking in the home. Although not essential, the family may facilitate recovery for anorexic and bulimic patients. Levenkron's main consideration in deciding whether or not to involve the family in therapy is a determination of the resourcefulness of the family (Levenkron, 1982).

Since the late 1950s, a team of therapists at the Children's Hospital Medical Center in Boston have been treating anorexic patients, first in the hospital and then on an outpatient basis. This group (Rollins & Blackwell, 1968; Piazza, Piazza, & Rollins, 1980; Rollins & Piazza, 1981) has utilized separate therapists for parents and child, using weekly interviews with each parent separately or together, and two to three interviews a week with the hospitalized patient, a procedure quite similar to our own. These clinicians found the team approach helpful in tolerating the emotional pressures created by the excessive demands of both parents and child, and it allowed the therapists to dilute the angry feelings aroused by these patient behaviors. During the early 1970s the group introduced family treatment, using Minuchin's concepts of pathological family structures, but most often retained individual psychotherapy for the anorexic child. They concluded, in 1980,

> that many . . . patients realistically did not fit with a redefinition of the anorexic symptomatology as exclusively a problem of family structure and interactional patterns . . . (p. 183). Predisposing vulnerability, intrapsychic conflict, and a developmental perspective must be added to family system considerations in formulating the pathology and appropriate therapeutic interventions in anorexia. (Piazza et al., 1980, p. 185)

Despite her compelling formulations about these disorders and their treatment, Selvini Palazzoli was disappointed with the results of her individual psychotherapy with these patients and abandoned that modality in favor of the paradoxical mode of family treatment. When one looks closely at the type of ancillary work Selvini Palazzoli (1978) did with parents in her pre-family therapy days, one can readily understand how her belief that "one must not probe too deeply into the family's psychological problems, let alone attempt to change their personality structures" (p. 108), significantly hindered the progress that the individual patients made. Selvini Palazzoli's current work, strategic family therapy, focuses on effecting alteration of the unhealthy interactional patterns of the anorexic family through the use of paradoxical behavioral instruction.

Minuchin and the structural family therapists who subscribe to his model for treating anorexics (Liebman, Minuchin, & Baker, 1974; Minuchin, Rosman, & Baker, 1978) also contend that anorexia can best be approached through a therapeutic focus on the structure of the patient's family. Treatment aims are to restructure dysfunctional family systems and replace them with more adaptive patterns, not to promote individual intrapsychic change. Therefore, the entire family is seen together, often for the whole treatment period. With older adolescents, when the developmental task of the adolescent is separation from the family, she may receive individual treatment and her parents couples therapy, after an initial period of family treatment.

While our treatment aims at disequilibrating the family homeostasis, a goal shared by family therapists, we also try to effect lasting intrapsychic change in the anorexic or bulimic patient. We do not believe that family therapy by itself will insure permanent changes in the child's pathology. The exploration of transactional patterns observed in early family sessions is achieved largely in the individual work with the patient or the parents.

THE METHOD

In working with anorexic and bulimic patients and their families, we divide the treatment responsibility among two therapists and a physician. One therapist assumes primary responsibility for work with the individual patient, the other for work with one or both parents. Both therapists and occasionally the physician are involved when the family is seen as a whole. The role of the physician varies with each situation. In all cases, however, the physician is a therapeutic agent and an ongoing participant in the management of the case. Clearly, we choose physicians who have an appreciation of and dedication to the psychotherapeutic treatment of these disorders. These physicians conduct the medical treatment in a manner which supports the psychotherapy, discourages splitting and frees the therapists from disruptive anxiety about the patient's medical condition. Our approach is predicated upon ongoing communication between the two therapists and the physician. Information is continually shared and the medical and psychological treatment coordinated.

The initial contact for treatment is usually made by telephone by one of the parents, and an interview is set up with both parents by the therapist who will work with the youngster. During this interview, the parents usually express their concern about the child's medical condition as well as her psychological state. We discuss the integration of medical and psychological intervention in our work and enlist the cooperation and participation of the parents. Because there are so many varied approaches to the treatment of these disorders, we take time to tell parents about our philosophy of treatment.

We explain that ours is a long-term psychodynamic approach aimed at not only alleviating the presenting symptoms, but also achieving lasting change in the underlying personality issues that helped to create the problem originally. We take care to share with the parents our feeling that no one is to blame in the situation and that their daughter's problem reflects not only her own difficulty but also a problem in the way the family as a whole is functioning. We suggest to the parents that their daughter's recovery depends on their learning to deal with the very difficult issues that arise when an anorexic or bulimic problem exists within a family. We tell parents that our goal is to help them to support growth and development in their child through an increased understanding of their child and of themselves. We explain that, should hospitalization become necessary, this is done on a medical unit and that the treatment team will continue work with the family throughout. Most parents feel quite secure in the knowledge that two therapists and a physician will be involved with them throughout the recovery period. The therapist also requests information about the history of the presenting problem, about the child's early development, and about her social and academic functioning.

Following this initial consultation, the patient is seen alone and her willingness to participate in the therapeutic process is explored. The therapist explains the procedure to the patient and begins to gather information. Then the parents are contacted by phone or seen in a second interview and given the name of the therapist with whom they will work. They are told that the results of the consultation will be shared with their therapist, so that they will not have to go over the same ground again.

This sequence of events is subject to some variation. If the patient is older (16 or over, usually), it may be advisable to see her before interviewing the parents. It is also a good idea to proceed in this manner if the initial phone contact with the parents suggests that the individual is highly resistant or embroiled in a power struggle with her parents. Under these conditions, we ask the parent to have the adolescent call and set up her own appointment. This has proven quite important to the future therapeutic alliance. When we see the adolescent first, we ask if she wishes to participate in the initial consultation with her parents. Although she usually opts not to participate, she is given the clear message that information will not be hidden from her; she can therefore begin to develop a therapeutic alliance.

At the outset, we inform the parents and the individual patient of the ongoing communication between us. The youngster's therapist tells her that although what she says to her therapist will not be shared with her parents, some things will be discussed with their therapist who will then use the information to better help them. The parents' therapist explains that the therapeutic relationship between their daughter and her therapist is confidential, but that their input is an important part of the work and will be shared with their child's therapist. When the treatment is framed in this way the child's therapist is then able to work freely with the child without pressure from the parents, and the parents can see themselves as collaborative agents in the treatment process.

Parents are also told that some information about their child may be used judiciously by their child's therapist, although we take care to keep this to an absolute minimum. It is usually much better for the child's therapist to let whatever information she knows from the parents guide her in her responses to the child, rather than verbalize it directly to her patient. When lies have been exposed by parents or when important information is being withheld by the child, we have resorted to having the child's therapist share her knowledge of the situation with the child. Considerable scrutiny is necessary before this is done, inasmuch as the child often feels cornered and betrayed by her parents and not protected by her own therapist. If done habitually, it also encourages the parents to "tattle" on the child, and fosters use of their own therapist for regressive purposes.

There have also been occasions when the child's therapist has learned through the child that the parents have been withholding important information. In such a case, the child's therapist may ask the child for her permission to have the information shared with her parents by their therapist. In general, when such potentially loaded issues arise on either side, we prefer to hold a family meeting at which the issue is shared and discussed. This has proven far more effective than our becoming intermediaries in the family's already indirect communicative style.

The therapist who has a fuller picture of an intrapsychic or interpersonal event, because she has information provided by the other therapist, can direct her questions in such a way that her patient's characterological problems can be expressed earlier and worked on more directly. The exchange of material between us often highlights specific trends much before they would have become apparent if the therapist knew only one side of the interpersonal equation.

The nature of the collaborative process changes as the work proceeds. More and more, the sharing of information recedes into the background and is replaced by a fuller exploration of dynamics of the transference and countertransference. It is obvious that the two therapists working in this way need to be compatible, share similar orientations to treatment, and want to work with a colleague. They must each have the courage to look at and modify their own way of working and the ability to be constructive when commenting upon the work of the other. The competitive issues which inevitably arise need to be addressed openly. The therapists also must be sufficiently aware of their own dynamics and be able to ascertain when they are reenacting with each other issues from their own lives and when they have been transformed into recreating the family's transactional patterns. Awareness of these nuances sharpens the therapists' skills and sensitivities, greatly enhancing each therapist's work and the collaboration between them.

THE TREATMENT

It is beyond the scope of this chapter to discuss in detail the ongoing analytic process with these patients and their families. The schematic overview that follows is an attempt to familiarize the reader with the nature of the analytic work, the relationship between individual, parent, and family work, and the role of the collaboration in facilitating positive treatment results.

Individual Psychotherapy

Analytic psychotherapy with these patients is extremely intense, both in frequency (two to three times weekly) and in scope. The work is geared toward structure-building or structural change, as the case requires. Although each of these patients suffers from both primary defects of the self and from later developmental failures, the earlier narcissistic and borderline problems and their behavioral manifestations must be analyzed and worked through before the later oedipal pathology can be seriously addressed.

Establishing and maintaining a therapeutic alliance are difficult — these patients are strongly distrustful, sensitive to narcissistic injury, and constantly need to act out their destructive and self-destructive impulses both within the treatment setting and outside of it. Their defensive maneuvers ward off their abandonment depression and are an attempt to counteract a fragmented sense of self. The fact that there coexists in these patients significant preoedipal and oedipal pathology makes the work especially difficult in both the initial stages and the long-term working-through of the major characterological issues. The potentially life-threatening nature of these conditions, and the effects of malnutrition, vomiting, and laxative abuse further complicate the work.

An important part of the therapeutic work with these patients is the manner in which food, weight, and eating are addressed in the treatment. Since we believe the specific eating disorder and the more general disorders in living are interrelated, therapeutic focus goes back and forth between the anorexic or bulimic symptomatology, its dynamic meaning and function for the patient, and other developmental problems.

A notable exception is the anorexic who begins treatment in a severely emaciated state and requires attention to weight gain before other issues can be effectively addressed. While the physician is the team member with whom the patient deals most directly about her weight restoration, the therapists and the physician formulate a basic treatment plan involving weight gain which depends upon the degree of emaciation, the presence of bulimic symptoms, the age of the patient, the willingness of the parents to support the plan, and whether or not the weight restoration will be carried out in the hospital or on an outpatient basis.

When a patient has to be hospitalized because she is so severely emaciated as to be of serious medical concern, a plan for weight gain is instituted upon admission. We prefer that the patient take food and any nutritional supplement, if necessary, by mouth. Generally, activity within the hospital and passes outside are made contingent upon weight gain.

The patient and parents are seen in therapy throughout the hospitalization period, which has not exceeded four weeks in our experience. This is a particularly stressful time for all concerned. The patient feels she is being punished, and tries to engage her parents in rescuing her by attempting to divide and conquer the therapeutic team. The parents often collude with their daughter's resistance and attempt to undermine the hospitalization plan in some way. During this period, the members of the treatment team need to communicate daily to share information, discuss the treatment plan, and be able to support each other's work with the patient and family. Usually by the end of the first week of the inpatient phase, the patient, the family, and the team are more aligned with each other and the rest of the hospitalization can proceed more smoothly.

Rather than determine a fixed discharge weight upon admission, we monitor the patient's progress quite closely and decide on discharge when the patient seems ready to maintain her weight as an outpatient. The weight at which this may occur is usually still about 15% below normal for her age and height. The patient, at this point, is not emotionally prepared for a full normal weight. If the patient is not able to maintain her discharge weight, we may continue a modified behavioral protocol on an outpatient basis until the patient is better able to control and slowly increase her weight as a result of the ongoing analytic work.

During the initial outpatient phase, the therapist is necessarily involved with the details of the patient's eating behavior, her strategies for managing her weight, and her thoughts and feelings about food and her body. The patient has now worked through much of her rage at not being allowed to continue to starve, the therapeutic alliance has been strengthened, and the content of the material begins to shift toward other areas of the patient's life. It is extremely important for the therapist to refrain from taking over for the patient at this point. She will ask for concrete advice about food in a manner that suggests that she has less competence than she really has. Focused ego-strengthening questions and genetic interpretation of the requests for therapeutic spoonfeeding go much further than gratifying the requests for concrete advice. It can be quite difficult to maintain a stance in which one is helping the patient learn to guide herself. These patients are clamoring for direction and rules, and there has been much control and limit-setting during the acute phase of the treatment. Performing parental rather than analytic functions is intensely gratifying for the patient in the short run but strongly interferes with the patient's developmental journey toward autonomy and independence.

The patient learns from the team approach that we believe that her problems are part of a larger field of family problems which we now address in the work with her parents and in the family sessions. The patient generally continues her progress and moves on to more mature, adaptive styles of relating to her parents and peers. As she begins to understand, explore, and work through the internalized and interpersonal conflicts that are displaced onto food, eating, and her body, she begins to address the question of her own identity. She wonders about how she came to be who she is, and what being a woman is all about. As these issues pertaining to the self are worked through, her menses will return or she will begin to menstruate for the first time. She also may begin to think about and form a close attachment outside the family. Although the therapeutic focus is less on food, weight, and eating, it is not unusual at later stages of the treatment to encounter regressions, when the patient will once again cling to these earlier preoccupations.

The collaborative method we employ has particular advantages for the individual work with the patient. The therapists' information about the parents and what goes on at home is an important ingredient in helping the child's therapist to understand who the parents are, what are the major issues and influences at home, and how the family operates. This knowledge helps her to better assess the nature of her patient's reality as well as the nature of the transference. Early discussions between the two therapists in which the details and impressions are shared allow some of the interlocking dynamics to be elucidated earlier and reduce the extent to which the almost inevitable countertransference reactions impinge negatively upon the treatment.

Our model is useful in handling the splitting that often goes on throughout the initial stages of the work, even if the patient is not hospitalized. The patient will often attempt to pit one parent against the other, her therapist against her parents, or her therapist against her parents' therapist. An example of this occurred repetitively with an anorexic teenager who exaggerated or misrepresented to her parents her therapist's communications. In order to get back at her parents, she depicted her therapist as the good, rewarding object and they as the bad, frustrating objects. This defense could potentially alienate the parents from the child's therapist. The child's therapist must be able to handle her countertransference therapeutically when she finds out that her patient has either been distorting her words or is actually using her therapist as a weapon in the battle with her parents. This knowledge helps the child's therapist become more sensitive to these issues with her patient and focus her questions more sharply to aid in bringing this material into the open.

The parents' therapist can help them understand the child's need for this defensive splitting. This therapist can also help them to try to evaluate for themselves whether their child is reporting to them accurately, or perhaps distorting what she has heard, either consciously or unconsciously. This way of helping parents to think about who their child is and why she may behave the way she does can increase their empathic responsiveness toward their daughter and facilitate more differentiation between family members. This, in turn, will help promote a higher level of functioning in their daughter thereby reducing some of the need for the defensive splitting.

The individual work can be reinforced at home by the parents if their therapist knows in detail about the nature of the individual work. Often in the beginning of treatment, the child's therapist can help make the patient aware that her need for her parents to prepare her special foods at all hours and her other demands for them to take care of her in an infantile manner are inappropriate and costly to her. When these issues arise in the work with the parents, they can be helped to collude less with the patient's regressive wishes and become more sensitive and responsive to the phase-appropriate needs and wishes of their daughter.

For example, early on in the treatment of an anorexic girl it was observed that the mother's buying of special foods for fear that otherwise the child would starve was perpetuating the rigidified eating habits of the daughter, as well as the daughter's overcontrol of the mother. Emphasis in both the individual work with the youngster and the work with her mother was on the need for the child to assume more responsibility for herself. Through an exploration of the mother's difficulty in permitting this, this mother was helped to see that, by refraining from overindulging her daughter and instead being empathically available without being infantilizing, she was actually parenting in a manner that supported her daughter's growth and independence.

At later stages in the treatment, information that the parents' therapist shares with her colleague can help the child's therapist gain more empathy for the parents, and thus help the child to do the same. She can come to see that her parents are both good and bad, just as she is, caught in their own tangled webs with their families of origin. Acceptance and forgiveness come late in the treatment, once the child comes to know and understand herself and her family.

As treatment proceeds toward termination, the patient moves up the developmental ladder, gains the capacity to separate from her parents, and comes to appreciate the nature of ambivalence. There may still be a tendency at times of regression for emotional issues to be centered around food, weight, and eating, but the patient has gained sufficient insight and structural growth so that these concerns no longer seriously interfere with self-esteem regulation. We have not worked long enough in this way with patients to know whether the analytic gains they have made will be sufficient to preclude further treatment. We do believe, however, that the patients we have treated have gained an empathic understanding of themselves and their families and have a degree of interpersonal competence and satisfaction far in excess of what could have been achieved through an individual model alone.

Treatment of the Parents

It has been our experience that, in order for change to occur and be supported and sustained, it is important to provide some intervention with the parents. Our working in this way has been influenced by Masterson's work with borderline adolescents and their families. His follow-up studies of hospitalized cases show that the greater the emotional growth of the parents, through therapy, the more they were able to provide positive support for their children's individuation (Masterson & Costello, 1980 p. 217).

Even if the parents drop out of treatment, which happened in one case in which the daughter moved out of the parental home and became financially and emotionally independent, the fact that the case began with environmental support through parental work had an enormous impact.

The reasons for our work with parents are threefold:

1) We began to see that the pathology of the adolescent patient was so intertwined with the pathology of the family that unless some attempt was made to untangle that web the patient could not improve. In some cases the intertwining takes the form of similarities between parent and child; in others the child is protecting her parents from marital difficulties by keeping attention focused on herself and away from the couple, or by coming between them.

2) We saw that the patient's progress was often impeded by the recalcitrance of the family system. This resistance may take the form of a parent who sabotages treatment, or of a particular kind of family interaction which precludes the possibility of change.

3) We came to appreciate the importance of establishing a therapeutic milieu in the home, as a means of supporting and reinforcing the gains achieved

in individual therapy with these difficult patients. Because of the severe communication problems in most of these families, the serious self-pathology in the youngsters, and the empathic difficulties of the parents, we found that substantial parent and family work had to be done to ensure that progress be sustained.

We have made the repeated observation that the most potent influence on anorexia seems to be the mother's projective identification vis-à-vis the anorexic daughter (Zinner & Shapiro, 1972). The latter is experienced by her mother as a part object, a split-off aspect of her own self. Unless the mother is helped to take back into herself these split-off aspects, she cannot free the daughter to improve.

In working with mothers, striking parallels are often discovered between them and their anorexic daughters. These mothers see this daughter as being most like them of all their children, and often the pathology of mother and daughter has taken on symptomatic similarity. The unconscious connectedness of these mothers and daughters is sometimes seen in their addressing similar issues with each of their therapists during the same week — for example, confessions about drug or alcohol abuse.

Mothers are often women who have seen themselves as helpless, project their helplessness onto their daughters, and cling to them because of their own unmet dependency needs. Both the mother's new object relationship with the therapist and the insight she gains into these processes within her allow her to relinquish her crippling hold on the daughter.

Over the course of our work with these families, we have gained an increasing appreciation of the importance of involving the fathers. Early on in our work, in response to a few highly resistant fathers, we agreed to work with the mother and daughter exclusively. In these cases, and in other situations in which the father was left out of the treatment for some time, we found that he typically would act in such a way as to sabotage his daughter's progress. The cases have gone more smoothly once the father has become reinvolved as an integral part of the treatment.

Generally, fathers have been seen as a member of the parental couple, rather than individually. By and large, fathers have been less receptive to intensive exploration of their own dynamics than have mothers. However, there have been some situations in which the father's pathology is particularly intertwined with the daughter's, and it may be that individual therapy for the fathers is as important in those cases as it is for the mothers.

We have repeatedly observed the pattern that the daughter comes between the parents, forms a coalition with one or another of them, and colludes with their own fears of being intimately involved with each other as a couple and as a parental subsystem. The parents may not initially see this as a problem, and we have found it untimely to address marital problems initially. In time, as the parents are able to make themselves more available to one another and function more cohesively, the marital problems may surface and the couple will then be ready to address them. This turn of events frequently does not occur until the patient begins to improve substantially.

Anorexics are usually aware of the major problems in their families, aside from their own difficulties. Realization that their parents are working on their difficulties with a person who is privy to important knowledge about the family enhances the patients' willingness to take responsibility for their particular role in the maintenance of the family's difficulties.

Although the content of the therapeutic work with the parents changes throughout the course of treatment, there is an underlying orientation in the work with the parents toward helping them to develop an empathic response to the child, so as to create a therapeutic milieu in the home which encourages change. The work with the parents can range from doing "therapy" to providing "counseling." In some cases sessions are held weekly with parents; in others, after there has been initial conjoint work with the couple, mother is seen as much as three times a week and father is included occasionally. The emphasis varies depending on the dynamics of the particular family, as well as the accessibility of the parents for individual work.

At the beginning of treatment, the parents need a great deal of support and direct guidance, because they are usually feeling helpless and hopeless about their parental functioning. The therapist explains in great detail the meaning of the child's behavior to the parents, in the hopes of enhancing their ability to empathize with the child. Parents may try to impose on their therapist an advice-giving role. Although, of course, some explicit advice is sometimes given, the need for it diminishes as time goes on; even in the beginning, the therapist tries to encourage the parents' own resourcefulness, as well as their exploration of their own behavior, rather than offer advice. Once the initial crisis has passed, effecting change in the families can be undertaken in order to foster, encourage, support, and maintain improvements in the child.

When a mother is seen on a regular basis, there is often a shifting back and forth between working on her personal difficulties and on her difficulties as a mother. The therapist must be alert to the mother's using or withholding material about herself or her daughter in any avoidant way. For example, if the mother's therapist is aware that a major crisis is occurring regarding the daughter and she does not mention it in her treatment, this may be brought to the mother's attention and explored. Conversely, if a mother is discussing painful personal issues and suddenly switches to some question about her maternal role, her resistance to looking into herself can be examined.

It has been our experience that the most effective work is done in cases in which the parents, in addition to the youngster, are open to an exploration of how their own dynamics impinge on their child's pathology. In cases in which there is significant psychopathology on the part of one or both parents, or a refusal by the parents to explore their own problems, the work with the youngster becomes that much more difficult. When parents are deeply involved in their own therapy, there is a parallel growth in parents and children, just as there was a parallel pathology at earlier stages.

Family Therapy

Therapy with the entire family, or with the identified patient and her parents, is a modality which we use to varying degrees depending on the particular case; however, in general, it is perceived by us as an adjunctive modality, even if it occurs on a fairly regular basis. Our basic approach is child-centered (Ornstein, 1976), as well as individual-centered. Although we do not minimize the contribution of the family system toward the anorexic pathology, our sense is that a major focus on family systems occurs at the expense of attention to highly significant intrapsychic factors. In addition, we have found that although the current family situation may change, the child may still respond to the "earlier" traumatic parents until her relationship with these internalized parents is completed through individual treatment. These internalized object relationships need to be explored, analyzed, and worked through in individual psychotherapy in order that the patient be able to free herself from her harsh, critical parental images.

Our interventions in family sessions range from observations on patterns of family interaction to comments on individual difficulties. These families need help in communicating directly with one another, in tolerating the expression of interpersonal conflict, in resisting the impulse to be caretakers of each other, and in differentiating the parental and sibling subsystems in the family.

More often than not, siblings are not included in family sessions in the initial stages of treatment. It has been our observation that the hub of the pathology is centered on the parent-patient relationship. When we have an indication that a sibling feels excluded, or that his/her involvement with the patient is problematic, we may include the sibling in a family session, or the parents' therapist may have an individual session with the sibling.

We often find in these families that the intense relationship between the parents and the anorexic child has prevented the normal kinds of sibling interactions that are seen in most families. As the patient begins to improve, and the parents begin to decrease their emotional investment in their "sick" child, we frequently see an increase in sibling interaction. This includes increased communication and sharing of experience, as well as increased sibling rivalry.

At that point we tend to include siblings in the family sessions. This helps the family to reconstitute itself as a viable unit in which there is a potential for interaction among all family members, as well as a clearer demarcation between spouse and sibling subsystems. In many of these families it is the first time in years that family members have been able to have satisfying involvements with one another.

We use family sessions in four different ways:

1) *Diagnostically*. We have found it useful to have a conjoint family session, i.e., with both therapists present, as soon as is feasible in the beginning of work on a case. It permits each therapist to obtain firsthand knowledge of the family members who are being seen by the other therapist. Early observation of family dynamics can be extremely helpful to both therapists, although the family may not continue to be seen together.

2) *In crisis situations, for the purpose of mobilizing the parents and modeling for them*. In this case, a single conjoint session may be held, in order to convey the message that forces must be joined. Such a session was used early in the treatment of a 13-year-old anorexic in order to extend and reestablish a behavior modification program she had needed during hospitalization to prevent continued weight loss and rehospitalization.

3) *For communication purposes*. Sometimes there is important information which should be communicated to the family or important planning that the family needs to do. Doing this via a family session offers the opportunity to simultaneously inform everyone concerned, thus minimizing the possibility of distortion and enabling the establishment of a unified family purpose. Family sessions often serve this purpose during the initial or final stages of hospitalization, when a hospitalization plan and a discharge plan must be addressed.

As discussed, we have occasionally held such sessions to create an arena for the communication of family secrets, which could not be exposed in other ways because of issues of confidentiality. For example, a 14-year-old had revealed to her therapist that she knew her mother was taking drugs, although the mother was not doing it openly and had not talked to her therapist about it. It was important for this issue to be brought out into the open, and a conjoint family session was held for that purpose.

In the three situations listed above, the presence of both therapists is important for a number of reasons. Having both therapists present in a session early in the treatment concretizes the impact of a team approach, and minimizes the opportunities for splitting, withholding information, forming coalitions, and other divisive behaviors. In some cases the pediatrician has been included in family sessions when there are issues addressed which are relevant to his/her role on the team. Having both therapists present in a crisis situation indicates that the therapists are mobilizing their forces as well as the family theirs. Having the family observe the therapists working collaboratively, perhaps disagreeing, in a family session, serves as a model for their continued interaction.

4) *As a major adjunctive treatment modality.* We have found that in a minority of cases it is necessary to have weekly family sessions for substantial periods of time, in order to maintain satisfactory functioning within the family and to facilitate the discussion of significant family issues. These are cases in which there is a high level of family dysfunction, with major dissension between the parents and significant acting out on the part of the youngster. Up until now, these sessions have been held with the child's therapist, essentially for pragmatic reasons such as finances and scheduling. However, we are rethinking the advisability of having both therapists present in these sessions. It has been our experience that in these cases there is a dramatic improvement in child functioning when family sessions are held, and we have seen repeatedly in these cases that in order to maintain a satisfactory level, sessions must be continued.

Although the presence of anorexic or bulimic symptomatology in their child causes the family members much distress, it creates a certain equilibrium in the family unit which is disrupted as the sufferer begins to improve. Clearly the child's illness satisfies the needs of one or more family members and for this reason the anorexic behavior is perpetuated. It is extremely important that those changes effected by the work between the youngster and her therapist be supported by the parents and that they be helped to understand and manage the impact upon them of growth in the child, which can be quite threatening. Sometimes the signs of changes are subtle, and the way in which the family responds has a major effect on whether movement continues or is arrested.

Sessions with these families can be extremely stressful both to family members and to the therapist, and pre- and post-session discussions between the therapists are crucial in order to plan strategies and assess results. These are often highly dysfunctional families with severe communication problems. The pervasive sense of hopelessness is a force to be dealt with in the early stages of work with the family. At that stage, we have found it helpful to have the sessions focused toward specific issues, to keep them from becoming diffuse and regressive. Often the youngster becomes infantile in the sessions, and the therapist is obliged to set limits for her. If this is done effectively, it can provide a useful model for the parents, whose difficulties in assuming the parental role are graphically seen in the sessions.

CONCLUSION

We believe that working collaboratively with a therapeutic partner in the way we have described is well worth the enormous expenditure of time and energy. The availability of a partner affords both the intellectual stimulation and the emotional support required for doing this type of psychotherapeutic work. We also think that this collaborative form of treatment provides the patient and her family with a more far-reaching treatment experience than could be accomplished by one therapist working alone in one therapeutic modality.

The depth and the breadth of the necessary work in these cases are evident. In some cases five or six therapy sessions per week are held for various combinations of family members, seen conjointly, concurrently, or consecutively. Needless to say, flexibility on the part of the therapists is extremely important as hypotheses are constantly being formed, tested, and reformed all in the space of a very short time. Switching from one treatment modality to another, and back again, is a common occurrence, based upon continual reevaluation of the needs of each particular case.

At certain times during the course of therapy, the main thrust of the work is accomplished in individual treatment. At other times, untangling the web of dysfunctional family patterns or opening up the lines of communication within the family must be accomplished before any meaningful individual work can occur. In still others, focusing on the arena of parental interaction then releases the youngster to pursue her own development, free from conflicting parental messages or regressive pulls from either parent.

Just as the therapeutic process with the patients has moved from confrontation of the acting-out defenses to the stage of interpretation and working-through, our collaboration has moved from much discussion of case management issues to a deeper exploration of interpersonal and intrapsychic issues. As we have become more comfortable with each other and with a mutual exploration of our feelings, both countertransferential and real, the collaboration has improved significantly, with a resulting increase in the progress of our cases.

Also, we have begun to find ourselves using conjoint family therapy as a treatment modality with greater frequency. We believe that this development is a result of greater ease in working together, a growing appreciation of the complex interaction between the individual and the family, and more skill in using this modality.

This multidimensional collaborative approach has challenged us on many levels and continues to do so. Perhaps the most basic ongoing challenge remains the logical and sensitive integration of the intrapsychic and interpersonal work. We expect that in the coming years our technique will continue to evolve and we look forward to the advances that are likely to come.

REFERENCES

Berlin, I., Boatman, M., Sheimo, S., and Szurek, S. (1951). Adolescent alternation of anorexia and obesity. *American Journal of Orthopsychiatry, 21*, 387-419.
Bruch, H. (1978). *The golden cage: The enigma of anorexia nervosa.* Cambridge, MA: Harvard University Press.
Bruch, H. (1982). Treatment in anorexia nervosa. *International Journal of Psychoanalytic Psychotherapy, 9*, 305-311
Grote, L. R., & Meng, H. (1934). Medical and psychotherapeutic treatment of endogenetic magersucht (anorexia). *Schweiz med. Wochenschrift, 64*, 137-139.
Levenkron, S. (1982). *Treating and overcoming anorexia nervosa.* New York: Charles Scribners Sons.
Levenkron, S. (1982). Personal communication.
Liebman, R., Minuchin, S., & Baker, L. (1974). An integrated treatment program for anorexia nervosa. *American Journal of Psychiatry, 131*, 432-436.
Lorand, S. (1943). Anorexia nervosa, report of a case. *Psychosomatic Medicine, 5*, 282-292.
Masterson, J. (with Costello, J. L.) (1980). *From borderline adolescent to functioning adult: The test of time.* New York: Brunner/Mazel.
Minuchin, S., Rosman, B. L., & Baker, L. (1978). *Psychosomatic families: Anorexia nervosa in context.* Cambridge, MA: Harvard University Press.
Ornstein, A. (1976). Making contact with the inner world of the child. *Comprehensive Psychiatry, 17*, 3-36.
Piazza, E., Piazza, N., & Rollins, N. (1980). Anorexia nervosa: Controversial aspects of therapy. *Comprehensive Psychiatry, 21*, 177-189.
Rollins, N., & Blackwell, A. (1968). The treatment of anorexia nervosa in children and adolescents: Stage 1. *Journal of Child Psychology and Psychiatry and Allied Disciplines, 9*, 81-91.
Rollins, N., & Piazza, E. (1981). Anorexia nervosa: A quantitative approach to follow up. *Journal of the American Academy of Child Psychiatry, 20*, 167-183.
Selvini Palazzoli, M. (1978). *Self-starvation.* New York: Jason Aronson.
Sperling, M. (1950). Children's interpretation and reaction to the unconscious of their mothers. *International Journal of Psychoanalysis, 31*, 36-41.
Sperling, M. (1978). *Psychosomatic disorders in childhood.* New York: Jason Aronson.
Sours, J. (1980). *Starving to death in a sea of objects.* New York: Jason Aronson.
Waller, J. F., Kaufman, M. R., & Deutsch, F. (1940). Anorexia nervosa. *Psychosomatic Medicine, 2*, 3-16.
Wilson, C. P. (1980). The family psychological profile of anorexia nervosa patients. *Journal of the Medical Society of New Jersey, 77*, 341-344.
Zinner, J., & Shapiro, R. (1972). Projective identification as a mode of perception and behaviour in families of adolescents. *International Journal of Psycho-Analysis, 52*, 523-530.

Chapter 10

Eating Disorders and the Family: A Model for Intervention

Barry Dym

Treating eating disorders is difficult and often frustrating work.* Any therapist who gains a reputation for good work receives referrals of anorexic and bulimic patients who have been seen by many other therapists who have "failed." If successful-where-others-have-failed, clinicians may become smug about themselves and evangelical about their method. Practitioners of psychoanalytic therapy, structural family therapy, cognitive-behavior therapy, and psychopharmacology have each laid claims to preeminence in the field.

Yet for all of our successes, we also have failures where others succeed. I have helped bulimic women who made no progress with psychodynamic therapy or with medication. I am certain that clinicians of other persuasions have worked well with patients I fail to help or help only temporarily. For that matter, I have made almost identical interventions in what appear to be almost identical circumstances, with widely varying results.

Considering this fickleness, I began to ponder the question, why do we succeed *when* we do? Several reasonable answers come to mind: the match between therapist and patient; the skill of the therapist; the therapist's enthusiasm for a new approach; the readiness of the patient. But if one assumes skill and experience, and if one acknowledges that all the modalities work sometimes, one is left with a disconcertingly broad statement: An approach will work if it is the right one at the right time.

Developing a useful way to conceptualize such an approach to interven-

---

*Most of the experience which provides the basis for this model comes from my own psychotherapy experience and my supervision of over 150 cases of bulimia and anorexia nervosa at the Boston Center for Family Health.

tion is the purpose of this chapter. The proposed diagnostic model is grounded in general systems theory and organized around three concepts.

The first is that there are many levels of organization in human experience, from cell to organ to person to culture. These systemic levels are hierarchically arranged, with each more complex than the one before. They are "a set of nested structures, like a set of Russian dolls" (Bronfenbrenner, 1979), and inextricably linked with each other. Most research studies and clinical modalities address only one level: the biochemistry of depression; the ego deficits of borderline personalities (Masterson, 1972); the enmeshment and rigidity of "psychosomatic families" (Minuchin, Rosman, & Baker, 1978). We need a conceptual framework which encompasses and relates information from all levels of systems. Clinical methods which consider only one level can be likened to the blindfolded fools who each argue that one part of an elephant is a tree trunk, a snake, or a mountain side. It is beyond my range to explore the entire biopsychosocial field (Engel, 1980) in this chapter. Instead, I will take a small part of that field to demonstrate the proposed diagnostic model.

The part focuses on the individual and her interpersonal field. This field is broadened at each level to include greater perspectives in both space and time. The levels which will later be described in more detail are as follows: 1) individual imagery and experience; 2) moment-to-moment interactional sequences; 3) interactional sequences which extend over hours, days, weeks; 4) patterns of adaptation to developmental stages; and 5) patterns of influence across generations.

The second concept, isomorphism, suggests a theoretical way to discuss the relationship among the five systemic levels. Isomorphism refers to deep organizational similarities at the different levels. Experience and images " . . . which appear widely unrelated in content will reflect the same patterning of form, will be . . . transformations or isomorphs of each other" (Levenson, 1972, p. 185). At another point Levenson describes isomorphism in this way:

> . . . the patient is a total aesthetic entity, for isomorphism is like a stone dropped into a four-dimensional pond. Its ripples extend in every direction in time and space. There is a continuous ongoing isomorphic repetition of the patient's (I would add, family's) patterns in the therapy room. . . . Everything—his past history, present behavior, fantasies, dreams and behavior in the treatment room— will reflect the same patterning. (p. 188)

This chapter will describe a series of isomorphic transformations. At the individual level, for example, it will describe the cognitive map which informs and guides an eating disorder as a behavior. At the level of moment-to-moment sequences, it will portray a recurrent interactional sequence in which the eating disorder behavior is an integral event.

The third concept, disequilibrium, helps the therapist to determine where to focus interventions. All living systems tend simultaneously towards equilibrium and disequilibrium. When the balance is more towards disequilibrium, the system is more vulnerable to change. Both natural causes, such as the developmental crisis of an individual family member, or random events, such as a job loss or car accident, can push the system beyond its capacity to return to a more stable state. Then, the family system adapts itself. It reorganizes in order to achieve a new balance between equilibrium and disequilibrium. The tendency towards disequilibrium and change, however, is not uniform throughout the family system; it may vary from level to level in the hierarchy.

In summary, the model set forth here proceeds in the following steps. First, the therapist organizes information about the patient and her family in terms of the five systemic levels. This is like placing a five-part grid over a complex and often confusing interactional field. Second, the therapist identifies a series of related patterns—isomorphs—at each of the levels. Third, he or she determines which isomorphs are in states of intense disequilibrium. Now the therapist is ready to plan and implement therapeutic interventions, beginning at that level of greatest instability.

The body of the chapter is an attempt to give substance to this diagnostic model. It is organized as follows. First, there will be a brief portrait of a young bulimarexic* woman and her family, the Antonionis. Then each of the systems levels will be explored with the following concerns in mind:

1) What are the general characteristics of each level?
2) What specific characteristics of eating disorders fit within that level?
3) How does one identify a series of related isomorphs throughout the levels?
4) How does one assess disequilibrium at each systems level?

Throughout each of these sections, case material from the Antonioni family will be used to illustrate the model.

ANNA AND THE ANTONIONIS

This is the story of a 17-year-old bulimarexic girl, who maintained a state of emaciation by taking laxatives or by vomiting almost all that she ate. When I first met Anna, she had already been hospitalized twice for anorexia, once for a psychotic episode and once because her colon seemed about to burst when she abruptly stopped taking laxatives. Since early puberty, Anna had also been both guided and oppressed by "voices."

Anna is a tall skinny girl with large, glistening eyes which look out of a

---

*I am using Boskind-White's definition for bulimarexia.

face as delicate and disarming as that of the young Audrey Hepburn. She is both intelligent and articulate. Socially, she combines skill and charm, though Anna disdains these virtues. She makes friends easily and, except during her time of frequent hospitalization, she does quite well in school. Before she became bulimarexic, Anna had seemed an almost perfect child, who required little focused attention from her parents—all in marked contrast to her brother, who did poorly in school, often misbehaved, and constantly worried his parents.

Throughout her teenage years, Anna has been very moody. At one moment she can be anxious and depressed. The next, she can be bright and cheerful. These mood shifts generally follow shifts in context. For example, she might sit sadly, sullenly, passively through 20 minutes of family discussion. If her parents left the room and she and I were left alone, Anna might become instantly animated.

The Antonionis are an American family who had lived in France for almost 10 years, the formative years for Anna and her brother Jonathan. The family is traditional, patriarchal, and closely knit. All describe the early years during which the family depended so much on each other in virtually idyllic images. "It was like paradise," says George Antonioni, the father. But the walls of paradise were breached when Jonathan went off to college in the United States. The family's sense of safety and security could not tolerate the loss of a member. On the other hand, the value placed on college was very high. The solution? A few months after Jonathan had left for Philadelphia, the family followed suit and moved to Washington, DC. At this point, Anna was 13.

To accomplish this move, George took a job which, while very prestigious, was hateful to him. He grew depressed and withdrawn. To his family, it seemed that the "rock of Gibraltar" had begun to soften and crumble. Judith, his wife and Anna's mother, stopped her own freelance writing and almost all other activities. She became utterly focused on her husband's welfare. Anna, who seemed to require so little guidance, was left on her own. She ran free, alternately feeling grownup and exhilarated or lost and frightened. To give a small snapshot of this time, imagine one summer weekend: George and Judith are traveling; Anna, with the house to herself, holds an impromptu party for hundreds of Georgetown residents, who dance and drink until dawn; upon return, George and Judith are so dispirited that they give Anna a small reprimand and get on with their business.

Within a year and a half, George felt "suffocated" by his business. As a

---

*Naturally, the names and the facts have been changed enough to protect the Antonionis' identities, but not so much as to distort the meaning or spirit of the case.

result, he took "leave" from his job and went traveling in Europe for three months. By the time he returned, he had resolved to take a new job. Judith objected, claiming that Anna had just adjusted to school in America and a second move might be hard even for her. But Judith would not strongly oppose George. His welfare was her greatest concern. Several months later, this once well-settled family was uprooted again and moved to Boston.

During the first year in America, Anna found ways to "fit in" with friends and to do well at school. However, this was the year her "voices" began, apparently to fill the void left by her formerly attentive parents.

The bulimarexia began when her father left to travel in Europe and intensified rapidly between the time he announced that they would move again and the actual move. This time, Anna had become very attached to friends and objected strongly. She also grew depressed. The combination of depression and weight loss alarmed her parents, who, with the resolution of the job situation, were in better spirits themselves. They hovered anxiously around Anna, spending innumerable hours trying to figure out exactly what she thought and felt. Anna alternated between snappish anger, extended tirades, and childlike dependency. Most of the anger was reserved for her father with whom she had been so close and adoring and from whom she now distanced. Much of the dependency was reserved for her mother. Judith sometimes felt caught in between, but made clear that her first loyalty was to her husband. It is no little irony, then, that the bulimarexia was the occasion for the family to pull together and to reconstruct its old close-knit patriarchy. They spent almost every free moment together.

The bulimarexia also ushered in several therapists, each of whom tried to "rescue" Anna from her parents. One performed what we in the trade call a "parentectomy," asserting that Anna and Judith were too close and that Judith should back way off. With their traditional respect for authority, the Antonionis followed the doctor's advice. Judith withdrew. Now Anna, who had been treated like a small child, was left alone. She grew frightened, then desperate, then despairing within a few months. When she threatened suicide and became more emaciated than ever, she was hospitalized. A new therapist advised the parents to express their love; Judith grew closer. Anna's condition stabilized. She recovered. The family was close again.

These alternations of distance and stability persisted through several quite different therapists with no substantial change in the bulimarexic condition, except during hospital stays. George and Judith occasionally switched positions: If Judith took too vehement a position on eating, for example, George would soften it and, for a time, he and Anna would be close, with Judith the outsider in the triangle. But usually Judith and Anna were closer and George was out. George and Judith, who never fought, remained close. If a coalition with Anna ever threatened their solidarity, Anna was temporarily dropped.

At these moments, her symptoms—weight loss, voices, depression—would flare, therapists would intervene to stabilize the situation, and the basic family structure would be reinstituted.

As I go on to describe each of the systemic levels, I will make references to the Antonionis for illustrative purposes, and I will elaborate different parts of the story.

LEVEL 1: THE INTRAPSYCHIC LEVEL

Analysis at this level focuses on identifying those images or cognitive sets which constitute one's view of reality, both consciously and unconsciously. The intrapsychic view informs and guides action; it forms much of the basis of what is thought possible and impossible, difficult and easy, right and wrong, futile and fulfilling. For example, many anorexics are closely and dependently attached to their mothers. An image informing this close connection might include the following monologue: "If I am independent, my mother will be angry. She will grow closer to my father and exclude me entirely from her life, and then I will fall apart." An image common to bulimia is as follows: "If I do not vomit this time, I will gain weight and begin an escalating cycle of weight gain which is out of my control."

The emphasis here is not on feelings, but cognitive sets, and particularly on those which constitute a bridge between the individual and the world around her. Feelings are considered, but primarily in terms of the amount of charge or intensity that attaches to the imagery.

The intrapsychic life of anorexic (and bulimarexic) girls has been richly portrayed in the psychoanalytic literature. The etiological focus of this literature is on irresolution in the separation-individuation stage of development. As a result of this irresolution, anorexic girls tend to feel helpless, confused, dependent, and filled with self-loathing. Theirs is a terrifying world in which they feel out of control. Anorexia may be seen as a maladaptive effort to cope with these feelings: by seeking self-mastery through a very literal control of one's body and by alternating sequences of fusion with and rejection of parents, especially mothers.

According to Selvini Palazzoli (1974), the anorexic does not experience her body as belonging to her. It is seen as a threat, which must be controlled. The body is taken as a "maternal object from which the ego wishes to separate itself at all costs" (p. 90). The anorexic therefore incorporates the maternal object in order to control it. Hence we find the extremely harsh consciences in eating-disorder patients and the radical swings from weepy, childlike dependence to angry, fiercely judgmental assaults on parents in order to distinguish themselves from their parents. The typical mother of an anorexic girl is herself insecure. Her overprotective attitude towards her daughter derives from her own difficulty in tolerating separation and autonomy. Symbiosis grows. The child becomes a confused and helpless victim who punishes her body and struggles to put off development of a woman's body.

Recently, Crisp (1980) has added some key dimensions of anorexia. First he has noted a "phobic" quality to the fear of fatness, a fear encouraged by modern culture. Second, he suggests that anorexia is not an inevitable outcome of the failed resolution in the separation-individuation phase. Different neurotic styles can develop. But if parents have great difficulty with adolescents or if they themselves had difficulty during that phase, then the phobic fear of fatness combines with the neurotic development to produce anorexia nervosa.

Assessment of Equilibrium/Disequilibrium

It is very difficult to describe a simple method for determining the degree of equilibrium or disequilibrium in the intrapsychic life of anorexic and bulimic patients. Richness of imagery and insight, for example, is not always a helpful indicator. Many young women have been in extensive individual therapy before coming to me, and the capacity of insight to move them often seems exhausted. Worse, the insights have been frequently repeated and assimilated into homeostatic process. In effect, they serve to reinforce the status quo: "I am dependent because of my parents. . . . There is nothing I can do about it," or "I have a neurotic need to take care of my mother. . . . " More naive patients, who have not yet become therapy veterans, may appear to have more stable intrapsychic lives, but are more susceptible to new understandings, and therefore more easily thrown into disequilibrium.

There are two major indicators which I use to determine the degree of equilibrium at this level. The first is simplest: How do people respond to reframing their understanding of what is wrong? For example, I said to a young woman that her bulimia seemed to be the only thing that she had that was entirely her own. She responded in two ways: First she said, "Yes." Then she was eager to begin discussion of methods for planning alternate forms of privacy. Other clients, however, are rather disinterested in such "insights," or rapidly include them in their established imagery. That mode would look like this: "I suppose that's right; my parents don't let me do anything by myself."

The second indicator has to do with the existence of alternative feelings and self-imagery. Some anorexic girls experience themselves differently in a context other than their families. One girl, for example, lived away from home at a boarding school. She generally felt good about herself at school: independent, competent, and likeable. At home, she almost immediately fell into the familiar opposite feelings. Two sets of images were at war. With her life increasingly taking place away from home, imagery supporting her "bulimarexic self" was losing the battle to imagery supported by her present experience. Her intrapsychic life was in disequilibrium.

Anna and the Antonionis

Anna fits well within the psychoanalytic portrait of anorexia. Although she was five feet, six inches tall and weighed 86 pounds when I met her, she felt fat and ugly. She was quite literally phobic about weighing herself on a scale, exhibiting all the phobic responses, like heart palpitations, rapid short breathing, nausea, and so forth. Moreover, Anna was sure that independence, which was so profoundly associated with the period of her parents' neglect of her, would lead to further neglect and rejection. Whenever Anna permitted herself to think too much of being out on her own, her "voices" warned her to stop. The voices were equally effective in limiting her budding battles with her parents and in forbidding her to make serious efforts to try to eat normally. Anna did not think that her skinny body was beautiful, but her voices warned her of the danger ahead if she put on weight and began to look more womanly.

By the time I met her, Anna had had about three years of individual, psychoanalytic psychotherapy, as well as extended use of lithium and antidepressant medications. Both she and her therapist felt stuck. They had explored present and past, and the intrapsychic road appeared barren. Anna seemed resistant to entering the therapeutic process. She confided to me that her voices gave clear and very restrictive instructions on how much of her inner life could be divulged to therapists. She seemed as angrily involved with her female therapist as she was with her mother.

Anna's intrapsychic life was essentially in equilibrium, supported by rigid patterns of interactional relationships, which restricted new experience and therefore limited the possibility of new information about herself. Her therapist, her parents, who alternately hovered and watched from a distance, and her friends treated her as a needy, testy, confused person, which reinforced the most debilitating side of her own self-imagery.

Anna did have some alternative imagery, based on an independent, fashionable life among sophisticated peers in Europe. While many initial interactions with people supported this imagery, it rapidly eroded as she grew insecure with strangers. Her voices condemned her for "kidding herself" and filled her with terrifying images of abandonment and physical harm. An alternative imagery was very undeveloped, therefore, and difficult for a therapist to tap.

As a new therapist, I had a great advantage in efforts to disequilibrate

Anna's self-imagery, since our experience together was automatically different. I permitted myself to respond to her charm and intelligence, hoping to build a relationship based on mutual respect instead of developing a transferential relationship. I allied with her voices, encouraging them to monitor the pace and content of her sharing of information. And Anna let it be known that the voices were more than mollified; they believed her parents needed protection against the vicious attitude that Anna had taken towards them during her individual therapy. In family sessions, I did treat her parents as reasonable people. By providing some safety against Anna's fear of her own excess and anger, I helped open the door for easy talking. When we were alone, Anna liked to confide in me.

However, the insights gained in years of therapy had become so deeply woven into the fabric of Anna's self-imagery that it was hard to shake the equilibrium at this level. The elaborate monitoring system of her voices, which had also been honed over a few years, added greatly to the difficulty. Perhaps intervention at this level, the intrapsychic level, might succeed, but I was not betting on it. This did not seem the best starting point for therapeutic intervention.

LEVEL II: MOMENT-TO-MOMENT SEQUENCES

These are repetitive sequences of behavior that are observable, for example, in the therapist's office. The sequences take the form of recursive cycles which are internalized as images. The images come to guide, perhaps govern, the behavior of the individuals as they act their parts in the recursive cycle. In this way, image and interactional sequence are isomorphic.

A familiar moment-to-moment sequence in a family with an anorexic daughter is as follows: The daughter nibbles feebly at her dinner; her mother anxiously offers to cook something else; the daughter snaps at her mother to "leave me alone"; the father tells his daughter to be more respectful of her mother; the daughter leaves the table in tears. This sequence may recur several times each week.

Since its publication in 1978, *Psychosomatic Families* has provided the most compelling portrait of family interaction with anorexia nervosa. Minuchin, Baker, and Rosman identify four major characteristics in these families: enmeshment, overprotectiveness, rigidity, and a lack of conflict resolution. These are familiar and easily accessible descriptions of family structure, and there is no need to describe them here. But they do provide an important backdrop to the prototypical moment-to-moment sequence which I would like to sketch.

Mother and anorexic daughter are intimately engaged in conversation, perhaps finishing each other's sentences, and acting as if they can read each other's minds. They are enmeshed. They are discussing whether it is reasonable for the daughter to apply to out-of-town colleges. The mother thinks this is a bad idea because her daughter is not very mature. While her daughter secretly agrees, she objects. Mother is being overprotective and, as in the past, will try to enlist her husband's support on this matter. At the moment, father seems preoccupied with his own thoughts and does not join the conversation. Then the conversation becomes heated. The father now enters in one of several ways. He may enter by saying something critical about his daughter. This is likely. But he may enter to criticize the way his wife is handling the situation. In either case, mother and daughter will temporarily suspend their heated discussion to defend the other. They will say that father does not understand. Anorexic daughters are often overprotective of their mothers as well. Often the father will leave in frustration at this point. Nothing will have been resolved about the specific issue of college or about how family members should treat each other. This rigid sequence will repeat itself endlessly, rendering the (rigid) family unable to adapt to the developmental crisis represented by the daughter's preparation to leave home.

While this moment-to-moment sequence should provide a clear picture of anorexic families at this level of interaction, it will be helpful also to see its isomorphic fit with the intrapsychic level.

Sometimes the father does not leave in frustration, but persists in his point of view. If he persists in criticizing his wife, she may cry or yield to his position. If he persists in criticizing his daughter and his wife is unable to act as a buffer but foresees that conflict may arise with her husband, then again she may yield. At this stage, the coalition has shifted from mother and daughter versus father to mother and father versus daughter, who is now abandoned. This scapegoating, however, may be extremely rapid, for the daughter may cry or threaten injury to herself, in which case the scapegoating turns instantly into concern and hovering attention. Potential parental conflict has been converted into concerned activity.

The daughter's positions in these sequences are important to note. She has been part of a powerful coalition with her mother against her father, which may frighten her. She has been overengaged, or fused, with her mother. She has been cast out of the parental system. She has been brought back in as a helpless victim and a dependent child. The positions support imagery noted in Level I and, in turn, the imagery guides her to play these roles. The interactional sequences at this level, then, are isomorphic to the imagery of Level I.

Assessment of Equilibrium/Disequilibrium

Assessment of equilibrium or disequilibrium at this level consists of at least three tasks. The first is to identify recursive cycles in which the eating disorder is a central event, or general interactional patterns of "psychosomatic families" such as are described above. The second is to search for deviations from those patterns, such as when a mother refuses periodically to mediate a fight between a bulimic daughter and her husband, or when she and her husband have a dispute without the bulimic daughter being enlisted to act as a buffer, thus recalibrating the metaphorical distance between parents. The third is to try to change the interactional patterns, such as instructing the mother not to mediate the fight in order to assess the rigidity of the recursive cycles.

Anna and the Antonionis

As we know, the Antonionis had been a tightly knit, rigidly organized family. Individual developmental crisis threw the family into great confusion, with its structure alternating between great lability and rigidity. At the time when I met the family, they had tightened their internal structure in order to combat what they felt to be the intrusions of Anna's incompetent individual therapist. The therapist had, for example, forbidden Anna and her mother from discussing "personal" matters. In keeping with the defensive tightening, moment-to-moment sequences in the Antonioni family were in a kind of brittle equilibrium.

At any particular moment Anna and one parent would be close. The other parent would enter and surreptitiously challenge the alliance — by worrying about Anna, by criticizing her, by making veiled competitive statements about parenting, by acting irritable or jealous. The surreptitious quality was essential because the implicit rule against marital discord was the strongest one in the family. Inevitably the challenging move of the entering parent was a signal for Anna to begin fighting with the parent with whom she had been allied. The entering parent would then protect the other from Anna. Anna would either withdraw, literally or emotionally, to a great distance, or begin to cry — in both cases she would feel (secretly) punished by her voices. In confusion, her parents would either leave her alone for an extended period of time or lecture her angrily. Eventually one would be assigned to mollify her or to lead her to professional help. An alliance would build with that parent, and the cycle would begin again.

This recursive cycle was isomorphic with Anna's imagery around dependence and independence, about being close, then cast out, about the necessity to fight and its perils, and about the need to have her voices, which served as a steady, if harsh, set of standards amidst the quicksand of shifting alliances in her family.

The recursive cycle was also very much in equilibrium. When I tried to block the process of shifting coalitions I was excluded from the family group. If I pointed out anger, a potential fight, even a real difference of opinion between the parents, I met the same resistance. Although I had a strong alliance with Anna, built in both individual and family sessions, she joined thoroughly with her parents to block my efforts to disrupt the recursive cycles of Level

II. The significance of this discovery is that if I came armed only with a here-and-now approach to family problems, I would likely fail to be helpful to the Antonionis. A strict "structuralist" approach, for example, might well have ended in a struggle for control between family and therapist.

LEVEL III: EXTENDED SEQUENCES

These repetitive sequences are similar to those in Level II, but take place over the course of hours, days, weeks, months. They do not take place in the observable moment. For example, imagine a hard-working father who is essentially out of the home for most of the week. During this time, tension gradually builds between mother and anorexic daughter. During the weekend, when father is home, the tension between mother and daughter peaks, ending in an angry shouting exchange, which appears out of control. Now father enters in order to mediate and conciliate both parties. He is successful and the tension declines. On Monday morning, he again leaves and tension begins to build between mother and daughter . . . and so forth.

The extension of recursive cycles into a broader context of time and space is significant. It means these cycles are not as tightly programmed, not as circumscribed and protected. The father's business trip may be longer than usual, leaving mother and daughter alone for a longer period of time; during the father's unanticipated absence, physical illness may temporarily throw the mother-daughter relationship into disequilibrium. Or, at the critical point of the parent's fight when the daughter normally enters to limit its escalation, she may be invited to stay at a friend's house for the weekend. The parents may have to discover alternate methods to regulate or to resolve their conflict. Often a random event (a member's inability to attend a given therapy session) presents the therapist with an unfamiliar family configuration (a father and his children alone). Such a random event can produce disequilibrium in the family.

Assessment of Equilibrium/Disequilibrium

Random events and long-term contradictory patterns appear to have their greatest, or at least most frequent, impact at Level III. Illnesses, accidents, business trips, vacations, family moves from one residential location to another or from school to school — these kinds of events are disruptive to family interactional patterns, and particularly to those patterns which take days and weeks to be completed. While families develop deviation-countering strategies to cope with such disruptions, generally the strategies cannot be as successful as those developed for moment-to-moment sequences. In large part this is because the field of possible disruptions is far broader and disequilibrium a more frequent possibility.

Experienced therapists have long known to sense and exploit opportunities to intervene in these cycles. For example, if a mother who has been in an enmeshed relationship with her bulimic daughter gets sick, the daughter may be terribly upset and her bulimia may worsen. The previously worried, incompetent, harsh, and/or distant father may temporarily move closer to his child, enabling him to be kind and competent. This strengthens an alliance which had been weak, helping eventually to break the enmeshment between mother and daughter.

In developing this five-level system grid it has been fascinating to note how pivotal are the disequilibrating events of Level III. It is as if one could conduct an extensive assessment in the other levels while waiting for a disruption in Level III as a signal to begin implementing intervention strategies. Furthermore, disequilibrium here will show itself in one of the other levels as well, thus opening opportunities for intervention there.

Anna and the Antonionis

George traveled a fair amount for business, and anticipating each planned trip caused considerable apprehension and anxiety in Judith and Anna. Mother felt that she could not control Anna, who was "stronger that I am," and Anna was terrified that "we will fight the whole time he is gone, and it will get out of hand because no one will stop us." Three times before, father's trips had been occasions for Anna's deterioration and hospitalizations. The health care system had to be brought in to fill father's place and to stabilize the conflict-avoidant triangle which was so much in disequilibrium. Six weeks into the therapy, George left for a two-week business trip which would precipitate a period of predictable disequilibrium. In therapy we could plan for this period: I could help mother and daughter develop new, less helpless, more competent ways to deal with both father's absence and with their own unmediated relationship.

Their success in this task, their great joy in their success, and their announcement to father on his return that they no longer needed him in his old rescuing capacity was the turning point in the therapy.

Following this, sequences in Level II loosened and Anna's alternative imagery (Level I) could surface and become more figural.

LEVEL IV: PATTERNS OF ADAPTATION TO DEVELOPMENTAL STAGES

It is a truism to say that open systems, like families, are adaptive to changes in their internal and external environment. It is also true that adaptation is not fresh with each unique situation. It becomes patterned. Over time families evolve patterned responses to events like developmental stages in the lives of their members. These responses may be described in terms of the recursive cycles ordinarily applied to more time-limited sequences of behavior.

One family, for example, repeated the following pattern. Each child is at first greatly encouraged to be more than usually independent. After a while the children feel and act entitled to their freedoms. However, with the first bit of trouble (for example, an adolescent missing curfew), the loose reins are pulled in tightly. A struggle ensues, during which the siblings dissociate themselves from the focal child who finds him/herself suddenly alone. She "acts out" by skipping school, abusing drugs, or not eating. Outside experts such as teachers or therapists are consulted and a compromise is successfully negotiated. At each subsequent stage and with each sibling a similar pattern is repeated.

The onset of anorexia or bulimia generally coincides with predictable adolescent markers, such as the onset of puberty and leaving home. Adaptive patterns which families have developed to meet prior moves towards separation and autonomy in their children are naturally activated by these adolescent developments. At the same time, parents encounter developmental challenges. These challenges may be stimulated by such events as the leave-taking of the oldest or by fears of an "empty nest" when the youngest child is about to leave.

Crisp (1980) has observed that it is now hard for adolescent girls to avoid some distorted response to food and fat, since our media has helped create a virtually phobic fear of fatness. This fear is greatest at adolescence. It seems apparent that the range and flexibility of adaptive patterns which a family can muster go a long way towards explaining how their daughters will navigate these treacherous waters. Not all adolescent girls become anorexic. Not all families with prototypical patterns (e.g., enmeshment, rigidity, overprotectiveness, lack of conflict resolution) produce anorexic daughters. Looking to the resourcefulness of adaptive patterns in families adds an important dimension.

Rosman has drawn an interesting distinction (personal communication, 1984). She hypothesizes that families who radically transform themselves to meet the needs of a chronically-ill child are likely to become inflexible. Those families who may appear less responsive, who take time to search their own repertoire of adaptive responses, and who appear to change less in response to major crises remain more flexible and stable over the course of time. The brittle family patterns of anorexic families seem to struggle to remain unchanged in the face of developmental crises but often change dramatically to meet such challenges. Such was the case with the Antonionis, of course, when they uprooted themselves to contend with their first child's move to college.

Assessment of Equilibrium/Disequilibrium

In assessing equilibrium and disequilibrium at this level, we must attend to such alternations of brittle stability and dramatic adaptations to past life crises, as well as to the onset of anorexia itself.

The pressure of an onrushing developmental event is so great that no family can fully halt its progress; its destabilizing qualities take hold in anticipation of the event itself. Disequilibrium is the rule. As with the extended sequences of Level III, the therapist should be alert to the potential of these crises. Therapeutic intervention seems more successful, for example, when its timing is coordinated with the timing of a developmental marker, such as a date for leaving home. When such dates are kept figural in family sessions, the disequilibrium inherent in the developmental crisis is amplified. The brittle anorexic family, lacking sturdy adaptive responses, is then likely to move into a transformational crisis.

Anna and the Antonionis

As we have seen, the Antonionis responded dramatically to developmental and other crises in their lives. Several times they uprooted the family to meet the father's professional crises. When their son left for college the response was similar. When Anna's first therapist told her parents she needed more autonomy, they virtually cast her loose. Following these dramatic shifts, there would be a troubled response by a family member. In the early years of the family, this would be the father, who would become immensely irritable, depressed, and restless. In recent years, Anna and her bulimarexia had taken over this role. Step three in these lengthy sequences would consist of a rallying around the troubled person, a general coming together, and a tightening of the boundaries against the outside world. Anna's hospitalizations temporarily disrupted this cycle, throwing the Antonionis into great confusion. But eventually they integrated the hospitalizations and professionals into the cycle, which took on the following character: 1) the anticipation of a crisis (developmental, professional, medical); 2) a dramatic family adaptation (family moves, mother stops working, etc.); 3) Anna's becoming ill (bulimarexia, psychotic, physically); 4) professionals' coming in to stabilize the situation, keeping the parents at a distance; 5) at first opportunity, the parents' rallying around Anna, closing ranks, and excluding professionals, such as therapists and teachers. To do this, they may move again . . . and the cycle starts over.

In one sense, the cycle had gone out of control by the time I met the Antonionis. Anna's crises were growing increasingly intense. Her body and mind were torn and anguished. On the other hand, the adaptive cycle, in which her bulimarexia was an integral event, was in place. And the scenario for the next cycle was already set in place. Anna was 17 years old and eligible for college application. In anticipation of this event her parents had made two apparently contradictory preparations. They had planned a year abroad for themselves, acknowledging the developmental stage. At the same time, they decided not to rent their home but to have someone "housesit." In this way, the family could rapidly reconvene if Anna experienced difficulties.

While it is clear that the adaptive cycle could and probably would repeat itself, there was also a difference: It had been escalating in intensity and seemed likely to continue escalating. The therapist interested in disequilibrium can of course push the escalation further, hoping a transformational event will be curative. But, as in cases of abuse, this seemed too dangerous.

An alternative is to support and to help consolidate the adaptive cycle. This has the effect of transforming the destructive escalation of the cycle, which required Anna to be ill, into a blueprint for a major move towards separation and autonomy. Practically, this meant encouraging the separation, establishing regular, ritualized times to come back together for intensive periods, and maintaining the house in Boston. Responses to Anna's difficulties would not require wild reactions.

The supportive cycle could now be more in keeping with those of the less reactive families whom Rosman identified as coping well with the chronic illness in a child.

At this point the ground seemed clear for me to conduct effective individual therapy with Anna, preparing her for her "inevitable" but stabilized separation. And I could take a psychoeducational approach with her parents, teaching them how to carefully lay the groundwork for the autonomy of their "chronically ill" daughter. These two approaches, in turn, gave added support, to the once escalating but increasingly sturdy adaptive patterns of the Antonionis.

LEVEL V: TRANSGENERATIONAL IMAGES AND SEQUENCES

At this level, we are concerned with the transmission of imagery and interactional sequences from one generation to the next. In families with chronically and psychosomatically ill children, for example, one often finds that the way one generation organizes to care for the ill child closely resembles that of the next. For example, mother and ill child are enmeshed and both are frequently close to the maternal grandmother. Like the maternal grandfather, the father tends to be distant and alternately appears negligent and harsh with his sick child. He sees his wife as overindulgent, perhaps ruining the possibility of growth for his child, and may attach strongly with his own hopes and aspirations to a second, well child. The reader should refer back to Levels I and II for a fuller discussion of just what is passed on.

One may speculate that the recursive cycles of one generation are internalized as in Level I (and reinforced by the repetition of the cycles as in Level II) and then carried out in the next generation. It is stunning to watch and wonder at this process. How do people manage to select and/or train their spouses to play roles so similar to their father's and mother's? How do people who vow never to permit the "crippling overindulgence" of a child in their family of origin manage to choose wives or husbands prone to enmeshment with children?

The transmission of basic images and family organization often appears more salient than specific symptoms. For example, in one generation the focally ill child may have severe eczema. In the next, it may be a boy with asthma. And in a third, it may be a child with an eating disorder. Considering how focused our culture is on eating and a fear of fatness, it is no wonder that psychosomatically organized families would frequently find eating disorders as the symptom of choice in this generation.

Assessment of Equilibrium/Disequilibrium

There appear to be two opposite conditions that increase the rigid transmission of images and sequences through generations. The first is the persistent pressure of the prior generation to support their images and forms of organization, as when grandparents live close by or in the same house or have twice-daily phone contact. The opposite condition, where grandparents are far removed — either by geography or death — often leads to rigidity as well. It is as if the images have been fixed in time, partly out of loyalty and partly because they could not change with new, ongoing experience between the generations.

Changes in these conditions signal disequilibrium. For example, I have several times observed the onset of anorexia in a child following the death of a grandparent or the entrance of a grandparent as a full-time household member. Sometimes a distant parent happens to be visiting. If that parent can be pulled into therapy for a moment, it can have a sudden and powerful disequilibrating impact on the family system. It is, of course, one of family therapy's most familiar interventions to try to establish stronger generational boundaries. Doing so permits not only greater autonomy for nuclear families, but also the surfacing of alternative, perhaps latent, images and sequences which were inadmissible with the older generation present. But I have generally found that initially this level is in quite rigid equilibrium, and the therapist is offered only limited and well-controlled access to information about past

Anna and the Antonionis

In many ways, Anna's family's patterns were isomorphic to those of her father's family of origin. In that family, the older brother died in a tragic accident and the parents reacted by overprotecting the surviving son. Yet for reasons unknown to him, they would also leave him alone for great stretches of time. Furthermore, when he was about 12 (close to the age when Anna had to leave Europe), they sent him thousands of miles away to boarding school in America. They then followed him and lived in the United States themselves. The conflict-avoidant triangle which we saw in Anna's family was an almost exact replication of the triangle operating in her father's family of origin.

This brief description is, in fact, only a small sample of what seems like an eerie transmission of images and transactional sequences from one generation to the next. In order to free himself from his family, George cut himself off from family members almost entirely. It was even difficult to get him to talk about them, although he would talk about almost anything else, and as far as he was concerned, there were no similarities between the two families. His wife at first differed mildly with this contention but retreated rapidly at his rebuttal. Therefore, Level V was very rigid and very much in equilibrium. Any attempt to reframe George's story met the same kind of disdain, anger or resistance that had been encountered at Level II. His perceptions were insulated and not vulnerable to revision through experience.

Anna's mother was more connected to her family, but in deference to her husband and the patriarchal patterns of their family, her family imagery had to remain in the background of the Antonioni family. Since hers was a matriarchy, which gave clear support to most of its women and their effectiveness, these images seemed an important alternative to make more figural in Anna's family. But it was only when the conflict-avoidant patterns of Levels II and III began to erode that the latent imagery of Mrs. Antonioni's family could become more available. Level V was in equilibrium for both parents, then, until the disequilibrium of other levels challenged it.

POSTSCRIPT TO THE ANTONIONI CASE

While sequences are more or less autonomous within each level, the levels which are isomorphically linked are also interactive. Change in one level frequently, though not always, leads to change in others. This was true in Anna's case. Change began most dramatically in Level III when father was absent and mother and daughter formed a competent female relationship. The ineluctable movement towards the day when Anna would leave home provided a continual source of disequilibrating pressure in Level IV. Interventions at these levels disrupted family patterns at the other levels, moving them into disequilibrium. The intrapsychic level was the first to shift, with Anna expressing a burst of optimistic self-confidence, which in turn was bolstered by her ability to stop vomiting and gain weight. However, the voices remained intact. Some restructuring in Level II then took place and with the establishment of a clear hierarchy, Anna relinquished her voices.

Application of this model in the initial assessment of disequilibrium provides a starting point for intervention. As the therapy proceeds, the five-level systems grid is helpful in organizing and tracking shifting areas of equilibrium and disequilibrium. These shifts can produce the kind of chain reaction which was critical in making the Antonioni's therapy successful.

REFERENCES

Beavers, W. R. (1983). Hierarchical issues in a systems approach to illness and health. *Family Systems Medicine, 1*(1), 47–55.
Boskind-White, M. & White, W. C. (1983). *Bulimarexia: The binge/purge cycle.* New York: Norton.
Bronfenbrenner, U. (1979). *The ecology of human development.* Cambridge, MA: Harvard University Press.
Bruch, H. (1973). *Eating disorders.* New York: Basic Books.
Carter, E. A., & McGoldrick, M. (Eds.) (1980). *The family life cycle.* New York: Gardner Press.
Crisp, A. H. (1980). *Anorexia nervosa: Let me be.* London: Academic Press.
Dell, R., & Goolishian, H. (1979). *Order through fluctuation: An evolutionary paradigm for human systems.* Paper presented at the Annual Scientific Meeting of the A. K. Rice Institute, Houston, Texas.
Engel, G. L. (1980). The clinical application of the biopsychological model. *American Journal of Psychiatry, 137*(5), 535–544.
Engel, G. L. (1977, April). The need for a new medical model: A challenge for biomedicine. *Science 196,* 129–136.
Erikson, E. (1963). *Childhood and society* (2nd edition). New York: W. W. Norton.
Garfinkel, P., & Garner, M. (1982). *Anorexia nervosa: A multidimensional perspective.* New York: Brunner/Mazel.
Guerin, P. J. Jr., & Pendagast, E. G. (1976). Evaluation of family system and genogram. In P. J. Guerin, Jr. (Ed.), *Family therapy.* New York: Gardnier Press.
Hoffman, L. (1981). *Foundations of family therapy.* New York: Basic Books.
Huygen, F. J. (1982). *Family medicine: The medical life history of families.* New York: Brunner/Mazel.
Levenson, E. A. (1972). *The fallacy of understanding.* New York: Basic Books.
Mahler, M., Pine, F., & Bergman, A. *The psychological birth of the infant.* New York: Basic Books.
Masterson, J. F. (1977). Primary anorexia nervosa in the borderline adolescent: An object relations view. In P. Hartocollis (Ed.), *Borderline personality disorders.* New York: International University Press.

Masterson, J. F. (1972). *Treatment of the borderline adolescent: A developmental approach.* New York: Wiley.
Minuchin, S. (1974). *Families and family therapy.* Cambridge, MA: Harvard University Press.
Minuchin, S., Rosman, B., & Baker, L. (1978). *Psychosomatic families: Anorexia nervosa in context.* Cambridge, MA: Harvard University Press.
Pelletier, K. (1977). *Mind as healer; Mind as slayer.* New York: Dell.
Prigogine, I. (1969). Structure, dissipation and life. In *Theoretical physics and biology.* Amerstam, Holland: North Holland.
Scheflen, A. (1981). *Levels of schizophrenia.* New York: Brunner/Mazel.
Selvini Palazzoli, M. (1974). *Self-starvation.* New York: Jason Aronson.
Watzlawick, P., Weakland, J., & Fisch, R. *Change.* New York: Norton.
White, M. (1983). Anorexia nervosa: A transgenerational system perspective. *Family Process 3,* 255-274.

Chapter 11

Eating and Monsters: A Psychodynamic View of Bulimarexia

Ana-Maria Rizzuto

A new syndrome, called variously the gorging and purging syndrome, bulimarexia (Boskind-Lodahl & Sirlin, 1977), and bulimia nervosa (Russell, 1979), has been described in the past few years. Some consider it a part of the wide spectrum of anorexia nervosa; others see in it a separate syndrome. In this chapter, I intend to show that bulimarexia forms a continuum with anorexia nervosa which can only be differentiated from it when detailed attention is paid to the character structure of the patient and the moment of development which has become the major stumbling block. Descriptively, the two syndromes have many characteristics in common, and most authors who have written about anorexia nervosa have not made any distinction between the two syndromes. Developmentally, bulimarexia appears as a consequence of interactions with the maternal object which affect the child slightly later than those related to anorexia nervosa; the child's interaction with the mother and parents is different and, as a consequence, the character structure of the child is also different.

Bulimarexia has acquired epidemic proportions in North America. Some statistics indicate that one out of every five young women with a college education binges and purges regularly. This fact should make us reflect on the cultural conditions in which this phenomenon takes place. In all times, fashion has been a part of medicine (Ackernecht, 1973) as it has been for clothing, manners, and attitudes. In Freud's days, any self-respecting woman who had a conflict would develop some original and interesting pain, cough, paralysis, anesthesia or another variation of a nonorganic physical symptom. Nowadays such a woman is an anachronism in medicine. The cultural changes make those symptoms laughable and good for cartoons, but useless to express psychic distress. People have to find symptoms which are personally and socially significant. Cultural changes create conditions for the unconscious selection of some psychic defenses over others and favor certain types of regressive human interactions originating in childhood as expression of psychic needs and conflicts in the present.

CULTURAL CHANGES

The history of medicine in the Western world until the beginning of the 19th century demonstrates that illness was conceived as something evil and foreign to the individual (spirit, demon, poison, bad substance, bad air, or vapor) which had invaded the body and made it ill. Eradication of the invasive factor was always the treatment of choice. Another possibility was that some normal internal humor or function had *increased* to the point of disturbing the equilibrium of the body. The expulsion of the excessive substance or the increased product was then the curative technique.

These general theories of the causes of human illness still prevail in many regions of the world, and among a good number of American citizens (American Indians, Puerto Ricans, several Asiatic groups, Chinese, Mexican-Americans, and others). The treatment of choice of illness conceptualized in this manner requires exorcisms, diet, purgation, vomiting, blood-letting, and any drug or potion that would cleanse the body. It is fascinating to learn that cathartics, emetics, clysters, and diuretics have been for several millennia the prevalent treatments in the West (Ackernecht, 1973; Castiglione, 1941), in China (Wong & Chimin, 1936), among Indians (Vogel, 1971), and in most ancient civilizations. A striking and extreme example quoted by the physician who carried out the treatment of an undiagnosed illness is the case of Jane Whitaker, who was told by some physicians that vomiting was contraindicated. Thomas O'Dowde, a firm believer in cathartics and emetics for all illnesses, who published her treatment in his book, *The Poor Man's Physician*, in 1665, describes the procedure with great pleasure:

> She took my Medicine and fell to Vomit and Stool without intermission, and to avoid trouble, laid herself along the Floor, and left both ends to their own discharge (as she merrily relates), till the stock was exhausted, by less than a grain of Medicine. (quoted in Singer, 1953, p. 60)

Freud himself started his therapeutic discoveries under the influence of this general concept of human illness. From 1880 to 1895, he used a method which he called cathartic. The word comes from the Greek and means purging or purification. Aristotle had used the word to talk about the purifying effects of participating in tragedy through the experience of pity and fear. Freud (1895/1955) explains his method, saying:

> It will now be understood how it is that the psychotherapeutic procedure which we have described in these pages has a curative effect. It brings to an end the operative force of the idea which was not abreacted in the first instance, by allowing its strangulated affect to find a way through speech. . . .(p. 17)

The language used by Freud is remarkable because it not only refers to the need to expel the affect but shows that, at least metaphorically, it is stuck in the throat!

Obviously, the understanding of human pathology in psychoanalysis went far beyond the simple idea of catharsis. However, it did not totally disregard it, and in so doing, it is possible that it paid attention to the unconscious and conscious human need for purgation, which all theories of illness in the course of history seemed to have taken for granted. Laplanche and Pontalis (1973) state:

> . . . catharsis remains one of the dimensions of any analytic psychotherapy. . . . Many treatments present us with intense revivals of certain memories, accompanied by a more or less tempestuous emotional discharge. . . . In other cases, speaking is itself an adequate reflex, when it is a lamentation or giving utterance to a tormenting secret, e.g., a confession. (p. 61)

Interestingly enough, the same mouth that eats and throws up is the one which, in the cathartic method, produces the secret unspeakable words. It is as though purgation can now be accomplished in psychotherapy by the uttering of hidden words.

Scientific medicine produced a radical change in the conceptualization of illness: neither "bad" humors nor "bad" spirits which had taken hold of a person were any longer responsible for someone falling ill. Natural processes which were part of man's biochemical nature explained it all. It was obviously a tremendous advance from the point of view of the causal and specific treatment of each disease. It had, nonetheless, psychological consequences. It deprived the patient and society alike of a very ancient and well-established way of projecting subjectively felt badness onto humors or devils, which, once expelled, would leave the person feeling purified. A scientific theory of illness leaves the individual alone with his or her feelings of being evil, bad, dirty. Science does not provide a cleansing ritual for the subjective feelings of the person who feels ill.

The next critical modern cultural change is the drastic disappearance of all the many bad and spooky creatures that used to inhabit the surroundings of humanity making it sometimes their plaything. Devils, spirits of the dead, monsters, and all sorts of unspeakable creatures have evaporated, together with their gracious availability to accept the badness we did not like as part of ourselves.

So, now, we are all alone with ourselves and know that we fall ill not because we are invaded by some "bad" thing, but simply because, like any other modern machine, we are out of order and have to be fixed. Unconsciously, we do not believe the causality of science. Then, when on account of our needs or conflicts, we feel we are bad, we have to accept that we are responsible and carry our ugly feelings about ourselves in whatever way we can.

Finally, the atomization of society, the decline of the extended family, and the prevalence of individualism and competition leave us all alone to deal with our subjective feelings of badness. Most among us have worked out well enough the developmental moment when those feelings acquire critical significance for the formation of character structure. We need not regress to infantile fears and resort to extreme measures of self-protection and purgation to deal with fears about our own badness. If, on the other hand, the early interaction with the maternal object and parents has gone wrong, the individual may regress to profound childhood fears and resort to extreme measures and primary psychic defenses in an attempt to deal with unbearable feelings.

At this point, a word of caution is necessary. I noted earlier the fashionable aspects of becoming ill. Not all those who binge and purge suffer from bulimarexia as a true psychological illness based on a pathological character structure. The behavior is easy to imitate and a very convenient means to alarm and horrify others. Many women nowadays who do not have a serious developmental disturbance seem to resort to binging and purging transiently as a way of expressing frustrations and conflicts which in Freud's day would have taken the shape of a paralysis, aphonia, or difficulty in walking. In this respect, they present a nonspecific symptom liable to appear in patients with many different character structures. As a symptom, it is not different from the use of drugs by many young people who would never be drug addicts.

THE CLINICAL PICTURE

The patients are usually young women in their early twenties or thirties who have been eating and purging in regular and ritualized form for a prolonged period of time. They have stabilized their body weight at a desirable level at either their normal weight or slightly less; some are underweight. They are usually employed, work steadily, are reliable and responsible, and stay in the same job for a long time. Often they are quite successful professionally. They dress well, are well-mannered, and are attracted to men as well as attractive to them. All the patients I know have had many boyfriends and are currently involved with one, or are married with or without children.

They come generally from affluent families who are interested in appearances, beauty, and stylized human relations, where good manners, poise, and the absence of angry manifestations are of great importance.

The fathers are, in general, very accomplished men; they are absorbed by their professions and remote emotionally. They tend to be the best functioning member of the family. The mothers are well-educated, bright, involved neither in a career nor in meaningful activities outside the home. In the home they are inefficient, scattered, and controlling of the behavior of the children; at the same time, they were alternatively remote or somewhat involved with only one aspect of their daughter's life, usually an irrelevant one such as her manners or her looks. I say "irrelevant" because the concern did not take into account the child's feelings or opinions about that aspect of herself. It only focused on the mother's involvement in that part of her daughter's life, not on her involvement with the child.

The parents as a couple relate to each other in emotionally limited ways. Withdrawal, denial, isolation of affect, and refusal to verbalize what is disagreeable seem to be the prevailing defenses used by the parents when dealing with conflict and family strife.

The ritual of binging and purging deserves careful description. Many women binge at least twice a day; some do not necessarily binge every day; some binge continuously for a period of time and then purge for another period. If this pattern allows for some variation, the actual eating and disgorging follow a completely invariable behavior, accompanied by the same subjective experience. These patients have constant thoughts about eating, food, weight, bodily appearance, and clothes. They spend a good part of their time thinking, planning, organizing, and reflecting about their food and their eating. They carry out their duties efficiently and responsibly while this thinking continues somewhat in their minds.

Then, suddenly, the thoughts become obsessively compelling, and the patient will get the urge to eat. She feels acute bodily tensions and almost unbearable restlessness. Following her established pattern, the patient eats voraciously (not infrequently, with her fingers) large quantities of food. An example may suffice: two submarine sandwiches, two hot dogs, two packages of potato chips, four brownies, three chocolate bars, two ice cream cones, and a drink. While the patient is eating, her total attention is on the food: the smell, taste, texture, flavor, and any other sensation of the mouth, nose, and throat. Any distraction from the eating irritates the patient; she experiences the interruption as a disruption of an action she must carry to completion. After eating, the patient becomes acutely aware of the size of her stomach, and after a period of time (from several minutes to an hour or more), the patient experiences an urgent need to throw up. Most patients talk about "getting sick"; the need is imperative. If the situation makes this difficult, the patient becomes frantic and extremely irritable. If the situation permits, the patient follows her own ritual. One example suffices: The person covers the floor around the toilet with paper towels, lifts the toilet seat, and kneels, embracing the toilet bowl with the head practically inside it. She induces the vomiting with her fingers until the stomach is completely empty. Then she proceeds to clean the toilet's edge and flushes the toilet. All this is done almost mechanically and with total absorption in the activity.

While eating or vomiting, the patient has no conscious fantasies, thoughts, or recognizable feelings. The whole experience has a quality of a dissociated state. The patient has no recollection of her subjective experience, if one excludes the physical sensations and the compulsion to act out the cycle.

To the behavior described, some patients add laxatives, diuretics, and occasional fasting. None that I know of uses emetics. Most of them smoke many cigarettes a day and drink more than the average person.

As for the clinical features distinguishing the "dieters" from the "vomiters and purgers," Beumont, George, and Smart (1976) have shown that it is possible to separate dieters from vomiters and purgers in their cases of anorexia nervosa. They consider these patients as suffering from anorexia nervosa but still can distinguish them. In their study, Beumont et al. found that the dieters have more obsessional traits then the vomiters and purgers, who in turn have histrionic traits which are practically absent in the dieters. The vomiters and purgers are also more socially outgoing, and smoke and drink more but are much less competitive with their peers. All the vomiters and purgers had had boyfriends, two-thirds had had intercourse, and half of them had used contraceptives. They were much more dishonest about their symptoms than the dieters, and in spite of the long duration of the behavior, close relatives did not know about it because part of the ritual involves extreme secrecy. The Beumont et al. sample includes 21% of vomiters with amenorrhea. (The cases I have seen menstruated regularly, even if they were underweight.) As for the precipitant, they found that disturbances within the family and concerns about examinations or pubertal changes were of lesser importance than in the dieters, but that being teased about their weight was more significant for the vomiters.

There is in my experience another essential difference: The patients suffering from classic anorexia nervosa are incapable of perceiving their body realistically (Bruch, 1973) and may or may not have a narcissistic investment in appearing attractive. Bulimarexics, on the other hand, have an intense involvement with their appearance, particularly the way they look to others. They not only feel seen by others but cannot do without having someone to approve of their appearance. This wish makes them very different from the patients with anorexia nervosa, who cannot believe that anybody is capable of seeing them as themselves beyond their bodily appearance (Rizzuto, Peterson, and Reed, 1981). The bulimarexic does not feel dissociated from her body and finds personal pleasure in being found attractive, and experiences deep narcissistic injury if people do not appreciate her looks. In brief, bulimarexics have a narcissistic investment in their bodies which is absent or very limited in anorexics.

THE DEVELOPMENTAL SIGNIFICANCE OF EATING

Spitz, in his paper about the mouth as the primal cavity (1955), related the sensations of the feeding situation and its gestalt to the beginning of perception:

> What appears to me significant in this phenomenon is that the *inside* of the mouth, *the oral cavity*, fulfills the conditions of partaking for perceptive purposes both of the inside and of the outside. It is simultaneously an interoceptor and exteroceptor. It is here that all perception will begin; in this role the oral cavity fulfills the function of a bridge from internal reception to external perception. (p. 220)

Spitz relates the primal cavity to the origins of the self:

> The site of the origin of perception and of psychological experience has far-reaching consequences. For it is here that the task of distinguishing between inside and outside has its inception; this discrimination becomes established much later and will lead in an unbroken development to the separation of the self from the non-self, of the self from the objects, and, in the course of this road, to what is accepted and what is rejected. (p. 222)

The significance of the primal cavity experiences for adult life is made explicit:

> The level of coenesthetic perception belongs to what I would call the experiential level of the primal cavity. It is the world of the deepest security which man ever experiences after birth, in which he rests encompassed and quiescent. It is to this world that man escapes when he feels threatened by pathological conditions in febrile states; also when in the waking state the ego becomes helpless through dissociation, as in toxic conditions. The method of escape has a double mechanism: the withdrawal of cathexis from the sensorium, on one hand, the hypercathexis of the body ego, on the other. The particular sector of the body ego representation which seems most highly cathected is the representation of the primal cavity. (p. 236)

Spitz clarifies that when we deal with the adult,

> . . . the approach to earliest orality is not a direct one, for the mnemic traces of earliest primal cavity experiences as such are not available to the patient and cannot be communicated to him by the therapist in terms of these experiences —

the terms for them do not exist in language, they can only be paraphrased. (p. 237)

Perceptually, the gestalt situation of feeding includes the maternal face and voice. The importance of this perceptual gestalt in the feeding situation of the infant is dramatically illustrated by a case discussed by Kreisler and colleagues (1974): Christopher H. was six-and-a-half months old when he developed acute vomiting which required hospitalization after he had lost 1500 grams. The child continued to vomit after hospitalization until it was discovered that he provoked his own vomiting by means of introducing his fingers into his mouth or by a direct effort to vomit. Intensive nursing care and restriction of the hands, plus some antiemetics, brought the child back to health. Careful questioning of the mother revealed that the child was perfectly normal until the mother, who was an apprehensive woman, had distanced herself from the baby and had worn a facial mask for eight days because she was afraid of giving the child a cold.

Fain, in discussing the case, observes that the facial mask partially transformed the mother into a stranger, with the end result that the infant confuses the good mother with the strange masked mother and experiences simultaneously the wish for closeness and the need to escape the frightening mother. In concluding his comments, Fain remarks that at that age food becomes confused with the mother and that in the case of this particular infant there must have been a need not to see the stranger's face, to repress it. Nonetheless, the child cannot ignore the awareness of the percept. At this point, the problem becomes an internal psychic struggle.

Soulé, in turn, comments that in his paper, *Negation* (1925), Freud had said that

> The original pleasure-ego wants to introject into itself everything that is good and to eject from itself everything that is bad. What is bad, what is alien to the ego and what is external are . . . identical. (p. 237)

He also quotes Spitz, who has said that at the age of three months the prototype for projection is regurgitation and vomiting. This manner of rejection remains deeply ingrained in our language and behavior, as demonstrated in everyday experience and vocabulary. A striking illustration is Chapter 3:16 of the *Book of Revelations*:

> Because you are lukewarm, neither cold nor hot, I would spew you out of my mouth.

The versicle makes a direct connection between human relations and vomiting.

Although Spitz (1955) and Kreisler, Fain, and Soulé (1974) make reference to the importance of the maternal face in the feeding situation, they do not mention the counterpart of that experience, that is, the child feeling perceived visually and otherwise by the mother. Indeed, there is very little written on the subject. Rizzuto, Peterson, and Reed (1981) found that patients with anorexia nervosa suffer from a particular form of pathology of the sense of self which leads them to feel that nobody can perceive them as people beyond their bodily appearance. This component of the feeding experience seems to have different consequences according to the level of development in which the feeding has become disrupted.

Anna Freud (1946) talks about the representational significance of food in the mother-child interaction:

> The image of food and the mother-image remain merged into one until the child is weaned from the breast.

She continues:

> Though food and the mother become separated for the conscious mind of all children from the second year onwards, the identity between the two images remains so far as the child's unconscious is concerned. Much of the child's conflicting behavior towards food does not originate from loss of appetite or lessened need to eat, etc., but from conflicting emotions towards the mother which are transferred onto the food which is a symbol for her. Ambivalence towards the mother may express itself as fluctuations between over-eating and refusal of food; guilty feelings towards the mother and a consequent inability to enjoy her affection as an inability to enjoy food; obstinacy and hostility towards the mother as a struggle against being fed.*
>
> Jealousy, if there is mother's love for the other children of the family, may find its outlet in greediness and insatiableness. At the stage of repression of the oedipus complex refusal of food may accompany, or be substituted for, the inner rejection of the phallic sexual strivings towards the mother. (pp. 125-126)

In following the child's development, Anna Freud refers to the sadistic tendencies towards the object and food alike which follow teething. She refers specifically to oral-sadistic fantasies (cannibalistic), which are:

> ... under no circumstances tolerated in consciousness, not even when the ego is immature. They are rejected with the help of all the mechanisms of defense available to the child in this early period of life. (p. 128)

Many significant events occur in the development of the child in the course of the second year of life. The most significant are the beginning separation

---

*Nowadays, when thinness is such a preoccupation, the reverse is possible. The child shows obstinacy by overeating, thus rejecting the maternal admonitions.

from the mother and the emergence of the anal phase. Concomitantly, the child's ability to fantasize begins to reach a high moment, and, in her efforts to deal with her representational world, as well as her wishes and fears, the child progressively creates a universe of nonexistent creatures ready to take any of the projections the young individual bestows on them. The child does not know how to talk about these beings until the adult world, usually through stories, provides the name of monsters. In between the ages of three or four, occasionally earlier, the child becomes able to verbalize her feelings about, and fears of, monsters. A good number of these creatures are monsters of assorted types.

It is interesting to look into the etymology of the word, monster, and its uses as presented by the Webster's dictionary:

> mon'ster, n. [ME. and OFr. *monstre*, from L. *monstrum*, any occurrence out of the ordinary course of nature supposed to indicate the will of the gods, a marvel, a monster, from *monere*, to admonish, to warn.]

The Latin origin of the word connects it with parental representatives (gods) and their power to punish. On the side of the childhood experience, it connects it with superego concerns about being admonished or warned.

The word attends to phenomena that do not conform with things as known in ordinary circumstances. The word relates to human experiences concerned with visible bodily shape, malformations (narcissistic preoccupation with appearances) or bodily completeness (oral dismemberment or castration). The word attends to the fear of or wish for fusion of two beings (centaur). At the superego level it considers the admonishing and punishing power of those in charge of things, and the preoccupation with and fear of wickedness, depravity, or cruelty on the part of the child.

Another facet of the monster concept is the enormity of the size or the ugliness of its looks. Finally, the aggressive, sadistic elements of cruelty and perversion appear in the implicit wish to horrify others. It is of great import to my argument that the visual components of the monster give it its sadistic (wish to inflict fear and suffering) and perverse (exhibition of something horrifying) aspects.

These characteristics of the monster do not include the intentions attributed to it as a living creature. Although monsters are dedicated to the following three tasks, most monsters specialize in only one: eating, maiming, or simply scaring people apparently just for the fun of it.

The description presented above not only points in the direction of the infantile origin of monsters, but also signals the kind of psychic services they may render to their young creator. As creatures brought to imaginary life to wear the projected looks of intolerable self-representations (the ugly, messy, angry, revengeful child), they illustrate well Freud's statement that "the pleasure-ego wants . . . to eject from itself everything that is bad" (Freud, 1925 p. 237). Obviously, at the age when the child is capable of self-representation, we are no longer talking exclusively about pleasure-ego but about the progressive development of the sense of self, and the need to project or repress ego dystonic self-representations.

The monster can also serve as a projected object for displacement of maternal or, later on, paternal traits which are not tolerable if perceived as part of a much needed maternal object whose presence, nurturance, and protection are indispensable to the child. The intent of this psychic maneuver, as Fain points out, is to avoid introjection (that is, the internal presence of the perceived or projected "bad" mother [Kreisler, Fain, & Soulé, 1974]). Clearly, this follows the same need to keep anything that is "bad" outside the self.

Notwithstanding the child's efforts, if the relationship with the mother includes consistent and persistent frustration of needs, the child cannot save the "good" mother from contamination with the "bad" mother as an internal representation. More active maneuvers are then required to rid oneself of the "bad" internal mother. In the feeding situation, the child may opt for two possible solutions to protect herself from taking in the "bad" mother, who is still inseparable from the food she provides. The child may refuse to eat, or vomit as a way of keeping out what she fears. Another option is the isolation of the pleasure of feeding from its source. Anna Freud (1946) writes:

> In the oral phase of libido development, oral pleasure, though originally discovered in conjunction with feeding, is sought and reproduced independently of the feeding situation in the numerous forms of thumb-sucking, as an autoerotic oral activity. As such, it may be pursued by the infant as a substitute for feeding (while waiting for food or when feeding has to be interrupted before the child is fully satisfied). It may enter into competition with feeding when infants are unwilling to remove the thumb from the mouth to take the teat of the bottle or the spoon filled with food. It further plays an important part, completely independently of feeding, as a general comforter (like food) before sleep, when the child is lonely, dull, etc. (p. 127)

I would like to suggest that this dissociated oral pleasure which bypasses the "bad" mother relates directly to the voracious eating of the bulimarexic who extracts intense sensual pleasure from her food without being encumbered by any mental representation or fantasy about the repressed maternal object.

Anna Freud (1946) links the acquisition of particular preferences for taste and consistency to the introduction of solid food. This seems to be a critical developmental moment for the future of oral satisfaction as well as for the mother-child relationship. Kreisler (Kreisler, Fain, & Soulé, 1974) has described two syndromes which infants can develop during this period. The first he calls the mental anorexia of the infant at the time of weaning. It is more frequently a five- or six-month-old baby, whose appetite diminishes noticeably, who loses weight, and shows marked intellectual precocity. The anorexia is not life-threatening, and may last for a brief period of time or for years. The second is a much more serious illness and implies a serious disturbance of the appetite, as well as a profound disturbance in the mother-child relation. Kreisler postulates that the type of relation these infants have with their mothers leads them to experience the feeding as a massive internalization of the mother, which has the equivalent of a true toxic condition (Kreisler, Fain, & Soulé, 1974). In this situation the child tries to keep the mother at a distance by refusing to eat. Kreisler postulates that excessive eating is based on the substitution of food for the unattainable maternal affection.

In summary, the relation of the child to the mother in the feeding situation decides early on the psychic significance of food at the conscious and unconscious levels of representation and the types of bodily oral satisfaction available to the individual in her future life. What is emotionally isolated from the maternal or self-representation may remain unconsciously linked to the feeding situation, to the fears of being invaded by the "bad" object or taken over by the internally experienced hungry (for maternal affection) monster. This monster is a later elaboration of partial self-representations of earlier feeding experiences. The elaboration of some aspects of the self-representation as a monster takes place during the anal period, when aggression is at the service of separation from the mother, the establishment of initiative, and the pleasures of smearing and manipulation of feces and foodstuffs alike. The monsters which are in the process of being concocted in the child's imagination to represent the disowned aspects of herself include those aspects of the young individual which she feels are disapproved of by the admonishments and warnings of the mother (remember the etymology of monster). They may include every aspect of the child's oral and anal "badness." These monsters are voracious, uncontrollable; their appearance is repulsive to the eye and their bodily surface is repulsive to touch. They are angry, vicious, and mean; therefore, they must be controlled at any price. Their meanness is represented by their large and deformed size, and their unsightly faces make them horrifying to look at. Sometimes they make frightening noises. Indeed, they must not be seen; that explains why they lurk in dark and hidden places, always avoiding open spaces and the light of day. Some monsters may lose their life if seen by a person. The destiny of a monster, in short, is to live in hiding, away from the maternal eye and the awareness of its creator.

The indispensably secret life of the monster links it to that aspect of development which reflects the need to feel "seen" internally by the mother beyond the visible aspects of the body (Rizzuto, Peterson, & Reed, 1981). A tentative developmental sequence for this need and its satisfaction is now discussed.

At the beginning of life, when the feeding situation is the only and essential component of the child-mother relation, the mother reaches the child internally through coenesthetic sensations of feeding satisfaction or dissatisfaction. The child's defenses are not yet organized and the only protection the child has are generalized reactions of distress. Perceptively, this is the first stage described by Spitz (1955).

> . . . when perception takes place in terms of totalities because it is mediated mainly through the coenesthetic system on one hand, through interoceptive and tango-receptors on the other. (p. 231)

These earliest percepts may provide generalized feelings of well-being or discomfort, thus becoming the first antecedents for the organization of the ego. At the second level of integration, Spitz describes:

> . . . diacritic perception, when distance receptors come into play, when visual images become available, but when the mnemic traces of these images are still impermanent, at least in the beginning. (p. 231)

The two most important percepts of this period are the human face and the human voice.* Both are regular components of the feeding situation. In the context of established eye contact, the child begins to discriminate different expressions in the maternal face. Winnicott (1971) suggests that at that moment in development, the child begins to interpret the variations of expression on the mother's face in a particular way:

> . . . What does the baby see when he or she looks at the mother's face? I am suggesting that, ordinarily, what the baby sees is himself or herself. In other words, the mother is looking at the baby and *what she looks like is related to what* she sees there. (p. 112)

Winnicott goes on to say:

> . . . I am linking apperception with perception by postulating a historical process (in the individual) which depends on being seen:
> When I look I am seen so I exist. I can now afford to look and see. I now look creatively and what I apperceive, I also perceive. In fact I take care not to see what is not there to be seen (unless I am tired). (p. 114)

Winnicott's subtle imagining of the baby's subjective experience refers not only to the child's perception of the maternal face, but its utilization for the

---

*I wish to thank Dr. Monique King of Cleveland for calling my attention to the importance of the auditory sphere.

formation of the sense of self around the maternal expression. Because most of these experiences, at least at the beginning, relate to the moment of feeding, there must be of necessity an apperceptive integration of the simultaneous perception of the maternal face and the coenesthetic gastrointestinal state of satisfaction, fullness, and satiation or their opposites. In this context, the baby begins to form a conception of himself or herself and an early affectual judgment of being good or bad. Then the need to get rid of what is bad requires either isolation of the "bad" aspects or later on, repression. This is a normal process which contributes to the emergence of the sense of self and the superego, mediated by the progressive sophistication of the ability to elaborate feelings about oneself in the context of seeing and being seen. The earliest decisions about what is "me" and what is "not me" are now being made. They require a certain judgment, as Freud (1925) describes it:

> The function of judgement is concerned in the main with two sorts of decisions. It affirms or disaffirms the possession by a thing of a particular attribute; and it asserts or disputes that a presentation has an existence in reality. The attribute to be decided about may originally have been good or bad, useful or harmful. Expressed in the language of the oldest — the oral — instinctual impulses, the judgement is: "I should like to eat this," or "I should like to spit it out"; and, put more generally: "I should like to take this into myself and to keep that out." That is to say: "It shall be inside me" or "it shall be outside me." (p. 237)

A moment arrives in development around age two and a half when the child begins to be aware that she can hide from the adult not only physically, but also psychologically. Obviously the child at this point has a long experience with dissociating herself from what is bad and unpleasant, and projecting it onto something or someone else. Most of these processes are unconscious. Nonetheless, in the course of a conflictual situation in which the child feels too extreme a discrepancy between her needs, wishes, and feelings and the sense of herself, a new type of self-conception dimly dawns on the child. The projection of felt badness onto the monsters does not suffice to bring about psychic balance. The child whose parents do not accept and do not help her to accept some of her own badness grows into a progressive sense of psychic isolation. The child now develops a compelling need *not to be seen*, psychologically, and in real life. Many of these children find favorite hiding places. However, even when they are not in hiding, they learn to hide psychically by complying with and obeying their parents without the subjective satisfaction of self-approval or the ability to accept some parental compliments; they are now convinced of their secret but unquestionable badness and feel constantly that they are fooling their parents.

The end result is an increase of superego demands, which does not provide a sense of worth but rather a ceaseless list of duties all experienced as burdens.

Subjectively, there is a progressive need to find some self-esteem. The parents who are basically pleased with a compliant child do praise the child or approve of her looks or accomplishments. The child in turn accepts the parental approval without much joy. What is most intriguing here is that the parental eye in these children does not get internalized. When these patients regress in the analytic situation and their language becomes more spontaneous, they refer to themselves as "she," indicating that they see themselves with the eyes of another person, usually the mother. A patient of mine could never imagine herself from the point of view of her own values. She could do nothing else but judge her appearance and behavior from her mother's way of thinking. If she did not try to visualize herself but tried to attend to some other feelings, she would refer to "a little person" within herself who had always been hidden.

A recent storybook for children entitled *Harry and the Terrible Whatzit*, by Dyck Gackenbach (1977), beautifully illustrates the conflict of the child with his monster. Harry *knows* that there is something terrible in the cellar and warns his mother not to go there. His mother disregards his warnings and goes, and sure enough disappears. Harry feels he has to do something. Armed with a broom, he courageously goes there *to find a horrifying monster*, whose size decreases by the minute under the punishment given to him by Harry. The monster explains that he is getting small because Harry is not afraid of him. The now miniscule monster is sent to the neighbor's cellar. Soon after, Harry finds his mother, who firmly states that she never saw a monster in the cellar (although she did go there, indicating that she was not afraid of what she could see) and that furthermore, she will never worry about such a thing as long as Harry is around.

The story is a new version, in modern and childish terms, of the descent into Hades, the underworld, the unconscious, facing the horrors of darkness, of internal darkness, and the monsters that inhabit it. The need to do so is compelling because the loved and indispensable woman has been devoured by the dark cavern (primal cavity). After victory over the powers of darkness has been achieved, the woman is recovered and the young hero earns her admiring love. In analytic terms, the child's victory over the monster provides self-integration and the concomitant enhancement of self-esteem and maternal love. The child can now accept parental praise because the secrets left in the cellar are under her control. The child, however, cannot do this alone. The parent has to be willing to go to the cellar and help the child face and tolerate her own badness. This, seemingly, is what is missing in the children who later on will be susceptible to developing bulimarexia. The avoidance of anger, the insistence on manners, and the neglect of the "monstrous" aspects of the young person lead to the disavowal of that particular self-representation. The angry, voracious, greedy child feels ugly and repulsive and has to hide.

SUMMARY

Some children, in spite of some early oral trauma and maternal deprivation, manage to feel seen as an individual by a mother who has some problems in feeding and relating to her child but who, unlike the other mother of patients with anorexia nervosa, is able to see the real child. These children may have had some mild anorexia as infants or vomited during a certain limited period. It is very difficult to document this fact because the mothers are poor historians when the children have this kind of history. When these children encounter a new trauma during the anal period and their natural aggressiveness is severely curtailed (not so much through punishment but through lack of acknowledgement of the intense libidinal and aggressive wishes typical of the anal period), the child attempts to hide and isolate the unacceptable aspects of her experience. The hidden aspects become identified with a subjective self-representation of a monstrous creature which is voracious and rejecting of anyone who wishes to know the child internally. The child fears that the parent can see the voraciousness and the anger she harbors secretly, while behaving unobjectionably. The compliance is a defense to cover up the monstrous self-representation. The parental pathology colludes with the child's defenses by approving of the latter's behavior, while neglecting to attend to the child's fears and concerns about herself. The voracious, angry monster, hidden behind good conduct, never meets the parental eye. The absence of this event does not permit the internalization of the parental eye in relation to the monster, leaving this aspect of the child isolated from a meaningful contact with the parent.

When the development has gone this way, the child is left with a profound wish for oral mothering, which is dissociated from the disapproving maternal representation but linked with the sensations provided by food. On the other hand, the child is afraid of the hidden voracious, aggressive, monstrous self-representation which is not to be seen by anybody—not even the child herself, lest final rejection occur. The defense of disavowal keeps these self-representations apart in what Kohut (1971) has called a "vertical split."

When the psychic situation is as described, the child's development may proceed normally on the surface or even apparently very successfully. Nonetheless, the conditions are there for the later development of bulimarexia. When the moment arrives for final separation from the internal representation of the primary objects in late adolescence (Blos, 1979), the adolescent is very ill-equipped. The hunger for oral mothering returns, and the adolescent tries *to satisfy* it through boyfriends, sexual relations, frantic activity, or to *control* it by more obsessive defenses and good behavior. A minimal disappointment (which touches deeply the apparently forgotten pains of childhood in a cultural context in which overeating and binging are very common) may precipitate an uncontrollable need to eat secretly, followed by an equally hidden need to vomit. I propose that the need to eat is the dissociated search for the orally approving maternal object, and the need to vomit, the urge to rid oneself of the monstrous creature who demands so much so frantically. The risk is that if the monster is not expelled, it may take over the total person. Soon a vicious circle of compelling need and fear is established and cannot be controlled until some help is provided either to repress the need once more and curb the monster, or to attend to the original needs and fears by means of prolonged psychotherapy.

These patients respond to classical psychotherapy or analysis, provided that the therapist respects the symptoms without demanding that the patient stop the eating and binging. The responsiveness is related to the type of defenses that prevail in the character structure. If schizoid withdrawal and secretiveness prevail, the treatment may be very difficult. If obsessive defenses are the most prevalent, then the treatment is less difficult.

REFERENCES

Ackernecht, H. (1973). *Therapeutics from the primitives to the twentieth Century.* New York: Collier-Macmillan.
Beumont, P. T. V., George, G. C. W., & Smart, D. E. (1946). "Dieters" and "vomiters" and "purgers" in anorexia nervosa. *Psychological Medicine, 6,* 617-622.
Blos, P. (1979). *The adolescent passage.* New York: International Universities Press.
Boskind-Lodahl, M., & Sirlin, Y. (1977). *Psychology Today,* March.
Bruch, H. (1973). *Eating disorders.* New York: Basic Books.
Castiglione, A. (1941). *A history of medicine.* New York: Alfred A. Knopf.
Freud, A. (1946). The psychoanalytic study of infantile feeding disturbances. In *The Psychoanalytical Study of the Child*, vol. II. New York: International Universities Press.
Freud, S. (1955). Studies on hysteria. In J. Strachey (Ed. and Trans.), *The standard edition of the complete psychological works of Sigmund Freud* (Vol. 2). London: Hogarth Press. (Original work published 1895)
Freud, S. (1961). Negation. In J. Strachey (Ed. and Trans.), *The Standard edition of the complete psychological works of Sigmund Freud* (Vol. 19, pp. 235-241). London: Hogarth Press. (Original work published 1925)
Gackenbach, D. (1977). *Harry and the terrible whatzit.* New York: Houghton-Mifflin/Clarion Books.
Kreisler, L., Fain, M., & Soulé, M. (1974). *L'enfant et son corps.* Presses Universitaires de France.
Laplanche, J., & Pontalis, J. B. (1973). *The language of psychoanalysis.* New York: Norton.
Kohut, H. (1971). *The analysis of the self.* New York: International Universities Press.
Russell, G. (1979). Bulimia nervosa: An ominous variant of anorexia nervosa. *Psychological Medicine, 9,* 429-448.
Rizzuto, A. M., Peterson, R. K., & Reed, M. (1981). The psychological sense of self in anorexia nervosa. *Psychiatric Clinics in North America, 4,*(3), 471-487.
Singer, C. (1953). *Medicine and history: Essays on the evolution of scientific thought and medical practice.* New York: Oxford University Press.
Spitz, R. A. (1955). The primal cavity: A contribution in the genesis of perception. *Psychoanalytic Study of the Child, 10,* 215-240.
Vogel, V. T. (1971). *American Indian medicine.* Norman: University of Oklahoma Press.
Winnicott, D. W. (1971). Mirror-role of mother and father in child development. In *Playing and Reality.* New York: Basic Books.
Wong, K., & Chimin (1936). *History of Chinese medicine.* Shanghai: National Quarantine Service.

Chapter 12

An Inpatient Model for the Treatment of Anorexia Nervosa

*Philip G. Levendusky
and Catherine P. Dooley*

The treatment of anorexia nervosa has been approached from a variety of therapeutic perspectives (Bemis, 1978; Russell, 1981) ranging from traditional psychoanalytic to purely behavioral. To date, it would appear that no single model has been demonstrated as an effective approach in treating this complex disorder. Therefore, rather than continue the pursuit of "proving" which orientation is best, the current chapter will describe a comprehensive approach that attempts to draw from the most effective aspects that each perspective has to offer for the inpatient treatment of anorexia.

It has been demonstrated (Agras, Barlow, Chaplin, Able, & Leitenberg, 1974; Garfinkel, Kline, & Stancer, 1973; Halmi, Powers, & Cunningham, 1975) that behavioral procedures have been productive in helping anorexics gain weight. Unfortunately there is little evidence to indicate that their gains have been maintained over time. Furthermore, in most behavioral approaches, weight gain has been the critical factor with little attention being paid to other variables that might also relate to anorexia. In particular, Bruch (1974) has criticized the behavioral approach as being dangerous because of its primary attention to weight gain and little effort being put forth to address the underlying issues that have contributed to the development of the syndrome. Without disagreeing with the Bruch position, the phrase "misuse is not an argument for disuse" comes to mind. In other words, rather than ignoring the

---

The authors would like to express their appreciation to Joan Zabarsky, Denise Block, Paul Laffer, Marty Kafka, Beth Murphy, Judy Taylor, and Members of Upham I Nursing Staff for their valuable contributions in helping shape the Therapeutic Contract Program.

demonstrated effectiveness of behavioral approaches in facilitating weight gain, because they fail to attend to etiology or have not been proven to provide a long-term maintenance, it is suggested that operant behavioral procedures should be one part of a multifaceted treatment approach that also includes exploratory psychotherapy, family therapy, group interventions, and cognitive behavior therapy.

THERAPEUTIC CONTRACT PROGRAM

The token economy has long been the staple of most behaviorally oriented inpatient psychiatric treatment programs. It was not until recently that alternatives to this model have been developed. One such alternative, the Therapeutic Contract Program (TCP), has been described by Levendusky, Berglas, Dooley, and Landau (1983). Using a general problem-solving philosophy, the TCP integrated a variety of treatment modalities in an individually prescribed inpatient therapeutic milieu. All patients admitted to the TCP develop treatment contracts designed to help them identify relevant long-term goals for their hospitalization and then, on a weekly basis, generate a series of short-term goals that are designed to help accomplish the long-term objectives. With the contract functioning as a general problem-solving procedure, all patients engage in individual psychotherapy, cognitive behavior therapy, psychotropic medication management, family therapy, group therapy, and, when necessary, contingency management.

The patient population treated in the TCP has been largely heterogeneous, with affective disorders and anorexia nervosa representing the most frequently appearing diagnoses. The average age of patients admitted to this program is 31 and the average length of hospitalization has been approximately 66 days. Patients are referred to this unit through the usual hospital admissions mechanisms. For anorexics treated in the TCP, they have had their illness for an average of seven years and have also had an average of at least two previous hospitalizations for this disorder. This chapter will describe more specifically the use of the TCP in the treatment of anorexia nervosa.

SETTING

Not only have anorexics been treated from a variety of theoretical perspectives, but these patients have also received treatment in a wide range of settings. Historically, when the syndrome was seen from a purely medical perspective, many patients were treated on wards of general hospitals. As the focus shifted toward a psychological etiology, both inpatient and outpatient psychiatric therapies were offered. In psychiatric settings, patients were often segregated into units that solely treated anorexia. While there may be something to be gained from anorexic patients being with others, given the nature of the disorder, a stronger argument can be offered for the treatment of these patients in a more heterogeneous environment. As a result, they have the opportunity to interact with a wide variety of patients and can, therefore, paradoxically learn from individuals who have a more "normal" approach to eating. Heterogeneous, however, is not to imply that, given the wide range of disorders, anorexics should be treated in a population that is primarily thought-disordered. On the contrary, it is recommended that, as in the above described TCP, the ideal patient mix include equal numbers of affective, anxiety, and character disorders, as well as anorexics.

TREATMENT TEAM

One of the clear advantages in treating anorexia on an inpatient basis is the opportunity available for the patient to deal with a number of members of a treatment team. In the current model the concept of "team" is critical and is not a euphemism for a "doctor and nursing staff." In the TCP all patients, anorexic or other, work with a range of professional staff including an individual psychotherapist, a behavioral contingency manager, a family therapist, a nursing staff coordinator, and an overall treatment administrator. To further clarify the role of each team member, an individual "job description" is in order.

Individual Psychotherapist

Few would argue that anorexia nervosa is a complex disorder with numerous etiological considerations. Without doubt, the understanding and resolution of the underlying etiology are necessary in a patient's ultimate recovery. However, in our experience it does not appear that a particular therapeutic orientation is critical, but, rather, that the therapist establish an intensive psychotherapeutic relationship with the patient that is designed to help facilitate a resolution of relevant psychological issues. Experience further suggests that, while a particular orientation is not critical, therapists with a more cognitive behavioral approach are more effective than those using a more traditional transferential approach.

Given an anorexic's symptom preoccupation, it is expected that in the early phases of hospitalization psychotherapy will not be effectively used by these patients. However, as the symptoms are more under control, the therapy often begins to "take off." Since these patients have difficulty in establishing relationships, it is recommended that therapy sessions be scheduled frequently, though seldom more often than three times per week. Ultimately, the relationship with the psychotherapist becomes the patient's primary therapeutic interaction, particularly as time of discharge approaches and on an outpatient basis. It is particularly important for psychotherapists to see themselves as part of a treatment team willing to respond to various administrative expectations that may become necessary over the course of treatment.

Contingency Manager (CM)

As indicated earlier, behavioral procedures are seen as being useful in assisting the anorexics in increasing their ability to put on weight and to maintain it. As with psychotherapy, there is an evolution of treatment over time with an operant focus evident early and a self-control and coping model evolving later. The role of the CM is that of pacer and gatekeeper. While the role of CM requires a basic understanding of behavior principles, no particular professional discipline need be necessary for this (i.e., in the past CMs have been psychiatrists, psychologists, etc.). The protocol that will be described later is actually implemented by the CM. Since anorexia is often conceptualized as a conflict of power and control, much of the "battle" in treatment is played out with the CM. The nature of this therapeutic interaction is task-focused and, while often supportive, is not designed to replace the primary psychotherapeutic relationship. Sessions with the CM are less frequent than with the psychotherapist (one or two times per week) and usually shorter (i.e., 30 minutes vs. 50). In further contrast, the CM's role is much more critical in early phases of treatment and becomes less so as discharge approaches.

Family Therapist

To say that family issues and conflicts represent a major and necessary focus for the effective treatment of anorexia is an understatement. It is hard to conceive of a clinical syndrome that is more influenced by or has more influences on the family unit than anorexia. As a result, family therapy represents a critical component in the current model. As with the interventions already described, the family therapy evolves over the course of treatment, usually starting with couple therapy between parents; as the patient becomes more able, a systems and communication approach including the patient begins to develop. While a range of issues is generally in evidence, separation and individuation usually predominate. Involvement in family therapy is an expectation of treatment, with members typically committing themselves, when deemed appropriate by the treatment team, to a weekly meeting prior to acceptance in the TCP.

Nurse Coordinator

Interestingly, upon discharge the member of the TCP treatment team who is rated by patients as being most important is their nusing staff coordinator. In the current model this person serves a complicated combination of roles with the patient, ranging from confidante and supporter to limit-setter and monitor. The intensity of this interaction is somewhat dictated by the fact that nursing staff members are in much more frequent contact with the patient and deal with them day-to-day on "nuts and bolts" issues, from eating to sleeping to going to the bathroom. It is further expected that the coordinator is the team member who actually implements the contingencies created by the contingency manager. Coordinators usually meet with the patient on a daily basis (i.e., five or six times per week) for moderate length sessions (30-45 minutes). While included in outpatient planning on a time-limited basis, the coordinator's primary function ends at the time of discharge.

Administrator

The most neutral and yet in some ways most powerful member of the treatment team is the administrator. This position has responsibility for the overall assessment and implementation of the treatment program. While this role is usually taken by psychologists or psychiatrists, no particular discipline affiliation is necessary. While the frequency of interaction with the patient is less than that of other team members, the patient's access to the administrator is usually precipitated by major conflicts such as program dissatisfaction, admission or discharge issues, and aftercare planning. Again, since control is such a critical issue with anorexics, the administrator attempts to occupy an objective and unimpassioned position on the treatment team.

While these five positions represent the core of the anorexic treatment team, patients are also involved with other therapeutic professionals including a psychiatrist for medication evaluation, a rehabilitation counselor for vocationally related issues, and various group leaders. All team members are in regular communication and need to be cognizant of the fact that the anorexic patients often have a tendency to "play" team members off against one another.

In summary, each member of the treatment team plays a critical role in the management of the anorexic symptomatology. By varying the roles of the members, a careful and critical balance can be maintained between the need for limits and control, support, understanding, and encouragement. Further, by having to deal with a number of personalities and roles, the patient has an opportunity to learn to manage a complex social network, which will serve to help her cope better once she has left the hospital.

TREATMENT CONTRACTS

Solving the various problems that may be contributing to an anorexic's symptoms is usually very difficult, particularly in patients whose condition is so severe that hospitalization becomes necessary. At the time of admission, a sense of helplessness is often predominant. The TCP teaches patients techniques for more effective problem-solving. As indicated earlier, each patient in a TCP program develops treatment contracts made up of relevant long- and short-term goals from the onset of hospitalization. In the early stages of treatment most of what appears on a patient's contract has been suggested by the patient's coordinator, contingency manager, and other members of the treatment team. Over time, however, the document becomes much more personalized and patients will take great pride in their improved abilities to develop effective contracts.

The actual process of contract development in the hospital occurs over the course of each week. Typically, at the beginning of the week, the patient, in consultation with the coordinator, will write a rough draft of a potential contract. The draft is presented in a "contract-setting" group made up of a wide variety of staff as well as other patients. The goal of the group is to help the patient further shape the contract into a final draft. This is accomplished by constructive feedback in the form of suggestions from those in attendance at the group. Following this meeting, a contract is formally typed. A copy goes to the patient, as well as into the medical record, and one is posted in a public area on the ward. Throughout the week the contract is referred to by patients and staff alike. At the end of the week all patients and staff attend a "contract evaluation" group in which each patient reads his/her contract identifying the accomplishment, or lack thereof, of each treatment goal. The contract process produces a set of treatment objectives that are redeveloped on a weekly basis. Each patient's goals are publicly discussed, and it is felt that such a declaration of goals on a regular basis increases the probability of compliance (Berglas & Levendusky, 1984, in press). In the treatment of anorexia, where control and secrecy are so often critical issues, this support through a public contract process is particularly important.

As is seen in Tables 1 and 2, the actual treatment contract is a complex document that addresses a wide variety of therapeutic issues. It can be noted in Table 1 that the patient, in the early stages of treatment, is attempting to deal with eight relevant long-term goals, only one of which directly focuses on the eating and weight symptoms. Other goals are related to interpersonal skills, affective factors, and family relations issues. While complex, the con-

Table 1
Example of Therapeutic Contract:
Low-Weight Anorexic, 40 Days of Inpatient Hospitalization

The following revised treatment plan was prepared by the members of the treatment team and the patient:

A. Long-Term Goals: Consistently implement behavioral techniques utilized on Behavior Therapy Unit because I am in the process of transition from a psychoanalytic framework.
  Short-Term Goals:
  1. Daily talks with patients about non-food-related topics.
  2. Attend groups as per schedule.
  3. Two·staff talks daily.
  4. Improved and explicit communication with staff.
  5. Continue decreased socializing when in Quiet Room (QR).

B. Long-Term Goal: Normalize eating patterns because with anorexia I developed abnormal eating habits and notions about food.
  Short-Term Goals:
  1. Continue limiting conversation about food.
  2. Follow prescribed behavioral program.
  3. Mood monitor after meals and p.r.n.
  4. Utilize 2 worry talks daily to discuss food obsession, increased body size and body weight p.r.n.

C. Long-Term Goal: Restructure family network because anorexia detrimentally alters family relationships.
  Short-Term Goals:
  1. Limit phone calls as prescribed.
  2. Refrain from calling out for Mom when upset in stressful situations.
  3. Attempt to realistically evaluate Mom's teaching, notions and concepts about food and food values for what they really are.
  4. Correspond regularly with sister.

D. Long-Term Goal: Increase self-esteem because negative personal feelings contribute to utilization of thinness as a façade to increase self-confidence and morale.
  Short-Term Goals:
  1. One positive self-statement daily.
  2. Write in journal as needed.
  3. Try to feel more comfortable with a more normal-looking, -feeling and physically functioning body.
  4. Avoid verbal or "thought-type" self put-downs.
  5. Utilize cosmetics and accessories to enhance appearance.

E. Long-Term Goal: Continue refinement of social skills because with anorexia I became isolated and lost finesse.

(continued)

Table 1 (*continued*)

Short-Term Goals:
1. Assume an assertive, not aggressive stance with people.
2. Do not interrupt ongoing conversations but interject if and when appropriate.
3 Appropriately participate in groups.
4. Remember to knock on door before entering a room and ask, "Are you free?"

F. Long-Term Goal: Begin to develop a sense of self-discipline because I have a tendency to "act out" when under stress and am unhappy.
Short-Term Goals:
1. Think without acting out.
2. Refrain from using testing behaviors.
3. Ask myself the question, "What will be the repercussions for such 'acting-out' behavior?"

G. Long-Term Goal: Begin developing an increased sense of maturity because the isolation imposed by anorexia caused me to become emotionally delayed.
Short-Term Goals:
1. Do not speak in a whiney tone of voice, especially when upset.
2. Accept apparently non-changeable situations and deal with them.
3. Attempt not to bargain when it is apparent that compromises will not be made.
4. Be patient and wait my turn when delayed.

H. Long-Term Goal: Do not take frustrations out on body because I have a tendency to "pick" at myself when agitated.
Short-Term Goals:
1. Refrain from picking sore on head.
2. Divert frustrations to constructive outlets such as journal writing, crafts, and reading.
3. Practice relaxation exercises.

Patient	Administrator

tract is written, as much as possible, in the patient's own language and reflects a personal priority of goals. Table 2 is a sample contract developed after approximately three months of hospitalization. Many of the earlier long-term goals have been either accomplished or consolidated into the remaining four. The eating symptoms continue to reflect a relatively small portion of the overall therapeutic attention. As a patient approaches discharge, the weekly contracts continue to evolve with more attention being paid to outside hospital

Table 2
Example of Therapeutic Contract:
Low-Weight Anorexic, 100 Days of Inpatient Hospitalization

The following revised treatment plan was prepared by the members of the treatment team and the patient:

A. Long Term Goal: Normalize weight by following program because dieting to the extreme of anorexia caused me to reduce my weight to a level where I was unable to function independently.
   Short-Term Goals:
   1. Gain 2 lbs. this week.
   2. Complete meals and snacks.
   3. Weighed by staff daily.
   4. Use worry talks for obsessions — others cue me when obsessing.
   5. Eat at a slower pace.

B. Long-Term Goal: Acquire new patterns of behavior to function in a normal and appropriate manner.
   Short-Term Goals:
   1. Attend all groups as per schedule and program
   2. Two staff talks daily.
   3. Be clear when communicating with staff.
   4. Refrain from picking at myself.
   5. Divert frustrations to constructive outlets, such as journal-writing, crafts, and reading.
   6. Practice relaxation.
   7. Practice "thought-stopping."
   8. Discuss transition from Quiet Room (QR) to patient community with staff and patients, especially roommate.

C. Long-Term Goal: Improve my interpersonal relations because I wish to "let go" of thinness as a mechanism to boost my self-esteem.
   Short-Term Goals:
   1. Initiate conversations in a non-abrasive manner with a modulated tone of voice and eye contact.
   2. Do not interrupt ongoing conversations in an effort to have my needs met immediately — others cue.
   3. Ask 3 people this week how I have been relating to them interpersonally.

D. Long-Term Goal: Meet regularly with members of my team so that I may benefit from the various modes of therapy utilized in my treatment.
   Short-Term Goals:
   1. See psychotherapist 3 times this week.
   2. See behavior therapist once this week.
   3. Meet with administrator once this week.
   4. Regularly meet with nursing coordinator this week.

Patient	Administrator

and aftercare maintenance issues. However, even after patients have been discharged, they are expected to continue their own weekly contracts.

Given the fact that all patients in the TCP program are expected to engage in the regular development of contracts, compliance with this expectation is usually not an issue. While anorexics likely have an intrinsic need to struggle with contracting, their being treated in a heterogeneous environment where the other patients do comply sets up a situation that fosters a norm of compliance, not one of struggle. It should be added that in a case where compliance does become an issue, it is made clear to patients that they will be discharged from treatment if they fail to engage in the contracting process. Paradoxically, taking control in this fashion results in patients grappling for control by spending more time personalizing and improving their contracts, than not.

GROUPS

While anorexia nervosa is usually viewed as an eating disorder, it is equally valid to view it as a social disorder. While physical symptoms of emaciation, amenorrhea, etc., are the most dramatic stigmata, significant social interaction deficits are also in evidence. In fact, it could be posited that, because of these social skill deficits and resultant lack of social control, anorexics develop their eating symptoms to allow themselves some degree of control in their lives. In any case, it is strongly recommended that the effective treatment of anorexia calls for a variety of group psychotherapy interventions.

To this end, the TCP involves patients in as many as 15 hours a week of various types of group therapy programs (Table 3). Already described are the contract-setting and evaluation groups, both of which have a clear focus on the problem-solving goals of the contracts program. In addition, patients are involved in social skills group, assertiveness group, communication group, sexual identity group, body awareness group, and job group, as well as the more usual ward government meetings.

Each group is designed to focus on the particular area reflected in its named agenda. The groups meet on a weekly basis and are usually co-led by two staff members. As with contracting groups, participation in these groups is expected and attendance is well over 90%. Specifically, the three groups in the social skills training sequence (i.e., social skills, assertiveness, and communication groups) are designed to provide patients with remedial and intermediate training in social interaction skills. If anorexia is at least partially conceptualized as having a social skill deficit component, then rudimentary didactic training is necessary. Specific protocols have been developed for each group, and there is heavy emphasis placed on role-playing, video-training, and facilitation of group interaction.

Table 3
Inpatient Treatment Groups

All patients are involved in the following groups programs:
  Contract setting meeting
  Assertiveness training
  Social skills training
  Relaxation group
  Body awareness group
  Job group
  Hall meeting
  Here-and-now group
  Patient government meeting
  Women's group
  Men's group
  Contract evaluation meeting

It should be emphasized, however, that these are both process- and technique-oriented groups, where attention is paid to both the explicit goals of the groups and interpersonal issues among members. This combined, behaviorally oriented process group has been described elsewhere by Belfer and Levendusky (in press). Process-oriented issues are also evident in sexual identity and body awareness groups. While each of these groups has an agenda, the group process becomes an even more major focus, particularly in the way in which members' problematic interactions affect one another. The focus of women's groups is on issues related to sexual identity and feminism, while body awareness is designed to assist patients in dealing with the physical and perceptual distortions seen in anorexia. As with other aspects of the program, all groups, with the exception of body awareness, have a heterogeneous membership and include all patients involved in the TCP.

INTEGRATED TREATMENT PROTOCOL

To this point, the program that has been outlined can be used as a milieu approach to the treatment of a wide range of psychiatric disorders including anorexia nervosa. While each of the components already described is seen as critical for the treatment of anorexia, none is specifically designed to manage the eating symptoms. To this end, the Integrated Treatment Protocol (ITP) was developed. Taking a rigorous operant approach, the following has been shown to be an effective method for managing the anorexic's disordered eating symptoms.

The ITP has three phases (Table 4), with each patient being evaluated for appropriate initial placement. At the time of admission all patients are in-

Table 4
General Stages of Integrated Treatment Protocol

Introduction	Self-Control	Staff Control
A) Admitted to hospital B) Oriented to program C) Initial involvement in groups, etc. D) Access to usual meals E) Access to bathroom, limited supervision	A) Expectation set B) Supervised meals C) Supervised baths D) 5 "meals"/day E) 2 lb/wk gain expected F) Quiet time G) Caloric expectations H) No food choice I) Initial goals set J) Mood monitor after meals K) No food preference L) Exercise limited and supervised	A) Expectations of staff-control B) Quiet Room restriction C) Isolation D) No groups E) Psychotherapies limited F) Slow pacing

volved in the introduction stage. Here, the patient is exposed to the usual orientation procedures available to everyone admitted to the TCP. This is done during the first two or three days of hospitalization and allows the staff to both observe the patient within the usual milieu and give the patient an unrestricted view of the treatment environment. In a small number of cases, particularly with slight to moderate symptoms, the introduction phase is a sufficient intervention. In other words, just coming into the hospital and being involved in a therapeutic community lead to an improvement in the eating symptoms. In such situations, these patients are then "mainstreamed" into the milieu and have little further involvement with the ITP.

However, the vast majority of patients show no improvement in the introduction stage and therefore move into the self-control stage. Here a series of expectations is established for the patient that includes, amongst other things, staff supervised meals, three meals and two snacks per day, caloric intake of 1500–2000 per day, staff supervised bathrooms, a 2 lb per week weight gain expectation, and a 15-minute quiet time after each meal for digestion and contemplation. This series of expectations may lead the reader to question, how is this self-control? In fact the self-control is evidenced by the fact that patients are given an opportunity to ask for the supervision described herein. While delineated, it is up to each patient to demonstrate the self-control needed to initiate each aspect of the program (e.g., inform staff when she needs to use the bathroom, etc.). Some patients with a moderate degree emaciation and other symptomatology are able to effectively use this stage and show improvement in their symptoms. In such cases where the patient demonstrates success, the degree of expected supervision is reduced (e.g., patients begin to eat breakfast and lunch). By the time they are ready for discharge, all activities related to eating are under their own control and, ideally, they have relearned how to appropriately use food and feed themselves. This, of course, is the ultimate goal of all phases of the program.

For the most emaciated and symptomatic patients, the self-control stage is not sufficient and, instead, it is necessary for them to be treated in the staff control stage. Here the overall program expectations are the same as in the self-control stage; however, it is recognized that the patient does not possess the necessary motivation or ability to use self-control. As a result, these patients are placed in a restrictive circumstance (i.e., an open-door quiet room or room restriction) and can only leave at prearranged times. In its most basic form, this would allow patients to be out of restriction for the three meals and two snacks each day. Patients are given 15 minutes to complete a meal, and, if successful, earn a 15-minute, out-of-restriction quiet time where they are expected to mood monitor (i.e., write down how they are feeling after eating and what this means to them). If patients accomplish this, then another 15-minute structured free time is made available.

In cases where patients fail to eat, either in the allotted time or in the quantity expected, they are immediately returned to restriction. Such noncompliance will often occur in early stages of the hospitalization and needs to be met with a straightforward business-like response in returning the patient to restriction without argument or discussion. Seldom does this pattern of noncompliance occur for more than two or three meals. Table 5 is a sample behavioral program for a low-weight anorexic in an early stage of treatment and exemplifies the specificity of both expectations and noncompliance contingencies.

If patients successfully comply with the program on a weekly basis, there is an opportunity for program change. For example, a patient who eats all meals during the week and gains the expected two pounds will earn an increase of 15 minutes in the structured free time after each meal. Two weeks of successful compliance would lead to another 15 minutes and, in turn, the patient would have enough time out of restriction to attend some part of selected groups or part of psychotherapy. It should be noted that neither group nor individual psychotherapy is available to patients in the most restrictive stages of the program. It is felt that if they are so symptomatic as to make these restrictions necessary, they would not effectively use individual psychotherapy and would likely be disruptive in groups. However, as their weight increases and the degree of compliance to program expectations is demonstrated, they can make use of other available therapies. It is important to note that the restrictive phase without therapies usually lasts about three to four

Table 5
Behavioral Program: Early Phase (Inpatient) Low-Weight Anorexia Nervosa

OPEN QUIET ROOM PROGRAM	Baseline Wt. —67 lbs.
EXPECTATIONS:	Goal Wt. —70 lbs.

Quiet Room
1. Patient will remain in the open quiet room (QR) with 6 possible 30-minute "out-times" per day.
2. Patient may have reading materials, writing materials, and one craft at a time in the QR. Needlepoint is to be kept in nursing station. Also may have transistor radio.
3. Time out is contingent upon:
    a. Completion of meal or snack in 10–20 min.
    b. Completion of mood-monitoring in designated observation area for full 15 min. — no talking.
    c. Thirty minute out-time should be scheduled ahead of time on daily schedule to include: group, quiet activity, social time, or staff talk (must attend group if available).
    d. If patient does not complete meal, she should mood monitor in QR and doesn't earn out-time. No cues to complete.
    e. If off-schedule or is acting inappropriately at any time out of QR, patient should be cued back to QR.
    f. Patient should be back in QR at the end of 30 min. on her own without cueing; loses next out-time if not.
    g. Out-time immediately follows mood-monitoring; nonnegotiable (may not save until later).
4. Worry talks daily in QR, to be scheduled at nursing staff discretion.
5. No patients in QR. No talking from QR; no standing on threshold; should stay at desk or on bed. Loses out-time if not.
6. May not go into room except for self-grooming needs; 10 min. time limit. Cue to put dentures in in the a.m.
7. Does not have free access to her room. May have 2 min. at start of out-time with staff member.
8. Out-time contingent upon meal completion and staying in QR.
9. If out of QR during in-time or doesn't return at end of 30 min., loses next out-time.
10. Relaxation on bed before meals 15 min.
11. Meal followed by mood-monitoring followed by 30 min. out-time. May not accumulate out-time(s). May attend portion of group available only during 30-min. out-time.
12. Picking head, vomiting, regurgitating, etc., will result in loss of out-time.
13. No more *cues*. Automatic loss of out-time for violations.
14. No water in QR.

Meals/Weight
1. 15 min. relaxation time on bed before meals. Three normal meals and three snacks will be prepared and supervised by staff. Patient should complete entire meal/snack each time. 20-min. time limit per meal, 10 min. per snack.

Table 5 (*continued*)

Optional glass of water with each meal and snack. Include beverage with meal. No water between meals.
2. Kitchen/dining room off-limits except during groups.
3. No exercise; no ping pong.
4. No food in room; no diet food or caffeine; no food/beverages on out-time.
5. No pork or ham; no milk—substitute Sustacal at meals. Does not follow strict kosher diet.
6. May have breakfast in dining room with other patients. Day-to-day contingent upon completion of entire meal, no food talk, no comparing meals, and time-limited.
7. Should spend entire meal time (20 min.) eating and mood-monitoring time (15 min.) writing or reflecting on feelings.
8. Should keep mood-monitoring sheets in folder of her own to be passed in with daily schedule at end of the day.
9. No cues on completing a meal. If not complete, then no out time.
10. No food requests on meals.
11. Has chosen normal diet with no pork or shellfish and no glass of milk with meat. Is expected to eat other dairy products, i.e., cheese, butter, etc. with meal.
12. Normal snacks three times daily—caloric equivalent (approx.) of Sustacal. (10:00 a.m.—2:00 p.m.—8:00 p.m.)

Obsessing/Complaints Re Program
1. Limit all obsessional material re: food, body, medical concerns, programs, etc., to daily worry talks. Refer questions re program to CM. Loss of out-time if obsessing about any of above.
2. If patient is obsessing/persisting on some point in discussion or staff talk, cue back to QR.
3. All *abnormal* behavior (i.e., gulping food, regurgitating, vomiting, hanging around nursing station, picking head, screaming, etc.) can be dealt with via loss of out-time.
4. No notes to staff except rounds day. Return notes to her.
5. Obsessing re: food, medical issues, body, program, etc., equals loss of out-time.
6. Terminate phone calls to parents Tuesday, Sunday, if obsessing.

Activities of Daily Living (ADL)
1. Bathroom supervision (5 min. each hour, on the half-hour, after checks are passed off); ADL supervision/shower and eve. ADL supervised.
2. Shower in the evening, 8:30 p.m., 25-minute time limit. This includes eve. ADLs.
3. Cue to sit on toilet if standing. Should not remove clothing at toilet.
4. Laundry done upstairs by another patient or by hospital, not in shower in p.m.

(*continued*)

Table 5 (*continued*)
Behavioral Program: Early Phase (Inpatient) Low-Weight Anorexia Nervosa

Staff
1. Daily schedule is to include in/out-time—one-half hour blocks—to be done on the evening shift the day before. Review in staff talk with staff signature.
2. Staff talks will focus on Therapeutic Contract, daily schedule, ADLs. Should bring agenda to talks.
3. No notes to staff until rounds day. Return notes to patient.
4. No formal appointments without program approval.
5. Will start twice-weekly therapy with psychotherapist.
6. Staff talk limited to 15 min. (longer at staff discretion).
7. Staff talk on out-time only.
8. Review weekly schedules with nursing coordinator.

Contingencies
1. Out-time contingent upon meal completion and staying in QR.
2. If out of QR during in-time or doesn't return at end of 30 minutes, loses next out-time.
3. At 70 lbs. may return to attendance of groups in their entirety.
4. Loses out-time for any program violation CND.
5. Baseline: 67   Goal: 70
   If below baseline: 1. 15 min. out-times.
                     2. MES porch.
                     3. Both discontinue radio in room.
6. Parents' visits non-contingent. Two half-hour out-time periods only.

Contingency Manager

weeks. At the end of this time, patients have usually increased their weight out of the critical range and are seen to be in a position to effectively use treatments offered.

Questions are often asked about the issues of "choice," particularly in the restrictive stage. It is our experience that patients should have no choice until they demonstrate their ability to handle the "no choice" situation. Most anorexics have some distinct food preferences (i.e., vegetarianism, fruititarian, etc.) that, on a surface level, may have some validity. Unfortunately, the validity is only at the surface and has more to do with the anorexic symptoms.

In initial stage of treatment, the only relevant weight goal is the weekly expectation of gain. A patient's ultimate weight range is not established until she has made substantial progress through the program. As with other components of treatment, an objective standard is used. Instead of an ideal weight being seen as a level where the patient is "medically stable" or is "beginning to feel fat," the TCP ideal weight is based on actuarial standards related to gender, frame, and height, with a plus or minus five-pound range.

As indicated above, compliance with the restrictive program gradually results in more access to the general therapeutic milieu. Over time, the patient also gradually earns more responsibility in dealing with such basics as meal supervision, meal preparation, and bathroom behavior. They also acquire onward, and ultimately off-ward, and out-of-hospital pass privileges, all of whose receipt is paced by demonstrated responsiveness to the treatment protocol. Realistically, it is likely to take an extremely symptomatic patient seven to 12 weeks to move from the highly restricted expectations to the more self-controlled and mainstreamed status in the milieu. Table 6 demonstrates the evolution of the behavioral program after approximately 100 days of hospitalization. While continuing to be quite specific, the expectations and contingencies are at a much greater degree of self-control than seen in Table 5.

It is important to emphasize that throughout the protocol, the rate of a patient's pacing through various steps is determined by the contingency manager. This team member's position is one of continued responsibility and authority over resisting a patient's effort to inappropriately accelerate her movement through the program. As has been reported elsewhere (Dooley, Landau, & Levendusky, in press), the contingency manager deals with much of the power struggle that is intrinsic in treating these patients and that in turn allows an opportunity for the members of the treatment team to deal with other issues.

With graduation to a stage of self-control (Table 6), the need for external contingencies is lessened; they are used only in cases where there is a reappearance of symptoms (i.e., weight loss, binge, or purge). At this point, the patient is actively using the available exploratory psychotherapy, as well as therapy groups. Eating symptoms are much more under the patient's control and the ultimate weight goal has been established and discussed. Ideally, patients should have an opportunity for continued hospitalization after these goals have been achieved so that they might consolidate their therapeutic accomplishments. Additionally, more time is spent away from the milieu with emphasis on part-time employment, looking for appropriate out-of-hospital residential situations and setting up appropriate aftercare plans.

Parenthetically, it should be noted that at later stages of treatment, there are several issues that, when they become relevant, can often lead to brief regressions and increases in symptoms. Particularly, achieving a weight of 100 pounds or achieving the ideal weight can be experienced as a time of considerable conflict and should be treated in a supportive but limit-setting fashion (e.g., reinstituting necessary contingencies). Similarly, leaving the hospital increases both anticipation and agitation. This is often a time when power struggles over where a patient will live, how much she will work, or

Table 6
Behavioral Program: Late Phase (Inpatient) Low-Weight Anorexia Nervosa

BEHAVIORAL PROGRAM	Range: 105–115 lbs.
	Baseline: 110 lbs.

Expectations
1. Patient may serve herself three normal meals/snacks with staff supervision of lunch and dinner only.
2. Unsupervised snacks/breakfast. Patient will let staff know when starting and finishing snack/breakfast. Any other time in kitchen or inappropriate use of snack privilege will result in resumption of snack/breakfast supervision the following day.
3. Hall dinner preparation at staff discretion.
4. May have her snack/breakfast off hall at staff discretion.
5. Daily weight.
6. May join skating group Sunday afternoons.
7. Exercise group at gym when within range 105–115.
8. Mutual escort (MES) on grounds with patients, family, friends.
9. Kitchen dining room off limits at times other than snacks.
10. No soda from machine.
11. No caffeine, diet food, or gum.
12. Call back (CBs) on grounds privileges.
13. MES off grounds with patients, family, friends.
14. Reinstate contingencies on baseline weight and use of privileges.
15. Hold cafeteria privileges if below baseline.

Contingencies
1. Failure to complete meal results in restriction area until next meal/snack.
2. Snack/breakfast unsupervised contingent upon appropriate use of this privilege and staying out of the kitchen at all other times. If in violation, staff will supervise snacks the following day.
3. All social privileges contingent upon maintaining 108 lb. weight. Rehabilitation appointments. Clinical vocational assessment program, body awareness group, van trip non-contingent.
4. No unsupervised cafeteria privileges if below 105 lbs.

Privileges
1. Call back (CB's) on grounds.
2. MES on grounds with patients, family, and friends.
3. MES off grounds with family and friends.
4. Midnight curfew Saturday.

Contingency Manager

when specifically she will be discharged occur. If such struggles are anticipated, and if the treatment team takes a unified position in regard to each member's recommendations, such conflicts can quickly be neutralized, with the patient then following therapy expectations.

Dooley, Landau and Levendusky (in press) report an outcome comparison of patients treated in the TCP with those treated on more traditionally oriented generic units of a well established private psychiatric hospital. Eight patients from each setting were compared. As is seen in Table 7, both groups were quite similar in measures related to the severity of their illness. However, length of hospitalization was apparently 50% shorter for the TCP group and, as can be seen in Figure 1, the treatment outcome for this group was considerably better. While no follow-up was available for the hospital group at large, all patients treated on the TCP maintained their weight within an objectively determined normal range. While not conclusive, these data clearly demonstrate that the TCP has been effectively used in assisting severely symptomatic low-weight anorexics in not just achieving a normal weight range, but also maintaining it for a significant period of time following discharge.

MEDICATION

There has been much recent speculation in regard to the usefulness of psychotropic medication in the treatment of eating disorders. While preliminary, the most encouraging results appear to be achieved with bulimics. Unfortunately, there is little to date to indicate that similar success has been achieved with anorexia. In our experience, medication adds a confounding factor to the treatment of these patients, and a factor that has not been demonstrated to be useful. It should also be noted that in the early stages of treatment, these patients often appear to be psychotic in the degree to which they are out of

Table 7
Comparison of Epidemiological and Demographic Variables
for the Two Samples

Sample	Age (years)	% Ideal Body Weight at Admission	Duration of Illness (years)	Duration of Hospitalization (days)	Previous Hospitalizations
Integrated Treatment Protocol	23.88	67.88	6.88	220.50	1.75
Hospital At Large	20.63	74.24	4.41	417.00	3.88

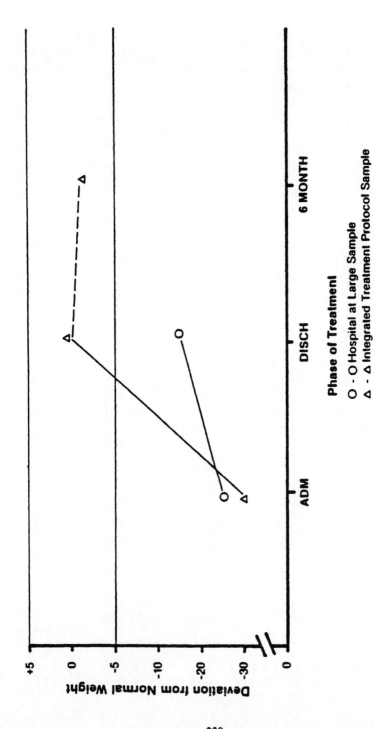

Figure 1. Comparison of weight change for two clinical samples.

control. As such, there is often a suggestion that the use of antipsychotic medication would be helpful. Again, this does not appear to be indicated since much of the "psychotic" behavior disappears as patients begin to put on weight.

AFTERCARE

Criteria for discharge are met when a patient has demonstrated an overall compliance and graduation up to and through self-control stage, has achieved an ideal weight, and has set up appropriate aftercare residential and treatment plans. It is expected that the therapeutic goals achieved during the hospitalization will be quite vulnerable after discharge. As indicated earlier, there is little evidence in the outcome literature on the treatment of anorexia to demonstrate that inpatient improvement is maintained on an outpatient basis. As a result, there is a considerable emphasis in the current model toward helping a patient set up and then participate in an active aftercare program.

The typical outpatient team is made up of the individual psychotherapist (who, by the time of discharge, has a strong therapeutic alliance with the patient), the contingency manager, who will monitor the patient's symptomatic status out of the hospital, and the family therapist, whose work at discharge is often critical, given the problems these families have with individuation and separation. In addition to the treatment team, it is expected that the patient will be living away from her family, be vocationally active for a minimum of 20 hours per week, demonstrate efforts to control eating symptoms, and maintain a plus or minus five-pound range around her ideal weight goal.

As might be expected, the greatest struggle is in the area of weight maintenance. To this end, a firm, but somewhat controversial, contingency has been established with these patients. Specifically, if their weight goes out of the plus or minus five-pound range for a week, the contingency manager instructs the psychotherapist to eliminate one therapy session for the subsequent week. The following week, if the patient remains out of range, then another psychotherapy session is eliminated. If, in the third week the patient is out of range, rehospitalization for a minimum of two weeks is required. The controversy about using psychotherapy as a contingency usually takes the form of "but when a patient is increasingly symptomatic, isn't this the time that she most needs therapy?" Our experience does not support this position; instead, it appears that when these patients become increasingly symptomatic, they are not able to use their therapy effectively. Just as most therapists would not attempt therapy with a patient who showed up for a session intoxicated, a similar response is necessary for the anorexic who is occasionally symptomatic.

During the outpatient phase of treatment, patients continue to complete contracts on a weekly basis. These and their specific behavioral expectations are reviewed regularly by their contingency manager. Further, in these sessions, weights are taken and the patients are closely monitored for potential symptoms. Since most patients treated in the TCP are in their early to mid twenties, vocational, residential, and independent living skill issues are particularly relevant for the outpatient. Because of past preoccupations with food, patients are discouraged from finding employment in food-related occupations. While most patients have what could minimally be described as an "avocational" interest with food, it is felt that employment should be separate from their food interests.

Attention to the anorexic's type of living situation after discharge is important. In our experience, there is often a desire for even adult patients to want to move home and live with their families. While family therapy will often focus on issues of separation, these are often so problematic, particularly when dealing with an outpatient treatment, that it is useful to administratively require patients to live away from home as a prerequisite for outpatient treatment. Ideally, the patient would then reside in a group living situation such as a halfway house or therapeutic apartment. If such facilities are not available, then roommates are an acceptable alternative.

The social skills deficits seen earlier in treatment are likely to reappear as the patient moves into such independent living situations. Such issues are often the focus of considerable attention in the treatment contracts and patients are often referred to self-help groups, such as the Anorexia Nervosa Aid Society, for support and assistance in regard to these matters.

Outpatient treatment of anorexia nervosa should be viewed as requiring a serious commitment of time and resources. Conservatively, two to three years of continued treatment are necessary for the resolution of the various factors that have contributed to this disorder.

SUMMARY

A multifaced model for the inpatient management of anorexia nervosa has been presented. This model integrates a variety of interventions into a comprehensive treatment approach that attempts to help patients acquire mastery in the area of self-esteem, social skills, independent functioning, family separation, and stable body weight. For severely symptomatic patients, a rigorous contingency management program represents a first step toward symptom control. Ultimately, all patients acquire an internally focused ability to control themselves in areas relating to the etiology of their disorder. They are discharged at an objectively determined "normal" weight and continue afterhospital treatment designed to help maintain their progress. To date, the success of the program has been impressive in achieving the goals outlined above.

REFERENCES

Agras, W. S., Barlow, D. H., Chaplin, N. H., Able, G. G., & Leitenberg, H. (1974). Behavior modification of anorexia nervosa. *Archives of General Psychiatry, 30,* 279-286.

Belfer, P., & Levendusky, P. G. (in press). Long-term behavioral group psychotherapy: A new model. In D. Upper & S. Ross (Eds.), *Handbook of behavioral group therapy.* New York: Plenum.

Bemis, K. M. (1978). Current approaches to the etiology and tretament of anorexia nervosa. *Psychological Bulletin, 85,* 593-617.

Berglas, S., & Levendusky, P. G. (1984, in press). The therapeutic contract program: An individual-oriented psychological treatment community. *Journal of Psychotherapeutic Theory, Research & Practice.*

Bruch, H. (1974). Perils of behavior modification in treatment of anorexia nervosa. *Journal of the American Medical Association, 230*(10), 1419-1422.

Dooley, C. P., Landau, R. J., & Levendusky, P. G. (in press). Integrated treatment protocol: a comprehensive approach to the treatment of anorexia nervosa.

Garfinkel, P. E., Kline, S. A., & Stancer, H. C. (1973). Treatment of anorexia nervosa using operant conditioning techniques. *Journal of Nervous and Mental Disease, 157*(6), 428-433.

Halmi, K. A., Powers, P., & Cuningham, S. (1975). Treatment of anorexia nervosa with behavior modification. *Archives of General Psychiatry, 32,* 93-96.

Levendusky, P. G., Berglas, S., Dooley, C. P., & Landau, R. J. (1983). Therapeutic contract program: Preliminary report on a behavioral alternative to the token economy. *Behavior Research & Therapy, 21,* 137-142.

Russell, G. (1981). The current treatment of anorexia nervosa. *British Journal of Psychiatry, 138,* 164-166.

Chapter 13

Structuring a Nurturant-Authoritative Psychotherapeutic Relationship with the Anorexic Patient

Steven Levenkron

PREMORBID AND PERSONALITY FEATURES

Who is most vulnerable to developing anorexia nervosa? As can be surmised from the title of my first book (Levenkron, 1978), it would be "the best little girl" in the family. She was the girl who, from outward appearances, seemed to be working very hard to please everyone, to achieve success, to be a positive influence, and, in fact, to assist her family so that they might be proud of her. She has been characterized as perfectionistic and mistrustful, while alternately compliant and rebellious. Superficially adult, she has never been especially relaxed about receiving support. She inferred from her parents that she was not supposed to need comforting or hugging. She rarely took advice, was often a tyrant at home, yet compliantly acquiescent away from home. The community viewed her as the best dressed and behaved little girl imaginable, and then she would return home only to assume a pleasant but unyielding dictatorial role.

I believe, as do growing numbers of therapists and professionals in the mental health field, that anorexia nervosa begins as an obsessional disorder (Levenkron, 1982). Many years ago most of the people who sought treatment were self-selected. Over time this situation has changed. Today we are seeing patients who, in fact, have been forced into therapy, coaxed into treatment, and sometimes have desperately desired help, not out of curiosity or the wish

---

Adapted from a lecture given at the annual national conference sponsored by the Center for the Study of Anorexia and Bulimia in New York City, November 1982.

to achieve greater happiness and self-understanding, but to be relieved of the terrible pain they experience.

Mental health professionals are going to see an increasing number of people who are termed obsessional. Indeed, I believe anorexia nervosa is symptomatic of an entire obsessional generation just growing into maturity. This is true, in part, because of what I call the premature offering of choices to children by their well-meaning parents. They are offered, for example, often by the age of five or six, a choice about which school they would like to attend, without any idea, of course, what this decision entails. This situation may stem from the fact that parents today are suffering from a kind of demoralization in their roles. I term them "exhausted" and "depleted." Today's mother faces enormous demands and, yet, what she is rewarded for least is nurturing. The caretaking of her children is often taken for granted. In our achievement-oriented society mothering is viewed by many as a low-status role. Today's full-time mother has no real spokesperson. The working mother, by virtue of having a job (i.e., identity, acceptability), can avoid this trap. But what about the woman who is "only a mother" or "only a housewife"? Nurturing—caretaking done when one person looks after another, not for status, not for prestige, not for gain—has been grossly undervalued by society.

Let us consider the children who have to grow up in such a society, in a culture where female appearance is scrutinized as never before, almost invariably with unrealistic expectations for thinness. Very often a family will "select" its strongest, the one whom both mother and father see as requiring the least attention, who puts up the least fuss, who manages the most independently. They identify that child and on a subtle level collude with her, praising and rewarding her for how little she needs and demands. That child quickly gets the message: "They love me for how little I need."

Now we, as parents, think we are offering our children choices and are helping them to grow up maturely by granting them more and more responsibility. The inferences made by that child are that she is loved and appreciated because she doesn't need all that much caretaking, because she doesn't need guidance, nurturance, advice, or comforting. An insidious, potentially illness-producing paradox develops: in order to get love, I must avoid needing love.

There is a certain prestige in seeing one's child being successful and creating achievements at earlier and earlier ages. Today, mothers are proud of their children for finishing their baby food first or for having the highest birth weight. And those mothers who are not working, who are not receiving a pay check, have to find other ways to feel self-esteem within their role as mother. The successful negotiation of each of her children's developmental tasks helps a mother feel better, helps her feel that she is doing a good job, so her need for her child's success becomes pressure on the child to become more independent sooner than ever. Sometimes there is too much independence, because I contend that the anorexic child, the obsessive youngster, is one who has not had enough time to behave dependently, and has not had that dependence and need for comfort accepted. So when the child is encouraged to be prematurely independent, the parent can feel highly successful and, at the same time, be relieved of the burden of "excess" nurturing.

What depletes and exhausts this kind of parent still further is anxiety about keeping up with society's expectations of what we should have materially — the big house, car, etc. Such parents are under enormous pressure and are assisted emotionally if the children raise themselves as quickly as possible.

What I think has happened in the family dynamics is that, as the parents gave "depleted" and "abandoning" communications to the child ("Honey, you decide for us," or, "We don't really understand you, and you have always known what's best for you"), these forms of praise demanded that the child not demonstrate need. As the child adjusts to implied demands that she not request emotional support, she becomes contemptuous of the parent. And if one considers transference in the anorexic, one finds that the anorexic produces a transference of contempt. The therapist would probably be harmless but not helpful. Also, one finds that most anorexics regard their parents with guilt, as well as contempt.

Within this family structure, the child receives considerable *abandoning* and *dependent* communication, and she becomes a highly independent person. Not only does she feel she has to protect her family, which she experiences as needing care, but she succeeds in school, she is pleasant, she is exemplary. She is exemplary for two reasons: 1) She has to protect the family; and 2) she has no trust.

I believe that this child does not trust either mother or father to comfort her emotionally. She will trust them for services, but not for support. Thus, since she has never learned to "get off the case" by receiving comfort, she attempts to comfort herself. This she accomplishes by organizing and ordering her external world.

For the most part, a lot of obsessive-compulsive behavior is evident in the anorexic because she derives security from her "no surprises" routine, from spatial symmetry, from order all around her. She also derives security from very high grades in school, because the "A" means she has fulfilled all that she must. The "A−," the "B+," and the "C" are experienced by her as personal failures. She does a lot of "splitting," seeing things in polarities. She sees adequacy, and she sees failure. She never sees success. She is hardly ever elated, and usually depressed. To feel barely adequate, she attempts to be as "perfect" as possible. When this compensatory activity fails, as it inevitably must, the typical feelings associated with dismal failure surface. Such fearful vigilance tends to foster defensive rigidity.

The anorexic has always possessed a rigid personality, yet she manages remarkably well. The anorexic was a happy child. She managed her neighbors, her teachers, her friends. Perhaps she always felt alone inside because she saw herself as a full-time *persona*. She saw herself as a person who is in charge of the world, who manipulates everyone, and suffers from deep feelings of inferiority because she suspects that if the world got to know who she really was, when she was not in that invulnerable, controlling role, they would disapprovingly cast her out. They neither love her nor care about her. So she redoubles her efforts at high achievement, never trusting in her worth. I want to emphasize "mistrustful" rather than "perfectionistic," because the anorexic is above all a mistrusting person. Most importantly, she does not trust her self—her impulses, desires, feelings, and perceptions. She is not thrilled with her achievements. She feels as if she is only coping, even when she is highly successful.

DEVELOPMENT OF THE ILLNESS

How does this obsessional person develop anorexia nervosa? Beneath a cloud of inadequacy, hampered by a sort of polarity tunnel vision, she struggles with the various developmental demands one regularly encounters along the path of maturity. She goes to school and she puts her puzzles together perfectly in kindergarten. She reads at the top of her class, she excels in math. She tries very hard at everything. Then she reaches puberty, a stage that implies many tasks. It first of all tells her that she may some day be separated from Mother and Father because she is beginning to develop an adult body. Along with this is a nagging fear that her childhood is, in fact, incomplete. Her fear of going ahead is very much a fear of separating from that incomplete childhood. So she needs new rules on how to achieve. And if she has watched television, if she has looked at fashion ads for clothing, if she has been involved in talk among women, she understands that the cultural ethic in Western society extols an unrealistically thin appearance for women.

Many years ago when a girl reached puberty she was relieved and delighted because then she could go to a party and look like a grown-up, and her nylons would not get baggy, because her thighs had filled out. That was before pantyhose, which fit any size legs. Even our death-weight patients would look all right in pantyhose.

But nowadays, instead of delighting in pubescence, most normal girls fret: "Oh my goodness, my thighs are getting fat." We have created something interesting. Aside from the pathological end of it, which results in anorexia nervosa, we have created a fear of one's own body in females growing up in this society. Surely there is no cultural reinforcement that says, "My thighs are getting thicker and my hips are getting rounder, and isn't it great, my bust is filling out." What should be a joy, what should be a source of pride, what should be praise for the body's natural achievement, in this society has become a condemnation. Why does society have such a powerful influence here?

The obsessive girl, who does mistrust, who must be perfect, who must achieve as highly as she can, will look at her thighs and say:

> I had better take care of these because it's clear that developmentally the world expected me to be a straight-A student, well dressed and pleasant. And surely, you can ask all my friends and neighbors, the world expects me to be thin. So I will diet in the same obsessive manner that I have achieved my "A's" and managed other things and people.

Now, anyone who has ever dieted knows that dieting makes one obsessive. One thinks about food a lot. And there are many studies to indicate that once an individual goes into a level of malnutrition, one goes far beyond "normal" diet-obsessing. There are certain chemical changes that cause such a malnourished person to think about food *all the time*. This is also what happens when a developmentally obsessive personality begins doing what can be termed "obsessogenic" behavior. She is in double jeopardy at this point. That girl has dieted back to prepubescence.

Here is the genesis of the anorexic condition: The girl begins her dieting, and she begins to feel a sense of achievement. She has begun dieting because she was a good little girl. She has begun dieting motivated by achievement, whether she has been a normal weight, slightly heavy, very heavy, or even thinner than normal. Anorexics come from a wide weight range. As she gets thinner, people start saying, "You're losing weight." If one says to the "average" person, "You're losing weight," that person smiles. If one says, "You've gained a bit of weight," the person frowns. But imagine what happens to this adolescent, in the midst of her identity crisis (and identity, of course, *is* appearance, for most adolescents), when she begins to lose weight and people say, "You're losing weight." She smiles because she believes that she is achieving, and she is going to keep on achieving. Now, since she is the kind of girl who has never been genuinely dependent upon other people for reassurance, for praise, for feeling good, for advice, for comfort, for emotional support, she really takes these comments as praise for her personal accomplishment. In other words, she is not competing with any other girls in a team sport. This is very much an individual sport. So as she loses more and more weight, people start saying, "Hey, you've lost a lot of weight." But they are not smiling anymore. Finally, her family, her physician, and perhaps her teachers and friends are saying to her, "You've lost too much weight."

But the anorexic does not respond to them. Since in her life experience she has never turned to others for help, why should she bother to listen to them on the very private, and to her precious, matter of her own body? She dismisses them and their advice and continues losing weight. Of course, everyone around her becomes alarmed, and then the family members begin to struggle with her. They struggle for her to eat more, as any family would do with a child they saw starving in front of them. But this girl has very little experience in confrontation. For the most part, she comes from a family of acquiescent parents.

Suddenly this family is saying, "We want to be authoritative with you." And the daughter says to herself, "You're attempting to thwart me and I'm going to struggle against you because, at this point, the external ways I have evolved for managing my life, all the rituals, all the special ways in which I am able to feel safe by ordering things outside of myself—the compulsively repeated exercises, the ever-lowered numbers on the scale—these are now invested in my weight and appearance."

By this time the anorexic is very involved in numerical systems for security. Drops in weight, whether it is from 110 to 100 or crossing that barrier from three digits to two, to 99, to 89, to 79, are victorious moments for the obsessive personality.

As anyone who has treated an anorexic knows, as soon as her weight goes up to 89 pounds she has a terrifying time crossing over into 90. The number system reigns supreme, and the anorexic is wedded to it more than to any person in her life. But when people start to struggle with her, her observing ego looks down at her and says, "Hey, you're struggling back, actually defying people, behaving assertively." Even though she is struggling, it is with a style she does not identify as defiant because she never wants to displease anyone. She feels she has to struggle with others because "I can't let them take away my numbers. I can't let them take away my bones."

So now a secondary benefit accrues to the illness that was not present at onset. The secondary benefit has evolved out of this girl's witnessing her own confrontations with the world, for the first time in her life, in defense of her illness. There is a victorious dimension to this new-found feeling of self-assertiveness, and it issues in difficult and complicated problems during treatment. The anorexic will sometimes confide, "You know, if I give this up, I'll be nothing." One can hear her saying, "If I don't dazzle people with my skinniness, then I will be a nobody."

What I hear is:

> This is the first time in my life I have ever been assertive, and, if I relinquish this assertiveness in defense of my illness or for whatever purpose, then I will be an unassertive person who can be dominated by others, and I will go back to being a passive, compliant girl who often learned to hate, secretly, inside. And my anger and my contempt for "her" is as the girl who had to please parents.

Once the anorexic has begun to confront her physician, her teachers, and her friends, then she becomes angry at her parents because she has proved that home is really not a very secure place; rather, home is a place where weak people dwell.

Anorexia nervosa, of course, does not only occur at puberty. The two other modal points where it develops are in the junior and senior years of high school and the first year of college. The years of high school warn one of a change in life. One will have to separate, spatially, from that childhood experienced as incomplete. In the junior year, this girl will go away and tour colleges, and come back and say, "Why am I frightened to go away to college? I'm a very independent person. Why do I have this fear of leaving home?" And in the first year of college, the separation has actually occurred. Indeed, college counselors are aware of the increase in the incidence of onset of anorexia nervosa in the freshman year.

Separation is a vital issue for these young women. Whether they are separating from their childlike body, which means childhood is coming to an end, or separating from their parents because they are going away to college, or graduating, or getting married, they become frightened, and they look towards some kind of foolproof achievement (i.e., weight loss) to protect themselves, since that has always worked for them previously.

IMPLICATIONS FOR MENTAL HEALTH PROFESSIONALS

The anorexic walks into the therapist's office and she sits down with an assumption: "The therapist, like my parents, is a 'good' person who needs care and reassurance, and my job is to take care of the therapist." Either parents or friends demanded that she go into treatment or she wants to get better, or she does not really want to get better but she wants to want to get better and she will tell you, "I really want to gain weight." But she does not want to gain weight. Again, she may only say it because she knows rationally that it is a good, acceptable thing to say.

Let us consider this girl on the first therapeutic interview. She comes in and she looks at the therapist, and she wants to know what it is the therapist wants from her. She begins to talk, if she has grown up in a family where there is talking. And the therapist will say to him- or herself, "Isn't that wonderful! I have developed a rapport with my patient." And the girl will say to herself, "Isn't this wonderful! I am meeting this therapist's needs."

Then, in the following sessions, the patient talks about her dreams. She talks about her fears. She talks about anything the therapist wants to talk about. Throughout this period, she is getting skinnier. And the therapist says, "I don't want to pressure you. Let me just understand who you are first, and then things will eventually get better." And the patient says to herself, "I'm going to make this person very happy. I will be the same wonderful caretaker of my therapist that I was of my parents."

So she establishes the same *reversal of dependency* in her mind that she has had at home. This reversal is very difficult to detect because she behaves like a productive patient. But she is again in a caretaking role. She is wearing her persona. Traditional, nondirective psychodynamic therapy will not suffice with such a person. A new approach is required.

THE NURTURANT-AUTHORITATIVE APPROACH

Twelve years ago a very skinny girl was admitted to Montefiore Hospital. She was 5'5" and she weighed 67 pounds. She had circulatory disturbances and a host of other problems. And I just looked at her and said what I would never be allowed to say in analytical supervision: "I'm going to be in charge of you and you'll be safe." She looked at me and replied, "Well, thank God somebody's going to be in charge of me. For the last five years my analyst said I would get better when I was ready." And there she was at 67 pounds. I said, "Dr. Z. and I will keep you alive and get you better. *You* obviously cannot get yourself better." I felt very guilty at the time for having said that.

I am proposing here the application of a highly directive model, one which is in direct conflict with the analytic mode of therapy with which most professionals are familiar (and comfortable). From the moment that I met that girl and she reinforced what I said, I could not decide if she was just trying to make me feel good or if she was sincere. But at the time she was incompetent, she was near death.

I tried to develop a repertoire of behaviors that would amount to reparenting the patient, establishing a regressive relationship, and when I did not know what to do with a patient, I would try to remember what I did with my daughters when they were two years old. The deficits that these girls present in therapy are so great that we dare not offer them dependent and abandoning communications. What we do offer them is nurturant and authoritative communications.

So we do not say, "Why do you think you really want to lose weight?" Otherwise the patient will think, "Oh, the therapist doesn't know why I want to lose weight. Well I don't know why I want to lose weight either, so I had better make up some answer." Anorexic patients have read much material on their own illness; most are anorexia nervosa buffs. So the therapist must know that the patient will say, "I'm afraid to become a woman. . . . I read that somewhere. And I think maybe I'm afraid of sex too (as is any immature personality, of course)."

We have to be extremely careful with this patient because we have to communicate something very important to her: We have to indicate that we are aware that she is not competent. This is a very painful statement to make to somebody who comes to seek help. She knows she is not competent but she does not want the therapist to know it. Also, she does not want the therapist to identify that in her. So in the first session I will typically say to someone, "You're apparently not managing. You're in a trap. You're helpless." Now these are distressing remarks to make. However, comments such as, "You are manipulative," "You are sneaky," or "You are lying," all can connote power. Such characterizations make the anorexic feel like a person who, even if she is bad for the first time in her life, is strong and and independent.

However, I tell the anorexic that she is not strong. I use no words that connote strength. I tell her that she does not understand why she has this illness, even though I understand why. In this way, I am intruding upon or influencing her own perceptions of herself, which is an authoritative approach. If I meet with parents before seeing their daughter, and I tell them how I will behave towards her, they tell me that she will leave my office "in two minutes flat." Interestingly enough, the patient never walks out after a meeting in which I sympathetically recognize that she is trapped, that she is helpless, that she is in fact a victim, that she has none of those manipulative, strong, difficult traits she has been accused of possessing. I communicate directly a perception of her as a very frightened person who is lonely and trapped.

She begins to believe that I have something to offer her, and that she cannot take care of me, that I, in fact, will be taking care of her. So I have no interest in taking history on first meeting her. I will weigh her on a medical scale in my office. I tell her to kick off her shoes and get on the scale. First she will tell me that she does not want to be weighed, that she weighs between five and ten pounds more than she actually weighs. But I do not dare to not weigh her. Also, I do not ask her open-ended questions. Above all, I do not sit in silence.

For the healthy personality who has been repressed by parents, authority figures, and a society which told her that her thoughts are dirty, bad, and evil, therapeutic silence is indeed a necessity. Silence to that person represents space, acceptance, and autonomy, a chance to rethink what she has been doing. But for the girl to whom society says anything is possible, all thoughts are legitimate, for that child, or adolescent, or young adult silence is not needed or helpful. She needs guidance. So when the therapist says nothing to her, she has two options. One, she can interpret that silence: "The therapist doesn't know what to say." Her alternate option is to think, "I am so worthless, this person has lost interest in me already." Thus, the therapist is sitting there waiting for the patient to blossom productively and she is sitting there feeling totally rejected.

Thus, it is important not to offer the anorexic silence because she is not, in fact, a repressed personality coming from a repressive society. She is an obsessional personality coming from an obsessogenic society, a structureless society. Her previous life experiences can be characterized as containing emo-

Structuring a Nurturant/Authoritative Psychotherapeutic Relationship

tional abandonment and dependence, which she has actually received from people around her.

She needs to be offered nurturance for her abandonment and authoritativeness to counteract her rigid self-reliance. It must be made clear from the very outset that it is the confident and competent therapist who will guide her and lead her out of her helplessness.

She may initially react quite negatively because at that moment she is going through a separation anxiety. She is being torn from the style in which her parents have always perceived her. The nurturant-authoritative (N-A) therapist is saying, "You're a young, confused child." Her previous messages have been, "Thank God, you're so independent and productive." So the task is not only to inform her as gently as possible about what kind of difficulty she is in, but also to promise to lead her out.

At this critical point in therapy it is necessary to make promises, to make assurances, and to risk attachments that cannot be blamed on the transference, because we, the therapists, are doing it. We are creating behaviors and attitudes within the patient. At those moments we are not neutral. We are nurturing that patient, being authoritative with her, and helping her to become dependent instead of independent. The message is: It is OK to be dependent; it is making progress to be dependent; you will still be loved even if you have need; it's marvelous to have mastered your independence but your basic education in dependence is lacking.

The N-A therapist may further state to the patient, "We're going to back up to that point, within our relationship, where you can be dependent upon me, so that you can ask me questions about yourself, instead of me asking you questions about yourself." There is *no one* who is less confident about his or her life than that anorexic patient who walks into the office. There is nothing wrong with making that clear in a supportive way. However, this produces dilemmas: Because we have to invite extraordinary attachments, we also have to shape and manipulate those extraordinary attachments.

Management of the nurturant-authoritative relationship is a balancing act between fostering dependence and setting limits on that dependence. Such a balance is well struck when, for example, at the end of a session, the therapist can firmly and comfortably indicate: "I'm going to take care of you within our therapeutic relationship . . . but our time is up, and you have to leave now. Your appointment is over."

Once we have become masters of inviting attachment, nurturance, and also controlling nurturance, we act as models. At this point we may say (usually after several months), "I will tell you what you should weigh, and I will tell you when you weigh enough. I am telling you now that you should be gaining weight. Someday I will be telling you that you should no longer be gaining weight. I am telling you now, too, that you may become attached to me within boundaries and I will, at the end of our session, tell you that that stops."

Whether it is in the individual session or throughout the entire therapy, what the therapist is doing is helping this patient understand flexibility. He/she is continuously moving back and forth, acting nurturant sometimes, being authoritative at other times. Later on in the therapy (after six months, a year or more, depending upon the severity of the deficits that the patient presents), the therapist will then begin to allow the patient to "grow up" within therapy, when she will be allowed to do some of that interpretive work. Then the patient will be offered her autonomy within therapy, the same way a parent gradually offers a growing child freedoms that come with responsibility and maturity. Ultimately, this is a reparenting model.

The therapist is telescoping a developmental relationship, regressing the patient, and then gradually offering her more mature behavior and a more mature relationship with the therapist. When she behaves obsessively and is slapping her thighs or hitting her head or saying that she is too fat, then it is necessary to revert to a nurturant-authoritative posture. When she is calm and able to reflect on her life, insight therapy is possible. But often, in mid-sentence, the therapist will have to switch because the patient will start to obsess. There is a very complex set of behavior choices we have. And there are so many choices to make that I think it takes most of us years to build up a repertoire of nurturant and authoritative statements that patients can hear. Once we allow ourselves as therapists to do that, though, it becomes easier. For those of us who are also parents, we truly have an advantage, because we have been nurturant with our young children.

MEDICAL ISSUES

Beyond all these choices the therapist has to make, there are additional responsibilities. The anorexic patient has a dangerous physical disorder as well. Therefore, it is essential for the therapist to work with a pediatrician or internist. Sometimes it may be necessary to tell the patient: "I'm afraid it's apparent that you cannot stop losing weight and I'm going to have to hospitalize you. I'm calling up the doctor and we're going to get a bed for you. I will come and visit you and we will do therapy in the hospital. And we may do something like hook you up to a machine that will intravenously feed you 2,000 calories a day, which will scare you very much, and we'll talk about that fright. It is not an assault on you; it is not punishment for failure. It's a rescue."

Now this is a difficult task for the therapist. I remember having my fears about it when first treating patients with this approach. So the therapist needs to be able to put the trauma of hospitalization in its true perspective — that is, as a temporary assistance and protection of the patient. However, her weight will be increased and she will be sent home. She may lose two to five pounds upon discharge, maybe more. So it is important for the therapist to see that the procedure is only a temporary life-saver and to communicate this fact to both the patient and her family. Hospitalization for the patient who does not trust anyone and is now having to turn herself over to those people who will change her most precious aspect — her weight — is scary and often overwhelming. The therapist should be reassuring in manner when having to say "I'm going to put you in the hospital and you'll be all right. And maybe the hospital will make it easier for you to think more clearly and be more comfortable, and I will help you see yourself and accept a normal body. And should that fail at first, we'll have to try again and again."

When we are dealing with true anorexia nervosa, it is most dangerous to treat it alone. We must have the assistance of medicine, understand the medical treatment, learn about hospitals, be knowledgeable about nutrition. We should know, for example, that it takes 3500 calories to gain a pound above maintenance and the same amount to lose it. Via such knowledge comes confidence, and through the projection of confidence we may engage the trust of the frightened, helpless people coming to us for treatment. It is through the creative balancing of nurturance and authoritativeness that this healing trust is best elicited.

REFERENCES

Levenkron, S. (1978). *The best little girl in the world.* Chicago: Contemporary Books.
Levenkron, S. (1982). *Treating and overcoming anorexia nervosa.* New York: Charles Scribners.

Chapter 14

Bulimarexia: Intervention Strategies and Outcome Considerations

William C. White, Jr.

This chapter is written primarily for the professional. It is intended as a brief synopsis of the work we have undertaken during the past eight years with hundreds of women who characteristically consume inordinate quantities of food over short intervals of time and later rid themselves of the dreaded calories via self-induced vomiting, laxatives, or extreme fasting.*

Throughout the course of our applied clinical research and treatment of the bulimarexic, we have encouraged professionals interested in our work to join us directly in the treatment process. To date, nearly 100 therapists (i.e., psychologists, social workers, physicians, nutritionists, and nurses) have participated in our treatment workshops throughout the U.S. Some were bulimarexic, most were not. As has been the case with our bulimarexic clientele, approximately 70% of these therapists have maintained contact with us over the years offering valuable criticism and insight which has enabled us to enhance the impact of therapy. Many of these clients and therapists have become sources of referral for women who might otherwise have been unable to locate a competent, well-informed colleague or professional. Their feedback has allowed us to troubleshoot our treatment program in much the same way as we conduct therapy with bulimarexics. Furthermore, we have borrowed from the therapies of Adler, Bandura, Berne, Ellis, Glasser, and Perls in the formulation of our treatment program and would like to acknowledge their contributions from the outset.

---

*The reader should consult our book (Boskind-White & White, 1983) for a more complete treatment of family dynamics, socialization rituals, etiological considerations and physiological implications relevant to this syndrome which we term *bulimarexia*.

EARLY FORMULATIONS

Back in 1976, when first confronted by women who binged and purged, we were unsure of how to proceed. Literature was essentially non-existent. In fact, DSM II defined *bulimia* in such a myopic fashion that women who characteristically binged and purged were classified as victims of anorexia nervosa. The resultant fear of hospitalization, the dire prognosis, and the stigma of a severe mental illness helped to negate honest confrontation of this pervasive problem for many years.

The bulimarexic's insistence upon secrecy no doubt led to our first treatment error. We agreed to honor and thereby reinforce this extraordinary commitment to secrecy by initially working with bulimarexics on a one-to-one basis. During this first year, work was slow and devoid of success experiences even among the most committed clients. Many of our clients had experienced a similar approach prior to reaching out to us. Most had found the obsessive pursuit of "why" and the primary focus upon etiologic-historic antecedents fascinating, yet continued to intensify their binge-purge ritual. Disenchantment soon led to missed appointments and we began to realize that these women needed a more compelling approach, at least initially, if they were to be part of the rehabilitative effort. At this point we decided to bring together those women who had sought our support in order to facilitate discussion and critique our initial treatment attempts. This first six-hour marathon ultimately led to our current mode of treating the bulimarexic.

This first group interacted with minimum facilitation. The sense of relief at discovering others consumed by the same ritualistic preoccupation cannot be overestimated. We were, however, fortunate in that our sample was diverse. Some of the women had just begun whereas others had been binge-purging for years. Some had made strides that others felt were next to impossible to attain. Still others had been binge-free for months only to succumb to stress and then resort, out of fear and desperation, to binging and purging once more. All were within expectation norms regarding their weight, so that models of perfection and beauty were immediately apparent. Nevertheless, even the most attractive were totally dissatisfied with their weight and bodily proportions!

Women agreed to meet weekly to help us formulate a more effective program. As might be anticipated, we began by looking for commonalities. We soon discovered that all of them were obsessed with their bodies yet maintained distorted body images despite honest feedback from significant others. Furthermore, they were perfectionistic, "good girls" who wanted desperately to please everyone. Finally, they chose to isolate and insulate themselves from major sources of stress by binging. How, when, where, and what they did seemed contingent upon situational events and prior socialization histories (Boskind-White & White, 1983). Such observations were not drawn from pilot groups exclusively. However, these early group experiences, coupled with the plethora of mail we were receiving daily, served to generate many hypotheses which were later confirmed or disconfirmed via questionnaires and direct therapy with scores of bulimarexics who reached out for referral and treatment (Boskind-Lodahl & White, 1978; White & Boskind-White, 1981).

Despite these commonalities, as psychologists we were equally impressed with the dramatic differences among our clientele. In fact, it is these nuances that dictate how a particular client is most effectively treated. For example, many co-eds are in control of their home situation so that binging and purging are rarely a problem over breaks. However, an equal number of bulimarexics are fine during school only to return to the rigors of home life and succumb to violent binge-purge rituals. Different antecedents in different situations under a variety of conditions serve to initiate and maintain binging. It is the task of therapy to help the client recognize and comprehend these seemingly complex behavioral patterns in order to help her fortify herself consistently in the face of stress. Success experiences are therefore crucial. This is particularly true in the case of the bulimarexic because she is, above all, an achiever. She has been reinforced for her many successes most of her life. Capitalizing upon her desire to succeed while helping to identify major precursors so that she can ultimately prevent binging represents a means of bolstering her self-concept and offering her opportunities to grow.

With time and experience we began to realize that bulimarexics are outcome-oriented. Therapy must transcend this shortsightedness by offering the bulimarexic the opportunity to become more process-oriented. It is the present that is the appropriate arena, not the past or the future. The essence of treatment involves developing effective, preventive strategies for the bulimarexic's current, day-to-day problems. This is most easily accomplished in a group context involving others with comparable problems. More often than we might realize, essential strategies which herald major breakthroughs are gleaned from interactions between group members within and outside of the group, either directly or vicariously. Furthermore, the group reinforces gregariousness rather than isolation. By providing innumerable opportunities for direct practice and vicarious learning, risk-taking within the supportive atmosphere of the group is enhanced. The development of alternative coping strategies in a wide variety of difficult situations often occurs with time and consistent group feedback.

With the advent of feminism, women have learned to support each other in their continuing struggle for equality. Group work capitalizes upon this obvious asset. It is, however, the therapist's responsibility to insure that a support network is generated and maintained during and *after* treatment. Our files abound with letters attesting to the prognostic significance of this support network. Equally important is the obvious fact that *showing beats telling*. The group should serve as a forum for honest communication, risk-taking, active participation and, most important, it must offer each participant ample opportunity for success experiences. Lest it become unrealistic, however, each member must also *learn to fail*, for this is a major stumbling block for the bulimarexic. To commit the slightest error is unacceptable to the perfectionist. Thus, learning to profit from inevitable mistakes, to troubleshoot specific aspects of her day without resorting to that premature, sabotage maneuver—the binge—is the ultimate goal of our group work. Let us now examine the process by which this goal has been attained by scores of women.

TREATMENT CONSIDERATIONS

Client Selection

In our experience, bulimarexics work best with other bulimarexics. In fact, many even object to the inclusion of therapists-in-training. We are, however, committed to such a teaching paradigm and have found the vast majority of bulimarexics receptive once the logic behind our learning modality is clear to them.

In our experience, the anorexic as well as the obese woman finds it exceedingly difficult to identify with the bulimarexic and vice versa. The anorexic who, in the face of stress, moves away from food, often cannot comprehend extreme food binging under such anxiety-provoking circumstances. Furthermore, her apathetic, irritable, and exceedingly angry response style is the antithesis of the bulimarexic's people-pleasing role orientation. On the other hand, the obese woman embodies both the anorexic's and the bulimarexic's greatest fear. The obese woman often envies her seemingly perfect sisters to the detriment of treatment. We have found that such "mixed groups" do not often remain together for very long.

Group Composition

As to optimal size of a group, we have found that a female-male co-therapist team can handle from eight to 10 appropriately selected bulimarexics comfortably. As we tend to facilitate interaction, homework, and role-playing within and outside of the group, an even number lends itself to pairing. Risk-taking opportunities are thereby enhanced and intimacy often develops. Nevertheless, we have worked effectively with as few as two and as many as 14 bulimarexics in a group.

Women of all ages, occupations, and educational levels may work together effectively in a group; however, these variables can subtract from the group experience when they become central. Care must be taken, for example, that participants do not attribute their tendencies to avoid involvement to their inability to identify with older or less educated group members. Such issues must be introduced and processed *prior* to the initiation of the group whenever possible to identify and avoid reluctance to participate. At this point many women admit that they would prefer individualized treatment. If this commitment is strong, they may be referred to colleagues who prefer to work on a one-to-one basis. We continue to work individually with such clients despite our commitment to group work primarily because we have found most of them eager to join a group at a later point.

There are at least three additional considerations relevant to group selection and composition. These include the clients' level of motivation, discipline, and willingness to take risks by attempting new strategies. By virtue of their socialization histories and recent media coverage, most bulimarexics are strong, well-informed women who are aware of the dangers of this syndrome. As a result, most are motivated to change. Those who would rather "fight than switch" are, however, often toxic in a group context; they represent a small contingent of "professional patients" who are rarely amenable to group therapy aimed at attenuating and ultimately eliminating binge-purge behavior. Such clients are perhaps better treated on a one-to-one basis. In our experience they must somehow be convinced that viable alternatives to binging exist *for them*.

With regard to discipline, it is somewhat ironic that most bulimarexics were and usually still are quite conscientious, controlled, and orderly. The problem is that such behavior is too concentrated and intense. It is as if the child within them has no avenue for expression except by binging and purging. Thus, we propose that they distribute this valuable asset more efficiently. By borrowing energy from daily activities which have become so habitual as to require very little discipline and applying it to activities related to food, the client is often capable of sustaining herself under considerable pressure. Most bulimarexics are willing to attempt this redistribution, particularly when they realize that they may be free to engage in more fulfilling, less destructive behaviors.

This leads us to the third and most relevant consideration: the willingness to develop new responses in situations that have consistently led to binging. It is our thesis that most women binge when they feel they have no alternative. Everything they have tried has ultimately failed to eliminate bulimarexia. However, they are hunting an insatiable beast with a BB gun! There is no single behavior which will consistently displace binging because it is such a well-entrenched *habit*. What will be necessary is a variety of alternative, high-valence behaviors which the bulimarexic learns to repeatedly engage in over time. Only then will she maintain control over this pervasive habit. Thus, the bulimarexic who engages in this process, first in the semi-controlled atmosphere of the group and later on a daily basis, is most likely to succeed.

Short-Term Group Format

Our commitment to a heterosexual, co-therapist team approach has received extensive consideration elsewhere (Boskind-White & White, 1983). Suffice it to say that the bulimarexic often transfers power to the men in her life. In fact, one of the few things that temporarily yet consistently curtail binging for most bulimarexics is a relationship with a man. Learning to cope with males is therefore critical and can be facilitated via interaction within a group when a male co-therapist who is attuned to the interpersonal dynamics of the bulimarexic is available. Even more important is the obvious need for feminist consciousness-raising. A significant part of every group we have run in the past five years involves an all-woman's component which emphasizes role redefinition, participant modeling, and behavioral rehearsal (White & Boskind-White, 1984). We are committed to such a treatment paradigm primarily because both aspects have been spontaneously cited as prognostically relevant by over 85% of those women whom we have treated to date.

Because our initial work involved women attending Cornell University, short-term therapy was undertaken. Our groups met for an hour and a half weekly during a semester. Thus, treatment consisted of from 15 to 20 hours of direct therapy. We have since found 15 to 20 hours of intensive treatment to be sufficient with older, more diverse groups of women (White & Boskind-White, 1981), where the goal is learning to ameliorate and ultimately eliminate binging and purging. Participants are always encouraged to spend time with one another outside the group engaging in specific "homework" which was generated during formal group sessions. Eating meals and spending time together afterwards in order to practice and devise new strategies to cope with old situations are particularly therapeutic. These interactions are often mutually beneficial in that they serve to show participants that they are capable of exerting control over their eating behavior with a minimum of support. Furthermore, resultant scenarios typically serve as focal points for group processing. The process as well as the outcome of such interactions is more apparent to all concerned under these circumstances. In addition, base rates against which to judge progress are more easily monitored when explicit contracts are entered into and later evaluated by participants. Finally, boredom is a major precursor to binging for most bulimarexics, so that efficient time management is an integral part of the bulimarexic's homework.

Effective therapy must therefore involve work outside the group. In fact, that work is most beneficial primarily because it is accomplished under conditions more commensurate with the real world and it requires *action in the present.* Even the chronic bulimarexic has proven herself capable of eliminating binging from her repertoire after short-term therapy because that is precisely what was addressed during the course of brief treatment. Myths are exposed, belief systems are modified, specific strategies are adopted, tested, and reapplied so that, in the final analysis, the client is fortified and more competent. It is not a matter of whether the bulimarexic can actualize her treatment goal but when and how she will choose to do so.

GROUP PROCESSES

Rewriting the Script

We typically begin each new group by asking each participant to explore what is initiating and maintaining her binge-purge response pattern. As a result, a number of irrational premises emerge and are processed by all concerned. Such basic misconceptions as the following are pathognomonic of the syndrome:

- Bulimarexia is a disease which must be cured;
- Bulimarexia has required years to develop and will therefore take years to cure;
- Only I can stop binging and purging, others can do little to help me;
- Bulimarexics are powerless in the face of food;
- Life will be great when I stop binging;
- I must know *why* I binge in order to stop.

Most therapists who subscribe to a broadly conceived behavioral/cognitive model can facilitate the expression and expulsion of these irrational beliefs with little difficulty. It is of paramount importance, however, that this be undertaken immediately and effectively or such unfinished business will constantly interfere with group process (Boskind-White & White, 1983).

The bulimarexic often believes that if she commits herself to new alternatives and fails, she will be in worse shape than if she had binged and purged. Since showing is more therapeutic than telling, the group can become a forum for illustration. For example, many a bulimarexic has averted a binge by taking a hot bath while enjoying her favorite music without realizing that several earlier efforts had failed to subdue this urge to binge. During the next group session, upon reiterating this new strategy, she is reminded of her earlier failures and the important role they played in helping her to arrive at a successful solution. Such experiential work serves to demonstrate to the client and other group members that making a decision to try something new and failing is rarely catastrophic and often productive.

Risk-Taking

In this same context, bulimarexics often choose to avoid the discomfort inherent in risk-taking and instead engage in that old, familiar habit of binging in the face of challenge. Again, they must be shown that pain is a precursor to change and that without risk-taking, growth opportunities are radically curtailed. However, much of this pain is exaggerated and self-imposed because the bulimarexic typically lives in the past or the future. She must learn to *remain in the present* when confronted by major stressors. By asking "What tense am I in?" many a bulimarexic has felt a remarkable sense of control upon realizing that she was rehearsing for future tragedy or condemning herself for past transgressions which she has not engaged in for years. It is our thesis that binging is an *avoidance behavior* and, as such, offers an opportunity to retreat from the rigors of life as they confront the bulimarexic in the here and now. By identifying herself within the context of her present situation, she is at least in a position to administer and even elicit strokes for so doing. With the help of the group she may then learn more effective strategies to overcome her present difficulties. Furthermore, such strategies often generalize to similar stressful situations, thereby enhancing her risk-taking repertoire and ultimately her self-concept.

Nevertheless, such strides are not likely to occur until the client recognizes that her reliance upon words such as "can't," "never" and "forever" is incapacitating. Helping the client to acknowledge that "can't" means "won't" and that use of "never" and "forever" assures continual binging and purging is therefore of critical importance. These words are commitments to a bulimarexic lifestyle. Inherent in such statements as "I will never binge again" or "I will stop binging forever" is the commitment to continue binging upon making even the slightest error. These expectations are toxic and must therefore be eliminated from the bulimarexic's verbal repertoire (White & Boskind-White, 1984).

BEHAVIORAL CONTRACTING

Goal Setting

Once women have identified major destructive behaviors contingent upon their irrational belief systems, they are encouraged to articulate and implement new strategies designed to overcome these major stumbling blocks. It is at this point that the concept of goal contracting is introduced. These contracts must, however, be explicated in specific "who," "what," "when," and "where" behaviors. For example, it is not sufficient that a client agree to call another group member when the going gets rough. The contract must be far more explicit. With whom should she contract? What will she *attempt* before initiating such a call? When is it agreeable to make such a call? How is a potential partner to respond to such a call? All of these important questions should be processed *prior* to the initiation of contracts if success is to be maximized.

When this homework is accomplished during the group, many obvious fringe benefits ensue. For example, "people pleasers" often say "yes" when they really mean "no." If one woman reaches out to another only to find the latter in dire straits and therefore unavailable, she is immediately reminded of several important considerations. First, her friend, in being honest, provides a model which is antithetical to that "yes-person" whom both have come to recognize as deceptive. Second, *one* alternative to binging is rarely sufficient. The bulimarexic must therefore contract with at least two well-chosen friends. Finally, as is often the case under such circumstances, both parties profit by helping each other over hurdles which neither might have mastered alone. Clients soon recognize that one way of stimulating their own growth is to help someone they respect, particularly under mutually stressful circumstances. Unless such commitments are made and practiced, the prognosis is guarded because the bulimarexic *is* what she *does*, not what she thinks and feels.

ALTERNATIVE STRATEGIES

There are a number of strategies that we have found essential to the elimination of the binge-purge ritual. Fundamental among these is the fact that the bulimarexic must avoid being alone, particularly during vulnerable moments. Most of our clients either live alone or isolate themselves whenever they encounter discriminative stimuli associated with binging. Thus, family therapy, a valuable mode of intervention, is often not possible except with the young woman who must live at home for socioeconomic reasons. In those cases where clients are or could easily reside with family members, we have found family therapy beneficial. Regardless of the living situation, however, to be alone, particularly during critical periods, is dangerous.

Binging is much more difficult when there is very little available to consume. Granted, most bulimarexics have a history of braving unbelievable odds when "consumed" by the urge to binge. As a result of therapy, however, it is now more difficult to deny the volition involved under these circumstances, so that many a bulimarexic has reported significant progress in the midst of such attempts at binging. Thus, at a minimum, those who are truly committed to alternative strategies will contract with significant others in order to avoid isolation at critical times and will get rid of the "food stash" which facilitates binging. These strategies, when adhered to relatively consistently, provide success experiences in situations where binging was considered inevitable.

The bulimarexic must also learn to constantly reward herself for approximations toward a particular goal if she is to replace rehearsing for tragedy (i.e., negativistic/pessimistic expectation) with a more productive, self-reinforcing response style. In the process the client often learns something even more valuable. By rewarding herself in the present, the bulimarexic's level of awareness is often heightened so that "mistakes" are more immediately identifiable and resolved, rather than neglected or accepted as inevitable. Such a coping strategy often elicits stroking from others, thereby further enhancing the bulimarexic's self-concept. These learning experiences, whether direct or vicarious, are often cited by former clients as turning points in therapy.

At this point in therapy, the well-educated client is asked to identify and then arrange major precursors to binging in a hierarchy. With the help of the group, each client then begins with her most difficult binge-precipitant and formulates at least two alternatives which she will attempt prior to resorting to a binge. These alternatives are explored by the group, thereby providing an arena for risk-taking, making overt errors, and experiencing reinforcement, albeit in a supportive milieu. Through the media of role-playing, participant modeling, and other group techniques (White & Boskind-White, 1984), trying out new strategies soon precedes and ultimately displaces binging for most group members. This is so primarily because effective strategies, although initially individualized and situation-specific, are also quite generalizable.

Following this learning paradigm, group members are encouraged to rehearse for tragedy in preparation for leave-taking. In order to make this as real as possible, the therapists interact minimally so that the group is left to its own resources. This technique has proven diagnostically and prognostically relevant. Women who perform well under these circumstances typically continue to learn and grow, ultimately overcoming their preoccupation with binging and purging. Those who falter significantly are much poorer prognostic risks. Nevertheless, with additional therapy and continued support from members of the group, they too prove capable of overcoming this insidious habit.

OUTCOME CONSIDERATIONS

In order to form a current composite description of the population of bulimarexics with whom we have worked and to assess changes in binge/purge practices, attitudes, lifestyle, and interpersonal relationships, we mailed a questionnaire to 206 bulimarexic women whom we had treated for a two-year period. These were mailed at different times in order to preclude possible invalidation of conclusions by the effects of one particular universal event (e.g., the holiday season, the beginning of the academic year).

Follow-up Questionnaire

Clients ranged in age from 17 to 42 and had been binging and purging for at least two years prior to the group. None of the women was clinically underweight, overweight, or in need of medical management when group therapy was initiated. A cover letter which accompanied each questionnaire stressed confidentiality and anonymity vis-à-vis the results and our hope that subjects would include any additional comments they felt were appropriate.

T-tests were used to assess significant changes in binging and purging frequencies, self-concept, and relationships with others, as well as significant differences between weight prior to group treatment and current weight and between current weight and (self-reported) ideal weight. The sign test (and its normal approximation) was used to test for significant changes in precursors to binging. The Bonferroni correction for multiple comparisons was applied where appropriate. Descriptive statistics were compiled to summarize and examine method of purging prior and subsequent to treatment, demographic data, family history variables, and type and duration of treatment received since our group. Verbal responses were analyzed to assess any changes in feelings associated with the actual act of binging or in number or type of leisure activities. Verbal responses were also examined to summarize perceptions regarding strengths and weaknesses of our treatment program as well as any subsequent treatment they might have received.*

Of the 206 women to whom questionnaires were mailed, 40 had relocated leaving no forwarding address and were, therefore, unavailable for comment. A total of 133 (80.1%) of the 166 women contacted responded to our questionnaire, including 26 who were interviewed during follow-up by telephone. While a response rate of 80.1% is exceptional in questionnaire studies of this type, we were disappointed that 19.9% of the women contacted chose not to respond to the questionnaire. If those women were, in any relevant way, different from those who did respond, this might constitute a threat to the validity of this study.

An additional limitation was the absence of a control group. We cannot therefore be certain whether reported changes were due to treatment or to some external, irrelevant event common to some or all of the women in our sample.

---

*The author wishes to express his gratitude to Amy S. Rubenstein for her assistance with methodology, design, and statistical analyses throughout this outcome research project.

Furthermore, positive changes could conceivably be attributable to regression to the mean since many of these women came for help when they were desperate. Thus any improvement might actually reflect a return from their lowest level of functioning to their usual or "mean" level of behavior or feeling state (and not a true treatment effect).

Finally, it should be noted that all data reported here are based upon respondents' self-reports, and, therefore, may not always represent completely accurate portrayals of true behaviors and measurements. With these limitations in mind, the results of our follow-up study were as follows.

Prior, current, and ideal weight. The respondents' weight prior to group treatment ranged from 67 to 180 pounds with an average of 122.4 pounds (see Table 1). Their current weights range from 92 to 170 pounds with an average of 123.0 pounds. The average current weight is not significantly different from the average weight prior to treatment ($t_{131} = .75$, $p = .454$). Self-stated ideal weights range from 90 to 150 pounds and average 116.8 pounds. This average is significantly less than the average actual current weight ($t_{131} = 9.62$, $p < .001$). Hence the women as a group have not decreased their weight significantly nor have they reached their ideal weights. Therefore, we can assume that any alterations in attitudes or behaviors are not simply the result of the long-awaited achievement of thinness.

In order to enhance and clarify the feedback from the self-report questionnaires, women were encouraged throughout the study to write at length regarding specific attitude and behavior changes they may have experienced. Although very few women attained their ideal weight (which was, typically, unrealistically slim), their anecdotal accounts on this dimension revealed a much more accepting and realistic appraisal of their bodies after therapy. In fact, 68% indicated that they no longer viewed a small weight gain (i.e., five to seven pounds) as catastrophic. Many spontaneously indicated that gaining weight was no longer the number one precipitant to binging. Furthermore,

Table 1
Prior, Current and Ideal Weight

	Mean	S.D.	Min.	Max.	N[1]
Weight prior to group	122.4	17.7	67.0	180.0	132
Current weight	123.0	15.2	92.0	170.0	132
(Self-reported) ideal weight (all reported in pounds)	116.8	11.8	90.0	150.0	132

[1]The total number of respondents was 133. In cases where one or more respondents did not respond to one or more questions, those respondents were included only in analyses of questions to which they did respond. Thus, the total N for the complete group does not always equal 133.

76% of the college students surveyed spontaneously indicated that before treatment they would consistently cut classes, hide out, and become social isolates during so-called "fat phases." In contrast, these women now report that although they weigh more than they would prefer, they view their weight gain as a challenge and respond by *doing* rather than *retreating*. In this same regard, 71% of the respondents surveyed indicated that they were pursuing a different kind of body ideal as evidenced by their regular involvement in aerobics and fitness programs.

Post-group binging and purging. Each woman's frequency of post-group binging and purging was assigned to one of five categories: 1) during the last month; 2) during the last six months; 3) during the last year; 4) since group treatment; or 5) none since group treatment (see Table 2). While only five (3.7%) of the women had not binged since the group, sixty-six (50%) had not binged at all during the last month. Nine (6.8%) of the women had not purged since the group, and 57 (42.9%) had not purged during the last month. In all further analyses involving binging and purging, "current" was defined as "during the last month."

Binge-purge frequencies. The average number of binges per month prior to treatment was 78.3 (see Table 3). The current average number is 14.1. This difference of 64.2 binges per month is stastistically significant ($t_{130} = 10.63$, $p < .001$). Likewise, the current average number of purges per month (11.8) is significantly less than the average number prior to treatment (78.7) ($t_{128} = 10.76$, $p < .001$). However, the distributions involved here are quite skewed (partially due to the large number of women who have not binged/purged at all during the last month). Therefore, statistics or significance tests involving means are not particularly meaningful. The changes in binging and purging frequencies can be seen, however, in the scatterplots of current frequencies plotted against prior frequencies.

Figure 1 shows the current number of binges per month as a function of

Table 2
Post-Group Binging and Purging

	Post-Group Binging N	(%)	Post-Group Purging N	(%)
During the last month	66	(50.0)	57	(42.9)
During the last six months	22	(16.7)	18	(13.5)
During the last year	22	(16.7)	27	(20.3)
Since the group	17	(12.9)	22	(16.5)
None since the group	5	(3.7)	9	(6.8)
	132	(100.0)	133	(100.0)

Table 3
Binging and Purging Frequencies

	Mean	S.D.	Min	Max	N
Binge frequency prior to group	78.3	72.3	2	390	131
Current binge frequency	14.1	27.6	0	150	133

	Mean	S.D.	Min	Max	N
Purge frequency prior to group	78.7	73.9	1	390	129
Current purge frequency	11.8	29.8	0	180	133

the number of binges per month prior to treatment. As evidenced by the multiple-case data points near the bottom of the graph, it is apparent that most of the women are now either not binging or binging very infrequently. This impact is clearly illustrated by Line 1 (slope = 1.0) which divides the women who have decreased their binge frequencies from those who have not. One hundred and eighteen (90.1%) of the women fall below Line 1, indicating that they are binging less frequently than before group treatment. Only 13 (9.9%), those falling on or above Line 1, have increased or maintained their binge frequencies.

In a similar manner, Line 2 (slope = ½) separates the women who are currently binging at less than half their previous rates. One hundred and nine (83.2%) fall into this category with 66 of them not having binged at all during the last month. Thus, more than 90% of the respondents have decreased their binge frequencies, and over 80% have decreased to less than half their previous rates.

Similarly, examination of Figure 2 reveals that 122 (94.6%) of the women fall below Line 1, indicating that they are currently purging less frequently than before group treatment. One hundred and fifteen (89.1%) women, those below Line 2, are currently purging less than half as often as before treatment. This group includes 76 women who have not purged at all during the last month. In summary, 50% of the respondents are not currently binging and 57.1% are no longer purging. Moreover, the majority of those who are still binging and/or purging have drastically reduced the frequencies of these behaviors.

Method of purging. The distributions of method of purging prior to group treatment and method of purging currently in use are shown in Table 4. For both the entire group previous to treatment and the group of women reporting purging during the last month, two methods—vomiting and a combination (primarily vomiting plus laxatives)—account for close to 90% of the total.

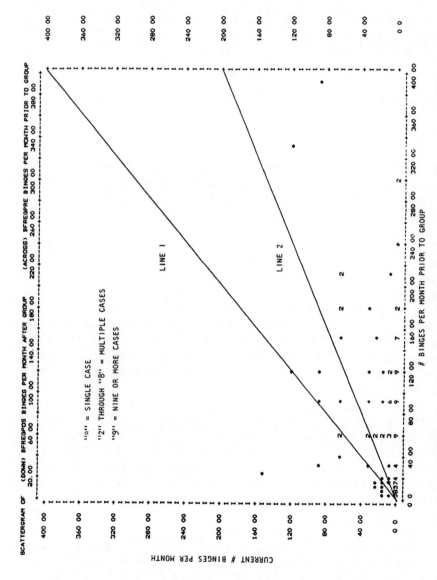

Figure 1. Binge frequency prior to group treatment vs. current binge frequency.

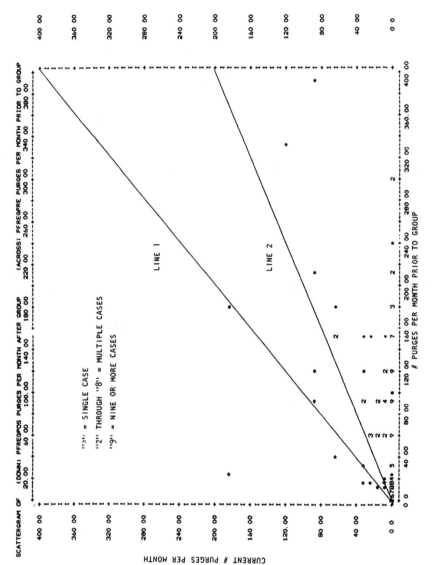

Figure 2. Purge frequency prior to group treatment vs. current purge frequency.

Table 4
Method of Purging

	# Reporting Method Prior to Group N	(%)	# Reporting Method Currently in Use N	(%)
Vomiting	66	(50.0)	35	(62.5)
Diuretics	1	(0.8)	0	(0.0)
Laxatives	5	(3.8)	1	(1.8)
Fasting	4	(3.0)	2	(3.5)
Other	2	(1.5)	3	(5.4)
Combination	54	(40.9)	15	(26.8)
	132	(100.0)	56	(100.0)

Two major changes in the distribution are the 13% increase in use of vomiting alone and the 14% decrease in combinations of two or more of the listed methods. This suggests the possibility that many women who were formerly vomiting and also using another method of purging have since given up that additional method. However, individual responses would have to be examined to test this hypothesis.

Precursors to binging. Table 5 shows the number of respondents citing each of several events or situations as likely precursors to a binge before group treatment and the number citing the events as currently leading to binges. For each of the specific events listed (i.e., excluding the category labeled "other"), the number of women citing the event as currently likely to cause a binge is significantly smaller than the number citing the event as a likely precursor prior to treatment ($p < .05$ for "interactions with children," $p < .001$ for all other specific events listed; all p-values were corrected for multiple comparisons within this group using a Bonferroni layering procedure). It should be noted, however, that these results are to be expected given the large number of women who are not currently binging.

When asked to describe their feelings prior to treatment, women consistently described themselves as anxious, depressed, lonely, angry, tired, or bored before resorting to binging and purging. At this point binging was obviously the number one response in their hierarchy when confronted by such feeling states. Most described binging as a way of anesthetizing themselves from such potentially painful experiences. On follow-up, however, respondents utilized a variety of strategies to curtail or prevent binging and purging. Top dog-underdog dialogues, reaching out to other group members, remaining in the present rather than preoccupying themselves with past and future considerations, administering self-strokes, cognitive restructuring, and look-

Table 5
Precursors to Binging

	Before Group N	(%)	Currently N	(%)
Parental interactions	86	(65.2)	27	(20.5)***
Interactions with husband/boyfriend	80	(60.6)	45	(34.1)***
Interactions with male peers	61	(46.2)	28	(21.2)***
Interactions with female peers	58	(43.9)	25	(18.9)***
Interactions with children	17	(12.9)	8	(6.1)*
Interactions with authority figures	73	(55.3)	31	(23.5)***
Other	56	(42.4)	47	(35.6)

*p<.05; **p<.01; ***p<.001
Note: All p-values were corrected for multiple comparisons within the group using a Bonferroni layering procedure.

ing at the bottom line (Boskind-White & White, 1983) were the most frequently cited alternatives. Furthermore, these particular strategies were consistently viewed as "crucial, essential, or necessary" by those who had significantly curtailed or eliminated binging from their repertoire.

Attitudes/relationships. All respondents were asked to describe any "significant" changes in their self-concepts and in their relationships with various significant others using a 7-point scale (1 = greatly worsened; 7 = greatly improved). The average ratings for the nine questions ranged from 4.9 to 5.8 (see Table 6). Each of these mean ratings is significantly greater than the "no change" rating of 4 (p<.001 for each question after correcting for multiple

Table 6
Attitudes/Relationships

	Mean	S.D.	Min	Max	N[1]
Feelings about self	5.8	1.1	1	7	131
Relationship with husband/boyfriend	5.1	1.6	1	7	99
Relationship with parents	5.3	1.1	2	7	126
Feelings about own body	5.2	1.2	1	7	130
Relationship with male peers	5.0	1.0	2	7	127
Relationship with female peers	5.2	1.1	3	7	128
Relationship with children	5.4	1.3	4	7	29
Relationship with authority figures	5.0	1.0	2	7	123
Feelings regarding gaining weight	4.9	1.1	1	7	130

[1]Ns vary because some questions were irrelevant for some women.

comparisons within this group using a Bonferroni layering procedure). Thus, as a group, these women perceive their attitudes and relationships in every one of the listed areas as having improved since their group treatment.

Family history. The number of women citing each of the family history variables is shown in Table 7. A primary goal of this section of the questionnaire was to explore the possibility that any of the events listed may have played a major role in the onset of bulimarexia. That is, we were interested in whether or not these women are more likely than the general population to have experienced these events. At first glance, most of the percentages reported appear relatively small. However, in order to better examine this question we must first obtain base rates for each question from the general population and then compare our data to these base rates.

Unfortunately, the collection of accurate data in this area is not simple. Different individuals as well as different groups of people have differing personal definitions of certain terms. What one group considers alcoholism, another may consider social drinking. Likewise, responses to questions regarding obesity may be influenced by societal norms as well as by distorted memories or distorted body image.

The "traumatic loss" question appears to be particularly problematic in this regard. While many women reported having experienced a "traumatic loss," the descriptions of these losses were quite diverse. It seems likely that, having been asked to search their memories for instances of traumatic loss, these women (or anyone answering this question) may have categorized some events as traumatic that might otherwise not have been viewed as such. Furthermore, the women in our study may also have a "motivation bias" to list instances of traumatic loss as a means of accounting for their eating problems.

A partial solution to both of these problems would be to pose this same question to a sample from the general population, asking both treatment and control groups for details of their "losses." "Blind" judges could then use a

Table 7
Family History

	N	(%)
Obese as a child	11	(8.3)
Mother obese	14	(10.5)
Father obese	11	(8.3)
Alcoholism in family	31	(23.3)
Incest in family	6	(4.5)
Traumatic loss	41	(30.8)

priori definitions of "traumatic loss" as criteria to eliminate questionable responses from both groups, leaving comparable data. Thus it is clear that, although it is not easy to collect accurate and comparable data in these areas, population base rates must be obtained before we can test conclusively for any associations between these family history variables and the occurrence of bulimarexia.

Strengths/weaknesses of the group. Respondents consistently cited the following aspects of the workshop as most beneficial:

1) Demystifying bulimarexia—Most felt that adherence to at least three of the major myths surrounding this pervasive habit (Boskind-White & White, 1983) had seriously impaired their progress prior to the group.
2) Interactions with other bulimarexics—Although therapy was typically 15 to 20 hours in duration, the amount of time these women spent interacting with one another was closer to 48 hours. The support network that was generated as a result of this group involvement was consistently cited as therapeutic. Eighty-two percent of our respondents remain in at least monthly contact with one other group member. Of this 82%, 69% either curtailed or eliminated the binge/purge ritual. The remaining 18% reported little or no progress in this regard.
3) Identifying precursors and adopting new strategies in old situations—Women not only reported this as extremely helpful but found it quite enjoyable. Such behavior rehearsal represented a large part of the "homework" undertaken outside the group.
4) Pain as a precursor to change—Most group members readily admitted to unwittingly avoiding challenge, risk-taking, and similar potentially painful experiences. Thus, they consistently indicated that feminist consciousness-raising and experiential exercises designed to enhance their risk-taking strategies served them well on a daily basis.

Although we encouraged group members to remain in touch and give us feedback regarding their difficulties and progress, many of them felt that we should have been more aggressive in this regard. Thus, despite the fact that almost 70% of the women with whom we have worked have written or called at least once subsequent to treatment, we are convinced that more structured follow-up would have been valuable. In fact, 97% felt that "booster treatment" would have been a worthwhile adjunct to our treatment program. Most felt that a one-year treatment follow-up with women who had already undergone the workshop experience would be quite valuable. We are therefore currently modifying our treatment program to include an opportunity for such a follow-up experience.

Follow-up considerations. Our approach to treatment began eight years ago and has grown significantly in response to the increasing numbers of women who reach out to us as sources of referral and treatment. Since these women come from all over the United States and Canada, logistical, financial, and interpersonal considerations impact the way in which we must work. Our workshop format at Cornell University is typically conducted over a semester and involves from 15 to 20, one-and-a-half hour weekly group sessions. However, many of our clients must leave families and work responsibilities and travel long distances in order to work with us. As a result, we have developed the massed, psychoeducational treatment format (Boskind-White & White, 1983).

This workshop format involves 15 to 20 hours of therapy over an intensive three-day period. These workshops were, from the outset, designed as psychoeducational, strategic-planning experiences for bulimarexics and the scores of therapists who wished to experience our work directly. They were never considered to be definitive treatment programs. Our primary goal was to share what we had gleaned from the scores of women with whom we had worked. Their effective strategies became the focal point of these treatment workshops. Goal-contracting was individualized and specific but binging and purging were always the primary issue addressed. We were indeed pleased to learn, therefore, that 68% of the women with whom we worked sought further therapy. Of these clients, 69% returned to their original therapists and reported significant progress while 86% of those who changed therapists reported progress in curtailing binging.

Finally, there was a small contingent of women (12%) who were quite negative regarding the group experience, as well as the therapy they received thereafter. In general, they were older (mean age of 36), had been bulimarexic for more than eight years, had been binging and purging daily, and were chronically depressed. All had been involved in long-term therapy (two years or more) prior to the workshop and 70% had been hospitalized at least once. Furthermore, all of these women had severe relationship problems with husbands and boyfriends and had made little progress in the development of intimacy. Such women did not appear to be appropriate candidates for the group. All were referred to therapists who were particularly good at working with the chronic depressive.

In conclusion, our data clearly indicate that the "cold-turkey approach" of giving up the binge/purge ritual abruptly is rare. Rather, reducing binge/purge practices in a gradual manner, while at the same time enchancing coping strategies, seems much more representative of the contingent of women surveyed. Unlike the classic addictive behavioral pattern, however, most women indicated that they were able to stop themselves in the middle of a binge, while others wrote that the amount of food consumed during a binge was considerably less than what they had consumed previously. More important, attitudes about the binge/purge seem to have undergone significant modification when viewed as opportunities to *reevaluate* and *learn*. It would therefore appear that, although many women made significant progress over time, most of them feel the need for ongoing therapy or, at the minimum, regular booster sessions aimed at enhancing coping strategies and dealing with new problems which often arise as one becomes stronger and therefore more actively involved in the process of living.

Until we address those deeper problems of society (see Chapter 6) that have spawned bulimarexia, most women will continue to obsess about their bodies. No matter how fortified a woman might be, as long as she continues to endorse and emulate the unrealistic and unhealthy models of womanhood with which the media continues to bombard her, she will not be free of this obsession. Rejection of such inappropriate models by refusing to conform to such rigid, restrictive role definitions therefore represents the most effective means of liberating women today. We can only hope that consciousness-raising, further research, and treatment will stimulate all of us to soundly reject such narrow and limited feminine role definitions.

REFERENCES

Boskind-Lodahl, M. B., & White, W. C. (October 1978). The definition and treatment of bulimarexia in college women—A pilot study. *Journal of American College Health Association, 27*(2), 84-96.

Boskind-White, M. B., & White, W. C. (1983). *Bulimarexia: The binge/purge cycle.* New York: W. W. Norton.

White, W. C., & Boskind-White, M. B. (1981). An experiential-behavioral approach to the treatment of bulimarexia. *Psychotherapy: Theory, Research and Practice, 18*(4), 501-507.

White, W. C., & Boskind-White, M. B. (1984). An experiential-behavioral treatment program for bulimarexic women. In R. C. Hawkins, W. J. Fremouw, & P. F. Clement (Eds.), *Binge eating: Theory, research and treatment.* New York: Springer.

Chapter 15

Therapeutic Dilemmas in the Treatment of Anorexia Nervosa: A Self-Psychological Perspective

Richard A. Geist

> *Looking for the fossilized, for something—persons and places thick and encrusted with final shape; instead there are many minnows wildly swimming, trembling, vigilant to escape the net.*
>
> *Elizabeth Hardwick*

To accompany an anorexic patient into her cachetic world of scattered memories is an arduous task. For the critical memories encountered as one begins this inward journey are not the usual ones—not those stored in the accessible reaches of the preconscious mind, nor even those hidden in the further purview of the unconscious. Initially, the memories which give form to the anorexic patient's life appear indelibly etched in the tissues of the body; they form a disconnected picture of the self which has become lost, as it were, in the interstices of cellular movement. Instead of using her memories as internal catalysts for the outward pursuit of precious ambitions and ideals, and thus achieving a sense of wholeness and vitality, the anorexic girl remains immured in her schoolgirl skin. She is bereft of appetizing pleasures, obsessively preoccupied with food, weight, and body, and inwardly driven to joyless, unrealistic perfection; thus, the therapist initially observes only isolated reminders of an enduring and cohesive self.

During the past century, the therapeutic schemas which have evolved to

---

The author would like to acknowledge the helpful suggestions of Dr. Anna Ornstein.

treat patients with anorexia nervosa represent a perplexing myriad of unconnected treatment modalities. There is no dearth of literature, for example, on the application of ECT, psychotropic drugs, pituitary implantation, administration of insulin, psychosurgery, various forms of forced feeding, psychoanalytic therapies, behavior modification, and family therapy (Barcai, 1977, Bruch, 1973; Green & Rau, 1974; Halmi, Powers, & Cunningham, 1975; Minuchin, Baker, Rosman, et al., 1975; Mitchel-Heggs, Kelly, & Richardson, 1976; Needleman & Waber, 1976; Thoma, 1967) to the treatment of anorexia nervosa. Such disparate approaches, coupled with the vociferous disagreements among their leading proponents, suggest that we have not developed a cohesive treatment focus around which clinical and theoretical thinking can crystalize. Rather, treatment recommendations seem to have their inception in the idiosyncratic blueprints of individual clinician's theoretical biases, personal responses, and countertransference reactions to starving adolescents. To use Anna Freud's (1971) phrase, the "essential unity" of a therapeutic approach still eludes us, despite a general agreement with Bruch's (1978) statement that "there are few conditions where treatment results are so closely linked to the pertinence of the therapeutic approach" (p. 121).

This chapter represents a search for the essential unity of individual therapeutic work with anorexic adolescents and young adults. It has as its theme not a review of the literature, of which there are many fine surveys (Cohler, 1977; Garfinkel & Garner, 1982; Levy, 1977; Waller, 1979), but a discussion of the therapeutic dilemmas inherent in the attempt to empathically seek out and rekindle the vestiges of the underdeveloped self through intensive psychotherapy. The purposes of such an effort are: 1) to understand anorexia as one major form of self-pathology in which there is a chronic disturbance in the empathic connectedness between parents and child; and 2) to demonstrate how the use of empathy as a methodological tool can lead to a cohesive treatment approach. I believe that it is the developmentally crucial empathy failures in the parent-child relationship—failures which prevent the internalization of psychic structure—as they are reproduced in the treatment situation that crystalize into the therapeutic dilemmas so often encountered during psychotherapy with these patients.

**EMPATHY AND THE NORMAL
DEVELOPMENT OF THE SELF**

The evolution of the child's cohesive self—his or her firm sense of wholeness, vitality, and self-esteem in the context of an independent feeling of unity over time and through space—requires that the child grow up in an empathically responsive environment. Such a milieu is one in which the parents, and others who perform structure-building selfobject* functions, are empathically available to mirror and echo the child's unique sense of perfection, exhibitionism, and vigor, and to offer themselves as idealizable models with whose calmness, omnipotence, and mature psychological organization the child is permitted to merge (Kohut, 1977). As Kohut has suggested:

> The child that is to survive psychologically is born into an empathic responsive human milieu, just as he is born into an atmosphere that contains an optimal amount of oxygen if he is to survive physically. His nascent self expects . . . an empathic environment to be in tune with his psychological need wishes with the same unquestioning certitude that the respiratory apparatus of the newborn may be said to expect oxygen to be contained in the surrounding atmosphere.(1977, p. 85).

Although phase-appropriate, empathic selfobject responses are most important for structure-building in the early parent-child relationship, the necessity for their continuing presence is felt throughout childhood and adolescence. For the empathic responsiveness contained in the parental mirroring and available idealized images are the external precursors which contribute to and foster development of the internal psychic structures of the self. In other words, empathy remains the guardian of the child's and adolescent's narcissistic equilibrium, a beacon which determines the quality, timing, and dosage of those selfobject functions (mirroring and idealization) that are necessary for growth and development. The resulting empathic connectedness promotes one of the most powerful bonds that exist between parent and child and, equally important, it serves as a baseline from which the unavoidable failures in parental empathy (i.e., the optimal frustrations) can foster internalization of those parental functions which lead to structure-building.

This process, which Kohut (1971) designates as transmuting internalization, is important for both developmental and therapeutic understanding. It allows us to conceptualize, for example,

> how the firm arm of the caretaker that calms the baby eventually becomes the child's capacity to calm himself; how the proud glow in the parents' eyes becomes the child's pride and pleasure in the assets and functioning of the self. (personal communication A. Ornstein, November 1981, cf. also A. Ornstein, 1981)

Such a process is easily observed through the image of the psychologically healthy three-year-old who falls and scrapes his knee on the driveway. In the

---

*A selfobject is a person (at times an idea, symbol, or thing) which or whom the child or adult experiences as a functional part of the self. The selfobject, through his or her mirroring, idealizing or partnering functions, provides those functions such as soothing, tension reducing and drive regulating mechanisms which have not yet been internalized as the child's own psychic structure, or which are needed to shore up the self structure.

absence of mother's direct presence (and assuming an ongoing empathic relationship), he begins to withdraw his investment in mother's immediate availability and begins a somewhat depersonalized internalization of one of her functions—in this case, a soothing function—which enables him to comfortably calm himself and resume playing. It is this process of transmuting internalization which promotes self-structures that enable youngsters to begin the lifelong process of caring for themselves physically and emotionally.

THE ANOREXIC PROCESS: FAILURES IN PARENTAL EMPATHY

To begin to comprehend how the anorexic patient's spindly presence contains a self which is severely defective in its soothing capacities necessitates an understanding of the patient's subjective history, the truth discerned through her own perceptions of reality. For empathic failures in a child's life are not evident from extrospective study; they are not easily recognizable from listening to parental histories, nor are they palpable through direct observational studies of child development. The essence of empathic failures is that they accumulate silently over time, and their effect on the individual child can only be appreciated from within that child's own experience. Thus a distillation of these patients' sentient narcissistic injuries can only be particularized via the therapist's empathic merger with the patient's present interpretations of her past actualities.

Without wishing to speciously elevate these patients' personal feelings to the level of objective happening, I would suggest that such use of empathy as a methodological tool for data-gathering and observation (P. Ornstein, 1979a), while not necessarily providing us with a metapsychological theory of anorexia nervosa, illuminates those intrapsychic themes which directly influence the treatment process. It is the elucidation of these themes to which we now turn our attention.

The Shattered Sense of Wholeness

In contradistinction to the child for whom parental touch, words, and gestures have led, via transmuting internalizations, to a cohesive self that allows for a feeling of wholeness, the anorexic patient reports a disturbance in the empathic connectedness with parents—a disturbance which precludes the selfobject functions from becoming internalized as psychic structures. Thus the patient who suffers from anorexia experiences herself as living in a milieu permeated by repetitive parental misunderstandings of her needs to be perceived in her totality. The coercive complaint, "I'm a person not an anorexic," embodies the essence of such perceived misunderstanding; it exists not only as a plaintive and reproachful projection of her own incapacity for meaningful relationships, but more important, the statement exists as a terse condensation of fragmented selfhood. If in treatment this need is recognized and interpreted, elaborations of the theme assume historical continuity. For example, Penny, a 20-year-old anorexic patient, recalled poignantly her adolescent attempts to dress up for special occasions—dates, academic affairs, and social gatherings. "It was hard to combine everything so it felt like me, and when I asked my mother how I looked she'd always find something wrong." Instead of the admiration, approval, and confirmation for which Penny yearned, her mother responded critically, isolating and negating a single element of her daughter's complete presence. "You'd look fine if it weren't for your hair; let me fix it," or "Yes, dear, you look nice, but that necklace ruins the whole thing. I'll get you another." Within the therapeutic space, patients relive a chronic history of such unempathic responses. In Penny's case her mother could not allow her daughter to weave makeup, jewelry, clothes, and hairstyle into a unique motif; rather, she splintered the synthesizing effort and then, in an attempt to reintegrate her daughter's wholeness, substituted a hairstyle and necklace of the mother's choosing. Only under this patchwork of imposed conditions could mother respond approvingly to the daughter she had "remade" in her own image.

Such interactions are reminiscent of Khan's (1979) description of the early mother-child relationship in patients with sexual perversions. Khan observes that "the child was treated by the mother as her thing creation rather than as an emergent growing person in his or her own right" (p. 12). Unlike mothers who foster perverse development by exhibiting the instinctual components of their children, anorexic patients experience their mothers as exploiting components of the self through continual failures in mirroring; that is, in failures to appreciate the daughter as a unique individual. The anorexic girl peers into the mirror of the mother and perceives not the reflection of her whole body self, but a prismatic image of isolated parts: Her stomach protrudes; her thighs are fat; her birthmark is too noticeable. When eating, the anorexic girl does not sit down to a whole meal—dinner; she dawdles before isolated pieces of meat, vegetables, potatoes, and their specific caloric content. Only when she allows mother to substitute the latter's own "thing creation" does she feel whole and alive, and then only by sacrificing her uniqueness.

How invasive and chronic such faulty mirroring can be was illuminated by a patient two years following the termination of a successful four-and-a-half year treatment. After receiving a low grade on a creatively written English paper in her first term at college, Laura telephoned, saying she was distressed and confused (a symptom which had previously expressed her inner fragmentation). "How do you know," she queried, "what I'm worth as a writer if he thinks it's a C paper and I think it's an A paper?" Following a brief interchange in which Laura decried her English teacher's recommendations for improving the paper, I reminded her of our previous discussions of her

A Self-Psychological Perspective

fragmented feelings and suggested that perhaps the combination of all her English papers and grades during the year might provide a more accurate index of her writing skills than an isolated fragment of a grade. "That's right," she replied, and the relief was audible in her voice, "it's just like my mother picking out little things she didn't like about me and trying to change them in her own image. I felt so hurt that I couldn't take the suggestions." What is perceived as a helpful suggestion from the observational vantage point is more often for the anorexic patient silently experienced as a hurtful, humiliating criticism of her developing resourcefulness and creativity as an emerging person.

The Subordination of Mirroring to Identification

When the anorexic patient has failed to internalize parental selfobject functions, and thus failed to have developed a sufficiently cohesive self, her defensive attempts to preserve her connectedness to her parents inhibits the normally balanced interplay between two deceptively distinct and necessary components of normal development: identification and mirroring.

Through identification the young girl, via incorporation, may begin to think, feel, or act as she perceives the mother or father to think, feel, or act. For example, the girl may begin to identify with her mother's femininity by incipiently imitating her clothing styles (in fact, many anorexic patients and their mothers share clothing). In contradistinction, however, mirroring involves the confirming, admiring activities of the parent in response to the girl's unique expression of her own way of dressing and her own expression of femininity (A. Ornstein, 1981). As Winnicott (1967) has emphasized in his description of the mirror role of the mother and family, " . . . each child derives benefit from being able to see herself in the attitude of the individual member or in the attitude of the family as a whole" (p. 118) Even more than Winnicott emphasized, mirroring involves an active responding to the unique aspects of the individual child. Only through such active confirmation can new structures form within the developing self—structures which guarantee its cohesiveness and protect its emerging uniqueness. Where a dearth of such mirroring exists,

> . . . the child very early on begins to sense that what the mother cathects and invests in is at once something very special in him and yet not him as a whole person. The child learns to tolerate this dissociation in his experience of self and gradually turns the mother into his accomplice in maintaining this special created object. (Khan, 1979, p.13)

In other words, identification without mirroring translates developmentally into a split-off sense of specialness combined with an excessive compliance, a collusive bond between mother and child which is reminiscent of what

Greenacre (1959) calls a focal symbiosis, a relationship in which there is a "pathological union of the child's special needs with the parents' special sensitivity" (p. 147). Within this collusive bond, compliance fosters subordination of the child's self to the subservient position of a narcissistic extension of the mother. The daughter perceives her mother as experiencing increasing difficulties mirroring any thoughts, feelings, or actions which differ from the mother's; and, *pari passu* we see mothers, whose daughters have anorexia, who increasingly need their daughters as a narcissistic extension of themselves in order to feel whole and alive. One of my patients dreamed that she was standing on a stage as a slave girl being sold to the highest bidder. While such a condensed image contained many meanings, one association was particularly revealing. Virginia stated, "I've always sold myself by being what they wanted me to be; when that happened, I lost everything; there was no me, no self left." The anorexic patient is not lacking in good enough mothering; she experiences a distortion of a very specific aspect of mothering—empathic mirroring. Such mirroring produces inner fragmentation and distorts her emerging self in a manner analogous to the child who gazes into a fun house mirror and receives a contorted misrepresentation of her own image.

The Development of Precocity

Defensive identification and compliance promote the substitution of precocious social and intellectual patterns of relating for the childish dependency so necessary to human development. In fact, the anorexic patient is typically described historically by her mother as "the best little girl in the family, mother's little helper," or "four going on 16." While most clinicians emphasize the intimate connection between such precocity and the development of a "false self" (Winnicott, 1958), we cannot overlook the fact that precocity in little girls is rarely limited to the premature development of intellectual and social skills. It also involves a pseudosexual advancement during their Oedipal years. The anorexic adolescent consistently recalls having been Daddy's favorite: memories of greeting father at the door (to the exclusion of mother); attending business dinners and other important social engagements as Daddy's date; cooking dinner and breakfast for him while mother sleeps. More important, the anorexic patient usually remembers her special connectedness with father, a relationship in which both acknowledged nonverbally the father's preference for his daughter in the context of their unwitting exclusion of mother.

Here we observe the integration of two developmental facts. First, the lack of mirroring by the mother vitiates the normal integration of exhibitionistic and grandiose fantasies; thus the secret Oedipal wish, the grandiose fantasy that father and daughter have an exclusive relationship which obviates mother's role, remains a psychologic actuality not subject to normal disappointment. Second, because the father at this stage of development fosters a uniquely exclusive relationship with his daughter, he provides (in an overstimulating manner) that echoing and mirroring for which the anorexic girl yearns. While not contributing to the progressive resolution of Oedipal conflicts, he does help his daughter build compensatory narcissistic structures (Kohut, 1977) which would otherwise be missing.* (It has been my experience that where fathers are unable to accomplish this task, we see borderline rather than narcissistic pathology.) For it is the exciting, stimulating relationship with the father which counteracts the fragmentation of the self. It is this very overstimulating relationship that serves as a "remedial stimulant" (Kohut, 1972) to the vitality, vigor, and uniqueness which the anorexic lacks in her self.

Such an overstimulating relationship, however, cannot continue following puberty; the guilt which exists in both father and daughter will, during adolescence, preclude the possibility of maintaining such stimulation in order to prevent fragmentation. It may, I believe, contribute to cessation of menses in anorexic girls previous to any significant weight loss, although we need to recognize that such amenorrhea is probably caused by a very complicated psychophysiological sequence of events.

Following the breakup of this intensified Oedipal drama, the anorexic adolescent seeks other forms of stimulation which preserve wholeness. For example, intense physical activity such as running and dancing can replace the eroticized father-daughter relationship and serve to maintain the integrity of the self. In touch with her body, she pursues this vital feeling of aliveness with a single-minded stamina of joyous ecstasy—still, however, without the self-regulating structure so necessary for taking care of herself.

Where activities such as running fail in their role as a remedial stimulant, the patient is once again threatened with the passive reexperiencing of the symptoms of fragmentation. In this situation youngsters frequently turn to the sexualization of their feelings as a defensive strategy. As Goldberg (1975) suggests,

> the passive experience of being overcome by painful affects . . . is handled by sexualizing the entire situation which can then be tolerated or mastered in this active, sexual manner. (p. 337)

As the anorexic girl describes her family eating patterns previous to the onset of her eating disorder, it is evident that mealtimes were perceived as devoid

---

*Gedo and Goldberg (1973) suggest that " . . . it becomes evident that a prerequisite for the resolution of the Oedipus complex is sufficient maturation along the paths of transformation of narcissism to permit the child to tolerate the mortification caused by the collapse of his phallic grandiosity."

of any empathic responsiveness. Patients describe an empty, depleted feeling at the dinner table coupled with heroic efforts to maintain contact with their families. How the precocious sexualization of eating can substitute for the missing relatedness at the dinner table becomes apparent through a clinical vignette.

Ginny came to her therapy session following a vacation weekend spent with friends of her family. She related her capacity to enjoy her meal without being preoccupied with caloric intake. That night, while the family slept, however, Ginny furtively consumed some ice cream from the freezer and then felt terribly guilty.

When I asked Ginny how she experienced this guilty feeling, she replied, "It was like breaking some taboo for which I'd be punished. It felt a little like when we were talking about sex." She then added, "I don't understand why I did it. It was such a nice meal. Everyone sat together and talked. Not like my family. In my house nobody ever ate together. Everyone just rushed around anxiously. You could never relate to anyone around food like in other families."

I told Ginny that the way she described taking the ice cream as a taboo made me wonder whether it felt sexually stimulating to her. "That's a weird question," she replied. "I've never told you this, but in junior high school when no one would relate to each other at dinner, I would sneak chocolate ice cream up to my room and mix it with all sorts of sweets, make it into soup and eat it. It was comforting to me because chocolate was always sexual."

I continued: " . . . As if the food excited you in place of the relationship; it helped you to feel alive again?"

Ginny said, "I always used to think at those times, if I had a boy friend here I wouldn't need this chocolate ice cream." She then went on to describe the one family holiday to which she looked forward. "Christmas," she said, "is the only one where we all sat down together. When I had them like that, food was food; it didn't need to be sexy."

Perhaps more than any theoretical statement, Ginny's description conveys how the disruption of the longed for empathic connection around mealtime threatened her with an empty depletion, a narcissistic insult which was defensively undone by sexualizing food and the eating process. Only as the therapeutic process mobilizes the internalization of structure can the patient tolerate the original painful and humiliating feelings without their precocious sexualization.

The Unavailability of Idealizable Images

Concurrent with specific failures in the mirroring process, the anorexic patient's retrospective perceptions suggest a chronic absence of parental availability as idealizable models with whose soothing, calming, omnipotent presence she would have been able to merge. Rather, she perceives her parents as having been intrusively panicky in response to anxiety signals.

For example, an anorexic adolescent attending college in a distant state telephoned her mother following an argument with a roommate. Anxious and upset, she told her mother about the petty quarrel, then added that she hated her dorm, her teachers, and her courses and that she intended to transfer schools. Instead of responding to her daughter with a calm and reassuring presence, a holding environment which contains the patient's anxiety, Mother interrupted saying, "Oh, wait till your father hears this; he'll be so upset. I just don't know what to do with you. Wait till I check my schedule and see when I can fly out and talk to the right people and straighten this out for you." The young woman perceives the parental reaction as chronically exacerbating her anxiety through the unwittingly communicated theme: You are helpless and need us to solve your problems.

The continual patterns of intrusive escalation of panic are experienced as an empathic failure in the protective shield (Khan, 1974) functioning of the parents (usually Mother) and thus as an impingement. As Khan (1974) and Kris (1975) have both demonstrated, chronic impingements disrupt " . . . the ego's subjective awareness and experience of itself as a coherent entity . . . " (Goldberg, 1973, p. 99). The primary defense used to cope with such disruption is disavowal, which

> involves a rift in the ego, an abandonment of its synthetic function. In one fragment of the personality behavior is based on the acknowledgement of the real state of affairs; in another on its disregard. (Goldberg, 1973, p. 99)

For the anorexic patient, the "splitting of the self in the service of defense" (Goldberg, 1973) has two important consequences. First, the real state of affairs is represented by the manner in which the anorexic patient treats herself. As in all real or libidinal losses, the child sustains a double identification. She identifies herself with the child who was treated unempathically, and she identifies herself with the unempathic adult. Therefore, she treats her split-off body self as she felt treated by her parents, e.g., she does not know how to care for herself (A. Freud, 1968). Unable to perceive her bodily needs—when she is hungry, when she is full, when she is tired, when she feels energetic— the anorexic girl possesses few soothing mechanisms; these products of transmuting internalizations remain fallow, potentially useful, but unused.

Galdston (1974) has accurately defined anorexia as a phobia of bodily pleasure. Expanding on his lucid discussion, I would suggest that the reason anorexic girls retreat from all pleasure involves the disparity between tantalizing satisfactions and a paucity of self-regulating structure capable of containing their appetites, for all those beatific and sensuous pleasures enjoyed by peers feel uncontrollable. As one patient suggested, "To enjoy myself would be like flying around a Maypole; I'd be terrified that I would eventually fly off into space." Thus the anorexic patient is not anchored in herself, but feels rigidly controlled by an intrusive environment.

If the manner in which the anorexic treats herself represents the real state of affairs, a narcissistic withdrawal and perfectionistic posture represent a disregard of reality. For the impingement experienced by the anorexic girl when parents react to anxiety signals by escalating panic leads not only to precocious development (James, 1960; Khan, 1974; Winnicott, 1958), but also to a particularly sentient narcissistic injury, a painful sense of felt hurt which is experienced intensely but not thought about. It is quickly disavowed and in its place occurs a narcissistic withdrawal, a personification of the "please Mother, I'd rather do it myself" slogan. The narcissistic injury leads to narcissistic rage, but instead of being directed at the mother (who cannot tolerate such expressions of emotion) it is used to lock the narcissistic retreat in place via perfection. As one patient said, "I not only can do it myself, I can do it perfectly so I certainly don't need you." Thus perfection, in the anorexic girl, substitutes for empathy and can only be relinquished when the patient is capable of empathizing with (soothing) herself.

PSYCHOTHERAPY

Inherent in therapeutic work with women with anorexia is a series of treatment difficulties which appear at first as a meaningless mosaic of unconnected problems. Resistance to the establishment of a therapeutic relationship, excessive compliance, perfectionism, omnipotence and narcissistic withdrawal, suicidal threat, and refusal to care for one's body all impede the therapist's efforts to rekindle those elements of the self which lie creatively dormant. Within the preceding contextual understanding of anorexia as a disturbance in the empathic connectedness between parent and child, however, the therapeutic dilemmas assume a unifying theme: the attempt to preserve the cohesiveness of the self while assiduously avoiding what is perceived as humiliating and unempathic responses leading to fragmentation.

> Empathy, as defined by Ornstein (1979b) and Schwaber, involves: the therapists's capacity to perceive and apprehend "how it feels to be the subject rather than the target of the patient's needs and demands . . . " (Schwaber, 1979). The crucial elements of this empathic vantage point are related to the observer's position inside the other person's psychic reality. . . . This also permits us to discriminate very sharply between various popular notions of what empathy is, such as kindness, acceptance, compassion, tact, friendliness, and sympathy— basic ingredients necessary for creating a proper average expectable climate for clinical work—and scientific empathy as vicarious introspection. In this latter sense empathy leads us to comprehend complex feelings and thoughts (needs,

A Self-Psychological Perspective

> wishes, conflicts, and fantasies, etc.) from the vantage point of the patient's own inner experience as contrasted with the vantage point of an external observer and that of a particular theory. (p. 99)

As the patient's attempts to defend her precariously established self-cohesion interface with the therapist's efforts to respond empathically, the therapeutic space becomes an arena which potentially facilitates or undermines the emergence of the anorexic patient's self-structure. The interwoven complexities of empathic relatedness and its failures determine the therapeutic dilemmas encountered during the treatment process.

Resistance

Bruch (1978) states that

> on principle, anorexic patients resist treatment. They feel that in extreme thinness they have found the perfect solution to their problem. . . . As a group they are manipulative and deceitful; anything goes in their effort to defeat a weight gaining program. (p. 137)

While I agree with Bruch that anorexic patients exhibit formidable resistance to treatment, experience suggests understandable reasons for such opposition, motives which transcend thinness as an all-consuming panacea. I have described previously how the anorexic's view of herself as mother's "thing creation" interferes with the consolidation of the self, how such out-of-tuneness is perceived as an impingement, an intrusion from which the patient defensively retreats. To the extent that the anorexic patient has experienced parenting as unempathic cumulative trauma, she will discern the therapist as a potentially traumatic "attacker of the integrity of the self" (Kohut, 1977). The manipulation and deceit observed in response to such a perception of the therapist are motivated neither out of negativism nor hostility; they reflect the unalloyed terror which accompanies a feared fragmentation of the self. As one patient stated, "I feel like a piece of mercury; if you drop me I'd break into so many pieces, no one would ever find them all."

In all the initial stages of therapy, then, one cannot overestimate the importance of establishing empathic contact by responding as subject rather than target of the patient's feelings, for such interaction allows the patient to feel understood. To respond as the subject of the patient's needs means that when she laments about the unfairness of the staff or her parents, we apprehend and explore how it feels to be so misunderstood, not how distorted are her perceptions; when she feels enraged at us, we explore with her those specifics of our behavior which made her feel so furious, not interpret the transference distortions of her anger; when she describes her power struggles with family and staff, we explore how it feels to experience the world as a constant battle for control, not delineate her provocative behavior. Toward the end of treatment one of my patients conveyed her appreciation of such empathy when she said,

> The first time I felt understood was when I came in and said I felt fat. You didn't tell me I didn't look fat, show me a mirror, or tell me I had to gain weight; you asked whether my whole self or just part of me felt fat.

Failure to respond empathically fosters intense resistance (often in the form of superficial compliance) in the patient and therapeutic exasperation in the therapist. It is just such frustrating impasses which promote punitive limit-setting and behavioral manipulation in the service of the therapist's need to effect change. How such ostensibly therapeutic efforts to coerce a patient to gain weight confirms a lack of wholeness and encourages the patient to eat her way out of therapy or the hospital without significant psychological change was illustrated by a patient through her associations to her hospital experience:

> ... That's just the way I felt in the hospital. I did what I had to do to get privileges, but it never felt like me. If you can't feel something as your own, it just has no meaning. I did what they said to get out of the hospital and then lost weight again. In the hospital I didn't know what I felt, so it felt all right to be or do what they said I should do or feel.

When I suggested that such compliance must have helped define who she was, she replied, "Yes, like when I was little, I did everything my mother wanted except I lost the real me in the process."

Behavioral manipulation of anorexic patients is by definition unempathic because it places the therapist in the position of target rather than subject of the patient's needs. Nowhere is the destructive use of behavioral principles more apparent than in the unwitting reinforcement of compliant behavior. For compliance in the anorexic patient—as in most narcissistic patients—represents an abortive attempt to substitute environmental directives, therapeutic interpretations, or parental wishes for the missing structure of the self (Schwaber, 1979). Such compliance, rather than being reinforced through any kind of token economy or intrusive interpretation, must be responded to in the same empathic manner described above. First, we must acknowledge the patient's attempts to comply with our wishes. Second, we must recognize with the patient that such compliance helps her to feel whole and alive because it provides self-definition. Third, we must explore with the patient her lifelong pattern of self-defining submission. Fourth, we must recognize the painful conflict inherent in compliance—how the patient wants to please in order to gain self-definition, while simultaneously resenting her compliance. And fifth, we must help the patient to understand the motivation for compliance — her intense fear of fragmentation and empty depletion when she fails to experience herself as whole. In my experience, such an empathic response to compliance as a resistance leads automatically to the patient's interest in rekindling the lost elements of the self.

Resistance in anorexic patients is too frequently explained as the patient projecting her unacceptable feelings onto the doctor and then attempting to avoid them by eluding the therapist (Cohler, 1977). We need to recognize that the patient's resistance emerges not only from "intrapsychic phenomena, but also . . . the unempathic responses of the therapist (P. Ornstein, 1979a). Whenever the patient experiences the therapist as an intruder into the integrity of the self, superficial compliance or active opposition to the treatment will remain the dominant theme of the psychotherapy. Only when the therapist demonstrates his/her understanding of this interpersonal aspect of resistance by allowing the progressive use of him/herself as an empathic selfobject which replaces the missing structure and functioning of the self can the patient begin to think of herself as an emerging person.

Internalization of Structure Through the Development of Soothing Mechanisms

Empathic understanding facilitates experiences of wholeness and vitality. These harbingers of narcissistic health regale the patient in teasings of aliveness at a time when she possesses very little experience of herself as the same person over time. Paradoxically, then, the empathic connectedness evokes complaints around the time pressures inherent in psychotherapy. For example, "I haven't got time for the real me to come out"; "Therapy isn't helping me fast enough"; "I'm not going to keep coming here for two (or three or four) more years." Such a discontinuous sense of oneself over time undermines the patient's understanding of growth — how the therapeutic process which leads from pathology to health can be a continuous one (Bach, 1975). If, however, the therapist tolerates the patient's complaints in a calm and empathic manner, she begins to merge with the therapist's soothing presence in an idealized transference. It is just this transference which heralds the patient's capacity for structure-building.

Following the establishment of an idealizing transference, the target of the patient's complaints begin to shift from therapist to mother (for parents are still typically responding to their daughter's fragmented self). Contrary to most psychotherapeutic training, it is important at this juncture for the therapist to sensitively explain to the patient her mother's dynamics. For such explanations, if couched in nonjudgmental terms, assist the anorexic 1) to understand how the mother's narcissistic equilibrium was contingent on her daughter's role as an appendage to her, and 2) to mitigate her guilt over felt responsibility for her mother's difficulties with empathic responsiveness. As the following example indicates, such explanations lead directly back to the experiential state of the patient.

Linda stormed into my office saying,

> I was so upset this weekend. I was depressed and hopeless. It felt like neither therapy nor anything else was helping. My parents were supposed to go away for the weekend and the more upset I got the more my mother tried to get me to come with them. Finally, when I refused, they cancelled the trip. I felt so furious, like I caused them to stay home. Why do they do that to me? Why? Can you tell me why?"

At this point I speculated to Linda that her mother needed her not to be depressed in order to experience herself as a good mother and that she probably would have felt too guilty to leave. Linda replied adamantly that she would have been okay. I agreed, by saying, "Yes, that's true, but she could only respond to a fragment of you, your depression; you must have felt like she couldn't see the healthy parts of you also." This comment brought forth a plethora of childhood memories concerning Mother's treatment of her as a "thing creation," followed by an insightful return to her own experiential state: "That's exactly what I do to myself, isn't it? I treat myself that way." I agreed, saying, "Yes, especially you treat your body the same way you felt treated by your mother – unempathically."

The anorexic's understanding of how she mothers herself critically directs her curiosity and attention to the process by which children learn to soothe and comfort themselves. Linda's attention concentrated on her lifelong inability to fall asleep at night without her parents', preferably her father's, presence. As we focused on her lack of soothing mechanisms and her fears of fragmentation when alone at night, Linda gradually began to internalize the therapist's therapeutic functions. Her illumination of this process was poignantly eloquent.

> I couldn't fall asleep last night, but I decided not to call my parents. Instead I began calling softly to myself, "mommy, mommy, mommy," and I began to cry and sob. I let myself cry and it was OK. It was weird, it was like putting a baby to bed only the baby was me; I was the adult and I was the baby.

I acknowledged that indeed she seemed able to soothe herself so that she didn't need outside help. Linda responded that she had never done that before and didn't know how to describe her feelings. I commented that presently she seemed alive and together. "Yes," she said, "it was like the whole feeling I have when I can get someone to actually hold me or like in here when your words help me feel together." Linda was then able to apprehend the importance of her ongoing reintegration process: "The child and the adult in me for the first time weren't living two separate lives."

The therapeutic mobilization of soothing mechanisms remains one of the paramount and pivotal occurrences in the treatment of anorexia nervosa. The developing capacity for self-comforting, or more accurately, for empathizing with the little girl in oneself, activates three developmental steps. First, self-comfort heals the "vertical split" (Kohut, 1971) which has been sustained by the persistent use of disavowal. Narcissistic insults no longer remain so humiliating because the anorexic girl now possesses a psychic structure which deflects their intensity. Rather than experiencing the symptoms of fragmentation in the presence of perceived criticism, she calms herself with the comforting reassurance that, for example, tomorrow will be a better day. Rather than assuming a narcissistically superior position, her moral righteousness and haughty denial of physical pleasure yield to empathic understanding. Empathy with oneself thus replaces the perfectionistic posture.*

Second, increasing cohesion of the self through the acquisition of self-soothing functions fosters reintegration of the split-off elements of mind and body, thus enabling the patient to slowly correct her distorted body image. For only as the body self becomes an integral part of the whole self can the anorexic patient harmonize bodily experiences and perceptual awareness into a coordinated and realistic body image. As Linda stated, following her realization that child and adult were no longer living separate lives, "for the first time I looked into the mirror and saw myself as skinny. I can't believe I've never seen myself that way before."

Third, as soothing mechanisms become internalized as psychic structure, we observe the subsidence of narcissistic rage and the concomitant need for omnipotent control over the selfobject environment. Originally such omnipotence is

> . . . indispensable because the maintenance of self-esteem—and indeed of the self—depends on the unconditional availability of the approving, mirroring functions of an admiring selfobject, or on the ever present opportunity for a merger with an idealized one. (Kohut, 1972, p. 386)

Similarly, rage is indispensable because in the absence of omnipotent control it promotes self-cohesion. As one patient said, "If I stop being angry, there'll

---

*We must as therapists recognize that those activities such as running, which serve as soothing mechanisms previous to the internalization of structure, will persist with their compulsive-addictive qualities until such structure is established. Within reasonable medical limits, they should not be curtailed.

be nothing left of me; my anger holds me together." With the development of a more cohesive self, however, there occurs a transition to that mature aggression which powers the healthy, self-assertive aspects of the personality. The following brief example captures the essence of this transition.

As Carol's rage at her parents for depriving her of numerous material objects reached a crescendo in one treatment hour, I asked whether she had ever considered the idea that her fury might be more related to her frustrated inability to force her parents to confirm that she was deserving of such items rather than to their depriving her of all those possessions. Carol left the hour without responding, but when she returned for her next session, she stated that, as a child, she remembered desperately wanting curtains for her room despite her parents' continual refusal to obtain them. When Carol moved out of her house, however, and a sibling appropriated the bedroom, curtains appeared on the windows. When I commented on the absence of rage in relating this memory, Carol stated,

> What made me remember it was the last few weeks I've been thinking that I really want curtains for my apartment. When you asked if I thought my anger was related to forcing my parents to value me, I realized I could go buy curtains for myself. When I feel I can give to myself and feel good, I don't get so angry with my parents.

Where narcissistic rage continues to exist and where the self remains fragmented, there is an ongoing risk of suicide; not active attempts to kill onself, but passive diffidence to life whenever the connection to the narcissistically perceived environment is disrupted. In this context, any attempts to determine when a patient may safely leave the hosptial should never depend on weight gain. Rather we must ask: 1) whether weight has been stabilized at a medically safe level; 2) whether a selfobject transference has been established with the therapist; and 3) whether there are clear indications that soothing mechanisms are becoming internalized. A positive response to these three questions suggests that the rekindling of dormant elements of the self has commenced and the patient is becoming capable of caring for herself.

The middle phase of therapy with anorexic patients is characterized by evidence that the therapist's empathy toward the patient's childhood self has permitted the internalization of soothing and tension-reducing mechanisms. The rage and omnipotence which frequently surface during this period can exhaust the patience of an already weary therapist, but when the therapist remains in an empathic position and the process succeeds, one observes an increasingly resilient self-structure developing in the patient. Although much turmoil remains, both patient and therapist experience enormous relief because the patient now possesses an ability to use the object, to place the therapist (and her parents) outside of her omnipotent control (Winnicott, 1971).

Transference and Its Interpretation

Loss of weight is the isolated element in anorexia which compels the environment to become important, that is, to respond to a part of the patient's self. The observation of diminishing body mass, as it percolates within the therapeutic space, focuses constant and unremitting attention on the patient's eating habits; for the nutritional patterns serve as a portentous reminder of the patient's inability to care for herself. Inherent in this symptom, however, are two contradictory messages. On the one hand, refusal to eat represents a tendency toward abortive self-cure as the patient defends her specious but indomitable belief that the body self can exist in vacuo despite the cumulative trauma which paralyzed the development of the self. On the other hand, the symptom serves as an idiom which communicates hope that the therapist will help her recover a cohesive self by responding to her whole person rather than the isolated function of eating. In such a therapeutic arena of contradictory messages the therapist's empathic capacities must inevitably be strained. As Schwaber (1979) states,

> The object's inability, for whatever reason, to serve as the needed selfobject supplying the missing structures or functions is experienced as a failure in empathy. . . . This may then result in a threat of fragmentation in the self. (p. 469)

At this juncture, when empathic connectedness between patient and therapist is broken, many therapists seem to panic and institute unwarranted and austere limit-setting interventions through intrusive interpretation, behavioral manipulation, active physical restraint, and forced feeding. While hospitalization, IV hyperalimentation, and restriction may at times be medically necessary, the active psychotherapeutic stance should be interpretation addressed to the interpersonal events which had temporarily broken the narcissistic bond between patient and therapist. As Schwaber (1979) continues,

> The sensitive elucidation of the meaning of rage or other fragmenting experience that occurs, of the meaning of the injury that led to it, understood in genetic perspective will permit the reinstatement of the positively felt narcissistic transference which is necessary for continued deepening of the analytic work. (p. 470)

The specific use of such a technique for transference interpretation is illuminated through a vignette from a young adult's psychotherapy. After three years of treatment, Nancy's weight had stabilized and her self was cohesive enough to begin to tolerate the emergence of sexual feelings without being overstimulated. In other words, drive-regulating structures had become sufficiently internalized to contribute to her growing sense of stability and wholeness, but these new structures remained vulnerable (Kohut, 1971). At this point, Nancy shared with me a short story which she had composed. It concerned the experiential state of being in my office and gazing at what she described as my "warm smile." Her associations to this story elaborated intense guilt over any felt excitement connected with me or her father. Almost as an afterthought she added, "Your smile feels reassuring like my father's." Our subsequent discussions focused on the guilt which accompanied any stimulating thoughts, wishes, and fantasies about me.

During this time, however, Nancy began to lose weight, a phenomenon which neither of us understood until she reported two dreams. In the first dream, Nancy was trapped in an office where radioactive gasses were poisoning her. In the second dream, she described a tale of her father's earnest promises to help her with an important task, while failing her at the last moment. Nancy felt so hurt in the face of this disappointment that she dropped a dish which cracked into many pieces. Following her many associations, which emphasized both her interest and disappointment in me, I told Nancy that my emphasis on the sexually stimulating elements of her original story at a time when she needed my reassuring presence must have made her once again feel misunderstood; that she must have felt as though she were in a dangerous place (radioactive gasses) and threatened with falling apart (broken dish).

Nancy replied by saying,

> It's nice to be in a place where I can feel crazy and have someone know I'm not. My supervisor at work is leaving too, just when I need her the most. It feels like the time I told you about when I needed my mother to help calm me down and she panicked.

We then discussed the specifics of my failure and how it resonated with her childhood memories of impoverished opportunities for merger with her mother's calming presence. In the weeks following my therapeutic failure and its elucidation, Nancy's weight increased, and she discussed both the sexualization of her eating and the Oedipal material, which she previously experienced as overstimulating.

Interpretation in this mode does not, as Bruch (1978) suggests with classic psychoanalytic interpretation, "confirm the patient's fear of being defective and incompetent, doomed to dependence" (p. 123). What do undermine the patient's emerging selfhood are transference interpretations offered from the vantage point of the therapist as target rather than subject of the patient's needs, wishes, and fantasies. If, in other words, we insist on " . . . correcting . . . [the patient's] distortions in terms of adult reality" rather than " . . . understanding the patient's childhood experiences as the precursor of [her] present-day, regressive responses in the [analysis]" (P. Ornstein, 1979b, p. 104), the patient will feel misunderstood and exacerbate her resistance to treatment (for we will have repeated the painful attempt to impose the adult's perspective onto the patient). Having done numerous consultations on anorexic patients whose treatment was at an impasse, I would suggest that the therapist's misuse and abuse of transference interpretation, either when verbalized or acted out through punitive limit-setting, directly contribute to such stalemates. Only when interpretations focus on the therapist's nontraumatic failures within the therapeutic relationship can the patient begin to withdraw the fractionalized bits of idealizing investment from the therapist and, via transmuting internalizations, transform them into viable psychic structure (Kohut, 1977; A. Ornstein, 1979b, Schwaber, 1979). It is just such psychic structure which presages the individual patient's capacity for lifelong emotional and physical self-care.

In conclusion, I would suggest that we must continue to patiently clarify the developmental deficits which contribute to the syndrome of anorexia. Only through such continuing clarification can we delineate the quality of the therapeutic relationship and specific treatment techniques which help to rekindle the lost elements of the self, without precipitately substituting weight for emerging selfhood.

REFERENCES

Bach, S. (1975). Narcissism, continuity and the uncanny. *International Journal of Psychoanalysis*, 56, 77-86.

Barcai, A. (1977, February). Lithium in adult anorexia nervosa. A pilot report on two patients *Acta Psychiatrica Scandinavica*, 55, 97-101.

Bruch, H. (1973). *Eating disorders*. New York: Basic Books.

Bruch, H. (1978). *The golden cage*. Cambridge, MA: Harvard University Press.

Cohler, B. (1977). The significance of the therapist's feelings in the treatment of anorexia nervosa. In S. Feinstein and P. Giovacchini (Eds.), *Adolescent psychiatry*, Volume 5 (pp. 352-386). New York: J. Aronson.

Freud, A. (1968). The role of bodily illness in the mental life of children. In *The writings of Anna Freud*, Volume 4 (pp. 260-279). New York: International Universities Press.

Freud, A. (1971). Difficulties in the path of psychoanalysis. In *The writings of Anna Freud*, Volume 7 (pp. 124-156). New York: International Universities Press.

Galdston, R. (1974). Mind over matter: Observations on 50 patients hospitalized with anorexia nervosa. *Journal of the American Academy of Child Psychiatry*, 13, 246-263.

Garfinkel, P. E., & Garner, D. M. (1982). *Anorexia nervosa: A multidimensional perspective*. New York: Brunner/Mazel.

Gedo, J., & Goldberg, A. (1973). *Models of the mind*. Chicago: University of Chicago Press.

Goldberg, A. (1975). A fresh look at perverse behavior. *International Journal of Psycho-Analysis*, 56, 335-342.

Green, R. S., & Rau, J. H. (1974, April). Treatment of compulsive eating disorders with anti-convulsant medication. *American Journal of Psychiatry*, 131, 428-432.

Greenacre, P. (1971). On focal symbiosis. In *Emotional growth: Psychoanalytic studies of the*

gifted and a great variety of other individuals (pp. 145-161). New York: International Universities Press.
Halmi, K. A., Powers, P., & Cunningham, S. (1975, January). Treatment of anorexia nervosa with behavior modification. Effectiveness of formula feeding and isolation. *Archives of General Psychiatry, 32,* 93-96.
James, M. (1960). Premature ego development. *International Journal of Psychoanalysis, 43,* .
Khan, M (1974), The concept of cumulative trauma. In M. Khan (Ed.), *The Privacy of the self* (pp. 42-58). New York: International Universities Press.
Khan, M. (1979). *Alienation in perversions.* New York: International Universities Press.
Kohut, H. (1971). *The analysis of the self.* New York: International Universities Press.
Kohut, H. (1972). Thoughts on narcissism and narcissistic rage. *The Psychoanalytic Study of the Child, 27,* 360-400.
Kohut, H. (1977). *The restoration of the self.* New York: International Universities Press.
Kris, E. (1975). On some vicissitudes of insight in psychoanalysis. In *The selected papers of Ernst Kris* (pp. 252-271). New Haven, CT: Yale University Press.
Levy, E. (1977, September). Introduction to special issue on anorexia nervosa. *Bulletin of the Menninger Clinic, 41,* 415-418.
Minuchin, S., Baker, L., Rosman, B., Liebman, R., Milman, L., & Todd, T. (1975). A conceptual model of psychosomatic illness in children: Family organization and family therapy. *Archives of General Psychiatry, 32,* 1030-1038.
Mitchel-Heggs, N., Kelly, D., & Richardson, A. (1976, March). Stereotectic limbic leucotomy—a follow-up at 16 months. *British Journal of Psychiatry, 128,* 226-240.
Needleman, H. L., & Waber, D. (1976). Letter: Amitriptyline therapy in patients with anorexia nervosa. *Lancet, 2,* 687.
Ornstein, A. (1981). Self-pathology in childhood: Developmental and clinical considerations. *Psychiatric Clinics of North America, 4,*(3), 435-453.
Ornstein, P. (1979a). The evolution of Heinz Kohut's psychoanalytic psychology of the self. In *The search for the self: Selected writings of Heinz Kohut, 1,* 1-106.
Ornstein, P. (1979b). The central position of empathy in psychoanalysis. *The Association for Psychoanalytic Medicine Bulletin, 18,*(4), 95-108.
Schwaber, E. (1979). On the self within the matrix of analytic theory: Some clinical reflections and reconsiderations. *International Journal of Psycho-Analysis, 60,* 467-479.
Thoma, H. (1967). *Anorexia nervosa.* New York: International Universities Press.
Tolpin, M. (1978). Selfobjects and oedipal objects. *Psychoanalytic Study of the Child, 33,* 167-184.
Waller, D. A. (1979). A clinician's guide to the psychological and medical diagnosis and treatment of anorexia nervosa. In T. Manschreck (Ed.), *Psychiatric medicine update. Massachusetts General Hospital reviews for physicians* (pp. 109-123). New York: American Elsevier.
Winnicott, D. (1958). Mind and its relation to the psych-soma. In *Collected papers: Through paediatrics to psychoanalysis.* London: Tavistock.
Winnicott, D. (1971). Mirror-role of mother and family in child development. In *Playing and reality* (pp. 111-118). New York: Basic Books.

Part IV

Conclusion

Chapter 16

Do Anorexics and Bulimics Get Well?

*Michael G. Thompson and
Margery T. Gans*

Research in the outcome of eating disorders produces confusing conclusions about the long-term prognosis of anorexia and bulimia. A review of this research shows that the confusion stems in part from the wide range and often contradictory findings related to recovery and in part from the methodological problems that beset outcome research in general and anorexia and bulimia in particular. The variety of findings and the methodological difficulties are, of course, interrelated problems. Thus it is not easy to conclude from the research how optimistic one can be about a prognosis for eating disorders or about treatments for those disorders.

The outcome literature on anorexia is substantial; research into bulimia is meager and outcome studies almost nonexistent. This chapter reviews both literatures, beginning with the work on anorexia and then addressing bulimia separately. One aim of the chapter is to introduce the reader to the many methodological problems of outcome research and to make him or her an informed consumer of outcome studies in the eating disorders field. From the ensuing discussion it should become more clear which questions need to be asked of future research in order to assess with more confidence the prognosis for sufferers from anorexia and bulimia.

OUTCOME OF ANOREXIA

The two basic questions that professionals and the public alike need to ask of the outcome literature on anorexia are: 1) Do anorexics get well?; and 2) if so, what makes a difference? The answer to the former question is that on follow-up, a majority of anorexics are relieved of some painful symptoms and are brought out of physical danger. Roughly 40% of anorexics are cured in a global sense; approximately 30% are significantly improved but lead symptomatic or impaired lives. Twenty percent develop an apparently stable but chronic anorexia, while another 9% die from various causes related to their condition. These figures reflect data summarized by Garfinkel and Garner (1982) in their comprehensive review of outcome studies in anorexia.

If the answer to "do they get better?" is yes, the next question has to be: What constitutes better? How has better been defined and measured? What have different researchers chosen to look for and how long have they waited in order to follow up their patients? In recent years some careful work has been done attempting to compile and compare the outcome literature on anorexia and address these questions. Since 1953 there have been 25 outcome studies in anorexia that have had sample sizes greater than 15. All told, 1075 patients have been followed for periods ranging from six months to 50 years. The 25 follow-up studies have a mean follow-up time of five years. Generally these studies have follow-up rates of over 90%; anorexics are extremely cooperative research subjects. These figures come from the three major reviews of the outcome literature published in the last few years by Hsu (1980), Schwartz and Thompson (1981), and Garfinkel and Garner (1982).

These three summary studies illustrate the difficulty of generalizing about anorexia outcome, because the criteria for what determines "better" are not uniform from study to study. For example, Crisp's 1965 study broke down eating disturbances into five categories: normal, overeating, undereating, mixed over/undereating, and vomiting. Garfinkel and Garner, in their own outcome study (Garfinkel, Moldofsky, & Garner, 1977), subdivided eating disturbances into moderate or marked food fads, bulimia, vomiting, and laxative abuse. How these categories are to be collapsed into one another is highly subjective. Clearly it is very difficult to compare data which have been collected in a variety of projects, designed and executed with different presuppositions and definitions. One result is differences in summation figures. Out of all this variability, however, one can proceed, category by category, to describe the condition of anorexic patients years after the onset of the illness.

Weight Maintenance

A majority of anorexics are within 15%-20% of normal weight after an average follow-up time of five years. Hsu and colleagues (1979) found that 62% of their patients were within 15% of normal weight four to eight years after admission to the hospital. Theander (1970) found 51% to be within 15% of average weight 16 years after discharge. On follow-up, a number of studies (Hsu, Crisp, & Harding, 1979; Garfinkel et al., 1977; Warren, 1968) have found 15%-25% of former anorexics to be still significantly underweight (defined as less than 75% of average body weight for height and age). Between 5% and 10% are significantly overweight. The remainder fall into an intermediate underweight or fluctuating weight category.

The range of findings on normal weight maintenance varies from 41% to 81%, depending on length of follow-up and age of patients. Thus the combination of treatments for anorexics is generally successful for a slight to large majority of patients with respect to the major symptoms—that is, if one chooses to look at the glass as being half full. If one chooses to see the glass as half empty, then anywhere from 20%-80% of anorexics continue on follow-up to be underweight, significantly underweight, or overweight.

Return of Menses

Approximately the same number of women who have achieved and maintained a normal weight on follow-up have regular menses. Studies report a range of from 40%-60% of subjects with regular menstruation, the remainder with erratic menses or amenorrhea. Despite returning to normal weight, between 13% and 50% of subjects were still amenorrheic on follow-up (Hsu, 1980), and many researchers have observed the phenomenon of regular menses not beginning for a significant period of time after normal or near-normal weight has been achieved (Crisp, 1965; Hsu et al., 1979).

Eating Behavior

Improvement in eating symptoms, gorging, vomiting, laxative abuse, and body concerns is not as favorable as that of weight itself. Bulimia is reported in all studies as present in 10%-15% of anorexic subjects; vomiting is reported in some studies, ranging from 10%-25%. Laxative abuse is reported, usually in the range of 10%, though Hsu et al. (1979) and Morgan and Russell (1975) report figures in the 30% range. Food fads, anxiety about eating with others, dietary restrictions, and random erratic eating afflict about 50% of patients in most follow-up studies.

Unfortunately, only a few studies report correlations between weight gain and other eating symptoms, so it is not possible to determine whether all of the eating difficulties occur in patients who have also failed to achieve normal weight. However, clinical experience and common sense suggest that achieving normal weight and displaying eating problems are by no means mutually exclusive. Therefore, we must conclude that a significant minority of those who have achieved normal weight and whose menses have returned may still lead lives afflicted by eating disorder symptoms. The extent to which this may be true—future outcome studies should examine this question more closely—may reduce the percentage of anorexics whom we can judge to be totally cured.

Chronic Anorexia

All outcome research has reported that a significant minority, approximately 15%-20% of anorexics, are chronically ill. In these women the basic features of anorexia are present years afterwards, but if they do not experience electrolyte difficulties, they can live self-sufficient though extremely limited lives until old age (Dally, 1969; Theander, 1970).

Recovery Time

For those patients who are cured or improved, the length of time from onset to eventual resolution of the illness is variable. Theander (1970) reports that of the sample on which he had reliable information 47% appeared to recover in less than three years, 31% in three to five years and 22% in more than five years. Dally (1969) reports that one third of normal weight patients may begin to lose weight immediately after discharge from the hospital. This is not strictly a reoccurrence of the disorder, but simply a case of premature discharge from treatment. Another small group of patients may relapse from three to 14 years after apparent recovery, often after a life stress such as pregnancy (Garfinkel & Garner, 1982).

Mortality

Reports of mortality from anorexia outcome studies range from 0%-24%, with 11 of the 25 outcome studies reporting less than 5% mortality. Most anorexics die from causes directly related to their disorder: inanition or severe electrolyte imbalances due to vomiting or purging. Suicide is relatively rare, constituting only 1% of reported cases (Garfinkel & Garner, 1982; Hsu, 1980; Schwartz & Thompson, 1981).

Psychosocial Adjustment

Relatively few investigators have examined social and marital adjustment. Social adjustment is difficult to measure and many researchers have preferred to focus on the more quantifiable features of the disorder such as weight and menstrual functioning. In general, psychosexual and interpersonal functioning are good only in those who maintain their weight (Morgan & Russell, 1975). Even among those of normal weight, however, social anxiety is common, especially in eating with others (Hsu, 1980; Morgan & Russell, 1975). And even among those who have achieved financial independence and lived away from home, a very high percentage still experienced intense hostile feelings toward their family. Among those who marry, Theander (1970) suggests that poor sexual adjustment is common.

Vocational Adjustment

It is in vocational adjustment that anorexics appear most normal. Theander (1970) reported that 63% of his patients were working full-time and expressed considerable job satisfaction, 23% were working in a limited way, 6% were students for a total of 92% who were working or were students. Seven of his patients worked successfully right up until their deaths from anorexia-related causes.

Psychiatric Symptomatology

In recovered anorexics, once the weight and eating issue has been put aside, other psychological problems seem to emerge. Theander (1970) reports that only 17% of his "cured" and improved anorexics could be judged mentally healthy. A number of other studies confirm Theander's finding that 37% exhibited severe psychiatric symptomatology (Hsu, 1980). Former anorexics principally manifest depressive and obsessive-compulsive symptoms, and social "phobias." Using established research criteria for depression, Cantwell and colleagues (1977) found that 12 of 26 patients had confirmed or probable affective disorder based on parents' report while, based on patients' report, eight out of 18 were given a diagnosis of affective disorder. Cantwell et al. conclude that anorexia may be a variant of affective illness.

For the most part, however, investigators have observed that the symptom picture in most anorexics remains consistent. Eating and body concerns continue to be the fundamental area of symptomatology. Schizophrenia is rarely an outcome of anorexia; it affects fewer than 1%.

Prognosis

There are a number of clinical features of anorexia that have prognostic implications. Garfinkel and Garner (1982), Selvini Palazzoli (1974) and Hsu et al. (1979) have written that binge-purge type anorexics carry a more guarded prognosis. Clinical wisdom suggests that vomiting, as well as bulimia, is associated with poor outcome; however, in many studies either this observation has not been upheld (Garfinkel & Garner, 1982) or vomiting behavior has not been assessed separately from bulimic behavior in general. Impulsive behavior such as stealing and self-mutilation has been associated with poor outcome. The entire complex of symptoms associated with the bulimic-binger pattern has a poor prognosis in the anorexic. It is the classic restricting anorexic—Bruch's "primary anorexic"—who has the better chance of making a full recovery.

Halmi and colleagues (1979) have described a "good prognostic subtype" of anorexia characterized by no previous hospitalizations, less denial of illness, less psychosexual immaturity, ready admission of appetite, and more overactivity before the illness. A number of investigators agree, logically, that very low body weight on hospital admission is associated with poor outcome (Garfinkel & Garner, 1982; Morgan & Russell, 1975). Premorbid obesity has been cited as a poor prognostic sign by some researchers, but this finding has been disputed by others.

Finally, it should be noted that while all anorexics tend to display distorted body-image perception, those with more severely distorted perceptions have a poor prognosis (Garfinkel et al., 1977; Halmi & Falk, 1982). Halmi and Falk also found that anorexics with neuropsychological deficits have a poorer outcome.

Of the demographic factors of age, sex, and social class, age of onset seems to have the most importance for outcome. There is a general agreement that earlier age of onset leads to a better outcome, though this may only be true down to the age of 14. Onset in adolescence has a better prognosis than onset after the age of 20 (Hsu et al., 1979; Morgan & Russell, 1975).

Males have a poorer prognosis than females, because they tend to show a binge-purge pattern. Also, more male than female anorexics manifest psychotic thinking. Bruch has theorized that males have a more severe underlying illness due to gender identity problems (Bruch, 1973). However, so few males have been followed on a long-term basis, it is not fair to generalize about the outcome in males. This is a question that will be answered by future work in the field.

Married women who develop anorexia have a less hopeful prognosis than single women (Crisp, Kalucy, Lacey, & Harding, 1977; Hsu et al., 1979), though this may only be due to the older age of the women.

No specific personality factors have been found to be associated with either a poor or a good prognosis in anorexia. Investigators have examined depressive, hysterical, and obsessive traits among others. Crisp and colleagues (1977) have discriminated among personality types on follow-up, but these had no bearing on outcome. Anorexics from families rated as more psychopathological have a poor outcome. Morgan and Russell (1975) and Hsu et al. (1979) have found that disturbed family or marital relations antedating the illness are related to a less favorable outcome.

Treatment Efficacy

One of the most interesting and perhaps important questions to be asked of the outcome literature is: "What treatment works best?" Unfortunately, there is as yet no answer to this question. It would be helpful and relieving if some treatment or combination of treatments could be demonstrated to be clearly superior to others. The sad fact is that it is not even known whether any treatment makes a difference in the long run, much less which treatment. Most practicing clinicians agree that treatment does make a difference, but it has yet to be empirically demonstrated. Garfinkel and Garner (1982) write that it is not known for certain whether treatment helps anorexics, but they believe that consistent weight-restoring approaches have reduced mortality and that long-term treatments which address predisposing factors do improve the prognosis for many patients.

It is worthwhile examining why the outcome literature has been unable to establish which treatments are effective in the treatment of anorexia. First, the sheer number of variables which arise over the years between discharge and follow-up make it impossible to draw causal connections between treatment and eventual outcome. Second, many anorexics receive not one but two, three, four, or a dozen treatments from different institutions and individuals with varying theoretical approaches. Even if the patient herself does not seek out a variety of treatments, most good inpatient programs are a theoretical blend of behavioral, medical, psychodynamic, and family approaches. There is almost complete unanimity among experts in the field that an eclectic approach is not only desirable but mandatory. This makes it impossible to compare one theoretical approach against another, except in the very short term. Third, of course, there can be no control group of anorexics who are untreated; it is the ethical obligation of professionals to try to treat these patients, and that obligation overrides any research need. There are a small number of anorexics who do not seek or seriously stay with one kind of treatment, but their numbers are fewer and fewer. Finally, even if anorexics only had one kind of treatment, the complexities of psychotherapy research are such that it may be a long time before it can be determined which therapies work for any person, much less the anorexic in particular.

Claims for the efficacy of one treatment versus another treatment are simply that: claims. The long-term outcome literature has yet to demonstrate the efficacy of one particular approach for the treatment of anorexia.

Methodological Problems

The problems of conducting long-term outcome research in general are staggering and any researcher who undertakes such a task must be respected.

However, there are numerous methodological difficulties inherent in such research and the informed consumer of the anorexia and bulimia literature should be aware of them. Four major questions need to be asked of any study: Who is being studied? How are they being followed? What is being asked? What claims are being made from the study?

The major difficulty in all studies is the variability of diagnostic criteria for anorexia. What is the definition of anorexia nervosa or bulimia used by a particular researcher? Nineteen of 25 researchers reviewed by Garfinkel and Garner (1982) define anorexia nervosa in terms consistent with the latter's definition, which in turn corresponds roughly to the definition found in the Diagnostic and Statistical Manual of Mental Disorders (American Psychiatric Association, 1980). Many of the earlier studies adopted only weight criteria for inclusion in the study, whereas the DSM-III criteria include both weight and psychological criteria. The fact that the early studies did not include such criteria is not a matter of sloppy research; it had to do with the historical growth of the field and the increasing specificity and accuracy of diagnostic criteria for anorexia since 1953 and the relative scarcity of patients in the early years. The latter problem meant that anorexia researchers—in order to get together a sample—grouped patients in studies though they differed significantly on important characteristics: age of onset, duration of illness, hospitalization, treatments, etc.

Part of the "who" question then relates to the diagnostic specificity for inclusion in the study. Other "who" questions relate to age of onset, age at presentation to the study, previous treatments, number of hospitalizations. It has been difficult to compare the results of studies in which the age of subjects has been markedly different. For example, Minuchin, Rosman, and Baker (1978) studied a group of anorexic girls with a mean onset age of 14.4 years and they were seen on average within six months of falling ill; by contrast, Garfinkel et al. (1977) studied a group whose average age at onset was 17.1 years and who had an average duration of illness of three years. One suspects that these were remarkably different groups at the time they were studied. The future work in outcome must further refine the vicissitudes of certain subtypes of anorexics, defined by specific behavioral criteria. In addition, different age and duration groups need to be compared with one another to illuminate differences between them.

How does a researcher follow his anorexic subjects? The method of follow-up has varied widely from study to study: some have involved long interviews, others short telephone interviews or brief phone interviews with relatives or physicians. Anorexia is notorious for its longevity. Patients have often been ill for a number of years before they come for treatment. Many drop in and out of different treatment programs, are discharged or terminated when they meet physical criteria for recovery, and relapse under stress in later years. There is reason to believe that the more prolonged the contact with the former anorexic patient, the more manifest are the persisting signs of the disorder (Theander, 1970). Therefore, a follow-up which involves only brief or superficial contact with the former anorexic is suspect. Similarly, studies which have relatively short follow-up periods show markedly higher success rates than those with longer follow-up periods. Mortality rates, obviously, are much higher for the longer term studies. For example, five studies of less than six years duration showed a mortality of 3%; Theander's study in Sweden, in which he followed 94 patients for an average of 16 years, revealed a mortality rate of 13% (Garfinkel & Garner, 1982; Theander, 1970).

What questions are being asked on follow-up? Researchers who ask only about weight maintenance or return of menses or general questions about functioning tend to present more optimistic pictures than more detailed studies of psychosocial and psychosexual functioning. Even today, too few researchers are exploring these important areas with sufficient detail. For example, in an otherwise excellent follow-up study published in 1983, Morgan, Purgold, and Welbourne make the traditional mistake of judging outcome largely by weight maintenance, without exploring psychosocial functioning. The study is excellent in that it uses a standardized outcome protocol which allows for comparison with two earlier studies utilizing the same protocol; however, its ratings were based on two scores—one an "average outcome score," the other a "general outcome score." The "general outcome score" was based entirely on weight and menstruation and the "average outcome score" included nothing about psychosocial or vocational functioning, but rather assessed socioeconomic status.

Finally, what does a researcher claim for his or her outcome research? Is the presence of the correlation of variables confused with the inference of cause and effect? That is to say, is the presence of a treatment feature simultaneously with improvement taken to mean that the feature caused improvement? Inferring cause and effect from a correlation is an elementary statistical error, but one that it is hard for the proponents of a single treatment modality not to want to make. However, as has already been noted, the complex character of anorexia makes it extremely difficult to isolate and identify all possible variables that may influence its etiology and course. It is important to stress that it is virtually impossible for one research project to account for every variable; it necessarily focuses on a certain set of variables. Therefore, the presence of, for example, a distant father or an overinvolved mother or an "enmeshed" family system does not necessarily mean that those factors caused the anorexia or that a particular family treatment is the cure. It may be so, but only repeated studies and long-term outcome research can provide those answers.

BULIMIA

Do bulimics get well? There is as yet no answer to this question. Clinicians know of bulimics who appear to have recovered and of others who have not. Clinicians experienced in the treatment of bulimics may even have an idea of the proportion of bulimics who do or do not improve. These clinical observations must serve until the outcome studies in bulimia are conducted.

Bulimia is defined as "binge eating" which is followed by a purging of the food by voluntary vomiting, laxatives, diuretic or fasting (American Psychiatric Association, 1980). The food is usually eaten rapidly, in secret, and often during times of stress and/or at the same unstructured or transitional times during the day, e.g., during the evening after work. Both binge and purge are associated with feelings of self-loathing and guilt, although some relief often accompanies the purge; the bulimic may experience intense anxiety if the cycle is interrupted before she can get rid of the food she has eaten. This behavior may accompany anorexia, but recently it has been identified as a disorder in its own right which afflicts women (primarily) who maintain normal weight and appearance (Crisp, 1981; Fairburn & Cooper, 1982; Palmer, 1979). The well-guarded secrecy of the binge-purge cycle and the normal appearance and behavior of bulimics in public makes them almost impossible to detect and treat until they are ready to disclose their symptoms. In this way they are quite different from the anorexics whose physical condition draws substantial attention. Bulimia, like anorexia, has a long course; women who come into treatment have often been suffering for three years or more. This fact, together with the relative newness of bulimia as an object of research, accounts in great part for the almost total lack of any outcome research on bulimia as a disorder distinct from anorexia.

Much of the slim literature on bulimia is anecdotal and qualitative (Boskind-White & White, 1983; Orbach, 1982). Most of the few controlled treatment studies involve the use of drugs, either antidepressant or anticonvulsants. Fairburn (1981) in England has recently explored the use of a cognitive-behavioral approach with bulimics and sees some ground for optimism with this approach.

Drug studies demonstrate a dramatic immediate improvement with the use of both antidepressants and anticonvulsants. Pope and colleagues (1983) found that 18 out of 20 subjects had a marked decrease in binge-behavior and changes-in-attitude report scales after a trial of imipramine. The follow-up period was one to eight months. Wermuth and colleagues (1977), in a study using the anticonvulsant phenytoin, achieved positive early results, but in a follow-up after 18 months found that only two of 19 original participants had both carried through on the treatment and experienced lasting improvement. Five others in that study appeared to improve with psychotherapeutic intervention or change in their life situation. Walsh et al. (1982), using MAO inhibitors, report a decrease in the frequency of binging behavior and improvement in eating attitudes as measured on a self-report task in five of six subjects, but provide no information as to length of follow-up. These findings have led some investigators to focus on the possible relationship between bulimia and affective disorders, though at this stage the findings are inconclusive.

There have been some psychotherapeutic approaches that have reported success. Johnson, Connors, and Stuckey (1983) reported success with a psychoeducational group therapy approach with 10 bulimics. In perhaps the largest "outcome" study of bulimia reported so far in the literature, Abraham, Mira, and Llewellyn-Jones (1983) report on the outcome of 43 patients 14 to 72 months after presenting for treatment. The treatment comprised counseling about binge eating and supportive psychotherapy when required. All bulimics were treated as outpatients. Bulimics were considered cured if they had no binge-eating behavior or less than one episode per month, no self-induced vomiting or laxative use, and had a stable body weight. Patients were considered improved if they were binge-eating or vomiting less than once a week. Depending on whether the outcome was assessed by questionnaire, interview, or self-rating, the number of patients completely cured was 29%–40%. On the questionnaire—a 19-item protocol completed by the patient—42% were considerd "cured," 37% still had bulimia, and 21% were classified as having anorexia.

According to Casper's (1983) interesting historical review of bulimia, the phenomenon of bulimia as one of medical interest is a fairly recent one, dating from perhaps 1940. The study of bulimia as a separate entity from anorexia is really no more than five to 10 years old at most. For now, bulimia research must rightly concentrate on exploration, description, and diagnostic discrimination. It is essential to seek for more accurate diagnosis that will help to distinguish between the subtypes of bulimics, and to distinguish them from anorexics on the one hand and normal, dieting adolescents and culturally expectable, weight-obsessed young women. Until the criteria for subgroups are agreed upon by researchers, bulimia outcome researchers will not know whom to follow up on. Obviously, patients who present themselves to clinics will be followed, but whether these represent the modal bulimic experience is not yet clear.

The field of bulimia research now needs what Chairman Mao prescribed: Let a hundred flowers bloom. Research is needed in all aspects of the disorder and all possible treatments for it. From the point of view of the outcome literature, it would be desirable if treatment studies could be designed with a long-term outcome portion in mind. It may take five or ten years, but by that time there will be an answer to the question "Do bulimics get well?" that is at least the equal of the answer we now have for anorexics.

REFERENCES

Abraham, S. F., Mira, M., Llewellyn-Jones, D. (1983). Bulimia: A study of outcome. *International Journal of Eating Disorders, 2*, 75-110.

American Psychiatric Association. (1980). *Diagnostic and statistical manual of mental disorders (DSM-III), third edition*. Washington, D.C.: American Psychiatric Association.

Boskind-White, M., & White, W. C. (1983). *Bulimarexia: The binge/purge cycle*. New York: Norton.

Bruch, H. (1973). *Eating disorders*. New York: Basic Books.

Bruch, H. (1977). Psychotherapy in eating disorders. *Canadian Psychiatric Association Journal, 22*(3), 102-108.

Cantwell, D. P., Sturzenburger, S., Burroughs, J., Salkin, B., & Green, J. K. (1977). Anorexia nervosa; An affective disorder. *Archives of General Psychiatry, 34*, 1087-1093.

Casper, R. C. (1983). On the emergence of bulimia nervosa as a syndrome: A historical view. *International Journal of Eating Disorders, 2*(3), 3-17.

Crisp, A. H. (1965). Clinical and therapeutic aspects of anorexia nervosa — A study of 30 cases. *Journal of Psychosomatic Research, 9*, 67-78.

Crisp, A. H. (1981). Anorexia nervosa at normal body weight — The abnormal weight control syndrome. *International Journal of Psychiatry in Medicine, 11*(3), 203-233.

Crisp, A. H., Kalucy, R. S., Lacey, J. H., & Harding, B. (1977). The long-term prognosis in anorexia nervosa: Some factors predictive of outcome. In R. Vigersky (Ed.), *Anorexia nervosa*. New York: Raven Press.

Dally, P. (1969). *Anorexia nervosa*. New York: Grune & Stratton.

Fairburn, C. G. (1981). *The place of a cognitive-behavioral approach in the management of bulimia*. Paper presented at the Toronto Conference on Anorexia Nervosa, 10-11 September.

Fairburn, C. G., & Cooper, P. (1982). Self-induced vomiting and bulimia nervosa: An undetected problem. *British Medical Journal, 284*, 1153-1156.

Garfinkel, P. E., & Garner, D. M. (1982). *Anorexia nervosa: A multidimensional perspective*. New York: Brunner/Mazel.

Garfinkel, P. E., Moldofsky, H., & Garner, D. M. (1977). The outcome of anorexia nervosa: Significance of clinical features, body image and behavior modification. In R. Vigersky (Ed.), *Anorexia nervosa*. New York: Raven Press.

Halmi, K. A., & Falk, J. R. (1982). Anorexia nervosa: A study of outcome discriminators in exclusive dieters and bulimics. *Journal of the American Academy of Child Psychiatry, 21*, 369-375.

Halmi, K. A., Goldberg, S. C., Casper, R. C., Eckert, E. D., & Davis, J. M. (1979). Pretreatment predictors of outcome in anorexia nervosa. *British Journal of Psychiatry, 134*, 71-78.

Hsu, L. K. G. (1980). Outcome of anorexia nervosa. A review of the literature (1954-1978). *Archives of General Psychiatry, 37*, 1041-1046.

Hsu, L. K. G., Crisp, A. H., & Harding, B. (1979). Outcome of anorexia nervosa. *Lancet, 1*, 61-65.

Johnson, C., Connors, M., & Stuckey, M. (1983). Short-term group treatment of bulimia: A preliminary report. *International Journal of Eating Disorders, 2*(4), 199-208.

Minuchin, S., Rosman, B. L., & Baker, L. (1978). *Psychosomatic families: Anorexia nervosa in context*. Cambridge, MA: Harvard University Press.

Morgan, H. G., & Russell, G. F. M. (1975). Value of family background and clinical features as predictors of long-term outcome in anorexia nervosa: Four year follow-up study of 41 patients. *Psychological Medicine, 5*, 355-371.

Morgan, H. G., Purgold, J., & Welbourne, J. (1983). Management and outcome in anorexia nervosa: A standardized prognostic study. *British Journal of Psychiatry, 143*, 282-287.

Orbach, S. (1982). *Fat is a feminist issue, II*. New York: Berkley Books.

Palmer, R. L. (1979). The dietary chaos syndrome: A useful new term? *British Journal of Medical Psychology, 52*, 187-190.

Pope, H. G., Hudson, J., Jonas, J. M., & Yurgelun-Todd, D. (1983). Bulimia treated with imipramine: A placebo-controlled double blind study. *American Journal of Psychiatry, 140*(5), 554-558.

Schwartz, D. M., & Thompson, M. F. (1981). Do anorexics get well? Current research and future needs. *American Journal of Psychiatry, 21*, 38-46.

Selvini Palazzoli, M. (1974). *Self-starvation*. London: Chaucer.

Theander, S. (1970). Anorexia nervosa: A psychiatric investigation of 44 female cases. *Acta Psychiatrica Scandinavica* (Suppl.), 214:1-194.

Walsh, B. T., Stewart, J. W., Wright, L., Harrison, W., Roose, S. P., & Glassman, A. H. Treatment of bulimia with monoamine oxidase inhibitors. *American Journal of Psychiatry, 139*(12), 1629-1630.

Warren, W. (1968). A study of anorexia nervosa in young girls. *Journal of Child Psychology and Psychiatry, 9*, 27-40.

Wermuth, B. M., Davis, K. L., Hollister, L. E., & Stunkard, A. J. Phenytoin treatment of the binge-eating syndrome. *American Journal of Psychiatry, 134*:1249-1253.

Chapter 17

Future Trends

Steven Wiley Emmett

> *If a man will begin with certainties, he shall end in doubts; but if he will be content to begin with doubts, he shall end in certainties.*
>
> Sir Francis Bacon,
> *Advancement of Learning*

In his introduction to *Future Shock*, the masterful study of our increasingly volatile world, Toffler (1971) draws upon the "deliciously ironic" words of what is purported to be an ancient Chinese proverb: "To prophesy is extremely difficult—especially with respect to the future" (p. 5). Indeed, accurate representation of the past is a formidable task; even more so is a reasonable depiction of some distant future. With this caveat offered, our concluding chapter will gaze forward in the belief that theoretical conjectures need not be incontrovertible to be useful. Indeed, as Toffler sagely observes, " . . . it is more important to be imaginative and insightful than to be 100% right" (p. 6).

Widespread basic research on eating disorders is beginning to flourish. Countless scholarly writings addressing many of the issues touched on in these pages are now just surfacing. Amidst the increased media attention and burgeoning self-help groups nationwide, there is a widening flood of information and discussion about the etiology of, and potential cures for, anorexia

---

The author wishes to thankfully acknowledge the contributors to this book whose many insights and suggestions helped in the preparation of this chapter.

nervosa and bulimia. As with any rapidly developing field, there has tended to be a somewhat chaotic current swirling about the substantial data already collected. The myriad medical and psychotherapeutic schools of thought clamor for our acceptance with various claims of treatment superiority. Unfortunately, there often seems to be more competition than creative communication.

This chapter will explore a number of potentially fruitful avenues for future research, utilizing as a guide the three perspectives—biomedical, sociocultural and psychological—considered in this collection of writings. Certainly there is sound cause to hope for the solution of many of the riddles posed by present studies. Answers may be gleaned more readily with heightened cooperation between the various fields of investigation and a greater standardization of definitions and diagnostic criteria. (Bulimia and its alternate spelling "bulemia" symbolically reflect the rapidity with which this particular syndrome has captured our attention and the disagreement it has spawned!)

It is hoped that the future trends briefly addressed below will highlight particularly important areas deserving further attention, thus abetting the growing number of helping professionals dedicated to controlling the eating disorder epidemic.

BIOMEDICAL TRENDS

The overlapping fields of neuroendocrinology and psychopharmacology represent, within this perspective, vehicles of hope for major advances in the understanding and treatment of anorexia and bulimia. Two primary areas of potentially fertile future research on the neuroendocrinological aspects of eating disorders involve the consequences of starvation (which may perpetuate the rigorously imposed need for self-control among anorexics) and the search for trait markers (the genetic underpinning of a susceptibility to the pathology).

With respect to the influence of starvation, it is suspected that alterations in the neurotransmitter beta-endorphin may accentuate a preoccupation with food: Hypothalamic beta-endorphin stimulates eating, while food deprivation increases cerebrospinal fluid opioid activity in cachectic anorexics. The increase may serve to augment their desire for strict self-control while precipitating bulimic episodes. Future studies with naloxone, an opiate antagonist, may aid researchers in unraveling the mystery of this phenomenon.

Another neurotransmitter facilitating understanding of the starved state is 5-hydroxytryptamine (serotonin). 5-HT is known to reduce carbohydrate craving when levels are centrally increased. Preliminary studies at the National Institute of Mental Health suggest that 5-hydroxyindoleacetic acid (a major metabolite of 5-HT) is lower in the cerebrospinal fluid of weight-recovered bulimic anorexics than in weight-recovered anorexics who exclusively fast (the "pure restricters") (Kaye, Ebert, & Gwirtsman, 1984). Recent reports of success with the drug fenfluramine (which releases 5-HT and may contribute to the diminution of bulimic binges) is also emerging and will be followed with interest.

The search for a specific genetic or trait marker continues to hold particular fascination for researchers. Locating and isolating such a hereditary link between eating disorder etiology/symptomatology and a certain chromosomal configuration would issue in a powerful specific biological indicator. Discovering the presence and influence of such a chromosomal trait could lead to the enhancement of refined controlled studies and thus promises to be a productive avenue of evidence leading into the future. For example, this knowledge would be employed in distinguishing "true" bulimics (individuals biologically at risk) from phenocopies (those manifesting bulimic behavior such as a wrestler attempting to make a desired weight level) without the distinctive chromosomal characteristics.

Other intriguing findings require further study: It has been found that norepinephrine activity as measured by cerebrospinal fluid levels appears to be low in anorexics long after recovery (Kaye, Ebert, Raleigh, & Lake, 1984); while the abnormal dexamethasone suppression test is observed both in patients with anorexia and depression, different neuroendocrine mechanisms may be contributing to the abnormality evidenced in the two conditions; nascent studies with a small sample of anorexic patients suggest a heightened adrenocorticotrophic hormonal response to CRF (corticotrophic releasing factor) as opposed to a blunted response found in depressives (unpublished data); still another challenging but potentially productive area of inquiry involves the chromatography of anorexic patients' urine (Trygstad, Foss, Edminson, Johansen, & Reichelt, 1978).

All of the above studies are based on preliminary results. Some research has served to call into question many of these initial findings. For instance, we would expect in studies conducted with identical twins and sisters (where one is afflicted with anorexia), given the conjectured component of organic dysfunction, to find evidence of genetic transmission of the illness. Such may not be the case. Certain results indicate that "women who have an anorexic identical twin or sister are not necessarily more likely to be anorexic than is the average woman" (Rohrbaugh, 1979, p. 412). Still other studies in the literature report anorexia nervosa occurring in monozygotic twin pairs. Despite such conflicting data, the search for contributing abnormal chromosomal factors will continue and with it countless possibilities for future biomedical advances.

In the field of psychopharmacology we will undoubtedly see the development of more effective antidepressant medications similar to those presently utilized in the treatment of bulimia. More placebo double-blind studies need to be conducted in order to discern which drugs, if any, most effectively counteract the underlying depression suspected by many neuropharmacologists to be the primary eating disorder precipitant. In addition to Pope and Hudson's work (see Chapter 4), two recent studies (Hughes, Wells, & Cunningham, 1984; Walsh, Stewart, Roose, et al., 1984) utilizing the antidepressant medications to combat bulimia revealed strongly positive results. Moreover, two-year follow-up data on patients treated in the Pope/Hudson placebo-controlled double-blind study showed that the patients maintained or even increased their degree of improvement since initial antidepressant treatment, an important finding suggesting that the antidepressant effect holds up over the long term (Pope, Hudson, & Jonas, 1984).

Anorexics, owing to their cachectic state, pose a more refractory problem vis-à-vis psychopharmacological treatment. Side effects such as lightheadedness and insomnia are severe and widespread and, to date, antidepressant medication has not proven particularly effective. Much greater refinement of such medication is required. Because of the rigorous safety standards imposed by the U.S. Federal Drug Administration, testing of an experimental drug takes many years. It is more likely that Europe, with its slightly more relaxed regulations, will be the source of such pharmacological improvements in the years ahead.

A bulk of the neuropharmacological research rests on the assumption that eating disorders are one of a number of pathologies (e.g., agoraphobia, alcohol and drug addiction) that are displayed as symptoms of an underlying major affective disorder. Indeed, in this weltanschauung, anorexics and bulimics are to be treated in an almost identical manner as depressed patients. Research statistics indicate that there is a higher incidence of depression in anorexic families than in the families of clinically depressed patients. Anorexia rivals manic-depression as a primary symptom in families with a history of depression. Thus, psychopharmacologists argue, anorexia nervosa may someday prove to be one of the most potent forms of major affective disorder in our society.

It remains to be seen whether, and to what degree, these sweeping reductionistic theorizations are born out by future research. We should not ignore the history of science, where complex, multifactorial theories have generally been proven wrong, nor the time-honored wisdom of the 14th century philosopher, Sir William of Ockham, who observed the essential simplicity of nature; it has been the simple, parsimonious explanation reducible to a single etiology that has usually been corroborated by scientific investigation. Thus, while discovery of a distinctive genetic marker as the primary contributor to eating disorders appears, at this stage, rather remote, many researchers remain convinced that unlocking the puzzle of the biological underpinnings of major affective disorders will provide illuminating data certain to revolutionize the field.

SOCIOCULTURAL TRENDS

Prognostication about sociocultural trends in our multifaceted society is a risky undertaking at best. Western culture is in the throes of what Toffler (1971) described as a "roaring current of change," its people suffering from a future shock in which "shattering stress and disorientation" are induced in individuals by "subjecting them to too much change in too short a time" (pp. 1-2). These rapid vacillations are in and of themselves an elemental force exerting an influence over our private and social existence. However, despite this reality, facts and figures available to us do permit the drawing of certain speculations. It is estimated that: 1) Americans spend approximately 10 billion dollars a year on dieting; 2) one in 10 Americans suffers from some sort of eating disorder; 3) approximately one in 250 adolescents and young women has anorexia nervosa; and 4) at least three-and-a-half-million people (predominantly female) are struggling with bulimia (NBC Nightly News, January 5, 1984). That the nation is obsessed by health, fitness, and especially the dread of fat is undeniable. One need only turn to our media with its barrage of diet-oriented advertising for corroboration. Simultaneously, in a truly stress-producing process, the same society devotes even more time and money lavishing attention on the joys of food and consumption. These twin national obsessions help engender classic approach-avoidance responses, particularly in the behavior of impressionable adolescents and young adults, who are primary recipients of the advertiser's message. At this point, given the developing trends of the past decade, one projection may be ventured: Eating disorders will probably continue to expand at all levels of society. As women continue to enter the workforce (increasingly with managerial status), marry at a later age, feel the pressure of competing role demands, and remain unprepared for the stresses accompanying these changes, such a disheartening pattern seems almost inevitable.

Should the proliferation reach epidemic proportions (as some experts already contend is the case with bulimia), it may not be too naive to expect some sort of demand for a consciousness-raising or grass roots counterculture movement (headed by concerned parents, educators, and health professionals) targeting the insidious advertising that abounds today. The most obvious and effective action might entail a boycott of companies and their products deemed particularly destructive, coupled with a call for an end to the display of near-emaciated models in their advertising campaigns. The obsessogenic marketing strategies forever admonishing us to "watch every calorie" should not go unchallenged.

The utilization of education is crucial when considering potentially creative pathways of change in the future. Be it in schools, parent effectiveness groups, churches, or community action committees, preventative and/or corrective educational experiences need to be made readily available. Early detection of and response to warning signs can make the difference between an illness of but a few months' duration or one following a chronic course. Mental health organizations can pave the way for this preventative endeavor by offering informational programs to the public at large. Health specialists have noted that the most successful prevention projects are those developed and implemented by concerned communities. Something modeled after the Alcoholics Anonymous approach might, for instance, be especially helpful for the growing bulimic population.

The aid of individuals with direct influence over adolescents and young adults, such as guidance counselors, teachers, pediatricians, coaches, college residence advisors, and youth ministers, must be actively solicited. A massive educational assault must be mounted at the college level where bulimia is emerging in an alarmingly high percentage of the female student population. This development would constitute the finest creative expression of responsible, in loco parentis control. Education can lead to prevention and change. Witness a recently reported study at Baylor University's Medical Center in Dallas, Texas. Upon learning that purging (via laxative abuse) resulted in but a minor (12%) decrease in absorbed calories, many bulimic women discontinued the practice (American Anorexia and Bulimia Association of Philadelphia Newsletter, 1984). Such convincing evidence needs to be widely disseminated so that others may be similarly influenced.

Future educational advancements must sway the thought and action of mental health practitioners and physicians as well. Increasing recognition of the intricate psychosomatic threads weaving throughout the fabric of many of today's illnesses has resulted in a far keener appreciation and understanding of the potent reciprocal influence of body and mind. The blossoming holistic health movement is an outgrowth of this belated acknowledgment. Recently, a directive was issued by the president of Harvard University (Boston Globe, 1984a). It called for, among other things, a greater respect in medical students' ongoing education for the impact of the mind on physical illness, and the infusion of future medical instruction with more holistic themes. (In this regard it should be noted, parenthetically, that doctors, too, are subject to cultural obsessions and prejudices. Known to possess streaks of perfectionism, while predisposed toward overachievement and repression of impulses, they are susceptible to "fat phobias" as well, and thus must be especially sensitive when treating the anorexic/bulimic.) These and other encouraging signs point to a rapidly approaching time in which the *entire person*, not just an objectively scrutinized diseased portion of the body (or mind), will be receiving care.

Yet another intriguing realm of conjecture involves what many sociologists today term the "androgynization" of culture (Kaplan & Bean, 1976). Evolving models of cultural esteem — from the macho image of the Marlboro man to the gentle and sensitive style of pop singer Michael Jackson — attest to a not so subtle change in values surrounding masculine identity. *People* magazine (1984), purveyor of middle America's tastes and interests, loudly proclaims (with its cover story on Boy George, a popular English punk rock star noted for his outlandish transvestism) the arrival of a "gender blender" society replete with unisex clothing and hairstyles, movies and plays celebrating the virtues of cross-dressing, and trend-setting entertainers of indeterminate sex. At the same time, advertising, taking its cue from the persuasive women's movement, asks the "new man," "Are you strong enough to be weak?" Perhaps the gradual merging of genders is a natural byproduct of a society bent on instituting universal depersonalization. Perhaps the fusion is inescapable in a land of glorified technology, where computers and ID numbers hold sway above humanity. Given the above, it is not surprising to find that a major complaint of patients in sex therapists' offices across the nation entails a lack of desire resulting in something akin to a collective asexuality. The implications stemming from this trend are manifold, particularly as they relate to eating disorder epidemiology. Foremost among these is the possible increased incidence of anorexia and bulimia in the male population. There is some preliminary evidence supporting such a development. In the case of bulimic men, the syndrome is surfacing noticeably in conjunction with occupational pressures (White, 1984), while recent attention has been paid to compulsive male runners and their psychic similarity to female anorexics.

Many important socioculturally-oriented questions remain unanswered. To what extent has our era inherited and been influenced by the legacy of past female mistreatment, e.g., the practice of binding feet in China or the corseting of women in Victorian times, and what may we come to understand in examining this mistreatment? As the superpowers lurch perilously close to nuclear annihilation, may not a case be made for viewing the country's obsession with "health" as a displaced fear of national proportion, one manifested in an attempt to control, at the very least, one's own body? Can a spiritual reawakening be generated across the land, one commensurate with a deeper appreciation and respect for *who* people *are*, rather than for *what* they *do* or how they look? There is ample documentation that women experience chronic and pervasive dissatisfaction with their bodies and, while we can delineate the broad cultural pressures feeding this unhappiness, we know little about specific conditions determining who will be most affected and who not at all. It would be enormously helpful to have studies (utilizing social and family background, psychological profile, etc.) involving women possessing a positive and realistic body image in contradistinction to women manifesting pronounced body distortion and dissatisfaction. Finally, with the turbulent upheaval in sex roles sweeping the country, we might see, as women continue to grow beyond the traditional femininity synonymous with dependency and passivity, an eventual *diminution* of eating disorders among females. These and other issues await exploration. Answers may someday shed light on the part sociocultural factors play in the formation of eating disorders. Clearly, with females comprising an overwhelming majority of those suffering from anorexia or bulimia, the argument for this being an integral component is a compelling one.

PSYCHOLOGICAL TRENDS

As biomedical and sociocultural elements receive closer scrutiny in the future, so too will the realms of psychological research and direct patient care continue to draw deserved interest from the nation's health professionals. This section will consider these dual aspects so crucial in a thorough understanding of eating disorder etiology and treatment.

The future directions of psychological research and theory encompassing anorexia and bulimia promise to be diverse. One such area may involve infant development studies. The data beginning to emerge from sources such as the Clinical Infant Research Unit at the National Institute of Mental Health suggest that certain inherent deficits in the early parent-infant relationship may be causally linked to the child's later difficulty in connecting with others, poor self-esteem, isolation, sense of personal ineffectiveness and marked inability to soothe the self—basic personality features of those struggling with eating disorders. The determination and detection of such potentially debilitating deficits may someday lead to early remedial action on the part of therapists.

Given the fact that anorexia/bulimia is found overwhelmingly in females, it should not be surprising to soon discover eating disorders being examined within the context of psychological theory directly informed by nascent women's development studies. Emerging from the work of women such as Chodorow (1978) and Gilligan (1982), this perspective may serve to enhance our understanding of not only critical male/female differences, but also (and more important for investigators of eating disorders) the complicated dynamics immanent within the mother/daughter relationship.

This perspective is rooted in the notion that gender identity, the immutable core of personality development, is firmly established by about the age of three for both sexes, but is experienced differently by boys and girls owing to the fact that the primary caretaker, ordinarily, is female. Thus, girls, sensing themselves as similar to their mothers, undergo a fusing process, whereby attachment and identity are merged. Boys, because of the sexual issues involved in distinguishing their male identity from Mother's female identity, are more imbued with a need for separation. Boundaries are more rigidly constructed for males in this ego-forming process, while females emerge from this period with a deeper felt need for, and ability to express, empathy. The end result possesses intriguing implications for students of eating psychopathology. Gilligan (1982) summarizes what this difference in male/female development engenders:

> . . . relationships, and particularly issues of dependency, are experienced differently by women and men. For boys and men, separation and individuation are critically tied to gender identity since separation from mother is essential for the development of masculinity. For girls and women, issues of femininity or female identity do not depend on the achievement of separation from the mother or on the progress of individuation. Since masculinity is defined through separation while femininity is defined through attachment, male gender identity is threatened by intimacy while female gender identity is threatened by separation. Thus males tend to have difficulty with relationships, while females tend to have problems with individuation . . . Women's failure to separate then becomes . . . a failure to develop. (pp. 8-9)

Greater appreciation of this psychodynamic matrix, from which flow identity issues so central to later ego development, is just beginning to appear. The full impact of such a perspective on the theory and treatment of eating disorders will not be felt for some time, but its mere existence is already prompting researchers and clinicians to reanalyze the possibly flawed formulations of psychoanalytically-based theory skewed by male bias.

Coupled with early development investigations will be broader epidemiological studies of the general population. Significant exploration of eating disorders in subpopulations such as diabetics and homosexuals, along with analysis of such factors as birth order and family history, will be undertaken. At present, subclassifications of bulimics are virtually nonexistent. Experienced clinicians are aware of the different types of bulimic behavior (witness the weekend "binge-aholic," the virtual nonstop binger, and the individual performing the binge/purge ritual on a regular but infrequent basis); however, the factors predisposing a person toward one symptomatic expression versus another, as well as potentially productive strategic therapeutic interventions ameliorating such symptoms, remain hidden.

As epidemiological research advances, so too will there be a refinement of outcome studies based on more thorough and explicit standards of recovery. In addition to simple weight gain and resumption of menstruation for anorexics and cessation of the binge/purge cycle for bulimics, measures of psychosexual and psychosocial adjustment, vocational satisfaction, improved self-concept, etc., must also be developed for consideration if complete recovery is to be documented. While symptoms may disappear, the ingrained anorexic or bulimic personality structure may long endure. These psychic orientations and the problems in living associated with them have not been adequately addressed in present outcome studies. In this regard, Minuchin, Rosman, & Baker (1978) ask,

> Has the weight gain been sustained? Has there been a personality change enabling the patient to cope with the world outside the therapy room and hospital? Have the processes of psychological and emotional development been reinstituted, so that new issues of growth can be met? (p. 126)

Such documentation must rely on long-term (five years of more) longitudinal and prognostic studies of high-risk groups who will be followed through the entire course of their illness, with projections as to who will and who won't respond to treatment based on predictive data (Morgan, Purgold, & Welbourne, 1983). Such future endeavors are not without problems, particularly in terms of design and application.

Research clarity also requires the development of more exact instruments for clinical evaluation and screening, tests which will measure the behavioral and psychological characteristics of anorexics and bulimics more precisely. At this juncture, the spectrum of normal and abnormal eating behaviors and the psychological, emotional, and cognitive features linked to such patterns are not well defined or delineated. Armed with more precise tests and finer standardized diagnostic criteria, researchers in the future may devise controlled studies involving cross-sectional comparisons between populations exhibiting healthy and destructive eating patterns, thus uncovering underlying psychopathologies applicable to clinical practice and other realms of pertinent research. Presently, we have few clues as to which, and to what extent, variables (e.g., depression, anxiety, self-perception) exert an influence over the genesis and development of pathological eating behavior. One such powerful variable, for instance, may be that of body image. The relationship between body image/weight obsession and overall functioning awaits analysis. Researchers Wooley and Wooley (1980) ask,

> To what extent, and in what ways, do insecurities over appearance affect the ability of women to assert themselves socially, professionally, and intellectually? Effects could be sought in global measures of accomplishments and level of functioning and in very specific behavioral observations which could point to the typical ways in which such insecurities are expressed in interpersonal or other behaviors (e.g. self-effacement, excessive compliance). (p. 155)

In future psychological research other important questions vis-à-vis treatment and theory will be addressed: What gender identity issues, for both male and female patients, are of greatest significance? Are particular purging methods related to specific emotional/cognitive impairments? Which predisposing factors (age, sex, marital status, socioeconomic level, race, chronicity, age of onset, etc.) are significant in understanding the course of eating psychopathology? How do such clinical features as body weight, history of obesity, thought disorder, purging methods, premorbid adjustment, family environment, and past treatment responses affect prognosis? Does the therapist's sex influence the content and outcome of therapy?

Research into such questions as those posed above must be linked to ongoing treatment programs to maximize relevance. The Wooleys, for example, note a glaring lack of treatment techniques aimed at specifically alleviating poor body image. Such an absence underscores the tremendous speed at which the entire field has progressed. If, indeed, history repeats itself, then we are likely to see unfold in the upcoming years new variants of treatment for eating disorders. Already we are besieged by competing claims of therapeutic success and superiority. Obviously, controlled studies contrasting different forms of treatment encompassing both anorexics and bulimics would greatly enhance our ability to creatively combat the disorders, but, as Minuchin et al. (1978) observe,

> . . . the vast majority of reports on the effectiveness of treatment describe programs . . . are conducted within clinical contexts. Thus, controlled comparisons of different treatments on matched populations are neither clinically nor ethically feasible. (p. 126)

Without such definitive comparative controlled studies, each approach must be judged on its own merit. It is hoped that this situation will engender increased dialogue between representatives of the many treatment modalities in the field. One trend we might look forward to involves improved teamwork between the various health professionals often engaged in treating the anorexic or bulimic. In an age where specialization is on the rise, the multifaceted eating disorder requires an integrative clinical perspective, one in which the medical doctor, nutritionist, psychotherapist/family therapist, nurse, and social worker—all of whom may at some point be involved in the therapy— can exchange helpful information by communicating openly and planning cooperatively. Just as an egalitarian cross-specialty approach is desirable, so too will there be adoption of more flexible multimodal treatment plans in the future.

In terms of inpatient care, we may expect a paring down of the time individuals spend in hospital, coupled with a quicker transition to structured long-term day programs. In this manner, ingrained debilitating feelings of dependency, helplessness, poor self-esteem, and ineffectiveness can be better combatted. Such a transition back into society might be facilitated by the supportive presence of residential centers similar in function and philosophy to the halfway house. Freestanding facilities for anorexics and bulimics, where an integrative, holistic treatment protocol is consistently applied, will soon become a reality. These transitional institutions would be staffed by individuals who have undergone a focused training (something sadly lacking at present), incorporating a thorough grounding in the dynamics of psychosomatic illness in general and, in particular, the distinctive aspects of eating disorders. Such an intermediate living situation would serve as a secure stepping stone as well, providing the anorexic/bulimic with a safe harbor from which to venture out into the environmental stresses impinging upon her daily.

Specific forms of therapy will continue to flourish and develop as time moves on. Group treatment, if preliminary results are representative, holds great promise, especially for bulimics. More long-term data with respect to group versus individual therapy effectiveness need to be compiled, in addition to assessment of such factors as ideal group size and impact of age and anorexic/bulimic mix in the group experience. Another crucial outgrowth of successful group treatment appears to be the importance of follow-up and the maintenance of support supplied to and by former group members. One major prognostic indicator found to be most relevant is the fact that women who remain in contact with one another after group treatment tend to progress more rapidly and ultimately attenuate their bulimic behavior better than those who do not (White, 1984). Whether this reflects a causal relationship or not remains to be explored. Regardless, it does provide support for the development of urgently needed self-help groups and aid societies across the nation. Such caring communities are essential for helping recovering anorexics and bulimics sustain healthy eating behavior.

Many therapists, influenced by growing feminist consciousness and a recognition of the pronounced sociocultural component to eating disorder etiology and symptomatology, may gradually shift the emphasis in treatment from the intrapsychic to the interpersonal and cognitive realms. Reeducation will play a major role in this trend, as women will be offered new models of a strong and independent femininity. (Indeed, perhaps someday we will be able to dispense altogether with the destructively confining habit of rigidly ascribing a select portion of what should be universal human attributes to one sex, and another antithetical set of qualities to the other!)

Further research into the functioning of bulimic family systems must also be conducted. To date most treatment results have incorporated therapy with anorexic families, largely because the identified patient is so noticeably disruptive to the system, and, in part, because bulimics, being secretive and tending to be older, often do not live in proximity to their families of origin.

Finally, less traditional treatment modalities should be considered. Psychodrama, body and movement therapies, for instance, aid inhibited anorexics and bulimics in releasing long-repressed feelings, while teaching them to redirect and channel their emotions in a more constructive fashion.

A FINAL PERSPECTIVE

This survey would be remiss if it did not at least cursorily acknowledge an important, but often overlooked, emerging perspective bearing on not merely the future of the eating disorders field, but all of society as well. It might be termed a spiritual perspective, philosophical/religious belief, or, as the originator of the relaxation response, Dr. Herbert Benson, in his recent book (1984) has dubbed it, "the faith factor." It is an exciting new field, awaiting scientific exploration, based upon the centuries-old acknowledgment by monks, ministers, and mystics of the mental and physical healing effects triggered by a deeply held faith. What some may view as simply the long established byproduct of the placebo effect is in fact a powerful influence which cannot be dismissed as merely a beguiling "mind-over-matter," unverifiable cliché. Indeed, the recent discovery of a neurochemical basis for the placebo effect offers intriguing possibilities for further investigation into this little researched area. Many of the problems doctors daily confront in their patients are self-limiting illnesses stemming from mind-body interactions. The future will find researchers actively investigating the possible emotional and physiological effects of personal belief systems.

In a land revering slimness over substance, in a culture extolling external appearance instead of soul, it is little wonder that we find our children and young adults literally starving themselves to death, manifesting a despair that, symbolically and symptomatically, results in an emptiness, a nausea, a sickness reflecting the pitiful obsession of a society brainwashed into believing that love and fulfillment are open to anyone managing to avoid the dreaded "pinch of an inch." Thirty years ago, psychotherapist and philosopher Rollo May (1953) observed of our society that " . . . the chief problem of people of the 20th century is emptiness . . . " (p. 14). He went on to note that

> the human being cannot live in a condition of emptiness for very long. . . . The pent-up potentialities turn into morbidity and despair, and eventually into destructive activities. . . . The *feeling* of emptiness . . . generally comes from people's feeling that they are *powerless* to do anything effective about their lives or the world they live in. . . . When a person continually faces danger he is powerless to overcome, his final line of defense is at last to avoid even feeling the dangers. (p. 24)

The rampant fat phobia we currently witness clearly constitutes a societal spiritual malaise. It is a vivid demonstration of an idolatrous cultural mindset where the worshipped slender body, like some miraculous icon, seduces unsuspecting vulnerable victims via TV and magazine covers. An advertising barrage tantalizingly and incessantly dangles before us the magical talismans of liquid diets and appetite-suppressing drugs. The theologian, Richard Niebuhr, accurately pinpointed this moral disease when he wrote of the "small 'g' gods" we create in a sterile effort at personally controlling every aspect of our often threatening existence. Thus has health and, more specifically, the often grotesquely slender frame come to dominate the altar of our collective unconscious. It sometimes seems as if a surreptitious force has entered our world in the guise of a civil religion heralding the arrival of an 11th commandment: Thou shalt be skinny! As a fetish, it reflects much of our rootless superficiality, formed as we drift from the core of life's ultimate meanings and concerns. The saddest commentary becomes the manner in which, all too often, children are raised in a conditional atmosphere of pseudo-acceptance, where love is doled out in a piecemeal fashion for achievement and appearance, rather than for the sheer simple fact of being.

In perhaps this century's most cogent inquiry into the nature of love, Fromm (1956) captured the essence of this destructive process and, in so doing, offers precious insight into the foundation of a world in which eating disorders flourish:

> Modern man's happiness consists of the thrill of looking at the shop windows, and in buying all that he can afford to buy. . . . He looks at people in a similar way. . . . [People seek] a nice package of qualities which are popular and sought after on the personality market. What specifically makes a person attractive depends on the fashion of the time. . . . In a culture in which the marketing orientation prevails . . . there is little reason to be surprised that human love relations follow the same pattern of exchange which governs the commodity . . . market. (pp. 3-4)

For Fromm, as with contemporary chroniclers of the spiritual state of humanity, there is unanimity over the fact that

> love is possible only if two persons communicate with each other from the center of their existence. . . . There is only one proof for the presence of love: the depth of the relationship. . . . (p. 103)

This elusive yet essential depth, the sole hope for not only anorexics and bulimics, but all of society's members, can never be generated in a land where the measure of a person's worth is judged by the shallow standards of wealth, weight, or the whiteness of a smile. As humans, as therapists, we must never lose sight of a central truth of existence: The wellspring of life is unconditional love; the bedrock of growth is the trusted knowledge that one is loved for who one is, not for what one does or how one appears.

This healing depth may be experienced in the therapeutic relationship. It is within this environment, marked by security, trust, and concern, that new life may be breathed into an apathetic soul. Indeed, it is a special process which, when etymologically understood, mirrors the essence of the modern day meaning of "spirit," deriving, as it does, from the Latin *spiritus*, "breath," and *spirare*, "to breathe." Thus does Webster's (1981) dictionary define spirit as "an animating or vital principle held to give life to physical beings." Is this not the ultimate goal in the arduous journey of psychotherapy? At the mysterious interface between mind and body, spirit is encountered and must be reckoned with. There is often a crucial point at which the evolving client arrives, a moment of truth (or, more accurately, a series of such potent moments) in which critical leaps of faith must be ventured, small yet terrifying risks taken, where habits long held are broken, and feelings long concealed are finally revealed. This marks the crisis time when a person, to continue improving, must act without the facilitative guidance and support of the therapist. It is not surprising that the venerable Alcoholics Anonymous organization has so successfully employed the concept of a "higher power" in steering alcoholics toward eventual recovery. It is based on the awareness that faith and courage are invaluable spiritual assets to be nourished and cherished during the struggle toward health.

In a recent interview, Benson observed that, owing to the dualism of mind and body promulgated by Descartes, science has "largely turned its back on healing and religion. . . . As a scientist and physician, I can observe . . . that when people believe in higher forces or factors that influence their lives . . . changes occur" (*Boston Globe*, 1984b, p. 2). The era of underestimating the mind/spirit's sway over the body and senses is rapidly drawing to a close. Widespread acceptance of such a perspective may provide a truly holistic foundation for the treatment of eating disorders in the future.

REFERENCES

American Anorexia and Bulimia Association of Philadelphia Newsletter (1984, March). *3*, 2.
Benson, H. (1984). *Beyond the relaxation response*. New York: Times Books.
Boston Globe, April 20, 1984a, p. 1.
Boston Globe, August 29, 1984b, p. 2.
Chodorow, N. (1978). *The reproduction of mothering*. Berkeley, CA: University of California Press.
Fromm, E. (1956). *The art of loving*. New York: Harper & Row.
Gilligan, C. (1982). *In a different voice*. Cambridge, MA: Harvard University Press.
Hughes, P. L., Wells, L. A., & Cunningham, C. J. (1984). *Controlled trial using desipramine for bulimia*: Paper presented at the annual meeting of the American Psychiatric Association, Los Angeles, CA, May 9.
Kaplan, A. G., & Bean, J. P. (Eds.). (1976). *Beyond sex-role stereotypes: Readings toward a psychology of androgyny*. Boston: Little-Brown.
Kaye, W. H., Ebert, M. H., & Gwirtsman, H. E. (1984). Brain serotonergic metabolism differentiates between patients with anorexia that fast or binge. (Abstr. 138) First Int'l Conference on Eating Disorders, New York, April 1984.
Kaye, W. H., Ebert, M. H., Raleigh, M., & Lake, C. R. (1984). Abnormalities in CNS monoamine metabolism in anorexia nervosa. *Archives of General Psychiatry, 41*, 350-355.
May, R. (1953). *Man's search for himself*. New York: Norton.
Minuchin, S., Rosman, B., & Baker, L. (1978). *Psychosomatic families: Anorexia nervosa in context*. Cambridge, MA: Harvard University Press.
Morgan, H. G., Purgold, J., & Welbourne, J. (1983). Management and outcome of anorexia nervosa: A standardized prognostic study. *British Journal of Psychiatry, 143*, 282-287.
People magazine, April 23, 1984.

Pope, H. G., Jr., Hudson, J. I., & Jonas, J. M. (1984). *Treatment of bulimia with antidepressants: A research update*. Presented at the annual meeting of the American Psychiatric Association, Los Angeles, CA, May 10.

Rohrbaugh, J. B. (1979). *Women: Psychology's puzzle*. New York: Basic Books.

Toffler, A. (1971). *Future shock*. New York: Bantam Books.

Trygstad, O., Foss, I., Edminson, P. D., Johansen, J. H., & Reichelt, K. L. (1978). Hormonal control of appetite: A urinary anorexigenic peptide. Chromatographic patterns of urinary peptides in anorexia nervosa. *Acta Endocrinologica, 89*, 196–208.

Walsh, B. T., Stewart, J., Roose, S. P., et al. (1984). *Phenelzine in the treatment of bulimia*. Presented at the annual meeting of the American Psychiatric Association, Los Angeles, CA, May 7.

Webster's seventh new collegiate dictionary. (1981). Springfield, MA: C. & C. Merriam.

White, W. C. (1984). Personal communication.

Wooley, S. C., & Wooley, O. W. (1980). Eating disorders: Obesity and anorexia. In A. M. Brodsky & R. Hare-Mustin (Eds.), *Women and psychotherapy*. New York: Guilford Press.

Index

Abraham, S. F., 301
Administrators, in Therapeutic Contract Program, 215
Adrenocortical hormones, 61-64
Adrenocorticotropic hormone (ACTH), 62-64
Advertising, 308
Affective disorder theory, 76-78
Aftercare
　for bulimarexics, 248
　in Therapeutic Contract Program, 231-32
Age, 119-21
　in prognosis for anorexics, 296
Alcoholics Anonymous, 318
Alimentation, 36-37
Amenorrhea, 6-7, 58-60, 293
　in bulimarexics, 199
Amitriptyline (Elavil), 86
Analytic psychotherapy, 162-66
Androgen, 64
"Androgynization" of culture, 310
Anorexia Aid Societies, 114, 232
Anorexia nervosa
　adrenocortical hormones and, 61-64
　antidepressant treatment of, 78-80
　biochemical effects of, 10-11
　bulimarexia and, 194, 249
　bulimarexia compared with, 199
　bulimia in, 21-23
　cardiovascular complications of, 12-13
　cyproheptadine (Periactin), treatment for, 74-75
　dental complications of, 15
　endocrine manifestations of, 6-9
　etiology of, 101-2
　feminist perspective of social considerations in, 127-37
　fluid and electrolyte complications of, 9-10
　gastrointestinal complications of, 11-12
　gonadotropins in, 7, 57-60
　growth hormone and, 7, 55-56
　hematologic and immunologic complications of, 13-14
　increase in, 98-101
　in infants, 204-5
　inpatient treatment of, 211-32
　intrapsychic level in, 179-80
　medical complications of, 5-6
　neuroendocrine aspects of, 51-52
　neuroendocrine regulation of appetite in, 52-53
　neurotransmitters and, 64-68
　nurturant-authoritative psychotherapeutic relationships for, 234-45
　nutritional assessment of, 30-35
　nutritional effects of, 20-30
　nutritional treatment of, 35-47
　outcome of, 291-99
　psychologic, neurologic, and ophthalmologic complications of, 14-15
　psychotherapeutic partnering approach to treatment of, 154-73
　risk factor model of, 102-4
　sociocultural context of, 95-98
　studies of treatments of, 73-74

Anorexia nervosa (continued)
  temperature regulation in, 56
  therapeutic dilemmas in treatment of anorexia nervosa self-psychological perspective on, 268-87
  thyroid hormones in, 53-55
  trends in biomedical research into, 305-8
  trends in psychological research into, 311-15
  trends in sociocultural research into, 308-11
  vasopressin and, 56-57
Anorexia Nervosa Aid Society, 114, 232
Anticonvulsant drugs, 75, 300-1
Antidepressant treatments, 76
  for anorexia nervosa, 78-80
  for bulimia, 80-88, 300
  trends in research in, 306-7
Antidiuretic hormones
  ADH, 9
  vasopressin, 56-57
Appetite
  anorexia nervosa and, 20-21
  neuroendocrine regulation of, 52-53
Appetite stimulants, 74-75
Apter, Nathaniel, 98-99
Archer, A. G., 14-15
Aristotle, 195
Armstrong, Lesley Hornby (Twiggy), 97, 115, 116, 122, 123
Arrhythmia, 5, 12
Asystole, 5
Athletics, 30

Bacon, Sir Francis, 304
Baker, L., 182, 298, 313
Ballet dancers, 110
Bassoe, H., 13
Beauty
  dieting and, 29
  sociocultural portrayals of, 97, 104
Behavior
  appetite and, 21
  avoidance of eating, by anorexics, 38-39
  impulsive, 23
  in life adaptation model, 108
  nutritional consequences of abnormalities in, in anorexia nervosa, 26-28
  obsessive, in dieting, 238
  in prognosis for anorexics, 295-96
  during severe starvation, 14
  sociocultural forces, personality and, 103-4
  of starvation subjects and anorexics, 52-53
  see also Eating behavior

Behavioral contracting
  in intervention strategies for bulimarexia, 253-54
  see also Therapeutic contracts
Behavior modification techniques, in nutritional treatment, 44
Behavior therapy, 74
  Bruch's criticisms of, 211-12
Belfer, P., 221
Bender, Marilyn, 122
Benson, April, on psychotherapeutic partnering approach to treatment of anorexia nervosa and bulimia, 154-73
Benson, Herbert, 316, 318
Berglas, S., 212
Berlin, I., 156
Beta-endorphin, 305
Beuf, A., 123
Beumont, P. T. V., 199
Binge eating
  by anorexics, 128
  antidepressant treatment of, 80
  in bulimarexia, 113
  neuroendocrine regulation of appetite in, 52-53
  norepinephrine and, 65
  paradoxical prescription for, 151-52
  as seizure disorder, 75
  in survey of bulimarexics, 258-59, 262-63
  see also Bulimarexia; Bulimia
Biochemical effects of anorexia nervosa and bulimia, 10-11
  trends in research into, 305-8
Biological treatments, 73-74
  affective disorder theory in, 76-78
  of anorexia nervosa, antidepressant, 78-80
  of bulimia, antidepressant, 80-88
  using cyproheptadine and phenytoin, 74-75
Biomedical research
  trends in, 305-8
  see also Medical complications of anorexia nervosa and bulimia
Blacks, 119
Blendis, L. M., 11
Blood complications, 13-14
Blood levels, in monitoring of antidepressant treatments, 86
Boatman, M., 156
Body awareness groups, in Therapeutic Contract Program, 221
Body image, see Self-image
Bone fractures, 8
Boskind-White, Marlene, on sociocultural perspective on bulimarexia, 113-25

Index

Boy George, 310
Bronfenbrenner, U., 175
Browning, W. Nicholson, on long-term dynamic group therapy for bulimia, 141-53
Brubakk, D., 13
Bruch, Hilde, xviii
  on behavioral approach, 211
  on concept of false self, 144-45
  on family in treatment of anorexia nervosa, 156-57
  on increase in anorexia nervosa, 99
  on lack of ego structures in anorexics, 101
  on male anorexics, 296
  on psychoanalytic interpretation, 286
  of psychological criteria for anorexia nervosa, 103
  on resistance by anorexics, 279
  on sociocultural forces in anorexia nervosa, 96
  on therapeutic approach to anorexia nervosa, 269
  on women in black culture, 118-19
Bulimarexia
  case history in, 176-92
  intervention strategies and outcomes for, 246-67
  psychodynamic view of, 194-210
  sociocultural perspective on, 113-25
Bulimia
  adrenocortical hormones and, 64
  amenorrhea and, 60
  in anorexics, 21-23, 293
  antidepressant treatment of, 80-88
  biochemical effects of, 10-11
  cardiovascular complications of, 12-13
  dental complications of, 15
  dexamethasone suppression in, 64
  DSM II definition of, 247
  endocrine manifestations of, 6-9
  fluid and electrolyte complications of, 9-10
  gastrointestinal complications of, 11-12
  gonadotropins and, 58
  growth hormone and, 56
  hematologic and immunologic complications of, 13-14
  long-term group therapy for, 141-53
  major affective disorder and, 78
  medical complications of, 5-6
  neuroendocrine regulation of appetite in, 52-53
  norepinephrine and, 65, 66
  nutritional assessment of, 30-35
  nutritional effects of, 20-30
  nutritional treatment of, 35-47
  outcome of, 300-1
  phenytoin treatment for, 74, 75
  in prognosis for anorexics, 295-96
  psychologic, neurologic, and ophthalmologic complications of, 14-15
  psychotherapeutic partnering approach to treatment of, 154-73
  sociocultural context of, 95-98
  studies of treatments of, 73-74
  thyroid hormone levels in, 55
  trends in biomedical research into, 305-8
  trends in psychological research into, 311-15
  trends in sociocultural research into, 308-11
Bulimia nervosa, see Bulimarexia
Bulimic anorexia nervosa, 21-23
  nutritional treatment for, 43-46
  see also Bulimarexia
Buvat, J., 59

Cannibalistic fantasies, 202
Cantwell, D. P., 295
Cardiac arrhythmias, 12
Cardiorespiratory function, 13
Cardiovascular system, 12-13
Carotene, 60
Casper, R. C., 10, 301
Cathartics, 195-96
Central nervous system neurotransmitters, 64-68
Chernin, K., 122
Children
  empathy in normal development of self in, 269-71
  failures in parental empathy for, 271-78
  independence encouraged in, 235-36
  obesity in, 98
  parental pathology in development of disorders in, 155-56
Chodorow, N., 311
Cholesterol, 11
Chronic anorexia, 294
Class aspects of female image, 117-19
Classical conversion hysteria, 104-5
Clinical intervention, see Intervention
Clinical observations, in nutritional assessment, 34
Clomiphene, 58-59
Clomipramine, 79
College, first year of, 240
Confidentiality, 161
Confrontation, by anorexics, 239
Connors, M., 301
Constipation, 11
  in recovering anorexics, 46-47

Contingency managers (CM), 214, 227
Contracts, therapeutic
  in intervention strategies for bulimarexia, 253-54
  paradoxical prescriptions in, 151-52
  in Therapeutic Contract Program, 216-20
Control
  as goal of anorexics, 133-34
  sense of, in bulimics, 143
Conversion hysteria, 104-5
Copeland, Paul M., on neuroendocrine aspects of eating disorders, 51-68
Corticotropin-releasing factor (CRF), 62, 63
Cortisol, 7, 61-62
Countertransference, 164, 165
Crisp, A. H.
  on anorexia nervosa as "fat phobia," 104, 180
  on cholesterol values, 10, 11
  on culturally distorted view of fat and food, 187
  on EEG abnormalities in anorexics, 14
  on effects of reduced estrogen in anorexics, 8
  follow-ups on anorexics by, 292
  on incidence of anorexia nervosa, 100
  on personality in prognosis for anorexics, 296
Cultural change, 195-97
Cyproheptadine (Periactin), 67, 74-75

Dally, P., 294
Death
  from anorexia nervosa, 292, 294
  by arrhythmia and asystole, 5
  causes of, in anorexia nervosa, 25
Dental complications of anorexia nervosa and bulimia, 15
  from self-induced vomiting, 26
Dependence, 243
Depression, 307
  as major affective disorder, 76-78
  neuroendocrines and, 63
  see also Antidepressant treatments
Desipramine (Norpramin), 86
Desyrel (trazodone), 79
Developmental stages
  empathy and, 269-71
  in life adaptation model, 107
  patterns of adaptation to, 186-89
  significance of eating in, 200-8
Dexamethasone, 62, 64
Diabetes mellitus, 12
Diagnostic and Statistical Manual of Mental Disorders (DSM-III; American Psychiatric Association), 298

Diet, patient involvement in monitoring, 41
Dieters, 199
Dieting, 308
  obsessive behavior in, 238
  popularity of, 95
  popular magazine articles on, 97
  as trigger of anorexia nervosa and bulimia, 29-30
Dietrich, Marlene, 122
Dilantin (phenytoin), 74, 75, 300-1
Dior, 122
Discipline, in intervention strategies for bulimarexia, 250
Disequilibrium concept, 175-76
  in adaptation patterns to developmental stages, 188
  in extended sequences, 185-86
  in intrapsychic level, 180-81
  in moment-to-moment sequences, 183-84
  in transgenerational images and sequences, 190
Diuretics, abuse of, in anorexia nervosa, 24, 26-28
Dooley, Catherine P., on inpatient treatment of anorexia nervosa, 211-32
Drug treatments
  for bulimia, 300-1
  in Therapeutic Contract Program, 229-31
  trends in research in, 306-8
  using antidepressants, for anorexia nervosa, 78-80
  using antidepressants, for bulimia, 80-88
  using cyproheptadine, 74-75
  using phenytoin, 75
Dwyer, Johanna
  on nutritional aspects of anorexia nervosa and bulimia, 20-48
Dym, Barry, on eating disorders and family, 174-92
Dynamic group therapy, for bulimia, 141-53

Eating
  avoidance of, by anorexics, 38-39
  developmental significance of, 200-8
  in Therapeutic Contract Program, 223
Eating Attitudes Test, 110
Eating behavior, 33
  neuroendocrinology of, 305
  in prognosis of anorexics, 293-94
Eating disorders
  biological treatments of, 73-89
  etiology of, 101-2
  family and, intervention in, 174-92
  increase in, 98-101

Index

neuroendocrine aspects of, 51-68
risk factor model for, 102-4
sociocultural context of, 95-98
trends in research into, 304-18
see also Anorexia nervosa; Bulimarexia; Bulimia
Ebert, M. H., 9
Edema, 25
Education, 309
Ego, 277
  Freud on ejection of "bad" by, 201, 203-4
Ego psychological theory on etiology of anorexia nervosa, 101
Ehrenreich, B., 124
Elavil (amitriptyline), 86
Electrolyte complications of anorexia nervosa and bulimia, 9-10
Emmett, Steven Wiley, on future trends, 304-18
Empathy, 269-71
  parental, anorexia nervosa and failures in, 271-78
  in psychotherapy, 278-84
Endocrine system, 6-9
  andrenocortical hormones, 61-64
  anorexia nervosa triggered by, 101
  antidiuretic hormone, 56-57
  appetite regulation by, 52-53
  central nervous system neurotransmitters, 64-68
  gonadotropins, 7, 57-60
  growth hormones, 7, 55-56
  neuroendocrines, 51-52
  starvation-induced changes in, 25
  temperature regulation by, 56
  thyroid hormones, 53-55
Endomorphy, 98
Energy intake, in nutritional treatment, 42-43
Energy needs, in nutritional treatment, 39-40
English, D., 124
Equilibrium, *see* Disequilibrium concept
Estrogen, 6-8
Etiology of eating disorders, 101-2
Exercise, 39
Extended sequences, 185-86

Fain, M., 201-2
Fairburn, C. G., 44-46, 300
"Faith factor," 316
Falk, J. R., 296
"False self" concept, 144-46, 274
Family
  of bulimics, psychological research into, 315

concept of false self and, 144-45
eating disorders and, intervention in, 174-92
in psychotherapeutic partnering technique, 155, 159-61
in survey of bulimarexics, 264
in treatment of anorexia nervosa, 156-57
see also Parents
Family systems theory of anorexia nervosa, 101-2
Family therapy, 73-74, 157-59
  often not possible for bulimarexics, 254
  in psychotherapeutic partnering technique, 169-71
  in Therapeutic Contract Program, 214
Fantasies, 202-3
Fashion, 119-21
  feminine and masculine trends in, 122-23
  feminist analysis of, 130-31
  in illness, 197
  in medicine, 194-95
Fathers, 167, 168
  of precocious anorexic girls, 274-75
  see also Family; Parents
Fatness, cultural context of, 116-17
Females, *see* Women
Femininity, 122-23, 131, 315
Feminism, 123, 248, 315
  in intervention strategies for bulimarexia, 251
  perspective of social considerations in anorexia nervosa, 127-37
Fenfluramine, 306
Fenichel, Otto, 144n
Fiber, in foods, 47
Flappers, 119-20, 122
Fluid complications of anorexia nervosa and bulimia, 9-10
Focal symbiosis, 274
Follicle-stimulating hormone (FSH), 58
Follow-ups, 99-100, 298-99, 315
Food
  anorexics' preoccupation with, 128
  cultural preoccupation with, 96-98
  determining intake of, 31-33
  developmental significance of, 200-8
  fiber in, 47
  monitoring intake of, 41
  as sexual stimulant, 276
  starvation subjects' preoccupation with, 52
  thoughts of, 28
  in women's social role, 131
Forced feeding, 36-37, 129-30
Fragmentation, 282, 283

Freud, Anna, 202, 204, 269
Freud, Sigmund
  on cathartic, 195-96
  on classical conversion hysteria, 104
  on ego's ejecting of "bad," 201, 203-4
  on forces shaping personality, 105
  on judgment of self, 207
Freudianism, 123
Fromm, E., 317
Fry, M., 11
Futterman, Linda, on psychotherapeutic partnering approach to treatment of anorexia nervosa and bulimia, 154-73
Future shock, 308

Gackenbach, Dyck, 208
Galdston, R., 277
Gans, Margery T., on whether anorexics and bulimics get well, 291-301
Garfinkel, P. E., 298
  ballet dancers studied by, 110
  on cultural norms regarding weight, 97
  on efficacy of treatments for anorexia nervosa, 297
  on outcomes of anorexia nervosa, 292
  on prognosis for anorexia, 295
Garland, Madge, 116, 119
Garner, D. M., 298
  ballet dancers studied by, 110
  on cultural norms regarding weight, 97
  on efficacy of treatments for anorexia nervosa, 297
  on outcomes of anorexia nervosa, 292
  on prognosis for anorexics, 295
Gastrointestinal system, 11-12
  recovering anorexics' problems with, 46-47
Gedo, J., 275n
Geist, Richard A., on therapeutic dilemmas in treatment of anorexia nervosa, 268-87
Gender, 310-14
Generations, transgenerational images and sequences, 189-91
Genetics, 305, 306
George, G. C. W., 199
Gestalt of mouth, 200-1
Getzels, Jacob, 105
Gilligan, C., 311, 312
Glamour, 114
Glucose metabolism, 11-12
Goals
  in intervention strategies for bulimarexia, 253-54
  in treatment contracts, 216
Gold, P. W., 9

Goldberg, A., 275, 277
Gonadotropins, 7, 57-60
Gorging and purging syndrome, *see* Bulimarexia
Gotch, F. M., 13
Grable, Betty, 120
Grandparents, 190
Greenacre, P., 274
Gross, H. A., 8
Group therapy, 315
  for bulimarexia, 247, 249-253
  for bulimia, 87-88
  long-term, for bulimia, 141-53
  in survey of bulimarexics, 265
  in Therapeutic Contract Program, 220-21
Growth, 7-8
Growth hormone, 7, 55-56

Halmi, K. A., 11, 59, 296
Hardwick, Elibabeth, 268
Hayworth, Rita, 120
Health, 123-24
Heart complications, 12-13
Heiman, M., 102
Heinz, E. R., 14
Hematologic complications of anorexia nervosa and bulimia, 13-14
Heredity, 306
High school years, 240
Holistic health movement, 309
Holmgren, S., 46
Homework, from therapy, 251-52, 254
Hormones, *see* Endocrine system; Neuroendocrines
Hospitalization
  inpatient model for treatment of anorexia nervosa, 211-32
  in nurturant-authoritative psychotherapy, 244-45
  of previously treated patients, 46
  in psychotherapeutic partnering technique, 163
  release from, suicide risk and, 284
Hsu, L. K. G., 292, 293, 295, 296
Hudson, James, 307
  on biological treatments of eating disorders, 73-89
Hughes, P. L., 86
Hunger strikers, 130
5-hydroxyindoleacetic acid, 305-6
5-hydroxytryptamine (serotonin), 67, 305-6
Hymowitz, C., 116, 118, 119
Hyperactivity, 28
Hypercarotenemia, 10, 60
Hyperkalemia, 28
Hypochloremic alkalosis, 27

Index

Hypoglycemia, 12
Hypokalemia, 10, 27
Hypophosphatemia, 10
Hypothyroidism, 54
Hysteria, 104-5

Identification, between mothers and daughters, 273-74
Identity, gender, 311-14
Illness, history of concept of, 195-97
Imipramine, 82-84, 300
Immaturity, 129
Immunologic complications of anorexia nervosa and bulimia, 13-14
Incidence of anorexia nervosa, 98-101
Independence, encouraged in children, 235-36
Infants, 204-5
Inpatient treatment of anorexia nervosa, 211-32
Insights, 180
Integrated Treatment Protocol (ITP), 221-29
Intervention, 135-37
  in bulimarexia, 246-67
  in family and eating disorders, 174-92
  in patient's environment, 155
Intrapsychic level, 179-82
Isomorphism, 175
Isomorphs, 176

Jackson, Michael, 310
Johnson, Craig L., 301
  on sociocultural context of anorexia nervosa and bulimia, 95-111

Kael, Pauline, 96
Kalager, T., 13
Kalucy, R. S., 100
Kaufman, M. R., 102
Kaye, W., 9
Kendell, R. E., 100
Keniston, K., 124
Keys, A., 14, 52
Khan, M., 272, 273, 277
Kim, Y., 13-14
Klinefelter, H. F., 10
Kluckholn, Clyde, 96, 109
Kohut, H.
  on anorexic's view of therapist, 279
  on empathy in child development, 270
  on soothing mechanisms, 283
  on vertical splitting, 209
Kreisler, L., 201-2, 204-5
Kris, E., 277

Laboratory tests, 34

for major affective disorder, 77-78
Lacey, J., 100
Landau, R. J., 212, 229
Laplanche, J., 196
Laxative abuse, 10
  in anorexia nervosa, 23, 26, 293
  in bulimarexia, 113
  minor calorie loss from, 309
  treatment for, 45
  for weight control, 30
Levendusky, Philip G., on inpatient treatment of anorexia nervosa, 211-32
Levenkron, Steven, 158
  on structuring nurturant-authoritative psychotherapeutic relationship with anorexic patient, 234-45
Levenson, E. A., 175
LH levels, 7
Life adaptations model of anorexia nervosa and eating disorders, 105-9
Lipid values, 10-11
Lithium carbonate, 79-80
Liver complications, 11
Llewellyn-Jones, D., 301
Long-term group therapy, for bulimia, 141-53
Lurie, A., 116, 122
Luteinizing hormone (LH), 58, 59
Luteinizing hormone-releasing hormone (LHRH), 58, 59

Major affective disorder theory, 76-78, 307
Major depression, 76, 77
Males, *see* Men
Manic depressive illness, 76, 77
MAO inhibitors, 301
Masculinity, 122-23, 312
Masterson, J., 166
May, Rollo, 316
Meal plans, in nutritional treatment, 40-41
Medical complications of anorexia nervosa and bulimia, 5-6
  biochemical effects, 10-11
  cardiovascular, 12-13
  dental, 15
  endocrine manifestations, 6-9
  fluid and electrolyte, 9-10
  gastrointestinal, 11-12
  hematologic and immunologic, 13-14
  in nurturant-authoritative psychotherapy, 244-45
  prognosis, 295-96
  psychologic, neurologic, and ophthalmologic, 14-15
  of starvation, 24-25
  trends in research into, 305-8

Medication, see Drug treatments
Medicine
  cultural change and, 195-97
  fashions in, 194-95
Men
  development of gender identity in, 311-12
  gonadotropins in, 59
  prognosis for anorexia nervosa in, 296
  as therapists, in intervention strategies for bulimarexia, 251
  Twiggy ideal rejected by, 123
Menstruation, 6-7
  gonadotropins and, 57-58
  in prognosis of anorexics, 293
Methodology, 297-99
3-methoxy, 4-hydroxy-phenylglycol (MHPG), 66
Metoclopramide, 11
Mianserin, 81-82
Michael, A. F., 13-14
Minuchin, S., 298
  on anorexic families, 101, 158, 159, 182
  on lack of controlled studies, 314
  on psychological outcomes for anorexics, 313
Mira, M., 301
Mirroring, between mothers and daughters, 273-74
Miss America Pageant, 97
Mitchell, J. E., 86
Moment-to-moment sequences, 182-85
Monitoring
  of blood levels in antidepressant treatments, 86
  food intake, 41
  weight, 42
Monroe, Marilyn, 116
Monsters, 203-5, 208
Mordasini, R., 10-11
Moreno, J. L., 151
Morgan, H. G., 293, 296, 299
Mortality
  of anorexics, 292, 294
  methodological issues in, 299
Mothers, 156, 167, 168
  of anorexics, 101-2
  anorexics complaints against, 281-82
  food in interactions between children and, 202-8
  lack of empathy for children by, 272
  see also Family; Parents
Motivation
  in intervention strategies for bulimarexia, 250
  in nutritional treatment, 37-38
Mouth, 200-1
Myerson, Bess, 121

Naloxone, 59
Narcissism, 278
Narcissistic rage, 284
Nardil (Phenelzine), 80, 84-86
Nasogastric feeding, 36
Nestel, P. J., 11
Neuroendocrines, 51-52
  andrenocortical hormones, 61-64
  antidiuretic hormone, 56-57
  appetite regulation by, 52-53
  central nervous system neurotransmitters, 64-68
  gonadotropins, 57-60
  growth hormones, 55-56
  temperature regulation by, 56
  thyroid hormones, 53-55
  trends in research into, 305-6
  see also Endocrine system
Neurologic complications of anorexia nervosa and bulimia, 14-15
Neurotransmitters, 64-68
Niebuhr, Richard, 316
Norepinephrine, 8-9, 65-66, 306
Norpramin (Desipramine), 86
Nurse coordinators, in Therapeutic Contract Program, 215
Nurturant-authoritative psychotherapy, 158, 234-45
Nutrition, 20-24
  assessment of, 30-35
  effects related to, 24-30
  in treatment, 35-47
Nylander, T., 100

Obesity
  bulimarexia and, 249
  cultural attitudes toward, 97-98
  in prognosis for anorexics, 296
  social class and, 118
Obsessional behavior, 237-38
  in bulimarexics, 247
  in bulimia, 142-44
O'Dowde, Thomas, 195
Oedipal complex, 274-75
Ophthalmologic complications of anorexia nervosa and bulimia, 14-15
Opioids, 59, 67-68
Oral pleasure, 204
Oral-sadistic fantasies, 202
Orbach, Susie, on feminist perspective of social considerations in anorexia nervosa, 127-37
Organic theory of anorexia nervosa, 101
Ornstein, A., 270
Ornstein, P., 278, 281, 287
Osteoporosis, 58
Outcomes

Index

of anorexia nervosa, 291-99
of bulimia, 300-1
Outpatients, in Therapeutic Contract Program, 231-32
Overweight, in medical articles, 123-24

Palmblad, J., 13
Palmer, R. L., 100
Pancreatic complications, 11
Paradoxical prescriptions, 151-153
"Parentectomies," 178
Parenteral nutrition, 36
Parents
  anorexia nervosa and failures in empathy from, 271-78
  of bulimarexics, 198
  of bulimics, 149
  concept of false self and, 145
  in family therapy, 169-71
  pathology of, in development of childhood disorders, 155-56
  in psychotherapeutic partnering technique, 159-61, 164-69
  in psychotherapy process, 157
  see also Family
Parnate (tranylcypromine), 79
Parsons, Talcott, 105
Partnering, in treatment of anorexia nervosa and bulimia, 154-73
Peptides, 67-68
Perfectionism, 144
Periactin (cyproheptadine), 67, 74-75
Peripheral neuropathies, 14
Personality
  features of anorexics, 234-37
  in prognosis for anorexics, 296
  sociocultural forces, behavior and, 103-4
Pertschuk, M. J., 14
Peterson, R. K., 202
Phenelzine (Nardil), 80, 84-86
Phenytoin (Dilantin), 74, 75, 300-1
Physicians
  "fat phobias" in, 309
  in therapeutic teams, 159
Playboy, 97, 116
Pleasures, 277-78
Pontalis, J. B., 196
Pope, Harrison G., 300, 307
  on biological treatments of eating disorders, 73-89
Potassium, 9-10, 26
Precocity, 274-76
Prediction of anorexia nervosa, 107
Premorbid features of anorexia nervosa, 234-37
Privacy, in children, 207
Prognosis, 105-7

for anorexia nervosa, 295-97
for bulimia, 300-1
Protein
  loss of, in starvation, 25
  in meal plans, 40
Protestantism, 123
Psychiatric symptomatology, in recovered anorexics, 295
Psychoanalysis, 155
  catharsis in, 196
  sociocultural factors ignored by, 115-16
Psychodramatic reenactment, 150-51
Psychodynamic approaches, 155
  to bulimarexia, 194-210
Psychological complications of
  anorexia nervosa and bulimia, 14-15
  effects of starvation and, 24-25, 28-29
  in methodology of follow-ups, 299
  psychiatric symptomatology of, 295
  trends in research into, 311-15
Psychology
  feminism and, 130
  intervention in eating disorders and family, 174-92
  long-term dynamic group therapy for bulimia, 141-53
  psychotherapeutic partnering approach to treatment of anorexia nervosa and bulimia, 154-73
  therapeutic dilemmas in treatment of anorexia nervosa, self-psychological perspective on, 268-87
  trends in research in, 311-15
Psychopharmacology
  trends in research into, 305-8
  see also Drug treatments
Psychosocial adjustment, of anorexics, 294-95
Psychotherapists
  anorexics and, 240-41
  anorexic's view of, 279
  in Therapeutic Contract Program team, 213-14
Psychotherapy, *see* Therapy; Treatment
Psychotic behavior, 229-31
Puberty, 237
Purging
  as compulsive behavior, 143
  minor calorie loss from, 309
  in survey of bulimarexics, 258-62
  see also Bulimarexia; Bulimia; Laxative abuse
Purgold, J., 299

Rage, 283-84
Recovery time, for anorexia nervosa, 294
Reed, M., 202

Remissions, spontaneous, 73
Research, trends in, 304-5, 316-18
  biomedical, 305-8
  psychological, 311-15
  sociocultural, 308-11
Resistance, 279-81
  by parents, 166
Rich, C. L., 80
Risk factor model of anorexia nervosa and eating disorders, 102-9
Risk factor models, 105-7
Rizzuto, Ana-Maria, 202
  on psychodynamic view of bulimarexia, 194-210
Robertson, G. L., 9
Rohrbaugh, J. B., 306
Rosman, B. L., 182, 187, 298, 313
Running, 275, 283n
  as compulsive behavior, 310
Russell, G. F. M., 60, 293, 296

Sadistic fantasies, 202
Saul, S. H., 11
Schizophrenia, 295
Schwaber, E., 278, 285
Schwartz, Donald M., 292
  on sociocultural context of anorexia nervosa and bulimia, 95-111
Secrecy, by anorexics, 132, 135
Self-control, 222-23
Self-help groups, 114, 315
Self-image, 114, 180-81, 237-38, 313
  class aspects of, 117-19
  cultural context of, 116-17
  lack of treatment attention to, 314
  in survey of bulimarexics, 263-64
Selfobject functions, 269-70
Self-psychological perspective on therapeutic dilemmas in treatment of anorexia nervosa, 268-87
Selvini Palazzoli, M., 101, 158-59, 179, 295
Separation issue, 240
Serotonin (5-hydroxytryptamine), 67, 305-6
Sexuality
  of adolescent anorexic girls, 275, 276
  classical conversion hysteria and, 105
  cultural androgyny and, 310
  in married anorexics, 295
  in precocious anorexic girls, 274
Sheimo, S., 156
Sheppard, Eugenia, 121
Sibling research, 306
Siblings, 169-70
Side effects
  of antidepressant medication, 307
  of imipramine, 82

of tricyclic antidepressants, 79
Silverstone, J. T., 118
Smart, D. E., 199
Social class, 117-19
Social skills, 220, 232
Sociocultural context of anorexia nervosa and eating disorders, 95-111
  of bulimarexia, 113-25, 194-97
  trends in research into, 308-11
Somatomedin C, 55-56, 66
Soothing mechanisms, 281-85
Soulé, M., 201-2
Sours, J., 157
Spack, Norman P., on medical complications of anorexia nervosa and bulimia, 5-15
Sperling, M., 156
Spirit, 317-18
Spitz, R. A., 200-2, 206
Splitting, 236
Spontaneous remissions, 73
Sports, 30
Starvation
  adrenocortical hormones and, 64
  behavioral changes during, 14
  gonadotropins in, 7, 57-58
  growth hormone and, 7, 55-56
  neuroendocrine aspects of, 51
  neuroendocrine regulation of appetite in, 52-53
  norepinephrine and, 65
  physical effects of, 24-25
  psychological effects of, 28-29
  studies of, 12
  thyroid hormones in, 53-55
  trends in research into, 305
Stuckey, M., 301
Suicide, 29, 284, 294
Superego, 207
Supervision of inpatients, 222-23
Symptoms, 104
  of anorexia nervosa, 128
  of bulimia, secondary autonomy of, 142-44
  psychiatric, in recovered anorexics, 295
Szurek, S., 156

Taylor, Elizabeth, 97
Teams
  in inpatient model for treatment of anorexia nervosa, 213-16
  in intervention strategies for bulimarexia, 249, 251
  in psychotherapeutic partnering in treatment of anorexia nervosa and bulimia, 159-73

Index

Temperature regulation, 56
Testosterone, 7
Theander, S.
  on incidence of anorexia nervosa, 99-100
  on mortality of anorexics, 299
  on recovery period for anorexics, 294
  on sexual adjustment by anorexics, 295
  on weight maintenance by anorexics, 292
Therapeutic Contract Program (TCP), 212
  aftercare in, 231-32
  medication in, 229-31
  treatment contracts in, 216-20
  treatment team in, 213-16
Therapeutic contracts
  in intervention strategies for bulimarexia, 253-54
  paradoxical prescriptions in, 151-52
Therapy
  for bulimic anorexia nervosa, 46
  intervention in eating disorders and family, 174-92
  long-term dynamic group, for bulimia, 141-53
  nurturant-authoritative psychotherapeutic relationships for anorexia nervosa, 234-45
  psychotherapeutic partnering approach to treatment of anorexia nervosa and bulimia, 154-73
  therapeutic dilemmas in treatment of anorexia nervosa, self-psychological perspective on, 268-87
  see also Treatment
Thinness
  cultural context of, 116-17
  cultural preoccupation with, 96-98
  in fashion and culture, 123
  as goal of anorexics, 128
Thompson, M. F., 292
Thompson, Michael G.
  on sociocultural context of anorexia nervosa and bulimia, 95-111
  on whether anorexics and bulimics get well, 291-301
Thomsen, K., 10
Thumb-sucking, 204
Thyroid functions, 7
Thyroid hormones, 53-55
Thyroid-stimulating hormone (TSH), 54-55
Thyrotropin-releasing hormone (TRH), 54-56
Thyroxine (T_4), 7, 53-54, 60
Toffler, A., 304, 308
Trait markers, 305, 306
Transference, 236, 281, 285-87
Transgenerational images and sequences, 189-91

Tranylcypromine (Parnate), 79
Trauma, in life adaptation model, 108
Trazodone (Desyrel), 79
Treatment
  affective disorder theory in, 76-78
  for anorexia nervosa, antidepressant, 78-80
  for anorexia nervosa, inpatient, 211-32
  for anorexia nervosa, therapeutic dilemmas in, self-psychological perspective on, 268-87
  biological, 73-75
  for bulimarexia, intervention strategies and outcomes for, 246-67
  for bulimia, antidepressant, 80-88
  for bulimia, prognosis for, 300-1
  for bulimic anorexia nervosa, 46
  feminist analysis of, 135-37
  for hypokalemia, 10
  long-term group therapy for bulimia, 141-53
  nurturant-authoritative psychotherapeutic relationships for anorexia nervosa, 234-45
  nutritional, 35-47
  nutritional assessment in, 30-35
  in prognosis for anorexics, 297
  psychological research needed into, 313-14
  psychotherapeutic partnering approach to treatment of anorexia nervosa and bulimia, 154-73
Tricyclic antidepressants, 79
Triiodothyronine (T_3), 7, 53-54, 60, 61
Tur, A. F., 12
Twiggy (Lesley Hornby Armstrong), 97, 115, 116, 122, 123
Twin research, 306

VandeWiele, R. L., 6
Vasopresin (antidiuretic hormone), 56-57
Victorian era, 116-17
Vitamins, 40
Vocational adjustment, in anorexics, 295
Vomiting
  in anorexics, 23, 293
  in bulimarexia, 113
  as compulsive behavior, 143
  effects on teeth of, 15
  in history of medical procedures, 195
  nutritional consequences of, 26
  nutritional treatment for, 43
  potassium loss from, 9-10
  in prognosis for anorexics, 295-96
  as ritual, 199
  in sample groups, 110-11

Vomiting (continued)
  in survey of bulimarexics, 259, 262
  for weight control, 30

Wallace, A., 96-97
Wallace, I., 96-97
Wallechinsky, D., 96-97
Walsh, B. T., 80, 84, 301
Warren, M. P., 6
Water balance, 9
  in weight gain, 42
Weight
  maintenance of, in aftercare, 231
  in methodology of follow-ups, 299
  monitoring, 42
  in nutritional assessment, 33
  in prognosis for anorexics, 292-93, 296
  in psychotherapeutic partnering technique, 163
  in survey of bulimarexics, 257-58
Weight gain
  in nutritional treatment, 42-44
  setting targets for, 35
  in Therapeutic Contract Program, 226-27
Weight loss
  obsessive dieting for, 238
  physical effects of, 24-25
Weissman, M., 116, 118, 119
Welbourne, J., 299
Wermuth, B. M., 300-1
West, Mae, 116
Whitaker, Jane, 195
White, William C., Jr., on bulimarexia intervention strategies and outcomes, 246-67
William of Ockham, Sir, 307
Wilson, C. P., 157-58
Winnicott, D. W.
  on child's perception of mother's face, 206-7
  on "false self," 144, 145
  on mirroring, 273
  on therapeutic relationship, 135
  on therapists' failures of understanding, 149
Women
  amenorrhea and endocrine effects in, 6-8
  in America of 1970s, 124-25
  attitudes towards own body of, 114
  class aspects of body image of, 117-19
  classical conversion hysteria in, 104-5
  cultural attitudes toward overweight in, 98
  cultural context of body image of, 116-17
  cultural origins of mistreatment of, 310
  development of gender identity in, 312
  dieting by, 29
  fashion for, 119-21
  femininity versus masculinity in, 122-23
  feminist perspective of social considerations in anorexia nervosa and, 127-37
  gonadotropins and menstruation in, 57-60
  incidence of anorexia nervosa among, 99-100
  sociocultural context of eating disorders in, 95-96
  studies of ballet dancers and students, 110-11
  trends in psychological research involving, 311
Women's groups, in Therapeutic Contract Program, 221
Women's Liberation Movement, 128, 129
Wooley, O. W., 98, 313, 314
Wooley, S. C., 98, 313, 314
Work, 118

Youth, 119-21

Zinc deficiency, 10